Discursive Framings of Human Rights

What does it mean to be a subject of human rights? The status of the subject is closely connected with the form and rhetoric of the framing discourse, and this book investigates the relationship between the status of the subject and the form of human rights discourse, in differing aesthetic and social contexts. Historical as well as contemporary declarations of rights have stressed both the protective and political aspects of human rights. But in concrete situations and conflictual moments, the high moral legitimacy of human rights rhetoric has often clouded the actual character of specific interventions, and so made it difficult to differentiate between the objects of humanitarian intervention and the subjects of politics. Critically re-examining this opposition – between victims and agents of human rights – through a focus on the ways in which discourses of rights are formed and circulated within and between political societies, this book elicits the fluidity of their relationship, and with it the shifting relation between human rights and humanitarianism. Analysing the symbolic framings of testimonies, disaster stories, atrocity tales, political speeches, and philosophical arguments, it thus establishes a relationship between these different genres and the political, economic, and legal dimensions of human rights discourse.

Karen-Margrethe Simonsen and Jonas Ross Kjærgård are both based in the School of Communication and Culture, Aarhus University, Denmark.

Discursive Framings of Human Rights

Negotiating agency and victimhood

Edited by
Karen-Margrethe Simonsen
and Jonas Ross Kjærgård

Routledge
Taylor & Francis Group
LONDON AND NEW YORK

First published 2017
by Birkbeck Law Press

Published 2017 by Routledge
2 Park Square, Milton Park, Abingdon, Oxon OX14 4RN
711 Third Avenue, New York, NY 10017, USA

First issued in paperback 2017

Routledge is an imprint of the Taylor & Francis Group, an informa business

British Library Cataloguing in Publication Data
A catalogue record for this book is available from the British Library

Library of Congress Cataloging-in-Publication Data
Names: Simonsen, Karen-Margrethe, 1962 – editor. |
Kjærgård, Jonas Ross, editor.
Title: Discursive framings of human rights: negotiating agency and victimhood/Edited by Karen-Margrethe Simonsen and Jonas Ross Kjærgård.
Description: New York, NY: Routledge, 2016. |
Includes bibliographical references and index.
Identifiers: LCCN 2016007805|
ISBN 9781138944503 (hbk) | ISBN 9781315671857 (ebk)
Subjects: LCSH: Human rights. | Victims of crimes – Civil rights.
Classification: LCC K3240. D574 2016 | DDC 342.08/5 – dc23
LC record available at http://lccn.loc.gov/2016007805

ISBN 13: 978-1-138-48191-6 (pbk)
ISBN 13: 978-1-138-94450-3 (hbk)

Typeset in Baskerville and Gill Sans by
Florence Production Ltd, Stoodleigh, Devon, UK
Cover design by Christian Salling and Peter Ole Pedersen

Contents

List of contributors

Marie Andreasen PhD, Italian Studies, School of Communication and Culture, Aarhus University. She has an MA from Aarhus University in Italian and European Studies 2012. MA-thesis title: *Stories of a Past with Political Violence: Self-Narratives of Italian Ex-Terrorists*, PhD thesis 2016: *Seeds of Understanding, Paths of Reconciliation: Remembering the Anni di Piombo in Italy*. Publications: 'Narrazioni autobiografiche degli Anni di Piombo: La violenza politica di sinistra'. *Conflictos de la memoria – Memoria de los conflictos/Conflitti della memoria – Memoria dei conflitti: Modelos narrativos de la memoria intergeneracional en España e Italia/Modelli narrativi della memoria intergenerazionale in Italia e Spagna*. Ed. Hans Lauge Hansen and Leonardo Cecchini, Copenhagen: Museum Tusculanum. *Etudes Romanes* 62 (2015), 349–362.

Leonardo Cecchini is Associate Professor, Italian Studies, School of Communication and Culture, Aarhus University. His research areas include life writing (autobiography), cultural products (fictional and non-fictional narrative, film and television programmes) about political violence and terrorism in Italy. Publications: Ed. with Hans Lauge Hansen: *Conflictos de la memoria – Memoria de los conflictos/Conflitti della memoria – Memoria dei conflitti. Modelos narrativos de la memoria intergeneracional en España e Italia/Modelli narrativi della memoria intergenerazionale in Italia e Spagna*. Copenhagen: Museum Tusculanum. *Etudes Romanes* 62 (2015) 349–362; 'Ethics of Conviction vs. Ethics of Responsibility in Cinematic Representations of Italian Left-Wing Terrorism of the 1970s'. *Terrorism, Italian Style: Representations of Political Violence in Contemporary Italian Cinema*. Ed. Ruth Glynn, Giancarlo Lombardi, and Alan O'Leary. London: Institute of Germanic & Romance Studies. University of London, 2012, 195–213; with Francesco Caviglia 'A Quest for Dialogism: Looking Back at Italian Political Violence in the '70s'. *The Discursive Construction of History, Society and Politics: Multimodal Approaches*. Ed. Torben Vestergaard, Inger Lassen, and Jeanne Strunck. Aalborg: Aalborg University Publishing House, 2009, 127–148; with Francesco Caviglia 'Narrative Models of Political Violence: Vicarious Experience and "Violentization" in 1970s Italy'. *Imagining Terrorism: The Rhetoric and Representation of Political Violence in Italy 1969–2009*. Ed. P. Antonello and A. O'Leary. *Italian Perspectives* no.18, Oxford: Legenda, 2009, 139–152.

Gale Coskan-Johnson is Assistant Professor of Writing and Rhetoric, Department of English Language and Literature, Brock University, Canada. She directs the Writing, Rhetoric and Discourse Studies Program (WRDS), edits the *Brock Review,* and is affiliated with the MA in Social Justice and Equity Studies. Her current research project is titled, '(Il)legal, (Ir)regular, (Un)documented: Rhetorics of Sovereignty and Transnational Migration', and it explores contemporary entanglements of transnational mobility and the rhetorics of sovereign power. Publications: 'American Rhetorics of Sovereignty and (Im)mobility in the Age of the Global Flow'. *Amerikastudien – American Studies* 61 (forthcoming); 'Osama bin Laden and the "Illegal" Mexican Immigrant: The Rhetorics of Death and Dying in the US National Imaginary'. *JAC: Journal of Rhetoric, Culture, and Politics* (forthcoming).

Lilie Chouliaraki is Professor of Media and Communications, the London School of Economics and Political Science, University of London. Her research areas include media ethics, broadly understood as the moral implications of mediated communication in contemporary public life and the mediation of human vulnerability. Publications: She has published extensively on the link between mediation, social action and cosmopolitan citizenship. *The Ironic Spectator: Solidarity in the Age of Post-Humanitarianism.* Cambridge: Polity Press, 2012; Ed. *Self-Mediation: New Media, Citizenship and Civil Selves.* London: Routledge, 2012; Ed. with Mette Morsing; *Media, Organizations and Identity.* Basingstoke: Macmillan, 2010; Ed. *Soft Power of War.* Philadelphia: John Benjamins Publishing, 2007; *Spectatorship of Suffering.* London: Sage, 2006.

Madeleine Dobie is Associate Professor of French, Columbia University. Her research areas include francophone/postcolonial literatures and cinemas of North Africa, the Middle East, and the Caribbean, and the cultural dimensions of migration and diaspora. She also teaches and writes about eighteenth-century French culture, particularly with regard to orientalism, colonialism and the history of slavery. Publications: *Relire Mayotte Capécia. Une Femme des Antilles dans l'espace colonial français, 1916–1955.* Paris: Armand-Colin, 2012; *Trading Places: Colonization and Slavery in Eighteenth Century French Culture.* Ithaca/London: Cornell University Press, 2010; *Foreign Bodies: Gender, Language and Culture in French Orientalism.* Stanford: Stanford University Press, 2001.

Costas Douzinas is Professor of Law, Pro-Vice Master for International Links, Director of the Birkbeck Institute for the Humanities. His research areas include British critical legal thought, the turning of legal scholarship towards ethical concerns and aesthetic considerations, law and visuality. Publications: Ed. with Conor Gearty *The Meanings of Rights: The Philosophy and Social Theory of Human Rights.* Cambridge: Cambridge University Press, 2014; *Philosophy and Resistance in the Crisis: Greece and the Future of Europe.* Cambridge/Malden: Polity Press, 2013; 'The Paradoxes of Human Rights'. *Constellations* 19.2 (2013), 51–67; *Human Rights and Empire: The Political Philosophy of Cosmopolitanism.*

Abingdon/New York: Routledge-Cavendish, 2007; *The End of Human Rights: Critical Legal Through at the Fin-de-Siecle*. Oxford: Hart, 2000; Ed. with Adam Gearey: *Critical Jurisprudence: The Political Philosophy of Justice*. Oxford: Hart, 2005; Ed. with Lynn Nead: *Law and the Image: The Authority of Art and the Aesthetics of Law*. Chicago/London: University of Chicago Press, 1999.

Nicolai von Eggers is a PhD Fellow, History of Ideas, Aarhus University. His research areas include political philosophy and the history of political and economic ideas. Publications: 'Radical Democracy and the French Revolution'. *Constellations*. 23.2 (2016); 'The Emergence of the Concept "Political Economy"'. *Intellectual History of Economic Normativities*. Ed. Mikkel Thorup, London: Palgrave Macmillan, 2016, forthcoming; 'A Critique of Giorgio Agamben's Abandonment of Sovereignty'. *Trópos* 8.1 (2015), 155–179; 'Governmentality, Police, Politics: Foucault with Rancière'. *KultuRRevolution* 64 (2013), 45–50. He has furthermore edited books in Danish on the American Revolution (2012), the French Revolution (2015), and the Haitian Revolution (forthcoming 2017).

Lena Halldenius is Professor of Human Rights and Director of Human Rights Program, Department of History, University of Lund, Sweden. Her research areas include human rights and the political thought of Mary Wollstonecraft. Publications: *Mary Wollstonecraft and Feminist Republicanism: Independence, Rights and the Experience of Unfreedom*. London: Pickering & Chatto, 2015; *Liberalism*. Stockholm: Bokbox Förlag, 2011; 'Freedom Fit for a Feminist? On the Feminist Potential of Quentin Skinner's Conception of Republican Freedom'. *Redescriptions: Political Thought, Conceptual History and Feminist Theory* 17.1 (2014), 86–103; 'Mary Wollstonecraft's Feminist Critique of Property: On Becoming a Thief From Principle'. *Hypatia: A Journal of Feminist Philosophy* 29.4 (2014), 942–957.

Isak Winkel Holm is Professor, Comparative Literature, University of Copenhagen. Co-founder of the excellence research project *Changing Disasters*, University of Copenhagen. Publications: *Tanken i billedet. Søren Kierkegaards poetik* (Thinking in Images: The Poetics of Søren Kierkegaard), Copenhagen: Gyldendal, 1998; *Stormløb mod grænsen: det politiske hos Franz Kafka* (Assault on the Border: the Political in Franz Kafka), Copenhagen: Gyldendal, 2015; articles on Rousseau, Schlegel, Kleist, Hegel, Nietzsche, Dostoevsky, Musil, Kundera, DeLillo, Sebald, McCarthy, disaster movies, etc. Translator of Franz Kafka, *Fortællinger* and *Efterladte fortællinger* (Stories and Posthumous Stories), 2007, and Friedrich Nietzsche, *Tragediens fødsel* (Birth of Tragedy), 1996.

Jonas Ross Kjærgård is Assistant Professor, Comparative Literature, School of Communication and Culture, Aarhus University. His research areas include eighteenth-century French politics, literature, and economy. Publications: *The Happiness of All: Balancing Money and Morals in French Revolutionary Human Rights*

Discourse (Dissertation 2015); 'Representation and Taxation: Fiscality, Human Rights, and the French Revolution'. *Intellectual History of Economic Normativities.* Ed. Mikkel Thorup. London: Palgrave Macmillan, 2016; co-editor: *Den Franske Revolution: En antologi* (*The French Revolution: An Anthology*). Aarhus: Slagmark, 2015.

Ingvild Hagen Kjørholt is Post.Doc. Fellow, NTNU, Norway. Her research areas include cosmopolitanism, Voltaire, and memory studies. Publications: 'Cosmopolitans, Slaves, and the Global Market in Voltaire's *Candide, ou l'optimisme*'. *Eighteenth-Century Fiction* 25.1 (2012), 61–84.

Elisa Kriza (Ruiz Velasco Garcia) has a PhD, Comparative Literature, Aarhus University. Her research areas include Russian culture and its interaction with the West. Publications: *Alexander Solzhenitsyn: Cold War Icon, Gulag Author, Russian Nationalist? A Study of his Western Reception*, Stuttgart: ibidem-Verlag, 2014.

Alexandra Schultheis Moore is Associate Professor of English, University of North Carolina at Greensboro. Publications: *Regenerative Fictions: Postcolonialism, Psychoanalysis, and the Nation as Family*. London: Palgrave Macmillan, 2004; numerous essays and book chapters on human rights in contemporary literature and film; co-editor of *Theoretical Perspectives on Human Rights and Literature.* New York/Abingdon: Routledge, 2012; *Teaching Human Rights in Literary and Cultural Studies.* New York: Modern Language Association, 2015; *Routledge Companion to Literature and Human Rights.* New York/Abingdon: Routledge, 2016; *Globally-Networked Learning in the Humanities: Theories and Practices.* New York/Abingdon: Routledge, 2015; and *Doubling the Voice: Survivors and Human Rights Workers Address Torture* (Republic of Letters, forthcoming).

Hanna Musiol is Associate Professor, NTNU, Norway. Her research areas include transnational American literature, visual studies, archive and curation, and digital humanities (DH), with emphasis on migration, political ecology, and human rights. She has published widely on literary and visual aesthetics and human rights in *Journal of American Studies*, *College Literature*, *WorkingUSA: Journal of Labor and Society*, *Routledge Companion to Human Rights and Literature*, and more. Publications: 'Museums of Human Bodies'. *College Literature* 40.3 (2013): 156–175; 'Sites of Human Rights Theory'. *Routledge Companion to Literature and Human Rights.* Ed. Sophia A. McClennen and Alexandra Schultheis Moore. New York/Abingdon: Routledge, 2016, 389–399. She is the creator of the (Im)Migrant Experience Initiative (IEI), an open-access digital archive devoted to the preservation of narratives of migration and displacement at the University of Massachusetts Boston (http://immigrantexperience.omeka.net/).

Peter Ole Pedersen is Assistant Professor, Department of Art History, Aarhus University. His research areas include the documentary film genre and the development of our current Net culture. Publications: *A Pixelated Reality:*

Documentary between Net-Distribution, Popular Culture and the Avantgarde. PhD dissertation, Aarhus University, 2014; 'Paranoid, moi? Surveillance and the Popular Cultural Documentary'. *Panoptikum* 12.19 (2014), 152–172; 'The Never-Ending Catastrophe: 9/11 Conspiracy Theory and the Integration of Activist Documentary on Video Websites'. *Acta Universitatis Sapientiae* 6 (2013), 49–64.

Devika Sharma is Assistant Professor, Comparative Literature, Copenhagen University. Her research areas include humanitarianism, modern cultural theory, contemporary American culture, and affect studies. Publications: 'The Predicament of Privilege'. *Critical Quarterly*, 2016. Co-edited with Frederik Tygstrup: *Structures of Feeling: Affectivity and the Study of Culture.* Walter de Gruyter, 2015; *Concepts for the Study of Culture*, Vol. 5.; 'The Captive Imagination: Inhumans, Animals, and Matthew Barney's Cremaster 2'. *Humanimalia* 6.2 (2015), 85–110; 'Visions of Punishment: On Susan Crile's Abu Ghraib Drawings'. *Invisibility Studies: Surveillance, Transparency and the Hidden in Contemporary Culture.* Ed. Kristin Veel and Henriette Steiner. 23 Peter Lang, 2015, 241–258; *Amerikanske fængselsbilleder: Kunst, kultur og indespærring i samtidens USA* (American Prison Images: Art, Culture and Confinement in Contemporary USA), Copenhagen: Tiderne Skifter, 2011.

Karen-Margrethe Simonsen is Associate Professor, Comparative Literature, School of Communication and Culture, Aarhus University. Her research areas include human rights and aesthetics, law and literature, and Spanish and Latin American Literature. Publications: 'Natural Rights and Power in the Spanish Comedia after the Conquest'. *The Routledge Companion to Literature and Human Rights.* Ed. Sophia A. McClennen and Alexandra Schultheis Moore. Abingdon/New York: Routledge, 2016, 279–288. Co-edited: *Sugar and Modernity in Latin America: Interdisciplinary Perspectives.* Aarhus: Aarhus University Press, 2014; Ed. *Law and Justice in Literature, Film and Theatre: Nordic Perspectives on Law and Humanities.* Berlin/New York: De Gruyter; Series: *Law and Literature*, 2013, Co-edited. *The Aesthetics of Human Rights, Academic Quarter*, 5, 2012, www.akademiskkvarter.hum.aau.dk/UK/05_12_2012.php; *Law and Literature: Interdisciplinary Readings and Perspectives* (ed. with. Ditlev Tamm) Copenhagen: DJØF Publishing House, 2010; 'The Politics of Universalism: Strategic Uses of Human Rights Discourses in Early Modernity'. *Journal of Aesthetics and Culture* 5 (2013), 1–12. www.aestheticsandculture.net/index.php/jac/issue/current.

Prologue

Human rights for Martians

Costas Douzinas

I Europe between two infant deaths

2015 has been a year marked by the heartbreaking images of a moving humanity of refugees and immigrants who leave the battlefronts of Syria, Iraq, Afghanistan and Libya to come to Europe, their imaginary Arcadia. More than one million people have braved the rough waters of the Aegean and Libyan seas, with the bulk landing on the Greek islands of Lesbos, Chios, Kos, Agathonissi, Farmakonissi and Lemnos. On the way to the islands, thousands have lost their lives. Photographs of drowned dead bodies lying on the beaches of Greece and Turkey have been published daily. The image of dead three-year-old Aylan Kurdi on a Turkish beach in early September went around the world and became the image of the refugee crisis. Britain's chief rabbi, Ephraim Mirvis, interviewed on radio, stated that:

> for far too long, we have related to these suffering individuals as if they are people who are living on Mars. Thanks to that image, that desperately sad and tragic image, it's moved our hearts . . . It's an image of that boy that has brought us to our senses and we must respond adequately.[1]

Yet the first known refugee casualty of 2016 was an unnamed two-year-old boy who drowned on 1 January when the crowded dinghy he was travelling in broke in the rocks off Greece's Agathonissi island. 'Nothing can prepare you for the horrific reality of what is going on. Today we came face to face with one of the youngest victims of this ongoing refugee crisis. It is a tragic reminder of the thousands of people who have died trying to reach safety in miserable conditions', said Christopher Catrambone, a migrant support NGO officer.[2]

1 See www.theguardian.com/commentisfree/2015/sep/06/photograph-refugee-crisis-aylan-kurdi.

2 See www.theguardian.com/world/2016/jan/03/toddler-becomes-europes-first-refugee-casualty-of-2016.

Between the first and the second dead infant, thousands braved the sea and hundreds drowned. The island of Lesbos has run out of burial space. Many graves are unmarked as the names and nationalities of the buried are unknown. Refugees are the unmourned and ungrievable victims of the latest humanitarian catastrophe. As Antigone knew, the dead must be honoured at all costs. Those who cannot, who do not deserve to be mourned form the most extreme case of bare life, live outside the protection of law and state, as Judith Butler reminded us.

The image of the little dead body floating on the waves and then lying on the beach was powerful. It was published and copied again and again around the world. Yet Aylan's death image did not have the same effect on European politicians as on the rabbi. Greece is a transit place on the way to Northern Europe for people fleeing the wars of the Middle East. Over a million refugees entered Europe in 2015, with some 820,000 landing on Greek islands. 950,000 applied for asylum in a European country but only 185,000 were granted refugee status. Germany temporarily opened its borders, receiving a large number of asylum seekers. But when the political climate started turning, the borders were closed again. Hungary built a fence on the border and declared that it cannot accept the moral blackmail of Germany, which initially welcomed immigrants. Croatia and the Former Yugoslav Republic of Macedonia built fences too. Poland declared that it would only accept Christian refugees. The European Union's response has been pathetic.

A number of high-level meetings of politicians and officials have reluctantly agreed a resettlement plan for 120,000 from the 500,000 or so refugees trapped in Greece, who will be distributed to the 28 EU states according to their population. At the time of writing, fewer than 200 refugees have been resettled from Greece to the rest of Europe. Immediately after the agreement, a number of states, including Hungary and Poland, have rejected participation and refused to take any refugees. Denmark, one of the most wealthy nations of the European Union, passed a law authorizing the confiscation of the pitiful valuables of refugees to cover the cost of offering basic services to them.

In September 2015, against wishes, expectations and predictions, I was elected a SYRIZA (Greek Radical Left Party) MP for the port of Pireas. As the President of the Defence and Foreign Relations committee of the Hellenic Parliament, I have to attend various inter-parliamentary conferences and meetings. In November, in a meeting at the European Parliament to discuss migration flows in the Western Balkans, I explained that the Greek position was to welcome the migrants, register them, start the asylum determination process for those who do not wish to leave immediately and let the others go while doing everything possible to make their lives bearable while in the country. The help of ordinary citizens and the solidarity of Greek and foreign NGOs has made this huge task for a small and economically devastated country possible.

A Northern European MP retorted by stating that the Greek port police should 'push back' the ramshackle refugee dinghies. I explained that 'pushing back' could only work if these vessels are rammed or sunk, something that the Greeks would not do. My interlocutor response was that the patrol boats should allow refugees to reach the islands but should turn back 'illegal' migrants. Again, I explained that the Greek government is not prepared to tolerate more deaths in the Aegean. Moreover, the separation of asylum seekers from economic migrants in rough waters is impossible even if some inhumane administration were to adopt the plan.

Jami and Barzo, two failed asylum seekers living in the London shadows, give a succinct answer to the Northern European politician. In a video accompanying coverage of a report by the refugee charity Parfras, which details the life of an underground humanity without shelter, food or the right to work and that survives in our cities on less than one dollar a day, Jami, who sleeps in parks, quietly contrasts himself to his friends who have 'papers' and implicitly to the rest of us. 'We both have two hands, two eyes, two legs. They are human like me'. Barzo ends his heart-rending description of destitution, homelessness and despair quietly, addressing people like us, who, from our comfortable houses, keep proclaiming 'human rights, human rights. But where are the human rights for the asylum seekers?'[3] In haunting and halting sentences echoing suffering humanity from Shylock to Primo Levi, these natural philosophers state an indisputably realistic truth: we may all be human but humanity has always excluded, despised and degraded some of its parts. Humanity is not one: it has always been split between full and lesser humans. The refugee crisis version distinguishes between refugees and migrants, placing the former in a precarious position of rhetorical protection while abandoning the 'illegals', as if there is any human being who is 'illegal' because of who they are.

2 Split humanity

How can we understand this paradox that not all humans have humanity in a human rights world? The inflation of rights-talk has obscured the terms. To understand what Jami and Barzo tell us and Aylan proves, we need to start again. 'Human rights' is a term combining law and morality. *Legal rights* have been the building block of Western law since early modernity. As *human*, rights refer to a type of morality and to the treatment individuals expect from public and private powers. *Human rights* are a hybrid category, which introduces a number of paradoxes at the heart of society by bringing together law and morality.

Let me start with legal rights, the part that really counts in power's treatment of people. Private property and contractual rights were introduced in early modernity. They were both the result of the emergence of market economy and contributed to its victory. Culturally, rights were precipitated by what Alasdair

3 See www.theguardian.com/uk/2009/mar/16/asylum-seekers-immigration-poverty.

McIntyre has called a 'moral catastrophe': the destruction of premodern communities of virtue and duty. Because the capitalist society of individualism and free will lacks a universal moral code, restraints on private egotism must be external. Crime, tort and legal rights achieve precisely that. The law empowers individuals to enforce their rights but also limits their exercise so that, in theory, we can all have an equal amount of rights. When disputes arise, it is the business of lawyers and judges to resolve them. These rule experts have propagated a commonly held view that laws and rights are like facts: they have 'objective' meaning, which can be discovered by the professionals. Legal rights turn social and political conflict into a technical problem about the meaning of rules.

Legal rules and rights, however, do not come with their meaning on their sleeve. Human rights provisions are commonly general and abstract. They must be interpreted to be applied. Most rights disputes involve at least two contradictory but plausible legal and cultural meanings. This is where the available discursive frameworks analysed in this volume become all-important. Take the 'right to life', which opens most bills of rights and human rights treaties. Its statement does not answer questions about abortion, the death penalty, and euthanasia, or indeed about whether this right protects the necessary prerequisites for survival such as food, shelter, healthcare or the safe passage to a place of asylum. In most cases, a human rights claim is the beginning rather than the end of a dispute about the meaning of the right or its relative standing vis-à-vis conflicting rights. At this point, moral, political or ideological considerations unavoidably enter legal argumentation. Deciding conflicts between liberty and security, which have become so important after the Paris terrorist attacks, involves assumptions about the way a democratic society works. These depend in part on decision-makers' ideological, political or moral views. Removing them from politicians and giving them to lawyers (with their usual homogeneous outlook) does not change this basic fact. Rights and law are supposed to use reason and precedent to make the exercise of power neutral and objective. But the repressed 'subjectivism' always returns: rights adjudication is ambiguous, open, and potentially radical. We should not forget that law's main job is to provide order, not to support morality.

Second, whether recognized or not by law, 'human rights' are moral claims. A Chinese dissident who asserts the right to free political activity or an asylum seeker who claims the right to secure passage to a place of safety are both right and wrong. The dissident's 'right' does not refer to an existing legal entitlement, but to a claim about what morality (or ideology, or international law, or some other higher source) demands. In this sense, the morality of human rights is always in potential conflict with their legal status. Human rights confound the real and the ideal. Take Article 1 of the Universal Declaration of Human Rights: 'All human beings are born free and equal of right'. But as Jeremy Bentham noted first, newly born infants depend for survival on their carers, while the statement that people are born equal flies in the face of huge disparities in the world. Biological and social nature distribute their wares unequally, an unavoidable result of the accidents of birth and history. Heredity, the standing and economic (dis)advantage of family and community largely determine our lives. Equality, on the other hand, is unnatural and must be fought for.

Similarly, the asylum seeker's claim to the right to life, as argued above, does not create an indefeasible expectation of survival. Depending on the political, legal or cultural discursive framework adopted, ramming a dinghy may be interpreted as a criminal act and a violation of the refugees' rights or a necessary protection of national interests. Human rights statements are therefore prescriptions: people are not free and equal, but they ought to become so; people do not have a right to life, they ought to be granted the necessary means for their survival. Their success depends on political will and the social conditions within which the equality and life maxims are to be fought for. Equality is a call for action, not a description of a state of affairs. Moral or legal philosophy no longer deserves the adjective 'moral' when they forget this simple fact.

Human rights are a subcategory of legal rights protecting important goods and activities. The standard claim is they are given to people on account of their humanity rather than membership of narrower categories such as nation, community or class. And yet this assertion is disproved by the history of natural and human rights. The French *Declaration of the Rights of Man and Citizen*, the political and legal foundation and manifesto of modernity, opens with the statement about free and equal rights that the Universal Declaration repeated, replacing 'men' with human beings. The Declaration proceeds to bestow these rights to French citizens only. From that point on, statehood, sovereignty and territory follow nationhood and its pathologies, nationalism, ethnic wars and cleansing, genocide. The gap between universal 'man' and national citizen is inhabited by foreigners – they do not have rights because they are not citizens and as a result they are not fully human.

The 'man' of the 'rights of man' has no concrete characteristics, except for free will, reason and soul. These universal elements secularized the Christian belief in the sacredness of life and endowed humanity with dignity and respect. But this 'man' is an abstraction without body, colour, gender or history, as Hegel, Burke and Marx agreed. Yet the empirical man who actually enjoyed legal rights was literally a man – a well-off, white, Christian, urban male. He condenses the abstract dignity of humanity and the privileges of the powerful.

Ever since, full 'humanity' has been constructed against a background of conditions of inhumanity (citizenship, class, gender, race, religion, sexuality). If rights are universal, refugees, *sans papiers* immigrants or the Guantanamo Bay detainees who have no country to protect them should have humanity's entitlements. But they have none – they are just bare, unprotected life. Human rights do not belong to humans; they construct a graded 'humanity'. Every historical age has used its (philosophical or empirical) definition of humanity to separate between rulers, ruled and excluded. Those who don't speak our language, share our religion, or belong to the wrong class, gender, colour or sexuality have always been left outside locally defined 'humanity'. These categories of exclusion are still active. They have been joined by the 'bottom billion', the 'human waste', the rejects of global neo-liberal capitalism.

3 The human rights paradox

The human rights movement can be seen as the ongoing but failing struggle to close the gap between the abstract man of the Declarations and the empirical human being. Has it succeeded? Yes and no. The concept of a common 'humanity' introduced the vocation of universal dignity. Jami, Barzo and Aylan teach us, however, that there is nothing sacred about any definition of humanity and nothing eternal about its scope. Refugees who have no state, nation or law to protect them should be the prime beneficiaries of human rights, recipients of the consolations of humanity. Despite the claims of liberal philosophers, however, bare humanity offers no protections. Human rights, we could conclude, do not belong to humans. They help construct who and how one becomes human. Jami, Barzo and Aylan have no rights at all. In their case, the paradoxical relationship between law and morality has been resolved through the elimination of the moral command. While they bleed and hurt like the rest of us, they are not fully human.

The ideological power of human rights lies precisely in their rhetorical ambiguity, the oscillation between real and ideal, between humanity and national citizenship, the only provider of legal rights. When human rights are part of the law, as with the British Human Rights Act, which the Conservative government has pledged to repeal, the law includes a principle of self-transcendence that pushes against the law's settled state. A legal system that includes human rights is paradoxically not equal to itself, since human rights call the whole of law to account everywhere, not just in totalitarian states.

In this sense, human rights become the latest expression of a human urge to resist domination and oppression and to dissent from the intolerance of public opinion. This was the case in the great revolutions of the eighteenth century, in the post-WWII 'never again' declarations, in popular uprisings against fascist and communist rule. They are part of a long and honourable tradition, which started in the West with Antigone's defiance of unjust law and surfaces in the struggles of the despised, enslaved or exploited. Those who defend Jami, Barzo and the thousands who arrive daily in the Greek islands belong to this tradition and redeem the value of human rights.

Those who use human rights rhetoric to defend the 'human' rights of powerful companies in the developing world contribute to the banalization and eventual atrophy of rights. This atrophy paradoxically follows the triumph of rights. Human rights have mutated, expanded and turned into a vernacular touching every aspect of social life. Rights have become ubiquitous at the cost of their specificity and significance. They are seen as key concept in morals, politics and subjectivity. Claiming rights is the main form of morality. Responsibility, virtue and duty, on the other hand, have been confined to backwardness and fanaticism. Similarly, rights recognition is the main tool and target of politics. Group claims and ideological positions, sectional interests and global campaigns are routinely expressed in the language of rights for individuals. But when rights become a 'trump card' that defeats state policies and collective priorities, allegedly to support the liberty of the individual, society starts breaking up into a collection of atoms indifferent to the common good. This way politics is depoliticized. Both liberty and security suffer.

In postmodern societies, rights are the main tools of identity politics. 'I want X' or 'X should be given to me' has become synonymous with 'I have a right to X'. This linguistic inflation weakens the association of rights with significant human goods. A government minister recently argued that we have a human right to properly functioning kitchen appliances. The right to choose our kids' school or our mobile phone is as important as the right to be free of torture or to have food on the table. But this has nothing to do with the Enlightenment tradition of emancipation and self-development or with the radical tradition of dissent both represented in human rights. When every desire can be turned into a legal right, nothing retains the dignity of right.

There is more. Rights talk has become an easy and simple way of describing complex historical, social and political situations, a type of 'cognitive mapping': particularly useful for media coverage. Take a workers' strike. When presented as a conflict between the right to strike and the right to work (as is often the case), a complicated set of relations, histories, traditions and communities is reduced to a simple calculus of right versus right, one of which must be wrong. This translation hinders both understanding and resolving the conflict. As the scope of rights increases, their inherent absolutism makes the antagonists intransigent.

Finally, human rights have become the last universal ideology globally. It unites the North and the South, globalizing imperialists and anti-globalization protesters, First World liberals and Third World revolutionaries. Human rights are used as a symbol or synonym for liberalism, capitalism or individualism by some, and for development, social justice or peace by others. In the South, rights are seen as primarily collective rather than individual, social and economic rather than civil, associated with social justice rather than liberty. Does the victory, universality and ubiquity of rights indicate that they transcend conflicts of interests and the clash of ideas? Have rights become a common horizon uniting Cardiff and Kabul, London and Lahore? It is a comforting idea, daily denied in news bulletins. If there is something perpetual about our world, it is the increasing wealth gap between the metropolitan lands and the rest, the yawning chasm in income and chances between the rich and the poor, the ever new and strictly policed walls that divide the comfortable middle classes from the 'underclass' of immigrants, refugees and undesirables, those pockets of 'Third World' in the midst of the First. If anything, our world looks increasingly hostile and dangerous, and the administration of justified or imagined fears has become a major and common tool of governments.

Human rights introduce morality into law and offer limited legal enforcement to moral claims. But as morality is not one and the law is not a simple exercise in reasoning, moral conflict enters the legal archive and legal strictures regiment and control moral responsibility. Jami, Barzo, and Aylan remind us what the purpose of human rights is. Their sad soliloquies attest to the fact that when seen as alien Martians, they are turned into subhumans without humanity or rights.

Introduction

Jonas Ross Kjærgård and Karen-Margrethe Simonsen

What does it mean to be a subject of human rights? Depending on the framework through which we regard that subject, he or she may be a victim, an agent, or something in between. This book investigates the relation between the status of the subject and the forms of human rights discourses in different aesthetic and social contexts. We want to better understand the framing of the schism between vulnerable victimhood and capable agency, its strategic purposes, and its consequences.

The approach of the book is interdisciplinary. Although the legal foundation of rights inevitably figures strongly, this book takes its point of departure in extralegal perspectives. This approach allows us to focus on the contextual framings of rights, and to emphasize the importance of aesthetics in human rights discourses and scholarship. In recent years, important work has appeared on the style and function of life narratives in the context of human rights (Schaffer and Smith), on human rights and literature (Maslan; Hunt; Slaughter; Goldberg and Moore), and on the role of the spectator in relation to atrocity tales or images of suffering (Chouliaraki; Sliwinski). This book adds to that literature by focusing explicitly on the discursive framing of human rights in multiple textual genres (atrocity tales, life narratives, testimonies, novels, short stories, etc.), in visual media (visual art, films, installations, documentaries, surveillance videos, etc.), and in political discourse in a broad sense (parliamentary debates, laws, declarations, activism, humanitarian campaigns).

Our underlying claim is that style *is* politics. With the title, *Discursive Framings of Human Rights*, we suggest that the human rights discourse is never objective and disinterested. Human rights are embedded in both small-scale and large-scale politics, and each chapter of this book investigates a specific *strategic* formatting of the human rights discourse. In *Frames of War*, Judith Butler writes that a 'frame does not simply exhibit reality, but actively participates in a strategy of containment, selectively producing and enforcing what will count as reality. It tries to do this, and its efforts are a powerful wager' (Butler, *Frames of War* xiii). What Butler emphasizes about the journalistic and political framing of war sheds light on the human rights discourse as well: in various contexts, different aspects of human rights are emphasized or strategically omitted. In this book, we present ways of understanding the workings and the implications of the selective usage of the human rights discourse.

We use the word 'negotiation' to specify both how frames are discussed and adjusted within different contexts, *and* to specify how positions of victimhood and agency may be negotiated according to the aesthetics of different texts.

The negotiation of the frame through which we experience catastrophes, human rights abuses, humanitarian interventions, and human rights campaigns is an attempt to discuss the limitations on our fields of vision. By adjusting the lenses through which we see, other aspects of reality may come into focus. Speaking less metaphorically, works of art, activist campaigns, and individual testimonies may supplement or criticize established versions of, say, the war on terror or the genocide in Algeria of the 1990s. They may see, interpret, and frame stories differently, and in the process cast those who used to be victims of atrocities as agents struggling to define their life situation. To negotiate the frame through which we see and speak about people who have suffered may alter our perception of their subjectivity; challenging established frameworks may turn victims into agents or agents into victims.

The concept of 'negotiation' is also used to designate the ways in which the aesthetic strategies of different kinds of texts treat extra-textual elements internally. As Stephen Greenblatt has explained, literature (or any other creative work) does not merely *reflect* social conflicts and class relations; rather, it intervenes in current discussions, it alters the meanings of phrases, and it creates models for an understanding of social life Through sometimes-subtle changes in style, semantics, narrative structure, and points of enunciation, texts complexly negotiate the subject positions of victims and agents. The very variety of styles and genres in which human rights abuses are told testify to the complexity of these negotiations. At times, these works supplement mainstream scenarios; at other times, they pick up on that 'rubbish heap' of 'debris' excluded from official frames of war, rubbish heaps that, according to Butler, may provide 'potential resources for resistance' against official narratives (Butler, *Frames of War* xiii).

Contributors to this book consistently seek to combine aesthetics and politics in critical and contextualized readings of human rights discourses. Human rights are not only dependent on specific laws; they are also dependent on the cultural and social recognition of rights-bearing individuals and a 'communicative arrangement' (Habermas 64). Thus, the social conditions for the victimhood and agency of the rights-bearing individual change all the time.

To understand the discursive framing of human rights, we must 'always historicize' (Jameson ix). But historicizing human rights is not necessarily creating long genealogies or philosophical histories. Rather, contributors to this book study human rights in their dynamic historical contexts because this approach allows us to see how rights talk has been used to negotiate the relations between the individual and the community, between the well known and the foreign, or between the agent and the victim. In short, we want to understand how human rights have been functionalized in specific political situations, and we want to use these contextualized analyses to critically investigate the ambivalent history of human rights. The high moral claims of human rights rhetoric have sometimes clouded the actual character of specific declarations and interventions, and made it difficult to differentiate between the objects of humanitarian aid and the subjects of political rights.

We position the discussion of human rights within a critical tradition that raises questions about the a priori legitimacy of human rights discourse (Douzinas; Douzinas and Gearty; Stamos), the possibility of solidarity (Butler; Rancière; Chouliaraki; Mouffe), and the role of human rights in national and international politics (Mignolo; De Sousa Santos; Robbins). We argue that historicized readings of relevant discursive framing allow us to follow the human rights discourse as it fluctuates in and out of parliaments, popular culture, social media, and law.

The book is divided into three parts, each of which discusses different types of negotiations of victimhood and agency in the human rights discourse. Part I investigates the problem of the manifold genealogies of human rights, Part II focuses on the relation between the nation state and the individual in political human rights conflicts, and Part III examines the affective patterns in response to human suffering. Articles within the three parts are organized chronologically, according to the dates of the examined material.

Part I. Troublesome origins: the genealogies of human rights

A prominent trend in the recent academic human rights literature is the genealogical approach. Where, scholars have asked, does the idea of human rights originate? In the many and often contrasting genealogies, influential answers have ranged from the Spinozistic thought of the early Enlightenment (Israel) to French classicist drama of the seventeenth century (Maslan), from eighteenth-century sentimentalism and natural law (Hunt; Edelstein) to the new 'moral world' of war protests and NGOs of the 1970s (Moyn 1). However, establishing genealogies of political concepts is no neutral endeavour. At their best, genealogies demonstrate historically shifting ways of reflecting on recurring problems. They may inspire new ways of approaching dilemmas that remain pressing over time. At their worst, genealogies are one-sided, and serve principally to legitimize specific normative stands on issues that are or ought to be debatable. The unvoiced assumption in this case is that if a persuasive genealogy may be established, then the nature of a political concept, such as human rights, has finally been defined. As Lena Halldenius demonstrates in her critical reading of James Griffin's *On Human Rights* (2008), selective readings from the vast historical material too often function to justify already established normative positions in contemporary debate. She invites us to read more broadly in the historical literature in order to nuance our positions and to seriously reflect on the questions and answers provided by figures from the past.

To read more broadly and thoroughly in the history of human rights is what Simonsen, Kjærgård, and Eggers do in the three remaining chapters of Part I. Instead of using the historical material to legitimize already-established normative positions, the three chapters aim to present conflictual moments in the history of human rights. The shared methodological assumption of these chapters is that the language of natural and human rights has been used to tackle historically demanding problems such as the inequality between the conquistadores and Native Americans in early modern globalization (Simonsen), the political rights of the poor (Kjærgård), and resistance to oppression (Eggers). The aim of the chapters is not to argue any one specific definition of human rights, but to demonstrate the ways in which the human rights vocabulary has been used in ideological struggles to come to terms with issues that remain problematic to this day. In these cases, historical figures struggle to determine whether or not American Indians should be considered political agents in their own right, whether the poor should have voting rights or merely be provided for by others, and whether the right to resistance is tyrannical or perhaps a democratic necessity.

In all four chapters, the political situations that motivate declarations of rights and broader human rights discourses demonstrate not the ideal, normative foundation of human rights, but the malleable and conflictual character of rights. Here, human rights are not presented as a stable list of principles that we may uphold or violate. Rather, the discourse of human rights is shown to be used in constant struggles to come to terms with urgent concerns. Depending on the political outlook of the historical figures invoking the language of rights, groups of people may be described as victims in need of protection, or as political agents. What the chapters bring to our attention are the ways in which the framing of rights has consequences, not only for our understanding of the history of human rights, but also for the subjects imagined to be or not be the bearers of rights.

Part II. Negotiating victimhood: the politics of contextual rhetoric

Many stories of human rights abuse are individual stories. Telling them may have a therapeutic effect and may in itself restore a sense of agency to the individual, but very often the transformation from victimhood to agency involves an act of making the suffering public. Published life narratives may be social, legal, or political claims, and the very publication of grief and suffering may itself be a political act. The reason for this is that the social vulnerability of our bodies partly constitutes us as political beings (Butler, *Precarious Life* 20). Thus, public stories of atrocities are not only about coming to terms with the trauma of violence; in becoming public, they play into the ongoing agonistic memory of the original situation of violence (Mouffe). They create the future by talking about the past. In both non-democratic and democratic nation states, not only perpetrators but also political actors may try, wholly or in part, to silence the stories of a violent past. Thus, telling your story against this background of selective national forgetting may be an act of political dissensus (Rancière).

In Part II, all articles discuss the politics of human rights in situations where the state has played a decisive *and* negative role in the understanding of human rights and the collective memory of human rights abuses. The examples range from Russia in the 1930s (Kriza), Italy in the 1970s (Andreasen and Cecchini), Algeria in the 1990s (Dobie), and present-day North America (Musiol and Coskan-Johnson). This section focuses both on the clash between the victim and the state, and on the ideological clash between national and international understandings of what human rights are. In some of the articles, the critical perspective on the state derives directly from the perspective of the victims and their traumatic experiences of violence (Cecchini and Andreasen; Dobie; Musiol); in other articles, the critical focus is on internal and external state policy (Kriza; Coskan-Johnson).

Based on historical reflections, scholars such as Arendt and Scarry have claimed that international law is weak when it comes to the protection of human rights, and that only the nation state in its democratic form may hope to defend the rights of human beings (Arendt 267ff; Scarry 40ff). However, this section raises a number of critical questions regarding the possibility of defending the rights of individuals within the nation state, even within the modern democratic nation state.

Part III. Responding to human suffering: affective space and aesthetic response

The aim of most humanitarian and human rights campaigns is to 'raise awareness' and to 'activate' people hitherto insufficiently engaged in political and humanitarian crises, be it politically or economically. The act of the successful campaign is to change the role of the spectator from passive to active, to increase his or her level of knowledge and generate involvement in a specific situation. Through text, image, and sound, the campaigners struggle to evoke a range of emotions stretching from empathy to rage, from sadness to culpability, but the ultimate goal is to make it possible for the spectator to 'find his or her feeling', making it possible to not only respond with adequate feeling to the suffering, but also to 'feel good' about helping, that is, finding the feeling that motivates action (Chouliaraki 1). It has been argued that literature and art are capable of eliciting empathy that may directly or indirectly lead to a consciousness of other peoples' suffering, and, eventually, action (Rorty; Hunt). However, the character of the response, both in humanitarian campaigns and in art and literature, is more complex and mixed than often assumed, and it has to be analysed in relation to specific aesthetic, mediatized, and social contexts. Also, it must be questioned whether it is possible to talk about a unidimensional and causal relation between certain stylistic choices and particular emotions; and even more urgently, whether it is possible to talk about a necessary relation between certain emotions and specific actions.

The common object of interest in Part III is the mix of affective responses to the varied aesthetic framing of human suffering. The articles raise these questions: How do spectators respond to human suffering and what are the stylistic means of producing these responses? How can we analyse the effects of the texts and media, and emphasize assumptions about agency and victimhood? What is the relation between the intention of the work or mediatized story and the responses of the spectator? And is there a relation between the reason and character of suffering, and the emotional response? In this section, the examples range from suffering due to natural disasters (Holm; Chouliaraki), to political persecution and genocide (Moore; Hagen; Kjørholt; Chouliaraki), poverty (Sharma), and war (Pedersen). The artists presented are Heinrich von Kleist, Joshua Oppenheimer, Binjamin Wilkomirski, Renzo Martens, and Rabih Mroué.

All the articles foreground the complexity of responses to human suffering. According to the contributions, far from producing unidimensional empathy and engagement, images of suffering may create baffled lingering, bewilderment, and indeterminacy of action (Winkel; Holm; Pedersen). A surplus of empathy may even create political paralysis (Hagen; Kjørholt). Instead of instigating action, they may invite critical reflection, and an active questioning of the relation between ethics and politics (Sharma; Pedersen). Sometimes, empathy may have less to do with the explicit presentation of suffering, and more to do with silences (Moore). Thus, in multiple ways, the articles investigate the complexities of effect and affect.

Works cited

Arendt, Hannah. *The Origins of Totalitarianism*. San Diego/New York/London: Harcourt, 1973. Print.

Butler, Judith. *Precarious Life: The Power of Mourning and Violence*. London/New York: Verso, 2004. Print.

Butler, Judith. *Frames of War: When Is Life Grievable?* London/New York: Verso, 2010. Print.

Chouliaraki, Lilie. *The Ironic Spectator: Solidarity in the Age of Post-Humanitarianism*. Cambridge: Polity Press, 2013. Print.

De Sousa Santos, Boaventura. *Toward a New Common Sense: Law, Science and Politics in the Paradigmatic Transition*. New York/London: Routledge, 1995. Print.

Douzinas, Costas. *The End of Human Rights: Critical Legal Thought at the Turn of the Century*. Oxford/Portland: Hart Publishing, 2000. Print.

Douzinas, Costas. *Human Rights and Empire: The Political Philosophy of Cosmopolitanism*. Abingdon: Routledge-Cavendish, 2007. Print.

Douzinas, Costas and Conor Gearty. *The Meanings of Rights: The Philosophy and Social Theory of Human Rights*. Cambridge: Cambridge University Press, 2014. Print.

Edelstein, Dan. 'Enlightenment Rights Talk'. *The Journal of Modern History* 86.3 (2014): 530–565. Print.

Goldberg, Elizabeth Swanson and Alexandrea Schultheis Moore, eds. *Theoretical Perspectives on Human Rights and Literature*. New York/London: Routledge, 2012. Print.

Greenblatt, Stephen. 'Resonance and Wonder'. *Bulletin of the American Academy of Arts and Sciences* 43.4 (Jan. 1990). 11–34. Print.
Habermas, Jürgen. 'Private and Public Autonomy, Human Rights and Popular Sovereignty'. *The Politics of Human Rights*. Ed. Obrad Savic. London/New York: Verso, 2002 (1999). 50–66. Print.
Hunt, Lynn. *Inventing Human Rights: A History*. New York/London: W. W. Norton, 2008. Print.
Israel, Jonathan. *Democratic Enlightenment: Philosophy, Revolution, and Human Rights 1750–1790*. Oxford: Oxford University Press, 2011. Print.
Jameson, Fredric. *The Political Unconscious: Narrative as a Socially Symbolic Act*. London/New York: Routledge, 2002. Print.
Maslan, Susan. 'The Anti-Human: Man and Citizen before the Declaration of the Rights of Man and of the Citizen'. *The South Atlantic Quarterly* 103.2/3 (2004): 357–374. Print.
Mignolo, Walter D. 'From "human rights" to "life rights"'. *The Meanings of Rights: The Philosophy and Social Theory of Human Rights*. Ed. Costas Douzinas and Conor Gearty. Cambridge: Cambridge University Press, 2014. 161–180. Print.
Mouffe, Chantal. 'Democracy, Human Rights and Cosmopolitanism: An Agonistic Approach'. *The Meanings of Rights: The Philosophy and Social Theory of Human Rights*. Ed. Costas Douzinas and Conor Gearty. Cambridge: Cambridge University Press, 2014. 181–192. Print.
Moyn, Samuel. *The Last Utopia: Human Rights in History*. Cambridge/London: The Belknap Press of Harvard University Press, 2012. Print.
Rancière, Jacques. 'Who Is the Subject of Human Rights?' *The South Atlantic Quarterly* 103.2/3 (2004): 297–310. Print.
Robbins, Bruce. '"All of Us without Exception": Sartre, Rancière, and the Cause of the Other'. *The Meanings of Rights: The Philosophy and Social Theory of Human Rights*. Ed. Costas Douzinas and Conor Gearty. Cambridge: Cambridge University Press, 2014. 251–271. Print.
Rorty, Richard. 'Human Rights, Rationality and Sentimentality'. *The Politics of Human Rights*. Ed. Obrad Savic. London/New York: Verso, 2002 (1999). 167–185. Print.
Scarry, Elaine. 'The Difficulty of Imagining Other Persons'. *The Handbook of Interethnic Coexistence*. Ed. Eugene Weiner, Alan B. Slifka, and Deborah E. Bing. New York: Continuum, 1998. 40–62. Print.
Schaffer, Kay and Sidonie Smith. *Human Rights and Narrated Lives: The Ethics of Retcognition*. New York/Basingstoke: Palgrave Macmillan, 2004. Print.
Slaughter, Joseph. *Human Rights, Inc. The World Novel, Narrative Form, and International Law*. New York: Fordham University Press, 2007. Print.
Sliwinski, Sharon. *Human Rights in Camera*. Chicago: University of Chicago Press, 2011. Print.
Stamos, David N. *The Myth of Universal Human Rights: Its Origin, History, and Explanation, Along with a More Humane Way*. London: Paradigm Publishers, 2014. Print.

Part I

Troublesome origins

The genealogies of human rights

Chapter 1

On the use and abuse of history in philosophy of human rights

Lena Halldenius

Anyone who is interested in human rights and history is called upon to engage in, or form an opinion on, the rapidly escalating and rather divisive academic debate about what a correct history of human rights looks like. Is 'our' concept of human rights ancient, medieval, early modern, modern, newer than modern? Did it find its shape in the late eighteenth century, as Lynn Hunt and several others claim, or is it a much later product of political and religious debates in the twentieth century, with little or no conceptual connection to anything prior to that, as another main mover, Samuel Moyn, argues? Sources invoked in these interventions span political struggles and rhetoric, legal developments, activism, pamphleteering, etc. The historiography of human rights has become its own vibrant research field.[1]

History also plays an important role in the philosophy of human rights, more so than in philosophical discussions focusing on related concepts, such as justice, and in a different way, as we will see. In philosophy, history tends to be used in order to make it credible that there is a tradition of rights as a moral idea, or an ethical ideal, that transcends national boundaries. In the example that I will investigate, this moral idea is tightly spun around the moral dignity of the human person.

I am sceptical of Moyn's strong discontinuity thesis, but agree with him that there has been a shift in conceptions of human rights during the twentieth century, from 'politics of the state to the morality of the globe' (Moyn 43). Rather than figuring in, or as, constitutional principles of the political life of a polity and the relation between a state and its members, the notion of (human) rights has come to serve as the name of a state- and politics-transcending ethical position on the status of the human person, and the relations between human persons. Amartya Sen represents this move towards personal morality, and away from contestation and politics, when he says that:

1 For an overview, see Alston.

> Human rights can be seen as primarily ethical demands. They are not principally 'legal', 'proto-legal', or 'ideal-legal' commands. Even though human rights can, and often do, inspire legislation, this is a further fact, rather than a constitutive characteristic of human rights.
>
> (Sen 319)

I find this move to be problematic, but at present am concerned with only one aspect of it, which has to do with the use of history in philosophy of human rights. If the move from politics of the state to morality of the globe is a recent one, it goes without saying that trying to ground a state-transcending morality of human rights with the help of early modern history is problematic. Still, philosophers of this kind of morality of human rights are prone to projecting it back onto an unsuspecting past, claiming to base their accounts on a long-standing human rights tradition that, frankly, is not there, at least not in that form. Examples of such influential contributors to philosophy are Martha Nussbaum, Thomas Pogge, Jeremy Waldron, and James Griffin. Griffin will be my main example, and the focus of my critical discussion. I zoom in on Griffin for two reasons. First, his reliance on what he refers to as a historical notion of human rights is not exceptional – he fits this pattern of invocations of history in support of a moral theory – but it is unusually explicit. Second, Griffin claims that 'our' concept of human rights is a product of eighteenth-century Enlightenment thought. If 'our' concept of human rights is Griffin's concept, then that is false – as we will see – but I agree that the eighteenth century is a pivotal moment, and that Enlightenment thinkers are a rich source that we do well to attend to.

As we will also see, the concept that we could build with Enlightenment sources as philosophical inspiration will not confirm, but challenge, the move from politics to morality, and will incorporate, as necessary components, principles that Griffin explicitly rejects. Even if there is no obvious tradition from eighteenth-century philosophers (I will, as we go along, articulate specifically who they are) to us, there are good philosophical reasons to excavate their commitments for purposes of challenging, rather than confirming, the moralized conception of human rights that, arguably, is 'ours'.

What is it that we are studying, and how?

What is it that philosophers do, or claim to be doing, when they study ideas from the past? What I have to say here is in no way radically new, but it provides us with a useful methodological context. One common view is that it is distinctive of philosophical, rather than historical, study of the past, that one engages with arguments and ideas directly. There are different rationales for this. One is that philosophical questions are perennial or time-resistant: when Aristotle, Rousseau, and Rawls address matters of 'justice' (or something that may be reasonably translated as 'justice'), what they say may be meaningfully analysed, compared, and assessed, without filtering it through differences in historical situation. Alternatively, one remains agnostic regarding the perennial nature of philosophical problems while excavating the philosophical past as a vast repository of possibly useful ideas. One could then consider the potential of Aristotle's, or Rousseau's, or Rawls's, or others' accounts of justice, for addressing justice-related issues in our own time.

The 'perennial questions' approach comes with deliberately discounting the historical, political, intellectual, or scientific context within which a text was produced. The 'vast repository approach' may be used with the same kind of discounting, but is not committed to it. It is perfectly possible to hold that the history of philosophy may be used as a bank of good ideas, while insisting that we cannot know what those ideas are, or understand what those philosophers are saying and conveying, without interpreting them in relation to their own intellectual milieu. This, roughly, is my position.

What we study in the history of philosophy are, strictly speaking, arguments, rather than texts, and we risk getting the arguments wrong if we do not attend to the relevant historical circumstances within which those arguments were made. What a philosopher could possibly have meant by the words used is constrained or shaped by whatever received and contested meanings of words that were available and so could have made sense to him or her, given the discursive context in which the arguments were formed.[2] Philosophers want to persuade; they have aims to promote and arguments to win, and even though a philosophical aim may be to transcend the present, the communication of that aim will be conditioned by whatever makes sense in that present. We need to be clear about what this does not entail: it is not to deny that there may be a continuity of concerns, a similarity of terminology, or even that ideas can survive, persist, and reappear, as it were. The point is a methodological one about what we need to do and know, if we aim to understand the philosophical content and purpose of what we are studying, rather than impose our own conventions and intuitions upon it.[3]

Both the 'perennial questions' and the 'vast repository' rationales require stringent attention to the sources, albeit in different ways. One cannot gesture vaguely towards the past and claim to have achieved something of philosophical significance. Why, then, is such gesturing common practice when the matter at hand is 'human rights', or 'rights', more generally conceived? This rhetorical question proceeds from the tendency in human rights philosophy to appeal to an evolving tradition of thought as support of one's own preferred conception.

First, let me note that vague gesturing or partial exploitation of the past is not a vice exclusive to those who invoke the trope of an evolving tradition. We may remind ourselves of the purposes to which Robert Nozick used John Locke's

2 For instance, see Skinner; Waugh and Ariew.

3 See Catana.

theory of natural rights and acquisition of property. The fact that Locke wrote property into the natural realm is exploited by Nozick in support of a near absolute right to private property against state intervention. Nozick was not concerned with the philosophical and political context within which Locke's account of rights and property took shape, or with who Locke's interlocutors were. Locke is employed to lend credence to Nozick's own position, while Locke's standing in the philosophical canon is supposed to convey authority. This is 'ipsedixitism', as Bentham put it with reference to Cicero: 'the master has said that it is so; therefore, say the disciples of the illustrious sage, therefore so it is' (Bentham, *Deontology* 323).

Nozick, at least, was clear about which source he was abusing. Such explicitness is not to be found when 'our' concept of human rights is placed within this kind of narrative: 'The moral notion of human rights has evolved from earlier notions of natural law and natural rights' (Pogge 54); 'there is a continuous, developing notion of human rights running through this history' (Griffin 2); '[t]he notion of human rights that emerged by the end of the Enlightenment – what can reasonably be called the Enlightenment notion – is the notion we have today' (Griffin 13). The moral concept of human rights as we know it, then, is the historical fruit of an early modern concept of natural rights, which in its turn was born of earlier, ancient and medieval concepts of natural law. Despite the historiographical struggles that I mentioned in the introduction, this smooth transmission of rights through history has remained an attractive idea in philosophy. History is now not a repository of ideas that might be useful and fruitful if we could only understand them properly, as much as a tradition that has been handed down to us, a tradition that not only allegedly explains, but also justifies, human rights as we claim to know them. We can appeal to this tradition in support of the existence, value, and correct explication of human rights. Despite all the work that the tradition is made to do, it seems to require little close attention to particulars in those historical sources in order to be taken as gospel. We already know what the tradition is, or what we need it to be. It is like oral history, or 'ipsedixitism', only now the sage is left vaguely unknown.

I will now introduce my main example and the focus of my critical discussion: James Griffin's much-lauded ethical account of human rights as grounded in dignity, conceived as 'normative agency', and claimed to express 'the Enlightenment project on human rights' (Griffin 152, 13).

The example: Griffin on history, rights, and equality

In *On Human Rights*, James Griffin claims to favour a bottom-up approach to human rights in ethics (29).[4] He does this by exploring what he takes to be the

4 Griffin does not hang anything on the terminological differences between human rights, natural rights, or rights of man. On these terminologies in the eighteenth century, see Hunt 22–26.

historical tradition of rights, with the aim of remedying the indeterminateness of the notion of human rights found in it. His account of the best ethics with which to make human rights determinate proceeds from 'normative agency': a person's capacity to form and pursue a worthwhile life. Human rights should be seen as protections of this capacity, which is alternatively referred to as the status of personhood. Griffin suggests that this way of understanding human rights is the ethically best way of making them determinate, given the historical tradition of human rights.

The historically evolving conception of human rights to which Griffin subscribes originated, we are told, in the doctrine of natural law in 'Greek and Roman antiquity' (9), and appeared in its 'modern' form in the twelfth and thirteenth centuries via Thomas Aquinas's theological account of man's innate disposition to reason (176). In the seventeenth and eighteenth centuries, this already-modern conception underwent a process of secularization, and the product of that process is the concept that is familiar to us today: there 'has been no theoretical development of the idea itself since then' (13).[5] A challenge for us now is that when God was taken out of the equation in the late seventeenth century, nothing was put in its place, leaving the term not only indeterminate, but 'nearly criterionless' (14). No wonder it needs a bit of reining in.

The one criterion that remains in Griffin's historical notion is that rights are entitlements that 'we have simply in virtue of being human' (13). Here, 'being human' is shorthand for a specific moral good that is inherently associated with being a person. This is common parlance. When Martha Nussbaum talks about human rights, 'human' is shorthand for an Aristotelian notion of human flourishing (72); for others, it refers to some set of human interests (Tasioulas 662ff), or equality of status or rank (Waldron 47–49). For Griffin, 'being human' stands for the moral capacity to form and pursue a worthwhile life (34). It is this moral feature – that human quality by virtue of which rights are held – that determines and limits what persons have a right *to*.

That Griffin's is a moral theory, where morality is logically prior to politics and law, is also evident in the fact that he defines rights as claims that human agents have, and which can be asserted against all other individual agents and groups, not against the political institutions of society, however conceived (Griffin 177). Rights are interpersonal norms of interaction. In Pogge's words (and against Pogge's own view), for Griffin, rights are 'interactional', not 'institutional' (Pogge 45, 64).

Now, if the term 'rights' really is nearly without criteria, what does it mean to proceed from a notion that it is nevertheless said to contain, not to mention to regard that notion as a side-constraint on the best ethics within which to embed it? Let me start with a brief reflection.

5 For an overview of evolutionary accounts of human rights throughout history, and various approaches to, defences of, and refutations of a 'diachronic transferability of language', concepts and ideas in the case of human rights in history, see Alston; McCrudden.

It would be rash to deny offhand that the process of abstraction from, or filtering, what actual philosophers have actually argued could yield something useful: a raw notion, perhaps, or a common presupposition. A question is how to perform such filtering without biasing the process towards an end result upon which one has already settled. Can we know that we have got the raw notion 'right', rather than missed it, by mistaking it for something else? Maybe there is no raw or core notion at all, only a jumble of ideas that could be structured and combined in a variety of different ways, none of which is necessarily more genuine or true to some kind of original sense (whatever that might be) than another. In Griffin's case, the procedure results in an extremely individualistic and private presupposition, before which an eighteenth-century protagonist of natural rights would stand baffled. To anticipate: Griffin does not allow for a human right to democratic participation since he believes that, in principle, the rights-grounding capacity for enabling one to form and pursue one's own path in life may be secured in societies without democratic institutions. Contrary to what he believes, this conclusion is in no way supported by eighteenth-century philosophy of natural rights.

The only conceivable way to go about trying to identify a 'historical notion' is, I maintain, by attending to the circumstances in which issues of rights have arisen, and to various points that philosophers have wanted to make by using a rights terminology. If there are historically prevalent and philosophically indispensable features of eighteenth-century accounts of rights, we find them in political presuppositions and conceptual features that Griffin either fails to see, outright rejects, or treats as contingent, notably the common good, the principle of equality, the fact of power in society, the threat that power represents, and the conceptual necessity of democratic accountability. Let's take a closer look at the matter of equality before the law.

In Griffin's theory of the best ethics within which to embed the historical notion of human rights (that is, the principle of normative agency), equality before the law is not necessary. His rejection of equality before the law as a human rights requirement goes back to his rejection of equality as a ground for human rights. Equality figures in the ground of human rights only to say that all human persons are 'equally endowed with rights', not that there is a right *to* equality (40). Moreover, Griffin insists that equality is not what ensures that all persons are equally endowed with rights. Equality is simply another way of saying that everyone who has rights has them for the same reason: because of their status as persons capable of normative agency. The egalitarianism of this is supposedly captured by the very notion of personhood.[6]

6 Here, Griffin may be usefully compared to Waldron, whose conception of dignity as grounds for rights proceeds from an old notion of 'rank', but in a modern, equalized way: 'the modern notion of *human* dignity [as opposed to the old hierarchical notion of nobles and commoners] involves an upwards equalization of rank' (Waldron 33, original emphasis).

There is, then, no interpersonal, comparative element in Griffin's account of human rights. His discussion of equality before the law, or rather his refutation of equality before the law, bears this out: each person has certain rights in relation to the law and legal procedure – for example, arbitrary detention is an infringement of personhood, and as such is counted as a violation of a human right – but that has nothing to do with equality before the law. How other people are treated under the law has no bearing on my situation; only the effects of law and legal procedure for my own normative agency can say anything about my own human rights situation. If I am treated worse than others, but am still able to exercise normative agency and pursue a worthwhile life, then no human right of mine is violated (see Griffin 194–199).

Discriminatory laws and practices concerning public services, healthcare, welfare, even legal processes, violate human rights only if they leave individuals below the threshold of what pursuing a worthwhile life requires, but when they do, the violation is not due to the discrimination – which is a comparative notion – but due to the result for each person in terms of normative agency, which is interpersonally non-comparative.

Griffin's reluctance to talk about rights *to* equality, rather than equality as part of our reasons for adopting a rights framework in the first place, does not make him exceptional in any way. For instance, few philosophers include patterns of distribution of resources under human rights, but, like Griffin, instead favour basic provision, or a threshold level, where each person's position is assessed independently of how others are faring. We see this in the influential works of Nussbaum and Pogge.[7] This is part of a popular commitment to minimalism, pruning what human rights are about.[8]

Griffin's refutation of principles of non-discrimination and of a right to equality of treatment under the law makes for a stark depoliticization of human rights. It is against the background of this private moral notion that we need to assess the claim that his ethics is the best ethics with which to make the 'historical notion' of human rights determinate. It is to this historical notion that we now turn.

The historical notion: where is it?

We now attend to something that is presumably of considerable importance to anyone relying on a historical notion to make a philosophical point: Where is it?

7 Pogge on the 'minimally adequate share' of essential goods (38), and Nussbaum on 'a *threshold level*' (6, original emphasis) of whatever is required for central capabilities. On human rights and economic inequality, see Moyn.

8 See the debate on 'minimalism' occasioned by Michael Ignatieff's book, *Human Rights as Politics and as Idolatry* (2001), for instance in Cohen.

The formative period of the Enlightenment idea of human rights (remember that Griffin makes nothing of the terminological differences between human rights, natural rights, and rights of man) that constitutes Griffin's historical notion tracks a period of secularization, represented by Grotius and Pufendorf. The Enlightenment idea is said to come to its fully formed self between the last 15 years of the seventeenth century (just in time to include Locke) through the end of the eighteenth. If this notion really is an idea of which there 'has been no theoretical development [. . .] since then' (13), then surely there must be plenty of manifestations of it in writings from that period. Remember that this is a notion of human rights such that rights are claims that all humans have, qua persons or normative agents, against all other agents.

Some Enlightenment thinkers seem to fall by the wayside from the start. Hume and Bentham would not agree that human agents have rights against all other human agents, simply by virtue of their humanity, for the simple reason that they explicitly rejected the idea that any such rights exist. This is unremarkable and well known, but, as it turns out, Griffin does not allow us that conclusion.

Over the course of the period in which the 'historical notion' was formed, the commitment to the naturalness of law and rights grew increasingly weak, Griffin tells us. It grew weak to an extent that it ended up claiming little more than the existence of 'moral principles independent of positive and social convention', leaving it compatible with 'virtually all conceptions of ethics', including Hume's, but excluding ethical relativism (12). What happened here? Hume and Bentham are now dragged kicking and screaming into the orbit of a more or less all-consuming natural or human rights paradigm. The historical notion of human rights is now a historical notion of morality. We might here want to remind ourselves of Lynn Hunt's warning that human rights may seem so self-evident to us that 'the risk is that the history of human rights becomes the history of Western civilization or now, sometimes, the history of the entire world', making it impossible to explain anything, not even the indubitable 'crystallization of human rights claims at the end of the eighteenth century' (Hunt 20). How did the idea of a right of all agents against all other agents – which is vague enough – turn into the same thing as anything to do with morality, except relativism?

If this is the historical notion, it is certainly true that it is 'nearly criterionless'. But if so, it is also incapable of constraining us to any particular conception. Let us, then, do Griffin the service of reining in his historical notion to what he needs it to be in order for it do the job he wants it to do. This is what you need to do if you want to claim to have history on your side.

To start with, there are at least a few things that Griffin's Enlightenment notion *cannot* be allowed to contain. If Griffin's ethics of personhood and normative agency are the best ethics to make it determinate, then the notion itself has to be compatible with that, in its foundations and necessary provisions. Consequently, the Enlightenment notion in question cannot be founded upon a principle of equality. Nor may it contain, as a necessary provision, a principle of non-discrimination or a right *to* equality of anything that is non-reducible to individual, non-comparative enjoyment. So, where do we find this partially reined in, and now less weak, historical notion of human rights? Where is it? Who holds it?

The start of the formative period seems to be set deliberately to include Locke, who also is Griffin's first reference when he sets out to explain what '*the* [Enlightenment] project' of human rights is (11, original emphasis). But further on, Locke seems to discredit himself, since his ground for human rights is a 'principle of equal respect', which, as we have seen, is the wrong kind of ground (214). Also, Locke might not be secular enough. But it may be reasonable to expect to find the most fitting proponents towards the end of the period, in eighteenth-century philosophy of rights.

The superstar of the Rights of Man doctrine – Thomas Paine – gets only a passing mention (Griffin 176); let us assume for now that he is supposed to pass the test (an Enlightenment notion of rights without Paine would be odd indeed). Rousseau and Kant are mentioned approvingly, sometimes together (cf. 32). Kant seems to be a particular favourite, which should not surprise, given the prominent place of the autonomy of the person within his system. Yet Griffin notes with a degree of concern that Kant's derivation of natural rights from respect for persons results in a broader range of rights than 'we have from the Enlightenment tradition' (219). This concern presumably concerns the extension, not the intension, of the term, so Kant stays.

Who else? One is at a bit of a loss, it turns out. We may have a negative criterion at least, so that we can know whose ideas do *not* fall under the historical notion of human rights. Not all Enlightenment thinkers favoured 'natural rights', after all. Bentham famously branded any talk of natural rights as a perversion of language (Bentham, *Anarchical Fallacies* 501). According to Hume's historical method in matters to do with morality, custom and experience are the only guide to knowledge about what people value. Natural rights, just as the social contract, are nothing short of fictions that obscure what really is at stake: the common interest in peace and security. Hume did not disagree with defenders of natural rights concerning human vulnerability to power, or concerning what people tended to regard as being worthy of protection. But he did discard any talk of natural rights as falsely assuming the existence of ideas that have no bearing on custom. Why assume that people are, in some metaphysical sense, 'born free', when, to be true to empirical experience, they are not? Everyone is born subject to law; securing peace and security (and freedom) in the face of that fact is what the challenge of political organization and the 'artificial' (that is, dependent upon custom) virtue of justice is about (Hume book III, section II).

Hume's and Bentham's careful rejections of natural rights are indicators, if any such were needed, that the Enlightenment debates about the existence, content, ground, and limits of natural rights were very far from criterionless catch-alls. These were conceptually meticulous and, more than anything, they mattered terribly. They mattered because the circumstances under which the issue of natural rights, or the rights of man, arose were the spectre of oppression and the abuse of power. A story of human rights as nothing other than a moral idea about individual capacities and interactions between agents misses the point of what eighteenth-century rights advocates were concerned about.

On equality, self-rule, and the abuse of power

Griffin says that, in writing the *Two Treatises of Government,* Locke's interest was in 'moral constraints on the arbitrary acts of rulers', and that this directed Locke's attention, in terms of which natural rights to focus on (11). Griffin claims it to be generally true of seventeenth- and eighteenth-century rights advocates that the pressing problem of autocratic rulers' abuse of power caused them to treat civil and political rights as the most important extensions of the concept of rights. However, this did not have any bearing on matters of 'sense', or what the concept of rights was. The concept remained indeterminate and thin (17). The problem of autocratic rulers, then, was merely a contingent seventeenth- and eighteenth-century concern that did not affect the concept of rights, only which examples of rights came to be listed as important. In order to further emphasize the irrelevance of constitutional matters to the intention of the Enlightenment concept of human rights, Griffin goes on to say, to the surprise of some of us, that 'seventeenth- and eighteenth-century writers' believed that respect for natural rights required no constitutional change. Instead, 'the monarchies of their day' could, in theory, respect a 'full range of human rights' (242). They were not likely to, but that is a contingent, practical problem, not a conceptual matter; nothing in the concept itself requires any particular constitutional form. At no stage are any examples given of anyone who actually subscribed to these views.

This rather startling assertion is used to legitimate, as true to the historical notion, Griffin's own position that human rights do not require democracy (or any particular constitutional form). In principle, a society in modern conditions could 'respect all human rights' without being democratic; it could instead be an 'aristocracy of the talents', where the talents in question would have 'a track record for soundness' (253).[9] The general public having a fair say in political decisions or means to contest the soundness of their governors is not required

9 The lure of aristocratic ideas is hard to shake, even for rights theorists. This is clearly visible in Waldron's 'egalitarian conception of dignity', with his prevalent use of hierarchical terminology, such as 'noble rank' and 'noble bearing'. Believing in equality of rights is to insist on 'nobility for the common man' (22), and 'upwards equalization of rank' (33). This is combined with a faith in modern society as already egalitarian in spirit: we no longer attribute to people different sorts of statuses ('We used to think there were many kinds: nobles, commoners, slaves, and so on. [. . .] The standard status for people now is more like an earldom than like the status of a peasant' (59)). Hierarchies, you will be glad to hear, are no longer a thing; they are 'imagined (or recollected)' (57), but not real, not anymore: 'things have changed'.

by human rights; it is required by 'the form of fairness relevant to democracy', which is a different form of fairness than the one relevant to human rights (249). Historical precedence is invoked again, when we are told that human rights and democracy 'have grown up' to meet different needs, the protection of the individual and the stable management of groups, respectively.

You do not need to go back to eighteenth-century sources to challenge a claim that full respect for human rights is compatible with denying the people political influence. But you do need to do so in order to show what some of the constituents would be of a conception of human rights that can claim Enlightenment provenance with any degree of credibility.

If we wish to understand natural rights in eighteenth-century thought, we need to grasp the fact that power over others, and the capacity of those who hold that power to also abuse it, was not a contingent concern, or merely part of the extension of a concept defined prior to, or independently of, any such concern. It was built into the concept itself; it was its very point.

We need to resist letting one smooth story replace another. It is crucial to emphasize that there was a battle over the meaning and point of rights. Rights were the focus of conceptual and political struggles, and we do well to attend to those thinkers who engaged systematically with the explication of rights, such as the French encyclopaedists.

The 'droit naturel' entry in the French *Encyclopédie* was written by Denis Diderot in 1755; Griffin does not mention it. We should first note that Diderot states as a philosophical starting point that rights are the foundation of justice, and that justice is 'declared equity', that is, fairness. Second, the object or point of natural rights is not the fulfilment of each person's life plans, but the good of humanity or the common interest. Third, the regulating principle of humanity is the conformity of one's own will to the will of all others; and fourth, the 'depository' that we consult in order to know what our natural rights are – that is, the rights of humanity – is the collected well of principles of written law, social practices, tacit conventions, and even feelings of indignation and resentment.

If we allow that a historical notion of an Enlightenment idea of natural rights should be at least compatible with the entry in the *Encyclopédie*, then we are left with at least these two general things that directly contradict Griffin's 'historical notion': first, justice, rights, and fairness are not different things, but conceptually stand and fall together; and second, the common good – not the good of each individual – is the criterion by which to assess what rights there are. Equally significant is Diderot's inclusion of a discussion of legitimate authority and restrictions on, and conditions for, the exercise of 'right over the lives of others'. This applies not only to governments, but to anyone who has power over another. What Diderot says about power over rights-bearing agents is that you do not gain legitimate authority – that is, the right to coerce others – simply by offering conditions that are advantageous to them. That would be magnanimity, not fairness.

The point to emphasize here is the centrality to Enlightenment natural rights discourses of the fact of power: that some are able to put others at risk and impose their will upon them. The centrality of this fact will likely be lost on us, unless we strive to remember that the doctrine of natural rights or the rights of man (the terminology was not consistent) in the eighteenth century was invoked to a large extent by republicans. The liberty of the person that is part of the foundation and object of the rights of man is the republican notion that a person is free only to the extent that he or she is not vulnerable to the risk of being subjected to the arbitrary imposition of someone else's will. An aristocracy of talents, however sound of judgement, cannot protect people's liberty, since a fair say in civic matters is part of the definition – not merely the extension – of republican freedom. This was Diderot's point, and it is one that is expressed consistently by eighteenth-century republican advocates of natural rights.[10]

Richard Price – whom Griffin does not mention either – lists as principles of 'sacred' rights 'the right to resist power when abused' and 'the right to chuse our own governors' (Price, 'A Discourse' 190). Importantly, these are not extensions of a prior and thin concept of rights; these principles are what rights meant according to Price. Rights are moral powers without which persons are not free; these principles operate under the general moral principle of universal benevolence. To the interests of mankind (truth, virtue, and liberty), all other interests are subordinate (180). Price's assertion, in the essay *A Discourse on the Love of Our Country* (1789), of a right to resist oppression and a right to civic self-government as sacred, natural, unalienable, held a priori as gifts from God, and his use of them to justify changes to the political system, initiated the so-called 'Revolution debate'. It prompted Edmund Burke to defend aristocracies (of the talented, no doubt) and custom in a refutation of natural rights as an abstract principle (Burke 151). According to Burke, the only rights that are 'real' are those that men hold as functions of the laws and conventions of their societies.

Adding to the flames of the debate about what rights mean, and necessarily require, in *Rights of Man* (1791), Thomas Paine (whose arguments Griffin does not discuss) argues against Burke and in support of Price that natural rights and civil rights are a conceptual package. Civil rights are not contingent examples of the extension of rights. The natural rights of men pre-exist in the individual – '[s]ociety grants him nothing' (Paine 116) – and civil rights are founded upon them, such that civil rights are the aggregate of the natural rights of all men, and pertain to those things in relation to which the power of the individual man is insufficient, such as security against attack.

In her *Vindication of the Rights of Men* (the first published commentary on Burke's *Reflections on the Revolution in France*, written in 1790, before Paine's *Rights of Man*)

10 For a more extensive analysis of eighteenth-century rights discourse, see Halldenius, *Mary Wollstonecraft* Chapters 2 and 3.

Mary Wollstonecraft (whom Griffin does not mention), defends the natural rights of man on republican grounds, and, like Paine, emphasizes that there can be no freedom, and hence no 'birthright', without a civic transformation establishing self-government and public accountability. Again, this is not a contingent item on a wish list of desirable stuff, but required by the definition of liberty. Wollstonecraft goes further than both Price and Paine, by also insisting that a 'mighty revolution in property' (Wollstonecraft, 'A Vindication' 5, 48)[11] – that is, a levelling of holdings of, and control over property – is required, unless the civic transformation is to turn out to be just a nominal change of masters.

Price stressed that the content of independence – the republican conception of freedom, understood as freedom from subordination to the will of another – are various moral powers: the power to act on what is right, to practice one's preferred religion, and the power of a civil society to govern itself (Price, 'Two Tracts' 22). These moral powers – rights – necessarily presuppose a personal independence that is only possible in political circumstances where no one is the master of another, however benevolent or sound of judgement. The liberty that is the natural right of man makes no sense outside of society and is inherently egalitarian. In *An Historical and Moral View of the French Revolution*, Wollstonecraft states explicitly that the 'natural and imprescriptible right of man' is freedom, and that the purpose of political society is to protect that right (Wollstonecraft, 'An Historical and Moral View' 6, 115, 221). That rights are natural is to say that equality between human persons is natural. Equality is built into the principle of rights such that the freedom that I can claim as my right is limited by every other person's equal claim to the same; freedom is violated per definition by vulnerability to the imposition of arbitrary power.

The concept of rights that the eighteenth-century republicans developed and promoted proceeded from a principle of equality; it presupposed a republican constitution (what we would today refer to as a representative democracy) as the only constitutional form that expresses political freedom and freedom of the person. If 'our' concept of human rights is ethical demands (as Sen puts it) of each against all, and if it is conceptually unconnected to equality between persons and to the structure and organization of political life (as Griffin claims), then our concept is not theirs. All the worse for our concept, I would add. Historically prevalent, conceptually integrated, and – in their own time – influential, yet contested, features of eighteenth-century accounts of rights support nothing like moral theories of the kind that Griffin advocates. On the contrary, they challenge them at their core. Rather than creating historical notions that cannot be supported by sources and are contradicted by scholarship, and using these figments to peddle one's own morality in lieu of sustained argument, I suggest that we explore the richness of eighteenth-century rights philosophy, and the

11 See also Halldenius, 'Mary Wollstonecraft's Feminist Critique'; Halldenius, *Mary Wollstonecraft*.

urgency that they convey. They are indeed a vast repository, but one that will make sense to us, and challenge our presuppositions of what rights are or can be, only if we attend closely to what they had to say about their own turbulent times.[12]

Works cited

Alston, Philip. 'Does the Past Matter? On the Origins of Human Rights'. *Harvard Law Review* 126 (2013): 2043–2081. Print.

Bentham, Jeremy. 'Deontology; or, The Science of Morality'. *The Works of Jeremy Bentham. Volume I.* Ed. John Bowring. Edinburgh: William Tait, 1843. Print.

——. 'Anarchical Fallacies: Being an Examination of the Declaration of Rights Issued During the French Revolution'. *The Works of Jeremy Bentham. Volume II.* Ed. John Bowring. Edinburgh: William Tait, 1843. Print.

Burke, Edmund. *Reflections on the Revolution in France.* Ed. C. Cruise O'Brien. London: Penguin, 1968. Print.

Catana, Leo. 'Philosophical Problems in the History of Philosophy: What Are They?' *Philosophy and Its History: Aims and Methods in the Study of Early Modern Philosophy.* Ed. Mogens Lærke, Justin E. H. Smith, and Eric Schliesser. Oxford: Oxford University Press, 2013. 115–133. Print.

Cohen, Joshua. 'Minimalism about Human Rights: The Most We Can Hope For?' *The Journal of Political Philosophy* 12.2 (2004): 190–213. Print.

Diderot, Denis. 'Natural Rights'. *The Encyclopedia of Diderot & d'Alembert Collaborative Translation Project.* Trans. Stephen J. Gendzier. Ann Arbor: Michigan Publishing, University of Michigan Library, 2009. Web. 03 Jun. 2015. <http://hdl.handle.net/2027/spo.did2222.0001.313>. Trans. of 'Droit naturel', *Encyclopédie ou Dictionnaire raisonné des sciences, des arts et des métiers*, vol. 5. Paris, 1755.

Griffin, James. *On Human Rights.* Oxford: Oxford University Press, 2008. Print.

Halldenius, Lena. 'Mary Wollstonecraft's Feminist Critique of Property: On Becoming a Thief from Principle'. *Hypatia: A Journal of Feminist Philosophy* 29.4 (2014): 942–957. Print.

——. *Mary Wollstonecraft and Feminist Republicanism: Independence, Rights, and the Experience of Unfreedom.* London: Pickering & Chatto, 2015. Print.

Hume, David. *A Treatise of Human Nature.* Ed. L. A. Selby-Bigge. Oxford: The Clarendon Press, 1978. Print.

Hunt, Lynn. *Inventing Human Rights: A History.* New York: W. W. Norton, 2008. Print.

Ignatieff, Michael. *Human Rights as Politics and Idolatry.* Princeton: Princeton University Press, 2001. Print.

Locke, John. *Two Treatises of Government.* Ed. P. Laslett. Cambridge: Cambridge University Press, 1988. Print.

McCrudden, Christopher. 'Human Rights Histories'. *Public Law and Legal Theory Research Paper Series.* University of Michigan, paper no. 448, 2015. Print.

Moyn, Samuel. *The Last Utopia: Human Rights in History.* Cambridge: Harvard University Press, 2010. Print.

12 I thank Eric Brandstedt, Frits Gåvertsson, the Human Rights Studies group at Lund University, the participants of the conference *Negotiating Human Rights* at Aarhus University, and the editors of this volume for useful comments and encouragement.

——. 'Do Human Rights Increase Inequality?' *The Chronicle of Higher Education*, 26 May 2015. Print.

Nozick, Robert. *Anarchy, State and Utopia*. Oxford: Blackwell, 1974. Print.

Nussbaum, Martha C. *Women and Human Development: The Capabilities Approach*. Cambridge: Cambridge University Press, 2000. Print.

Paine, Thomas. *Rights of Man*. Ed. Mark Philp. Oxford: Oxford University Press, 1995. Print.

Pogge, Thomas. *World Poverty and Human Rights*. Cambridge: Polity Press, 2002. Print.

Price, Richard. 'A Discourse on the Love of Our Country'. *Political Writings*. Ed. D. O. Thomas. Cambridge: Cambridge University Press, 1991. 176–196. Print.

——. 'Two Tracts on Civil Liberty'. *Political Writings*. Ed. D. O. Thomas. Cambridge: Cambridge University Press, 1991. 14–100. Print.

Sen, Amartya. 'Elements of a Theory of Human Rights'. *Philosophy and Public Affairs* 32.4 (2004): 315–356. Print.

Skinner, Quentin. 'Motives, Intentions and Interpretation'. *Visions of Politics. Volume I. Regarding Method*. Cambridge: Cambridge University Press, 2002. 90–102. Print.

Tasioulas, John. 'Taking Rights out of Human Rights'. *Ethics* 120.4 (2010): 647–678. Print.

Waldron, Jeremy. *Dignity, Rank, and Rights*. Ed. Mair Dan-Cohen. Oxford: Oxford University Press, 2012. Print.

Waugh, Joanne and Roger Ariew. 'The Contingency of Philosophical Problems'. *Philosophy and Its History: Aims and Methods in the Study of Early Modern Philosophy*. Ed. Mogens Lærke, Justin E. H. Smith, and Eric Schliesser. Oxford: Oxford University Press, 2013. 91–114. Print.

Wollstonecraft, Mary. 'A Vindication of the Rights of Men'. *The Works of Mary Wollstonecraft. Volume 5*. Ed. Janet Todd and Marilyn Butler. London: Pickering & Chatto, 1989. 1–60. Print.

——. 'An Historical and Moral View of the French Revolution'. *The Works of Mary Wollstonecraft. Volume 6*. Ed. Janet Todd and Marilyn Butler. London: Pickering & Chatto, 1989. 1–235. Print.

Chapter 2

The political agency of victims in atrocity tales by Bartolomé de las Casas

The Spanish origin of human rights

Karen-Margrethe Simonsen

> Being a spectator of calamities taking place in another country is a quintessential modern experience.
>
> (Sontag 16)

The human rights debates in Spain in the sixteenth century grew directly out of the Spanish encounter with the American Indians after the discovery of the New World.[1] The question of whether the Native Americans were human beings, whether they could claim ownership of their land, and whether it was legitimate to enslave them was at the core of debates. The colonization of America was a colonialism *avant la lettre*, chaotic, brutal and unsystematic *and* calculated, morally debated, and legally regulated by numerous laws. According to Anthony Pagden, not only did the Spanish change; the encounter changed 'the moral geography of the world' (Pagden, *European Encounters* 7).

The above-mentioned moral 'geography' was conditioned by uneven power relations, and it was developed and reflected upon in irregular ways in genres that shifted between law, literature, anthropology, religion, and politics. In this article, my analytical focus is one of these genre-shifting texts, often considered to be one of the Western world's first atrocity tales, *Brevísima relación de la destrucción de las Indias* (*A Short Account of the Destruction of the Indies*) (1542), written by the Dominican monk Bartolomé de las Casas, who is very often regarded as a forerunner of modern human rights. I argue that this atrocity tale is split between ethical universalism and international politics, and that the image of the 'victims', that is, the American Indians, shifts just like they do in a puzzle picture.

1 I follow Mauricio Beuchot in calling the early rights *human* rights, and not only *natural* rights. As Beuchot argues, this is no anachronism, because they are based on a universal conception of an integral human being with basic freedom (Beuchot 13). Further reasons for calling them 'human rights' are that they are both individual and collective (or subjective and objective), they are born of globalization, and they are codified. Early globalization and contemporary globalization share the foundation of radical inequality and a fundamental insecurity regarding the moral order of the international community.

The victims are both helpless, universalized beings who are slaughtered by the Spanish, and thus in this way display what Judith Butler has called a 'primary helplessness (Butler 32), and they are potential political agents, inhabitants of defined political communities in the New World, who have the right to protest against the violent invasion of the Spanish with a just war. Both the primary vulnerability and the potential agency of the victims are or may be political in their essence, but they are political in different ways. Additionally, I will discuss the engravings that Flemish artist Theodore de Bry made for a French publication of this book in 1598.

Through an analysis of this account, I hope to contribute to a more nuanced understanding of the politics of the genre of the *atrocity tale* and the way it discusses human rights. Las Casas' atrocity tale is particularly interesting, because it situates the discussion of human rights within a situation of a violent clash between nations. The implication is that ethical universalism is challenged in its foundation.

I argue that the human rights discourses in early modern Spain are directly related to a new international situation at the time. The most important lawyer of that age, Francisco de Vitoria, claimed that rights ought to be based not only on a traditional sense of *jus gentium* ('law of nations'), a divine or natural moral law that 'hovers' above any particular nation, and by which every nation should abide, in order to secure their moral foundation, but also on law *inter gentes* ('law between peoples'), that is, international law that 'gives' rights to the people, not because of their status as human beings, or because of their cultural customs, but because they belong to recognized political unities (Vitoria xxv).[2] In his writings, Las Casas draws on some of the same ideas.

From identity politics to performative politics

In early modern times, the specific understanding of the identity of the American Indians was decisive for their political rights. In the famous debate in Valladolid in 1550, where the moral foundation of the conquests were debated on the initiative of King Charles V, the royal historian and Aristotelian Ginés de Sepúlveda argued that the Indians were different from the Spanish. In fact, they were unreasonable creatures, and therefore they could be enslaved, and their land and gold could be taken from them (de Sepúlveda 305–306). Las Casas argued that the Indians were similar to Europeans, and therefore could be christened (Las Casas, *In Defense of the Indians* 26–27).[3] The discussion of similarity

2 The idea of a *jus inter gentes* opposed to *jus gentium* was not new. It already existed in medieval law. But Vitoria gave it a new meaning in his lectures on modern international law (see Schmitt 129).

3 For a further discussion of the debate in Valladolid and the politics of these early human rights discourses, see my article on 'The Politics of Universalism'.

versus difference pervades the many different types of texts about the Indians, but always in a disturbing way that questions the ethical foundations of the understanding.

As Tzvetan Todorov has demonstrated, these doubts about the identity of the Indians troubled many of the first conquerors, and constituted one important barrier to an encounter on equal footing. Columbus was not able to conceive of the Indians as free, autonomous subjects, since he always saw them through a European conceptualization. However, seeing the Indians as Others was just as bad. Finding the right moral foundation in the encounter with the American Indian was like sailing between Scylla and Charybdis:

> Either he [Columbus] conceives the Indians (though without using these words) as human beings altogether, having the same rights as himself; but then he sees them not only as equals but also as identical, and this behavior leads to assimilationism, the projection of his own values on others. Or else he starts from the difference, but the latter is immediately translated into terms of superiority and inferiority [. . .]. What is denied is the existence of a human substance truly other, something capable of being not merely an imperfect state of oneself.
>
> (Todorov 42)

An unavoidable trap of 'identity thinking' haunted the rights thinking. Whatever strategy was chosen, when thinking about the identity of the Indians – similarity or difference – they would come out as inferiors, and therefore not as autonomous rights-bearers.

However, apart from the problem of having enough or the right kind of knowledge in a persuasive form, there is also the problem of *wanting* to understand the 'other' as autonomous. And this problem is much greater in an uneven power situation. Seen from the European side, the question is: How can you (the powerful, beneficiary culture) acknowledge the autonomy of another (weaker) people? Or: How can you restrain the violence of a dominant culture, tempted by the economic advantage of exploiting a (militarily) weaker culture?

In a historical context, there were many attempts to enlarge the knowledge of the Indians. Bartolomé de las Casas, who made four journeys to America, contributed greatly to this knowledge, together with a number of other intellectuals, monks, foot soldiers, conquerors, and such, who gave more or less accurate accounts of the American communities and their strange customs, and wrote voluminous books, full of wonders and empirical knowledge. But, I argue that ultimately, knowledge of the American communities did not protect them, since this knowledge was asymmetrical, and the political and economic interests in their land and gold were too great.

In the midst of the debates, a very different solution to the problem of solidarity appeared, namely to dissolve the relation between rights and identity, and instead of thinking about the *Other* in terms of identity, think about him or her in terms of autonomous, political agency. This meant substituting the discussion about similarity or difference with a discussion about others' rights to sovereignty.

This change in reasoning may be seen in Francisco de Vitoria's *De Indis* and *De Jure Belli*, of 1532. In these books, the most important question is not whether the Indians are rational beings or barbarians, but whether they have a prince, and may be considered the 'true owners in both private and public law [of their land] before the arrival of the Spanish' (Vitoria VI). To both questions, he answers affirmatively. In fact, he argues that even if the Indians are barbarians, heathens, radical sinners, cannibals, and appear somewhat unintelligent, they still possess enough reason to have 'orderly arranged' polities, overlords and lords (Vitoria xiii), and it would not be appropriate to 'deny to those, who have never done any wrong, what we grant to Saracens and Jews, who are the persistent enemies of Christianity' (Vitoria xiii).

Francisco de Vitoria had never travelled in America. He was not able to understand Indian cultures, and in his evaluation of the capabilities of the Indians he followed Spanish prejudices, yet despite this negative evaluation of their natural capacities and cultural identity, he argued that they possessed the right to their own land. This made all the difference. The fact that he saw the American Indians as inferior to the Christians did not hinder his arguing in favour of their legitimate *dominion*, which includes both private and public ownership (Pagden, 'Dispossessing the Barbarian' 81).[4]

Las Casas' *A Short Account of the Destruction of the Indies*: political context

Bartolomé de las Casas' *A Short Account of the Destruction of the Indies* describes in approximately 100 pages, and in gruesome detail, the Spanish torture and killing of American natives from Mexico to Peru, from 1492 until approximately 1542. The account is addressed directly to the Spanish King, intended to persuade him to change his politics. The French edition of 1598 (in Latin), with illustrations by the Flemish artist Theodore de Bry, has since then circulated as a kind of archetypical, and ethically appealing *memory freeze* of atrocity.[5] Both the book and the images greatly contributed to creating the Black Legend of the Spanish conquest.

Taking into account that this was a peak period of the inquisition, it is remarkable that this highly damaging book (damaging to the Spanish reputation) was not censored in Spain until more than 100 years later (1659). Abroad,

4 In this particular passage, Vitoria is more radical than Francisco Suárez and Hugo Grotrius, both of whom argued that the fact of cannibalism legitimized invasion (Boucher 9).

5 I borrow the term *memory freeze* from Susan Sontag.

it was one of the most published and read books. Between 1578 and 1648, 21 Dutch, eight Italian, six French, four German, two English, and two Latin translations were published. All in all, 43 translations appeared in 70 years (Varela 50). According to Consuelo de Varela, in the hands of the British, the Dutch, and the French, this legendary book turned into a 'political weapon of the first order' ('un arma política de primer orden') (Varela 50). Yet, it passed by the critical eyes of the censors, and, in fact, until his death in 1566, Las Casas was allowed to freely publish his fierce criticism of Spanish cruelty in the New World.[6]

Lewis Hanke has suggested that the reason for this liberal attitude was that the King (especially Charles V, but also Philip II) had a genuinely Christian concern for the moral legitimacy of the conquest (Hanke 10, 174).[7] A more critical view would be that the King encouraged these debates because he had a political interest in them. The brutal and undisciplined behaviour of the Spanish conquerors challenged the stability of both the political and moral orders. Borrowing the vocabulary of Carl Schmitt, what the King needed was for the land appropriated in America to not only be considered a *free space* for individual conquerors, but be organized according to a *nomos* subject to Spanish law (Schmitt 81).

In his Prologue, Las Casas comes as close as one can get to criticizing the King for not preventing the slaughter of the Indians. He explains the King's lack of interference as being due to lack of knowledge. If the King had been informed earlier, 'Your Highness would not have delayed for even one moment [. . .] to prevent any repetition of the atrocities which go under the name of "conquests"' (Las Casas, *A Short Account* 6). Las Casas quotes the Bible, to remind the King of his moral responsibility. Even though the King is sovereign, he is politically vulnerable, if he does not abide by the 'divine' norms of natural law.[8]

6 This is especially interesting, since Ginés de Sepúlveda, who had defended the conquerors and the *encomenderos*, was not allowed to publish any other book after the debate in Valladolid in 1550.

7 According to Lewis Hanke, the discussions of the problems of America reveal 'both the highly developed individualism of the Spaniards and a deliberate, imaginative, and courageous attempt by the crown and the Spanish people to shoulder the heavy burdens placed on Spain by her political and ecclesiastical dominion in America' (10). Hanke later states that even when the '[i]mpatient conquistadores champed at the bit while intricate discussions were held concerning the applicability to the Indians of the Aristotelian doctrine of slavery', 'The crown continued to listen to those idealists who had been responsible for the experiments [of making peaceful, farming settlements in America] and even for a time suspended conquest in America while its justice was being debated at Valladolid' (174).

8 Las Casas depicts the ordering of the world into kingdoms, with sovereign and benign kings as an order established by 'Divine Providence', and quotes the words of Solomon: 'A king that sitteth in the throne of judgment scattereth away all evil with his eyes', to convince the King of his moral *and* legal and political responsibility (Las Casas, *A Short Account* 5).

The genre of the atrocity tale: ethics and politics

The genre of the atrocity tale is by definition an ethical genre. It documents violence and brutal abuses, beyond social acceptance, against defenceless victims, and on this basis makes an affective appeal to an audience that is supposed to feel moral indignation. In order for this indignation to arise, the violence has to be seen as an injustice, and not just as a misfortune (Shklar 14). Atrocity tales are not about natural disasters, nor about contingent violence done by some individuals to other individuals (which would be ordinary crime). They are about systematic violence, by a stronger party, to several people. The ethical appeal is meant to be clear and one-dimensional. This is due to the fact that the atrocity tale is also an accusatory genre that aims to accuse more or less defined perpetrators, forcing them to acknowledge their responsibility, and, if necessary or possible, to change politics. According to the sociologists Bromley, Shupe, and Ventimiglia, who were some of the first to attempt a definition, the pure atrocity story must do at least these three things: 'a) evoke moral outrage by specifying and detailing the value violations, b) authorize, implicitly or explicitly, punitive sanctions, and c) mobilize control efforts against the alleged perpetrators' (Bromley, Shupe, and Ventimiglia 43). Thus, moral outrage and political (or legal) persuasiveness go hand in hand. However, it is remarkable that Bromley *et al.* do not mention documentation as an integral part of the genre. They even write that it 'is of no importance whether the allegations made in atrocity stories are actually true or false' (43). I would argue that this is only partly true. If the spectator believes the atrocity to be totally untrue, he or she may still feel the horror, but the atrocity tale will hardly be able to persuade the spectator to punish or mobilize control effects.

The atrocity tale, in order to be persuasive, must insist on veracity, not only on the truth of suffering, but also the truth of the violation. Owing to its accusatory character, the atrocity tale is close to *forensic aesthetics*, as defined by Eyal Weizman. Within a forensic framework, the teller of atrocity stories will try to be convincing through material evidence, and/or through a neutralization of the subjectivity of his or her own statement, and of any individual testimony that is included in the story: any witness will be cross-examined, to determine the truth of his or her claims, any object will be made to speak (Weizman 14).

The dual intention of making facts vivid and subjectivity neutral, far from making the veracity of the story clear, blurs the distinction between subjectivity and objectivity. While there is an explicit intention of objective presentation, there is also a necessary subjectivity in this presentation, even of objects. Subjects are turned to objects, and objects to subjects.

In atrocity tales, the problem of subjectivity and objectivity is duplicated at the level of articulation. Atrocity tales are normally not written by the victims or by the perpetrators, but by bystanders, helpers, or advocates who were spectators or second-degree witnesses. This means that the atrocity tale is based on a mediation of the experiences of others. This is also the case with the atrocity tale by Bartolomé de las Casas. He speaks on behalf of the victims.

The simple fact of this displaced subjectivity raises a political question: How does the voice of Las Casas filter/manipulate the voice of the American Indians? It also raises a question about publicity, which, according to *forensis*, is at the heart of the political treatment of human rights.

The word 'forensic' literally means 'pertaining to the forum', and, as Weizman explains, the forum in its original sense is a 'multidimensional space of politics, law, and economy' (Weizman 9).

The atrocity tale's depiction of suffering takes the suffering itself out of any private arena in which it may have taken place, and makes it a public affair. Yet, the sometimes cruel intimacy of torture adds ambiguity to its public exposure, and the character of the public is also ambiguous. As already mentioned, Las Casas' atrocity tales were addressed directly to the King, but they were read by a numerous and divided public both in Spain and outside of Spain, in the new colonies, and in competing nations, where they served different political goals.

The success of the atrocity tale as a 'speech act', its persuasiveness, has to be measured against both its double aim of creating outrage and showing documentation, and against very different political contexts, or, to put it differently, a very complex 'forum'.

Two kinds of politics in *A Short Account of the Destruction of the Indies*

A Short Account of the Destruction of the Indies has the official form of a *relación*, meaning an official report, framed as an eyewitness account, presented to the King, describing real happenings in America. In the Prologue, Las Casas claims that his report is based on 'more than fifty years' experience of seeing at first hand the evil and the harm, the losses and diminutions suffered by those great kingdoms' (5).

Las Casas explicitly aims to *present* the atrocities without interpretation, the implicit idea being that the atrocities may 'speak for themselves'. He conscientiously reports from every region of the New World, and includes a little bit of the geography, the name of the region, the King and the people, and how the atrocities were committed in that particular region, thus adding credibility to his 'documentation'. However, his neutrality is dubious, both at the level of the statement and at the level of rhetorical framing.

At this point in history (1542), Las Casas was an acknowledged intellectual, a famous defender of the Indians, and an urgent voice in the debate. The fact that an atrocity tale was written by him implicitly bestows authority on it. Without this authority, the account would have been much less convincing. In this very direct way, subjectivity and objectivity are intermingled in a complex manner, at the level of the statement.

Looking at the rhetorical framework, it is complex in the sense that it not only documents, but also dramatizes or allegorizes. The accurate descriptions of scenes of torture and killing are placed inside a framework of moral allegory:

> [. . .] over the years I have time and again met Spanish laymen who have been so struck by the natural goodness that shines through these people that they frequently can be heard to exclaim: 'These would be the most blessed people on earth if only they were given the chance to convert to Christianity'. It was upon these gentle lambs, imbued by the Creator with all the qualities we have mentioned, that from the very first day they clapped eyes on them the Spanish fell like ravening wolves upon the fold, or like tigers and savage lions who have not eaten meat for days.
>
> (11)

The brutal conquest is thus inscribed into a religious allegory of good (Native Americans) versus evil (Spanish conquerors). This Manichean framing adds melodramatic tension to the violation, and the affective dramatization of opposites is underlined in Theodore de Bry's illustrations.

One of the first engravings by Theodore de Bry in Las Casas' book is this one.

Figure 2.1 Illustration by Theodore de Bry 1552, published in 1598 in the Latin version of Las Casas' *A Short Account*.

Source: Las Casas, *Narratio Regionum* 31.

The illustration is based on the following two passages in Las Casas' work:

> They spared no one, erecting especially wide gibbets on which they could string their victims up with their feet just off the ground and then burn them alive thirteen at a time, in honour of our Saviour and the twelve Apostles, or tie dry straw to their bodies and set fire to it.
>
> (15)

And:

> [. . .] they grabbed suckling infants by the feet and, ripping them from their mothers' breasts, dashed them headlong against the rocks.
>
> (15)

The torture is accurately described but the devilish character of the Spanish conquerors is underlined. Not only are they brutal; they mock Christianity by choosing to burn 13 at a time, a blasphemous mockery that turns the American victims into Jesus and the 12 apostles, and the Spanish conquerors into bloodthirsty devils.

De Bry follows Las Casas quite closely in the antithetic mode of depiction of the innocent victims and the evil perpetrators. In the image, the victimhood of the Indians is emphasized by their helpless, fragile nudity. It is interesting that the nudity of the woman hanging second to the right, and of the child who is about to be killed, at the left, is especially accentuated, women and children typically being considered more defenceless than men. By accentuating their nudity, the affective impact of the image increases.[9] The genitals of the Indian men are covered by small pieces of cloth, which means that they are 'protected' a little bit, but this hopeless protection, in combination with the fact that their bodies are small and fragile, hanging helplessly from the gallows, only emphasizes their humiliation.

The elegance of the Spanish torturers' clothes signals a social class of distinction, their larger body size, and their physical, muscular strength emphasize their agency. Their exaggerated movements seem to suggest that they are more than eager to torture. Their feet only touch the ground lightly as though they were performing a macabre ballet of death. At the left, a man is slaying a baby against a stylized Indian hut/house. This hut seems to be an immense tombstone that mirrors the dark body of the murderer but blurs the reflection of the 'white' bodies of the dead or dying Indians. It is as though the murderer's own death

9 This analytical point should not be overemphasized, because of the 18 engravings made by Theodore de Bry, only four underline the suffering of women and children. This also has to do with the fact that Las Casas particularly depicts the extermination of kingdoms, and therefore he describes the killing of the kings or governors, in particular.

is already inscribed in the tombstone, while the Indians' bodies are kept in the light. But the tombstone may also be read as a tombstone over the grave of memory itself, since the sufferings of the Indians are not reflected in it. In order to underline the scale of the slaughter, you can see multiple killings going on in the background.

In the image above, and the other 17 engravings in the book, the torturers are 'caught in the act', and fully exposed to the moral indignation of the spectator.[10] Any spectator will be horrified, and as mentioned above, in the centuries to come, the images came to function as 'memory freezes' of atrocity. The images are archetypical in the way they combine preciseness and moral indignation, and they seem to be based on the idea, repeated by Susan Sontag as a general trait of atrocity tales, that, if 'the horror could be made vivid enough, most people would finally take in the outrageousness, the insanity of war' (Sontag 12). Horror *in itself* is supposed to be persuasive.[11] We will 'automatically' identify with the sufferings of the Indians.

Yet, the paradox is that the illustration elicits more than an abhorrence of the Spanish torturers and sympathy with the suffering victims. As James Dawes has pointed out, drawing on Freud and Adorno, the exposure of the victims' pain may in fact add insult to injury, and may create an appeal not only to the moral indignation of the audience, but also to their voyeuristic pleasure (Dawes 8–9). And, in fact, there are several characteristics in the image that invite 'identification' with the Spanish torturers rather than with the victims, not least their elegance and self-assurance.

In de Bry's images, the Indians are almost anonymous, their faces are blurred, some of the faces even seem to be grotesque masks that represent stereotypical visions of either extreme suffering or of death. In contrast, the Spanish man whose face may be seen has an individual, recognizable face. Anonymizing the victims and presenting the perpetrators in a more recognizable form (sometimes with name and title) is very often seen in atrocity tales, owing to their inherently dual moral and accusatory character.[12] In a certain sense, you do not have to give the victims an individual character, for it is outrageous that *any* human being should suffer as the Indians in De Bry's images suffer. What is exposed here is what Judith Butler has called a 'primary helplessness' (Butler 32) or

10 Only one engraving does not show a scene of torture or of killing: this is the scene where the Spanish meet Montezuma, the powerful King of Mexico.

11 The historical context is also important. Theodore de Bry was a Flemish Catholic who had recently converted to Protestantism. He had more than one reason to underline the cynical character of the Spanish Catholics' slaughter of the Indians.

12 Sharon Sliwinski points this out in her reading of atrocity tales from the Congo Reform Movement: 'The maimed children's stories were obsessively repeated at hundreds of meetings, although usually without proper names' (Sliwinski 79). She is critical of this tendency, since it dehumanizes the victims.

'"common" corporeal vulnerability' (Butler 42). Once you see and feel this vulnerability, you will understand that the perpetrator must be stopped and punished. Therefore, this strategy seems to be in line both with the moral and the political aims of the atrocity tale. This is an understanding that grounds politics in ethical universalism, or in the words of Francisco de Vitoria, *jus gentium*. According to this understanding, the Spanish slaughter is not consistent with (Christian) natural law. It is a crime against humanity, and therefore it must be stopped by the sovereign.

However, I argue that it is an ethical problem that the Spanish perpetrators of these crimes are depicted as vital agents, and the Indians as helpless, dehumanized victims. Only if we see the victims as potential agents is it possible to acknowledge their autonomy. But how is it possible to show such agency, while vividly depicting the destruction to which they were exposed? One answer to this question may be found in Las Casas' different depiction of the victims.

Whereas the murderer is recognizable and the victim is anonymous in De Bry's illustrations, it is the other way around in Las Casas' writing: the perpetrator is anonymized, and the victims, especially local governors, are given names. This naming of governors is interesting, because it underlines and rhetorically restores the political position of the Indians. It is further significant that nowhere is this political position related to their cultural identity. Even when anecdotes are told about the deaths of local kings, and they are attributed with especially honourable traits, these anecdotes serve to illuminate the unequal war scenario, rather than any substantial cultural traits. For instance, this is the case with the anecdote about Hatuey of Cuba, who, tied to the stake, was asked to convert to Christianity, in order to be saved, and go to Heaven instead of Hell. On hearing that Heaven was full of Christians, he said he preferred Hell (Las Casas, *A Short Account* 28). The book is quite clearly *not* an anthropological guide to local culture. The information given in the book about the local communities is political, in the sense that it is information about politically divided kingdoms and communities and their legitimate governors.

Through the dual strategy of omitting the name of any conqueror, and providing the names of the local kings, Las Casas diminishes the direct accusation of any specific conqueror, and he makes us feel the presence of the Indian governors/*caciques*. One could argue that he does not have to mention the names of the conquerors, since which conqueror was responsible for which conquest is common knowledge, but behind this fact there also lies the intention to both generalize and to narrow the responsibility. Very often, the Spanish are just called 'the Spanish' or 'the Europeans', or, more bitterly, 'the Christians', meaning that they all are, *or* each of them is, responsible for their acts in the conquest. The main responsibility is attributed to the King, who has the political power to stop the atrocities.

On the other hand, the mention of the local kings in America creates a sense of familiarity with the victims. Whereas the Spanish conquerors in the time of Las Casas were often seen as heroic conquerors of a vast land inhabited by unknown, 'savage' Indians, the conquest is now seen through the eyes of *specific* Indians, who can be named.

The most important effect of the dual strategy of anonymization (of the Spanish) and familiarization (of the Indians) is often overlooked, namely that by using this strategy, Las Casas places his morally founded atrocity tale within a framework of international politics. It is still most important for him to denounce the violence in the name of universal humanitarianism or Christian natural law, but he also argues that the American Indians have a right to property and self-defence. Thus, there is a radical difference between the framing of the atrocities in De Bry's images, and Las Casas' text.

The Legacy of Las Casas

The critics of Bartolomé de las Casas very often claim that his knowledge of the Indian communities was superficial – for instance, he never learned any Indian language – and that his egalitarianism was a double-edged sword that, ideally, could save the Indians' lives, but would ruin their cultural and religious identity, since Las Casas' belief in the superiority of the Christian religion would necessarily reduce the Indians' religion to a status of fatal error. Within Las Casas' ethical universalism, the Indians are, so to speak (still), undeveloped children waiting for the Christian father to bring them eternal truth. Following up on Daniel Castro's critique of Las Casas' 'ecclesiastic imperialism' (Castro 153), Daniel R. Brunstetter has recently strengthened this criticism. He argues that, contrary to what is often understood, Las Casas is much closer to his opponent, Ginés de Sepúlveda. Sepúlveda's argument that the Indians were natural slaves or 'permanently unequal' remains 'salient given the disquiet with alterity that emerges when the Other challenges so-called universal truths' (Brunstetter 47). Thus, Brunstetter argues that even though Las Casas grants the Indians equal status as humans, he cannot look upon their heathen religion as equal to Christianity. And the limits of his solidarity are to be found in the situation where the Indians, after having had Christianity preached to them in a peaceful manner, continue to reject the Christian religion. This will not be met with benign tolerance. Therefore, Las Casas repeatedly reassures himself and his audience that the Indian has a special *natural* proclivity to Christianity that will lead him, without force, to convert. Only if he converts will the American Indian be part of the true universal community. Thus, Las Casas' moral ground, which includes the Indian within the universal community, excludes him as a true member. The Indian's cultural and religious specificity (his belief in foreign gods), and the impossibility of accepting his sticking to these gods, hinder his full admittance to the universal community.

The strength of Brunstetter's argument is that not only does he demonstrate how Las Casas is trapped within a non-egalitarian morality; he also argues that Las Casas is an example of how this non-egalitarian 'egalitarianism' persisted after Christianity ceased to be the foundation of human rights. This continued in the French Enlightenment and the American Revolution, where God generally is replaced with modern natural law, enlightenment, or democracy. As Brunstetter says, to be included in post-Revolutionary North America, the Native Americans had to adhere to Enlightenment principles, and if they resisted this, they were not accepted as full members. In fact, in the post-Revolutionary context, the situation grew even worse for the Indians than it had been in the early modern era:

> Before 1776, it was understandable, or so the argument went, that the Indians failed to follow Las Casas' example given his ideals were overpowered by the actions of his fanatical countrymen and the system of oppression that characterized Spanish colonialism. However, following the triumph of American democracy, such an excuse was no longer justifiable. After the American Revolution, a Las Casasian faith in the Other was no longer philosophically acceptable because the true colors of Enlightenment philosophy – the marriage between natural liberty and politics – had been revealed. The Indians retained the chance to assimilate to an enlightened proto-European culture, but those who did not assimilate and chose to persist in their traditional ways ceased to be worthy of defending, and became the other Other – true barbarians.
>
> (Brunstetter 12)

The problem with this kind of argument, and Brunstetter is probably aware of this, is that it assumes some kind of 'super-idealism', supposing that it is possible to have a completely neutral and all-inclusive position. Or, to put it differently, against Brunstetter's claim, one could argue that the fact that Sepúlveda's physical Otherside (emphasizing non-inclusion) also somehow haunts the discourse of Las Casas' cultural Otherside (emphasizing inclusion) does not necessarily make Las Casas completely similar to Sepúlveda, just as there are also crucial differences between Enlightenment strategies and early Christian conquest.

However, following Brunstetter in this line of thought is rewarding in more than one sense. The logic of his argument is that the final test of the egalitarian content of egalitarianism is whether or not the 'other' has the right to resist the moral foundations of your inclusion of him. Thus, according to Brunstetter, the paradoxical legacy of Las Casas is not the idealism of his defence of the Indians, but the conditional pragmatism of his tolerance. Brunstetter states that by 'linking his defense of the Indians to assimilation, [he] establishes the conditions for legitimized illiberalism at some point in the future' (Brunstetter 11). He argues that European and North American modernity is founded on an idea of peaceful, inclusive 'conversion' that blurs the mechanisms of exclusion, rather than admitting to them openly, as Sepúlveda does, and this peaceful exclusion by inclusion is already present in Las Casas' writing.

An extreme consequence of the foregoing circumstance might be that Indians would have 'preferred' Sepúlveda to Las Casas, since at least he openly confesses that he sees them as inferior beings, thus he makes visible the prejudiced power that turns them into subjects of the Spanish Crown, whereas Las Casas' humanitarian approach conceals the weapons that are turned against them under a veil of egalitarianism. However, as I have argued, Las Casas does not only argue for a universal egalitarianism on the basis of a common human identity; he also argues for the respect for the political autonomy of the American Indians. And, in fact, he argues that because of their immoral excesses, the Spanish risk losing any moral right to autonomy that they may have had.

Political autonomy?

At the beginning of *A Short Account*, Las Casas says that the Spanish people involved in the torture and killing of the Indians had been 'anaesthetized to human suffering by their own greed and ambition that they had ceased to be men in any meaningful sense of the term [. . .]' (3). Later, Las Casas calls the Spanish 'perfidious crusaders'. So radical are their sins that the only rights they have earned, and that 'can be upheld in human, divine, or natural law are the right to eternal damnation and the right to answer for their offences and the harm they have done to the Spanish Crown' (53–54).

According to Las Casas, the Spanish Crown has been harmed through the dehumanized, bestial behaviour of the Spanish. Thus, Spanish power is being undermined from within, whereas, in principle, the Indian position is as strong as it has 'always' been, or was before the arrival of the Spanish:

> Any reasonable person who knows anything of God, of rights and of civil law can imagine for himself what the likely reaction would be of *any people* living peaceably within their own frontiers, unaware that they owe allegiance to anyone save their *natural lords*, were a stranger suddenly to issue a demand along the following lines: 'You shall henceforth obey a foreign king, whom you have never seen nor ever heard of and, if you do not, we will cut you to pieces' – especially when they discover that these strangers are indeed quite prepared to carry out this threat to the letter.
>
> (Las Casas, *A Short Account* 53, my emphasis)[13]

Las Casas adds: 'Such a recognition of suzerainty has no standing in law whatsoever' (53). If the Spanish trespass on the frontier of a foreign community,

13 Here, Las Casas mocks the *requirimiento* (of 1513), which was a declaration that was read to the American Indians in Spanish upon arrival in new territories. The declaration refers to the Papal Bull of 1492 that gave the Spanish the divine right of sovereignty in any land west of Cape Verde. The Indians were given the choice of surrendering to Spanish rule, or being killed. Lewis Hanke states that whenever the Indians saw the Spanish take out a piece of paper, they fled, since they knew the immediate consequences.

and they want to force the citizens of that community to submission, that community has the right to fight back. This is a just war. And because the Spanish act so cruelly, the Indians have a right that 'they quite properly enjoy under natural, divine, and Roman law to defend themselves by cutting the Spanish forces to pieces [. . .]' (70). The Spanish are not only 'inhuman beasts' or 'devils in a human form'; they are also, and more extremely, called 'outlaws' (129). They are not within the political order or the order of civilization (128) that respects national borders 'anywhere in the world'. Thus, Las Casas frames his moral and religious tale in the context of international politics, and in this particular sense he moves away from identity politics and away from universal egalitarianism. No matter who the Indians are, they have a king and own their land, and no one has the right to intrude upon them. Here, Bartolomé de las Casas concurs with the radical aspect of the argument made by Francisco de Vitoria.

The rights of the Indians include both the individual right to not be exposed to cruel treatment, and the collective right to national sovereignty. The respect for the first right might be incorporated within a benign form of imperialism; respect for the second right worked directly against the idea of imperial expansion.

What the Spanish discourses about human rights teach us is an interesting lesson about human rights and power. They show us an early sense of 'cosmopolitanism'. This cosmopolitanism is hardly developed and one could argue that it only encompasses two partners in a very uneven power-position (the strong self-confident absolutistic state of Spain backed up by the Pope and different and militarily weak Indian tribes). But it is a modern form of cosmopolitanism because it is not based on sheer idealism, but on a dependent relation between nations. As Francisco de Vitoria calls it, the Spanish sense of justice was based not only on a traditional sense of *jus gentium*, but on a modern sense of *inter gentes*. Both of these exceed the discussion about the barbarous culture of the Indians, but whereas the first is grounded in ethical universalism, the last one points to a new international cosmopolitanism.

In this article, I have tried to show that the atrocity tale, despite its religious, allegorical form is political in two ways: one takes its point of departure in universal, individual vulnerability, which, exposed to a larger political audience in itself, makes a political appeal for action by responsible political actors. The other aims at respecting, and, if necessary, restoring the political autonomy of the victims, without any evaluation of their cultural identity.

In a recent book, Sharon Sliwinski argues convincingly that it is time 'for the history of human rights to be retold as a special mode of thinking of the spectator' (33). A central point of her re-evaluation of the global *sensus communis* and the reception of mass-produced atrocity tales in a broader public is that the sensory, aesthetic framing of the atrocities (distant suffering) influences the political character of the human rights discourse. This article is a contribution to such a new history of human rights, with a special focus on the spectator.

The importance of the Spanish use of human or natural rights discourses is not normally acknowledged in histories of human rights. Even though the debates in Valladolid in 1550 are well known, and Bartolomé de las Casas is sometimes seen as a forerunner of human rights thinking – a philosopher who inspired Voltaire and Bacon – with a few exceptions, the Spanish origins of human rights or natural rights hardly ever makes it into standard histories of human rights, and Las Casas, when praised, is often considered to be only a 'beacon of light' in an ocean of utter darkness (Brunstetter 11). Likewise, it is well known that Francisco de Vitoria significantly inspired Hugo Grotius, but Grotius is considered to be more important in founding European modernity (Anghie 321).[14]

In this article, I have argued that the Spanish development of human rights discourses is important, because it is exemplary in showing how modern human rights grew out of the atrocities and the deep political conflicts related to early globalization. Thus, these modern human rights are not founded on an ideal philosophical or religious truth, but on the experience of brutality that made it necessary to rethink the political foundations of natural rights.

Works cited

Anghie, Antony. 'Francisco de Vitoria and the Colonial Origins of International Law'. *Social & Legal Studies* 5.3 (1996): 321–336. Print.

Beuchot, Mauricio. *Los fundamentos de los derechos humanos en Bartolomé de las Casas*. Barcelona: Anthropos, 1994. Print.

Boucher, David. *The Limits of Ethics in International Relations: Natural Law, Natural Rights, and Human Rights in Transition*. Oxford: Oxford University Press, 2009. Print.

Bromley, David G., Anson D. Shupe, Jr., and J. C. Ventimiglia. 'Atrocity Tales, the Unification Church, and the Social Construction of Evil'. *Journal of Communication* 29.3 (Sept. 1979): 42–53. Web. 25 Aug. 2015.

Brunstetter, Daniel R. *Tensions of Modernity: Las Casas and His Legacy in the French Enlightenment*. London/New York: Routledge, 2012. Print.

Butler, Judith. *Precarious Life: The Powers of Mourning and Violence*. London/New York: Verso, 2006. Print.

14 The history described on the United Nations' home page goes directly from the Magna Carta to the Petition of Right (1628), to the US Constitution (1787) and the French Declaration of the Rights of Man and the Citizen (1789 ff). The Spanish history of human rights is totally omitted from handbooks, such as Michael Freeman's *Human Rights*, from theoretical books that discuss origins, such as Lynn Hunt's *Inventing Human Rights: A History*, and from histories, such as Micheline R. Ishay's *The History of Human Rights*. It is especially remarkable that the Spanish history of human rights is almost entirely absent from this last book, since it wants to situate the discussions of human rights within the context of globalization. A quotation from Bartolomé de las Casas is inserted, but the main development is centred on the 'four great historical events in the Western World: the Reformation, and the English, American and French Revolutions' (65). Important exceptions are James Brown Scott, Carl Schmitt, and Lewis Hanke.

Castro, Daniel. *Another Face of Empire: Bartolomé de las Casas, Indigenous Rights, and Ecclesiastical Imperialism*. Durham/London: Duke University Press, 2007. Print.

Dawes, James. *That the World May Know: Bearing Witness to Atrocity*. Cambridge: Harvard University Press, 2007. Print.

De Bry, Theodore. 18 engraved illustrations, printed in Bartolomé de las Casas. *Narratio Regionum indicarum per Hispanos quosdam devastatarum* verissima, 1614, Typis Hieronymi Galleri, Biblioteca Digital Hispánica, Biblioteca Nacional de España. Web. 17 Sept. 2015. <http://bdh-rd.bne.es/viewer.vm?id=0000172864&page=1>.

Freeman, Michael. *Human Rights: An Interdisciplinary Approach*. Cambridge: Polity Press, 2002.

Hanke, Lewis. *The Spanish Struggle for Justice in the Conquest of America*. Dallas: Southern Methodist University Press, 2002. Print.

Hunt, Lynn. *Inventing Human Rights: A History*. New York/London: W. W. Norton, 2008. Print.

Ishay, Micheline. *The History of Human Rights From Ancient Times to the Globalization Era*. Berkeley/Los Angeles/London: University of California Press, 2004. Print.

Las Casas, Bartolomé de. *Brevísima relación de la destrucción de las Indias*. Madrid: Ed. Castalia, 1999. Print.

——. *In Defense of the Indians*. De Kalb: Northern Illinois Press, 1992. Print.

——. *A Short Account of the Destruction of the Indies*. London: Penguin, 2004. Print.

Pagden, Anthony. 'Dispossessing the Barbarian: The Language of Spanish Thomism and the Debate over the Property Rights of the American Indians'. Ed. Anthony Pagden. *The Languages of Political Theory in Early-Modern Europe*. Cambridge/London: Cambridge University Press, 1987. 79–98. Print.

——. *European Encounters with the New World*. New Haven/London: Yale University Press, 1993. Print.

Schmitt, Carl. *The Nomos of the Earth in the International Law of the Jus Publicum Europaeum*. New York: Telos Press Publishing, 2006. Print.

Scott, James Brown. *The Origin of International Law: Francisco de Vitoria and His Law of Nations*. Oxford/London: The Clarendon Press/Humphrey Milford, 1934. Print.

de Sepúlveda, Juan Ginés. *Democrates alter, sive de justis belli causis apud Indos/Democrates Segundo, o, De las justas causas de la Guerra contra los indios*. Trans. Marcelino Menéndez y Pelayo. 1781. Alicante: Biblioteca Virtual Miguel de Cervantes. Web. 17 Sept. 2015. <www.cervantesvirtual.com/buscador/?q=democrates+segundo>.

Shklar, Judith N. *The Faces of Injustice*. New Haven/London: Yale University Press, 1990.

Simonsen, Karen-Margrethe. 'The Politics of Universalism: Strategic Uses of Human Rights Discourses in Early Modernity'. *Journal of Aesthetics and Culture* 5 (2013). Web. 17 Sept. 2015. <www.aestheticsandculture.net/index.php/jac/article/view/23157>.

Sliwinski, Sharon. *Human Rights in Camera*. Chicago/London: University of Chicago Press, 2011. Print.

Sontag, Susan. *Regarding the Pain of Others*. London/New York: Penguin, 2004. Print.

Todorov, Tzvetan. *The Conquest of America: The Question of the Other*. New York: Harper & Row, 1984. Print.

Varela, Consuelo. 'Introducción Biográfica y crítica'. *Brevísima relación de la destrucción de las Indias*. Ed. Bartolomé de Las Casas. Madrid: Ed. Castalia, 1999. Print.

Vitoria, Francisco de. *De Indis et De Juri Belli*. Trans. James Brown Scott. 1917. Web. 17 Sept. 2015. <https://en.wikisource.org/wiki/De_Indis_De_Jure_Belli>.

Weizman, Eyal. 'Forensic Architecture: Only the Criminal Can Solve the Crime'. *Radical Philosophy* 164 (Nov/Dec 2010): 9–24. Web. 12 May 2016 <www.radicalphilosophy.com/article/forensic-architecture>.

Chapter 3

The inequality of common utility

Active/passive citizenship in French revolutionary human rights

Jonas Ross Kjærgård

Article 1 of the French 1789 Declaration of the Rights of Man and Citizen states that '[a]ll men are born and remain free and equal in rights' (*L'an 1* 198).[1] Is it not obvious that French revolutionary human rights are characterized by their 'universalism' (Ishay 4) or by their 'unqualified moral universalism' (Israel, *Democratic Enlightenment* 937)? Does the phrasing of article 1 not prove that the 1789 Declaration describes 'universal human rights' (Hunt 17) and that there is a 'direct echo' between the 1789 text and the 1948 Universal Declaration of Human Rights (Sliwinski 17–18)? If eighteenth-century men and women did not always actually experience this universal equality, is it not because the declaration should be read as 'prescriptive' rather than 'descriptive' (Douzinas 10)? Put differently: Even if they were not always applied, were the universal principles not *in* the 1789 Declaration, and is it not precisely these universal principles that make the Declaration a crucial document in the history of human rights?

In this article, I answer the foregoing questions in the negative. I argue that French revolutionary human rights, as they were developed between 1789 and 1791, were non-universal. What this means is not only that there was a discrepancy between revolutionary practice and principle. Undoubtedly, inconsistencies between ideals and reality existed, but my point is a different one: the rights presented in the Declaration, as well as in its immediate legal and political context, were non-universal in the sense that certain rights were assigned to some, but not to others. As seen from the perspective of human rights historiography, the consequence of my argument is that French revolutionary rights are not a precursor to present-day universal human rights (if any such thing exists). Rather, French revolutionary rights establish a distinction between those with the right to protection and security, and those with the additional right to political influence. To use the vocabulary of this anthology, I read the 1789 Declaration as an early example of how the agency/victimhood schism is embedded in the human rights discourse.

1 Unless anything else is indicated, translations are mine.

My focus is the distinction between active and passive citizens, a distinction that was presented in the debates preceding the 1789 Declaration, but eventually omitted from that document. The active/passive schism was introduced into the Declaration debates by the revolutionary Abbé Sieyès, and I analyse its function in his political philosophy, as well as the significant role it came to assume in the 1789 Declaration debates. Whereas passive citizens had the right to protection, to private property, and to equality before the law, only active citizens had the right to take part in the formation of *la chose publique*; only they had the right to vote and to hold public offices. In order to be included among the active citizens, a number of objective criteria had to be met, one of which was the payment of a certain fiscal contribution. What I am interested in is the logic behind the division between active and passive citizens, and the ways in which it entered the 1789 Declaration, albeit in different linguistic clothing. Phrased differently, my primary concern is to argue that French revolutionary human rights are non-universal, and my secondary aim is to describe the logic behind this specific kind of social inequality. Often, the first part of the 1789 Declaration's article 1 is quoted as an example of the universalism of that document, but the second part of it is more important to my argument: 'Men are born and remain free and equal in rights. Social distinctions may be based only on common utility' (*L'an 1* 198). What exactly does 'social distinctions' mean here, and in what way are they legitimized by 'common utility'?

The beginnings of an answer to the foregoing questions may be found in Gail Bossenga's book *The Politics of Privilege*. Her point is that rather than bringing an end to social inequality, the French Revolution altered the premises of social conflict:

> The Revolution created new possibilities and patterns for mobilization and social conflict. As a result of the Revolution, membership in the national state, or citizenship, became the source of all civic rights. Although in theory the rights of citizens were inalienable and universal, in fact they were inequitably distributed. Thus, after the Revolution, conflict was to revolve significantly around the acquisition and definition of the full rights of citizenship by disenfranchised groups. [. . .] Thus the Revolution laid the foundations for future battles waged by disadvantaged groups, whether defined by class, gender, belief or race.
>
> (Bossenga 206–207)

Bossenga argues that the French Revolution, in spite of its libertarian and egalitarian ideology, was fundamentally unsuccessful in inaugurating a free and equal society. However, it was successful in abolishing the Old Regime *kinds* of inequality, which were based on privileges and feudal principles. Rather than postulating absolute uniformity between revolutionary ideology and practice, and rather than suggesting a revolution without consequences, Bossenga claims that the Revolution facilitated new types of political struggle. The struggle against

Old Regime privileges was replaced by one centred on the definition and acquisition of citizenship or membership in the nation state. True to her revisionist interpretation of the Revolution, Bossenga argues that these new political conflicts cannot be reduced to class struggle; some were class-based, but others were structured around gender, race, or religion. Tightening this argument, she writes that 'the formation of a society of classes, essentially an economic issue, may best be seen as a problem analytically distinct from the creation of a society of citizens, a matter of political membership' (206).

I agree with Bossenga that the formation of a society of classes is an economic issue that *may be* distinct from the problem of political membership. In other words, I think she is right to identify political struggles centred on other kinds of disagreements than specifically economic ones, but the argument I want to make is that those other kinds of political struggles were often decisively influenced by economic concerns. Even though it may be analytically solid, I consider her distinction between the economic problem of a class society and the political problem of citizenship too binary in a historical perspective, because the issue of political membership was most frequently *also* an economic one. In the attempt to better understand the role of economy in these new kinds of political struggle, I argue that the addition of social distinctions to the Declaration's article 1 had a profound influence on the establishment of a social hierarchy based on the ability of the members of the state to contribute to the public, on their ability to be of 'common utility'. I argue that common utility was principally an economic term, and that it factored crucially in the political micro-machinery of the grand transition towards 'the happiness of all', the Revolution was meant to bring about (*L'an 1* 198; Kjærgård). During the Revolution, the acquisition of citizenship came to depend on gender, religion, and race, but also, and in a complicated interrelation, on decisively economic questions of fiscal contributions and paid work. I argue that the non-universality of French revolutionary human rights may be explained by analysing that form of social inequality that is based on economic conceptions of common utility.

Before delving into the details of the active/passive distinction, I want to sketch the political atmosphere and the institutional framework within which the Declaration debates took place.

Debating the Declaration

The French Revolution was triggered by the monarchical regime's inability to raise sufficient fiscal income (Kaiser and Van Kley 1). In particular, their involvement in the Seven Years' War (1756–1763) and the American Revolutionary War (1775–1783) had prompted the French state to take out massive public loans (Riley; Kwass; Sonenscher). Because the payments and the interest on these loans amounted to sums far outweighing the state income, successive finance ministers of the 1780s were keen to impose new taxes. In order to do this, they summoned the Estates General. The Estates General was an assembly consisting of representatives from all three estates – the clerics, the nobles, and the commoners – and it had not been assembled since 1614. Even though it had not always been respected in the past, formally the Estates General was the only political institution with the authority to impose new taxes. Politically, however, it was a hazardous move to summon this institution, because its assembly signalled an element of popular sovereignty. During the eighteenth century, Enlightenment *philosophes* had done much to develop the intellectual foundation for a move from absolutist monarchical sovereignty to popular sovereignty, and to assemble the Estates General turned out to be equal to establishing the institutional foundation for realizing this shift.

King Louis XVI summoned the Estates General in January 1789, and four months later representatives from all the regions of France arrived in Paris. When this happened, what had initially been an economic question of avoiding state bankruptcy became a distinctly political problem. Should the members of the Estates General vote by head or by estate? Should the Third Estate – the commoners – have more members, since they represented roughly 99 per cent of the French population? Should the King be allowed to veto any decision that the Estates General might reach? The impossibility of reaching a satisfactory compromise for these questions prompted the Third Estate members to officially declare themselves the National Assembly in June 1789, a decision that was confirmed on 20 June with the Tennis Court Oath. The establishment of the National Assembly marks the beginnings of the French Revolution, and is a crucial element in what has been called a process of 'political apprenticeship' (*L'an 1* 8; Tackett 77–117). Most of the deputies were lawyers and, despite their obvious interest in politics, they lacked knowledge of its practicalities. The downside to this unfamiliarity with politics, and the learning process it necessitated, was a slow legislative procedure in the early years of the Revolution, but the democratic benefit was a debate in which the ways of politics were continuously discussed.

Once the National Assembly was founded, the first question on the agenda was the problem of the New Regime's constitution and a declaration of the rights of man.[2] After lengthy negotiations, the deputies decided to realize the idea of a declaration of rights, and to use this declaration as a preface to the as yet unwritten constitution. The choice of this composition meant that the declaration would state the basic principles of the New Regime, whereas the constitution would then specify these principles at greater length. When this structural question was debated in early August 1789, there was no unanimous agreement on either that a declaration of rights should preface the constitution, or that it was even a good idea to have such a document. Arguing against the

2 For literature on the Declaration debates, see *L'an 1*, Rials, Gauchet, and Baker. In addition to containing valuable scholarly essays, *L'an 1* is primarily a source collection of all the speeches and documents of the Declaration debates.

idea of a declaration of rights, Pierre-Victor Malouet, an outspoken slave owner and Riom's elected Third Estate member, said: 'A declaration of rights is not necessary for breaking the chains of tyranny; the Constitution suffices and the metaphysical maxims could be dangerous' (Malouet, *L'an 1* 117). In other words, giving liberty and equality the status of absolute and universal rights might give people the wrong impression. Malouet acknowledged that this was precisely what the Americans had done 13 years earlier in their *Declaration of Independence* (1776), but France was not America:

> [A]s co-citizens we have an immense multitude of men with no property. Before anything else, they expect their subsistence to come from a secure job, a thorough police, and continuous protection, and sometimes they are frustrated, not without just cause, with the spectacle of luxury and opulence. (Malouet, *L'an 1* 105)

Malouet's argument was that France, and especially the propertyless classes, was not prepared for universal rights. What the nation needed was not equality and liberty, but stability and order. For that very reason, Malouet asked rhetorically: 'Why, then, start by transporting [the Frenchman] to a high mountain and show him his limitless empire, when he will soon have to descend and find limitations for every step he takes?' (Malouet, *L'an 1* 106).[3] Other deputies similarly argued that it was preposterous, and potentially dangerous, to promise people universal, natural rights (the high mountain) in the declaration, when everything they would meet in society would reveal inequality and limitations. Thus, Delandine quoted Malouet verbatim on 1 August (*L'an 1* 110); on 4 August, before the famous night session, the influential Abbé Grégoire suggested that a declaration should not only show the citizen 'the circle that he can cover but also the barrier that he cannot cross' (*L'an 1* 123); and Baron Joseph-Henri Jessé stated that '[f]reedom is an ample liquor that needs a solid vase to contain it' (*L'an 1* 134). Despite this criticism, the 4 August morning session ended with the deputies deciding that they did want a declaration, and that it should preface the constitution.

Two things should be kept in mind from the analysis thus far. First, the fact that the declaration would preface the constitution meant that any phrasing, however minuscule it might be, was seen to potentially grow in size, as the corpus of New Regime legislation would later expand. The declaration would set out the basic principles, meaning that the importance of any specific wording would grow exponentially, as further legislation was added in accordance with the

3 Susan Maslan discussed the distinction between the limitless rights of the 'high mountain' and the 'limitations' of the real-life rights, in her talk 'Human Rights between Enlightenment and Post-Modernity', at the *Negotiating Human Rights: Cultural, Legal, and Political Framings* conference, Aarhus University, 23–25 January 2014. Her publication on the subject is forthcoming.

initially stated, basic principles. The consequence of this relationship between the 1789 Declaration and the 1791 Constitution is not only that the two documents influence one another and should be read side by side, but also that the National Assembly Declaration debates would focus on minuscule linguistic details. The Declaration debates are all about linguistic finesse and the politics of semantics. Second, even though critics of a declaration, such as Malouet, were unsuccessful at a general level, they were active participants in the Declaration debates. The 1789 declaration was a collective document with numerous compromises, and the fact that a significant portion of the National Assembly opposed the idea of a declaration and the far-reaching principles of equality and liberty would have consequences for the remainder of the debate. Equally important was the fact that among the proponents of a declaration, there was a will to preserve some element of social inequality, albeit in a distinct, New Regime way, something that Abbé Sieyès exemplifies better than anyone else.

Emmanuel Joseph Sieyès and active/passive citizenship

Abbé Sieyès has been called 'the key to the French revolution' (Bredin; Sewell, *A Rhetoric* 8–9). Even if such a claim is overstated, he did have a remarkable influence on key phases of it. Not only was he an influential member of the National Assembly with manifest influence on the 1789 Declaration and the 1791 Constitution; he was also the most successful political pamphleteer of the pre-revolutionary years, *and* aided Napoleon in his *coup d'état* on 18 Brumaire 1799, which is usually regarded as the close of the Revolution. Sieyès was born in Fréjus, a small town in Provence, in 1748, and was ordained as a priest in 1772. Despite his theological education, he seems to have never been a truly religious man (Sewell, *A Rhetoric* 9; Forsyth 33). Instead, his interests were political economy, Enlightenment philosophy, and politics. In 1788 and 1789, he published three pamphlets with the titles *An Essay on Privileges* (1788), *Views of the Executive Means Available to the Representatives of France in 1789* (1789), and, most famously, *What Is the Third Estate?* (1789). All three pamphlets demonstrate a blend distinctive of Sieyès. They all are principled and philosophically advanced, on the one hand, and politically poignant and tied to the specific French historical situation, on the other. This blend of systematized reason and historical specificity makes Sieyès a difficult philosopher to understand today, and it gave him the reputation of being a metaphysician in his own time.

On 19 July 1789, the National Assembly established a *Constitutional Committee*, and assigned it the task to 'present a constitutional project, which will then be discussed in the bureaus and carried to the general assembly for deliberation there' (*L'an 1* 70). Because of the political authority he had at this time, Sieyès was an elected member of this committee, and two days after its establishment he presented his proposal for a declaration of rights: *Preliminary of the Constitution:*

Recognition and Reasoned Exposition of the Rights of Man and Citizen. It was immediately published, and when it was presented to the National Assembly it was described as brilliant, but also as problematic, because it supposed 'much more than it is permitted to expect from the generality of those who have to read and understand it; and everyone has to read and understand it' (Champion de Cicé, *L'an 1* 85). What is interesting is the proposal's distinction between active and passive citizens:

> All the inhabitants of a country should enjoy the rights of the *passive* citizen: all have a right to the protection of their person, of their property, of their liberty, etc., but not all have the right to take an active part in the formation of public powers; not all are *active* citizens. Women, at least in the current state of things, children, foreigners, those also who contribute nothing to the maintenance of the public establishment, should not actively influence the public weal. All can enjoy the advantages of society; but only those who contribute to the public establishment, are like the true stockholders in the great social enterprise. Only they are true active citizens, the true members of the association.
>
> (Sieyès in Fauré 100–101; qtd. in Sewell, *A Rhetoric* 176–177)

Whereas the citizen's *passive* right to protection, property, and freedom are equally enjoyed by every member of the state, the *active* right to help shape the contours of the public is reserved for those contributing to the social enterprise. This distinction excludes women (at least for the time being), children, foreigners, and those not contributing, by way of taxes, to the public establishment from the political sphere. These excluded groups have the right to protection, but not the right to take an active part in political decisions. The distinction between groups of people with and without specifically political rights is familiar from contemporary politics, but what interests me is the exact logic of the active/passive schism in this context, and the ways in which it influenced the 1789 Declaration. When analysing the genealogy of human rights, I argue that this active/passive distinction should be seen as a key element not in the history of universal rights, but of that schism between agency and victimhood that repeatedly surfaces in contemporary humanitarianism and human rights politics.

Historians have long debated the questions of whether or not the active/passive distinction conforms to the general political outlook of Sieyès and the Revolution. William Sewell has argued that it reveals not only a 'deep contradiction in Sieyès's argument', but also allows a glimpse into 'a chasm that reaches to the core of the "bourgeois" revolutionary project' (*A Rhetoric* 152). Sewell writes that Sieyès argued consistently that the Third Estate should have greater political influence than the aristocracy, because, in effect, the members of the Third Estate did all the useful labour in society. Nonetheless, he argued that only those making a specific fiscal contribution should be allowed to vote, and only those with sufficient funds to pursue a political career without being paid for it, the group of people whom Sieyès called 'available citizens', should be allowed to legislate in practice (Sewell, *A Rhetoric* 164–174). In other words, if you are useful to society, you can vote, but you have to prove your utility through financial means, and, Sewell argues, this mandatory economic proof makes it doubtful whether useful labour was actually sufficient grounds for acquiring political rights in the first place.

While Sewell sees a contradiction in Sieyès's thinking, Sieyès himself did not. In the paragraph immediately succeeding the passage on active and passive citizenship, Sieyès writes: 'The equality of political rights is a fundamental principle. It is sacred, like that of civil rights. Privileges would soon emerge from the inequality of political rights' (Sieyès in Fauré 101). Sieyès makes it very clear that unequally distributed political rights would reintroduce privileges, which, at this point, he states are 'unjust, odious, and contradictory to the true goal of society' (101). In contrast to Sewell, and more in line with Sieyès himself, neither Murray Forsyth nor Michael Sonenscher sees any inconsistency in Sieyès's political philosophy, with regard to the active/passive distinction. Implicitly disagreeing with Sewell, Sonenscher argues that, rather than resembling a 'property-based qualification for participation in political life' (which was Sewell's argument), Sieyès thinks along the lines of a 'voluntary payment of a membership fee to join a political party or [. . .] the purchase of a share in a public corporation in order to be able to vote for the membership of its board of executive directors' (Sonenscher in Sieyès xxxi). According to Sonenscher, what is important in Sieyès's concept of active citizenship is not wealth, but rather that people have to demonstrate an interest, in order to vote, and an ability, in order to be eligible (Sonenscher 233–234). Forsyth makes a parallel argument, as he warns against understanding the active/passive schism as an attempt to limit suffrage to a small elite:

> Seen as a whole Sieyes' views are not those of a man determined at all costs to exclude the lower strata of society from the suffrage, and to reserve it for those with substantial property. On the contrary, they are the views of one who believed that the exercise of the most elementary political right called for certain moral and intellectual qualities, that not everyone in the society of his own day possessed these qualities, but that they ought to be encouraged to acquire them.
>
> (Forsyth 163)

I agree with Sonenscher and Forsyth that there is no 'deep contradiction' in Sieyès's thinking, but in my opinion they underestimate the importance and the political implications of the active/passive schism. According to the calculations made by the members of the *New Constitutional Committee* in 1789, the proposed distinction would mean that of a total French population of 26 million, only 4.4 million would have political rights and be active citizens (Thouret in *AP* 9:203).

This distinction signals a kind of social hierarchy that functions in a way wholly different from the Old Regime system of privileges, but that nonetheless grounds political inequality among the French citizenry, and reveals the non-universality of French revolutionary human rights. However, when there is no contradiction in Sieyès's thinking, it is because the logic of the active/passive schism is grounded in the social philosophy that Sieyès put forth in the opening passages of *What Is the Third Estate?* Here, he listed 'the activities that support society', and I think this list explains both why Sieyès would be so critical of the nobility, *and* why he would exclude the poor from full political membership (95). Sieyès stated that the work necessary for any society could be divided into four categories:

> 1) work on the land.
> 2) the handiwork [that] adds further amounts of additional value to these primary goods.
> 3) the merchants and dealers.
> 4) the liberal and scientific professions.
>
> (Sieyès 94–95)

I agree with Sewell that the logic behind this list is the foundation of Sieyès's whole argument (*A Rhetoric* 57). Inspired by the political economists of the century (the physiocrats), Sieyès starts out by mentioning agricultural work. Without the riches of the earth and of the water, mankind would have nothing. Next, and here Sieyès departs from the physiocrats, come the efforts of man to improve the value of objects that he can gather from nature, through industry and labour. Third, merchants and dealers function as necessary intermediate links between production and consumption. And finally, society needs something that is not immediately connected with the circulation of goods, namely teachers, researchers, priests, and others who are 'useful or agreeable' not to the objects of society, but to its subjects (Sieyès 94–95). This is Sieyès's positive description of useful work. Since the nobility performs none of these tasks, Sieyès states that the nobles are 'a heavy burden to impose upon a nation!' (Sieyès 96n3). But his strong emphasis on useful work as a basis for political membership works two ways. While it may be (and very often was) directed at the useless nobility, it may equally be directed at the lower social classes, whose members, for whatever reason, do not contribute to society in a way that corresponds to Sieyès's primarily economic conception of utility. Hence, basing political membership on 'public utility' may function as an attack on the privileged but useless nobility, *and* as a way of depriving the impoverished and uneducated classes of political rights. The result is a society that achieves order by emphasizing a specific kind of utility, and that accepts the political exclusion of those unable to meet these social requirements. In what follows, I pursue this logic into the Declaration debates and the 1791 Constitution, in order to better describe the non-universality of French revolutionary human rights.

Limiting political rights

In the 1789 Declaration, article 6 is the one most directly addressing voting rights. It was also among the most difficult ones to pass in the National Assembly, where it elicited 'very lively debates' that resulted in 'disorder' and 'sinister blows' (*L'an 1* 158). The reason for these heated discussions was that the deputies were caught in a dilemma, which they were unable to solve, the very same dilemma regarding the universality or non-universality of political rights with which Sieyès struggled in his active/passive distinction. Let me quote article 6, and then proceed to explain how it came into existence:

> The law is the expression of the general will. All citizens have the right to take part, in person or by their representatives, in its formation. It must be the same for everyone whether it protects or penalizes. All citizens being equal in its eyes are equally admissible to all public dignities, offices and employments, according to their ability, and with no other distinction than that of their virtues and talents.
>
> (*L'an 1* 199)

In trying to understand the content of this article, one place to start is the Rousseauian term 'the general will'.[4] In his *Of the Social Contract* (1762), Jean-Jacques Rousseau made a distinction between the will of all and the general will, writing:

> the latter looks only to the common interest, the former looks to private interest, and is nothing but a sum of particular wills; but if, from these same wills, one takes away the pluses and the minuses which cancel each other out, what is left as the sum of the differences is the general will.
>
> (60)

To define the general will as that which is common to the members of the polity has consequences with regard to the political organization of society. Hence, Rousseau wrote: 'Since the law is nothing but the declaration of the general will, it is clear that the People cannot be represented in its Legislative power' (115). In other words: The general will cannot be represented because no individual has the ability to determine what is common to everyone. This results in a somewhat ambiguous relation between the political philosophy of Rousseau and article 6 of the Declaration. The article reiterates Rousseau's

4 To align this article's notion of the general will with Rousseau's ideas seems quite straightforward. Nonetheless, Jonathan Israel has argued – unsurprisingly, to readers of his work – that in the context of the Declaration, and specifically Sieyès's draft proposal, the general will 'actually pivoted on the Spinozist doctrine' (Israel, 'Philosophy' 116). Dan Edelstein has cogently criticized this claim (131).

determination of the relation between the general will and the law, but it manifestly departs from Rousseau, as it acknowledges that representatives, as opposed to the individual members of society themselves, might legitimately perform the task of legislators. In more general terms, it is characteristic of the Declaration debates that it resonates with elements of Enlightenment philosophy, but transforms the key concepts and ideas of Enlightenment *philosophes* to fit the specific needs of the immediate debate.

If article 6 is not a mere reiteration of Rousseau's words, how should it be understood? And, more importantly in this context, what precisely was meant by the clauses, 'according to their ability, and with no other distinction than that of their virtues and talents'? In his exposition of the Declaration debates, historian Antoine de Baecque suggests mixed origins for article 6, mainly comprising elements from the drafts and comments of M. de Talleyrand-Périgord, Marquis de Lally-Tollendal, Comte de Mirabeau, and Abbé Sieyès (*L'an 1* 31). Baecque does not explain how these deputies influenced the article, but here I want to focus on the contributions of bishop Talleyrand-Périgord and the noble Lally-Tollendal, both of whom were active participants in the 21 August debate on article 6. At this point, it may be worth repeating that the Declaration debates were all about the politics of minuscule linguistic details.

The precise wording of the Declaration's 17 articles was agreed upon in the week between 20 and 26 August 1789. At this point in the debate, the deputies used a draft proposal made by a subgroup of the assembly called the 'sixth bureau' as the point of departure of their discussion. At least 30 official draft proposals had been submitted at this time, but the one made by the sixth bureau had the benefit of being relatively anonymous.[5] Precisely because it was not a strong draft made by any of the most influential deputies, such as Compte de Mirabeau, Abbé Sieyès, or Marquis de La Fayette, it served well as the starting point for a compromise-seeking National Assembly. What became article 6 in the final version was initially the three following articles:

> Article 11. Since the first duty of every citizen is to serve society according to his capacity and talents, he has the right to be called to any public office.
>
> Article 12. Since the law is the expression of the general will, every citizen must cooperate immediately in the formation of the law.
>
> Article 13. The law must be the same for everyone; and no political authority is binding for the citizen unless it commands in the name of the law.
>
> (*Projet de déclaration des droits de l'homme et du citoyen. Discuté dans le sixième bureau de l'Assemblée nationale* in *L'an 1* 268–269)

5 For collections of these draft proposals, see Fauré, *L'an 1*, and Rials. The estimate of 30 official drafts is from *L'an 1* (219).

The sixth bureau proposal used three articles to cover the content, which was eventually collected in one article: first, the right of every capable citizen to hold any public office; second, the right of every citizen to *immediately* take part in the formation of the law (a phrasing resonating with Rousseau's criticism of political representation); and third, equality before the law. After some debate, the deputies decided to combine these articles into a single one, and the most successful of these combination proposals was that of Talleyrand-Périgord:

> The law being the expression of the general will, all citizens must contribute personally or by representation in its formation; it must be the same for everyone whether it protects or penalizes. All citizens being equal in its eyes are susceptible to every position and to every public office, according to their ability.
>
> (*L'an 1* 158)

With the inclusion of the idea of political representation, this phrasing resembles the final version, but actually it was only at this point in the debate that the real trouble began. The wording, especially of the last sentence, generated heated debate, and a number of clauses were suggested. One unknown deputy suggested adding 'with no distinction' at the very end of the article, and another proposed adding 'with no distinction by birth' (*L'an 1* 158). The reason for these proposed additions was the ambiguity of the word 'ability', which could suggest the prevalent, Old Regime idea that some had a natural, birth-given capacity to perform specific tasks, such as a natural aristocratic ability to rule. Fittingly, the assembly was filled with 'outcries against the aristocracy' at this moment (*L'an 1* 159). Lally-Tollendal eased the tension of the debate when he suggested a different kind of addition: instead of 'without distinction by birth', he proposed 'with no other distinction than that of their talents and their virtues' (*L'an 1* 159). This addition made it into the final version.

What Lally-Tollendal did may seem a small adjustment, but he changed the logic of the clause in a way that recalls elements of Sieyès's political philosophy. Instead of negatively stating that the nobles could not legitimately claim an a priori right to specific offices, he positively stated the requirements for holding an office: talents and virtues. Similarly, Sieyès did not just criticize the privileges and the political power of the aristocracy in the Old Regime. He listed the necessary tasks to be performed in society, and claimed that those performing these tasks ought to be the ones with political power. This positive way of stating the requirements for political influence was not only a massive blow to the Old Regime privileges of the nobility, but also the beginning of the establishment of another kind of social hierarchy, one based not on birth, but on the ability of citizens to be of common utility (article 1), or to demonstrate talents and virtues (article 6). This is a different way of legitimizing social hierarchies, and one consequence of this new logic of social distinction is that the definition of terms such as 'common utility', 'talent', 'ability', and 'virtue' becomes a crucial means of societal inclusion and exclusion. Some central actors of the French Revolution understood the potential of linguistic finesse, and used it to develop rhetorical weapons against Old Regime privilege. Simultaneously, however, they were involved in creating the positive ideological basis for new kinds of social distinctions, which in turn resulted in the political exclusion of the 'useless'. I will continue this analysis of the non-universality of French revolutionary human rights by following the active/passive distinction into the 1791 Constitution. This is where it gets a bit more technical, and where the problem of political representation resurfaces.

The active/passive schism was omitted from the Declaration, but included in the Constitution, in which it had two main functions with regard to the national election process. In contrast to a system of direct election, where citizens would cast their votes for whomever they wanted as their representative, the 1791 Constitution was based on an indirect system of election. It held that active citizens should assemble in Primary Assemblies in the various cities and cantons of France, every other March, to appoint electors. Two weeks after the electors were appointed, they were to meet in Electoral Assemblies, and only at this point would representatives for the National Legislative Assembly be elected. In addition, only active citizens could be elected as deputies of the Assembly. In other words, active citizens should appoint electors who would afterwards elect the deputies from among those active citizens who were running for office. In order to qualify as an active citizen, one would have to fulfil the following seven requirements:

- to have been born, or to become, a Frenchman;
- to be fully twenty-five years of age;
- to be domiciled in the city or canton for the period determined by law;
- to pay, in any part of the kingdom whatsoever, a direct tax equal at least to the value of three days' work, and to present the receipt therefore;
- not to be in a position of domesticity, that is to say, a servant for wages;
- to be inscribed upon the roll of the National Guard in the municipality of his domicile;
- to have taken the civic oath.

(Stewart 236)

Besides these conditions, and besides being a man, which was implicit, anyone who was accused of a crime, and those who, after having gone bankrupt, were unable to prove that they had been acquitted by their creditors, were also 'excluded from the exercise of the rights of the active citizens' (Stewart 236) (for the gender aspects of active/passive citizenship, see Sewell, 'Le citoyen'). Manifestly, here, the active/passive distinction illustrates the economic aspects of political membership. But there is more. The requirements for qualifying as an elector are listed in the Constitution's first chapter, section II, article 7.

Depending on the place of residence, an elector must be the proprietor or usufructuary of a property assessed at a worth equal to the local value of 150 or 200 days' labour, depending on region. These qualifications should be seen against the background of the seemingly universal suffrage stipulated in article 6 of the 1789 Declaration, which stated: 'The law is the expression of the general will. All citizens have the right to take part, in person or by their representatives, in its formation'. The assembly deputies are in reality the representatives of representatives, and monetary and proprietary requirements function to limit the field of representatives in both election phases. When it is necessary to not only be an active citizen, but also to dispose of quite valuable property to qualify as elector, it is clear that the notion of 'all citizens' has been decisively narrowed by the economic qualifications stipulated in the Constitution. In other words, the technicalities of these election processes demonstrate that the inclusion of the possibility of political representation in article 6 of the Declaration was not a mere practicality, but also served as the basis for establishing a distinction between those with and without the right to political participation.

Conclusion: the non-universality of French revolutionary human rights

Commenting on the 'almost unimaginable extension of political rights to groups previously disenfranchised' occurring in the early years of the French Revolution, Lynn Hunt locates an 'inner logic' of human rights (149–150). She argues that as the deputies moved from deliberating the abstract principles of the Declaration to concretizing these in actual legislation, they developed a 'conceivability scale'. It was one thing, Hunt claims, to grant voting rights to Protestants, but another, more difficult step, to grant suffrage to Jews. Similarly, it was less conceivable to allow women and slaves rights than it was to acknowledge the rights of free blacks. Stating her general point, she writes: 'The declaration was designed to articulate the universal rights of humanity and the general political rights of the French nation and its citizens. It offered no specific qualifications for active participation' (Hunt 151). While Hunt is certainly right to emphasize the significance of the extension of political rights during the early Revolution, from the perspective of this article's analysis of the active/passive schism, there is something truly puzzling about her phrase 'no specific qualifications for *active* participation' (my emphasis). Granted, the active/passive distinction did not make it into the 1789 Declaration, but it did influence the Declaration debates, and it did function as a qualifier for citizenship in the 1791 Constitution, which the Declaration was designed to preface. Furthermore, the often economically defined ideal of 'common utility' in article 1 relativizes the egalitarian principles of the Declaration. Even though Hunt's account of the early history of human rights is compelling, it is too celebratory, because it neglects the malleability of the rights discourse, as well as the possibility for new kinds of social inequality sanctioned by the 1789 Declaration.

As I hope to have made clear, numerous histories of human rights take the universalism of French revolutionary rights for granted, without considering the ways in which the Declaration made possible new kinds of social distinctions. When read carefully and in its political and legal context, the 1789 Declaration is not universal, because it facilitates a distinction between those with and without political rights. The division between those two groups is based on the idea of common utility, and this notion has the effect of making political membership dependent on fiscal contributions, among other things. The conclusion I draw from my analysis is that the 1789 Declaration should not be read as a founding document in the history of universal rights. This document and the attendant debates teach us a lesson in the politics of semantics, they demonstrate how linguistic details may alter the meaning of words and ideas that we thought we knew, and they reveal how the distinction between those with political rights and those with only the passive right to protection and security was written into in the human rights discourse more than 200 years ago. As such, the Declaration helped to pave the way for a society in which social inequality was legitimized by referencing the citizens' capacity to be of common utility.

Works cited

Archives parlementaires de 1787 à 1860. 127 vols. Ed. M. J. Mavidal *et al.* Paris: Librairie administrative de P. Dupont, 1862–. [*AP*]. Web. 23 Nov. 2015. <http://frda.stanford.edu/en/ap>. Only volumes 1–82 available online.

Baecque, Antoine de, Wolfgang Schmale, and Michel Vovelle. *L'an 1 des droits de l'homme.* Paris: Presses du CNRS, 1988. Print. [*L'an I*]

Baker, Keith Michael. 'The Idea of a Declaration of Rights'. *The French Idea of Freedom: The Old Regime and the Declaration of Rights of 1789.* Ed. Dale Van Kley. Stanford: Stanford University Press, 1994. 154–199. Print.

Bossenga, Gail. *The Politics of Privilege: Old Regime and Revolution in Lille.* Cambridge: Cambridge University Press, 1991. Print.

Bredin, Jean-Denis. *Sieyès, La clé de la Révolution française.* Paris: Editions de Fallois, 1988. Print.

Douzinas, Costas. *Human Rights and Empire: The Political Philosophy of Cosmopolitanism.* London: Routledge-Cavendish, 2007. Print.

Edelstein, Dan. 'A Response to Jonathan Israel'. *Self-Evident Truths? Human Rights and the Enlightenment.* Ed. Kate E. Tunstall. New York/London: Bloomsbury Academic, 2012. 127–137. Print.

Fauré, Christine, ed. *Les déclarations des droits de l'homme de 1789.* Paris: Éditions Payot, 1988. Print.

Forsyth, Murray. *Reason and Revolution: The Political Thought of the Abbé Sieyes.* New York: Leicester University Press, 1987. Print.

Gauchet, Marcel. 'Rights of Man'. *A Critical Dictionary of the French Revolution.* Ed. François Furet and Mona Ozouf. Trans. Arthur Goldhammer. Cambridge/London: The Belknap Press of Harvard University Press, 1989. 818–829. Print.

Hunt, Lynn. *Inventing Human Rights: A History.* New York/London: W. W. Norton, 2008. Print.

Ishay, Micheline R. *The History of Human Rights: From Ancient Times to the Globalization Era.* Berkeley: University of California Press, 2004. Print.

Israel, Jonathan. *Democratic Enlightenment: Philosophy, Revolution, and Human Rights 1750–1790.* Oxford: Oxford University Press, 2011. Print.

——. 'Philosophy, Religion and the Controversy about Basic Human Rights in 1789'. *Self-Evident Truths? Human Rights and the Enlightenment.* Ed. Kate E. Tunstall. New York/London: Bloomsbury Academic, 2012. 111–127. Print.

Kaiser, Thomas and Dale K. Van Kley, eds. *From Deficit to Deluge: The Origins of the French Revolution.* Stanford: Stanford University Press, 2011. Print.

Kjærgård, Jonas Ross. *The Happiness of All: Balancing Money and Morals in French Revolutionary Human Rights Discourse.* PhD dissertation. Aarhus University, 2015. Print.

Kwass, Michael. *Privilege and the Politics of Taxation in Eighteenth-Century France: Liberté, Égalité, Fiscalité.* Cambridge: Cambridge University Press, 2000. Print.

Rials, Stéphane. *La declaration des droits de l'homme et du citoyen.* Paris: Hachette, 1988. Print.

Riley, James C. *The Seven Years War and the Old Regime in France: The Economic and Financial Toll.* Princeton: Princeton University Press, 1986. Print.

Rousseau, Jean-Jacques. *The Social Contract and Other Later Political Writings.* Ed. and trans. Victor Gourevitch. Cambridge: Cambridge University Press, 2012. Print.

Sewell, William H., Jr. 'Le citoyen/la citoyenne: Activity, Passivity and the Revolutionary Concept of Citizenship'. *The French Revolution and the Creation of Modern Political Culture Vol. 2.* Ed. Colin Lucas. Oxford: Pergamon Press, 1988. 105–125. Print.

——. Jr. *A Rhetoric of Bourgeois Revolution: The Abbé Sieyes and What Is the Third Estate?* Durham/London: Duke University Press, 1994. Print.

Sieyès, Emmanuel Joseph. *Political Writings.* Ed. and trans. Michael Sonenscher. Indianapolis/Cambridge: Hackett Publishing Company, 2003. Print.

Sliwinski, Sharon. *Human Rights in Camera.* Chicago/London: University of Chicago Press, 2011. Print.

Sonenscher, Michael. *Before the Deluge: Public Debt, Inequality, and the Intellectual Origins of the French Revolution.* Princeton/Oxford: Princeton University Press, 2007. Print.

Stewart, John Hall, ed. *A Documentary Survey of the French Revolution.* New York: The Macmillan Company, 1951. Print.

Tackett, Timothy. *Becoming a Revolutionary: The Deputies of the French National Assembly and the Emergence of a Revolutionary Culture (1789–1790).* Princeton: Princeton University Press, 1996. Print.

Chapter 4

The right to resist in the 1793 Declaration of Rights

Nicolai von Eggers

The right to resist plays an enigmatic role in the history of human rights in general, and in the French Revolution in particular. Although it is an integral part of the first wave of human rights declarations – US Declaration of Independence (1776), the Declaration of the Rights of Man and the Citizen (1789), and the Declaration of the Rights of Man and the Citizen (1793) – it completely disappears in later rights declarations. It is deliberately not mentioned in the 1795 Declaration of the Rights and Duties of the Man and the Citizen, and the 1948 Universal Declaration of Human Rights defines resistance (or rebellion) against oppression in purely negative terms; that is, resistance not as a right, but rather as a mechanical effect of a loss of rights: 'it is essential, if man is not to be compelled to have recourse, as a last resort, to rebellion against tyranny and oppression, that human rights should be protected by the rule of law' (Preamble).

What, then, is the right to resist? Is it a human right? One way to answer this question is to go back to the initial declarations of the right to resist, and reconstruct the rationale behind them. The 1776 Declaration of Independence speaks of the 'right' and 'duty' of mankind to 'throw off' a despotic government (Preamble). The 1789 Declaration declares 'resistance to oppression' to be one of the four 'natural and indispensible rights of man' (*art. 2*), although without defining this right any further. However, it is with the 1793 Declaration that we get the most comprehensive definition of the right to resist, and the most elaborate attempt to institutionalize this right (if not in practice, then at least in theory).

This article is a commentary on the final three articles of the 1793 Declaration of Rights defining the right to resist oppression. These are as follows:

> Art. 33. Resistance to oppression is a consequence of the other rights of man.
>
> Art. 34. There is oppression against the social body when a single one of its members is oppressed. There is oppression against each member when the social body is oppressed.
>
> Art. 35. When the government violates the rights of the people, insurrection is, for the people and for each part of the people, the most sacred of rights and the most indispensible of duties.

Two things should be noted here.

First, in my commentary, I will seek to explain the above-mentioned articles through a contextualization of them on two accounts: their historical context in the spring of 1793, during which the fall of the King had left behind a power vacuum to be filled by some sort of republican rule, *and* the context of the political theories of Condorcet and Maximilien Robespierre. The 1793 debate on the human rights declaration, including the right to resist, was based on the *Projet* of Condorcet, who presented his commissioned draft to the National Convention in February 1793, and which included a definition of a right to resist (*art. 31–33*). The wording of the final declaration of the right to resist, however, is based on Robespierre's very different conception of the right to resist in his *Projet* (*art. 27–31*). Thus, understanding the different and competing conceptions of the right to resist expressed in the 1793 debates requires an understanding of the different political theories underpinning these differing conceptions of the right to resist, as proposed by Condorcet and Robespierre.

Since both Condorcet and Robespierre developed and modified their political theories, along with their politico-intellectual trajectories, during the course of the French Revolution, absorbing input and adapting their theories to the situation, I have attempted, as much as possible, to interpret their differing conceptions of the right to resist, in light of their writings and speeches from the period immediately preceding and surrounding their declarations of the right to resist – that is, the years 1792 and 1793. This is not to say that some sort of epistemological break occurs within their respective theories in the year of 1792. In fact, as I will argue, their conceptions of political economy, in particular, which are essential to understanding their conceptions of the right to resist, display great continuity. However, the second revolution of 10 August 1792, and the beheading of the King in January 1793, created a situation of what we might call the 'facticity of republicanism' or the 'facticity of popular politics' to which both authors had to respond, which they in fact did. As Keith Michael Baker and Albert Soboul have demonstrated for Condorcet and Robespierre, respectively, the second revolution caused a reorientation of their respective political theories towards more popularized models of political rule. Unlike the abstract formulations of the right to resist in the 1776 and 1789 Declarations, then, *in the 1793 Declaration, the right to resist should be understood as part of an attempt to integrate popular forms of politics – different modes of dissent – into republican rule (whatever its specific form), based on popular sovereignty.*

My second point is that considering the right to resist today is important, because it questions the intrinsic connection between rights and the rule of law, as expressed in the 1948 Declaration, quoted above. This relation rests on the definition of 'oppression'. If we can conceive of a form of oppression occurring under and within the framework of the rule of law, then the right to resist oppression becomes a right beyond the rule of law, consequently challenging, possibly shattering, the conception of the relation between rule of law and rebellion against tyranny and oppression as envisaged by the 1948 Declaration.

Furthermore, if – and again, this is an 'if' – the rule of law is potentially oppressive, then the right to resist has as its consequence that the state does not hold a monopoly on legitimate violence. Instead, violence – popular or not – becomes legitimate, whenever it addresses and seeks to correct that which brings oppression. The 1793 debates on the right to resist, the two different conceptions of it, concern, as I will show, the struggle between two variants of republican rule administering popular sovereignty, that is, two models of democracy. The one, that of Condorcet, emphasizes the state's monopoly on legitimate violence, and attempts to subsume all forms of dissent to state regulation. It does so in order to secure and enforce the rule of law. The other, that of Robespierre, rejects subsuming all actions to the rule of law, warning against the inherent tendency of governments to become authoritarian, oppressive, and dismissive of dissent. Consequently, according to a Robespierrist conception of the right to resist,[1] the right to resist must be declared, so that citizens know that their resistance may be legitimate, even though it goes against the rule of law. Consequently, *the right to resist concerns the state's supposed monopoly on legitimate violence and the inherent legitimacy of the rule of law*. This may also explain why it is omitted from the 1795 and 1948 declarations.

I argue that the right to resist marks a significant point of difference, if not *the* point of difference, between two competing models of democracy: professional (rule of law) and popular (right to resist). Chantal Mouffe has portrayed this tension in the following way:

> On one side we have the liberal tradition constituted by the rule of law, the defence of human rights and the respect of individual liberty; on the other, the democratic tradition, whose main ideas are those of equality, identity between governing and governed, and popular sovereignty.
>
> (Mouffe 3)

At a certain point in history, these two became intrinsically linked: 'liberalism was democratized and democracy liberalized' (ibid.). Mouffe has called this tension the 'paradox of democracy' – one she fully embraces, by the way. However, as I will argue, it is perhaps much less a paradox of democracy than a genuine struggle over democracy, between two irreconcilable understandings and practices of democracy. Or rather, we do not simply have a tension between liberalism (rule of law, human rights, respect for the individual), on the one side, and democracy (equality, identity of rulers and ruled, popular sovereignty), on

1 'Robespierrist' in the sense of the Robespierre of the *Projet*, heavily influenced by, and oriented towards the popular movement of Paris (cf. Soboul). The actual policies pursued by Robespierre after the Jacobins' rise to power in the summer of 1793 are a different question, which will not be discussed in the present article. Here, I focus on political theory and its complications only.

the other. Instead, each side radically redefines the meaning of the other not only in theory, but also in practice, so that, for example, a political order taking the rule of law as its sacred basis will have a wholly different conception of what equality and popular sovereignty mean, than would a democratic one. Similarly, one starting from the dogma of equality[2] or popular sovereignty would not be opposed to the rule of law or individual human rights per se, but would understand them in a very different way than would a liberal. Thus, we are not dealing with an antagonism between equal opposites – a paradox – but with a genuine struggle in which one's position radically redefines the very definition of the other, and in which there is no neutral or common ground.[3]

The struggle over how to define the relation between the people and its government in a democracy goes back to the French Revolution. After the overthrow of the monarchy on 10 August 1792, and the execution of the former King on 21 January 1793, two different models were increasingly developed and proposed to fill the power vacuum left by the fall of monarchical sovereignty. In the debate over the 1793 constitution and declaration of rights, commencing less than a month after the beheading of the King, the struggle between the two models of republican rule – professional and popular democracy – broke out into the open, represented by Condorcet's and Robespierre's respective proposals for a rights declaration. As Yannick Bosc has argued, the differences between the two models primarily concerned their respective models of political economy, and subsequently their conflicting definitions of property (Bosc 65). Although I agree with Bosc, when it comes to understanding the different political models Condorcet and Robespierre propose, which again reflect their respective definitions of property, we should turn to their definitions of the right to resist. This is therefore what I will do here.

In what follows, I will go over the three articles of the 1793 Declaration defining the right to resist, one by one, focusing on how to read the key concepts surrounding the right to resist, and thus defining it. These concepts are 'oppression' (*art. 33*), 'the social body' (*art. 34*), and 'the people' vis-à-vis its government (*art. 35*).

Oppression

> Resistance to oppression is a consequence of the other rights of man.
>
> (art. 33)

The first thing to note when reading Condorcet's and Robespierre's conceptions of the right to resist oppression are the ways in which 'oppression' is defined.

2 For models assuming actual equality as the unqualified precondition for politics, see Badiou (447) and Rancière (45).

3 For this logic of struggle and its relation to the French Revolution, see von Eggers, 'Reappropriating Sovereignty'.

To put it concisely, their different conceptions of oppression revolve around the question of whether cases in which the right to resist is legitimate and the way it may be expressed may be exhaustively defined by law. According to Condorcet, the right to resist should be given a legal form (*mode légal*), so that it could be easily defined when we discuss oppression, and so that acts of resistance themselves do not become oppressive. On the other hand, for Robespierre, the right to resist rests on the right to exist, meaning that whenever one's existence is threatened (for lack of food, work, or education), then there is an absolute, unregulated right to resist. In fact, Robespierre argued, clearly directed at Condorcet, 'subjecting resistance against oppression to legal forms [*mode légal*] is the ultimate refinement of tyranny' (*art. 31*). Let us take a closer look at their respective positions.

For Condorcet, oppression is directly related to law. All cases of oppression defined by Condorcet in article 32 of his *Projet* relate directly to positive law: positive laws violating natural rights (*art. 32, sec. 1*), particularly as opposed to the universal or general application of law (*art. 32, sec. 2*), and the violation of law (*art. 32, sec. 3*). In other words, there is oppression when the law is not followed, when it is applied only in individual cases, and not in general, and when it is sometimes applied and other times not. Only in these cases would resistance be legitimate, and only if it is performed according to the way to be described in the constitution.

As we can see, the pivotal point here is Condorcet's understanding of the law. According to Condorcet, there is an intrinsic connection between natural law and positive law. The natural light of reason makes man capable of discovering the natural rights of man. These rights, as declared in article 1 of Condorcet's *Projet*, are: liberty (not being a slave, and freedom of opinion and thought; *art. 3–6*), equality (having the same rights as everybody else; *art. 7*), security, property, social guarantee (popular sovereignty that will ensure the rights of man are sustained; *art. 25–28*), and the right to resist oppression. The sole purpose of the constitution and the political administration is to 'maintain' the natural rights discovered by natural reason, in a political state (*Preamble*). In other words, the challenge of political rule is to ensure congruity between natural and positive laws. Consequently, resistance is only legitimate in cases where positive law is not in accordance with natural rights. If positive law is in accordance with natural law, then resistance to law must be avoided at all costs.

In *On the Nature of Political Powers in a Free Nation*, Condorcet argues that once the law has been drafted by the legislators, it shall be executed by 'a force that acts upon the actions of individuals independent of their will and their reason' (Condorcet, *Œuvres complètes de Condorcet: Tome XVI* 122). The primary function of this force is to act 'against resistance to law' (ibid. 123). Whether it is performed by an individual, by a group, or even an entire class of people, resistance to law must be avoided at all costs (ibid. 125–128). If resistance to law is accepted, we are de facto in a state of 'internal war, a veritable dissolution of society' (ibid.

124). In other words, particularity and particular interests are both unimaginable and unacceptable. Either laws are just – that is, in accordance with natural law and useful for preserving natural rights such as liberty and property – or they are not. A law cannot be oppressive to some and not to others; either it is oppressive, or it is not. Consequently, there are no such things as legitimate acts of resistance by individuals, groups, or classes of people, and the only legitimate form of resistance is when the people as a whole insurrect against universally oppressive laws.

What is, then, the relation between law and resistance? This question clearly troubles Condorcet throughout his writings of 1791 through 1793. Before 1791, he simply dismissed the issue of resistance (Baker 264–285), but with the events of the French Revolution, especially the second revolution of 10 August 1792, Condorcet begins to accept the necessity of resistance in creating a just political system. And, in the speech preceding the presentation of the *Projet* to the Convention, he finally develops a theory of the relation between law and the right to resist.

As the right to resist is declared to be one of the natural rights of man, Condorcet argues that there should be, for all laws, a *mode légal*, 'for the people to express their objections' (Condorcet, 'The Principles' 413). Such objections would be presented at primary assemblies. At a given primary assembly, a single citizen may propose 'that a law be re-examined, or that a new law be passed to rectify the problems that have become apparent to him' (ibid. 419). He should then collect 50 signatures, and the issue will be raised before a primary assembly. If the assembly agrees, the matter should be discussed in a meeting among 'all the assemblies within one of the territorial division':

> If the decision of the majority of these assemblies is in agreement with its own, then all the assemblies within a larger circumscription will be summoned; and, if the sentiment of the majority continues to support theirs, the assembly of representatives of the people will be obliged to examine, not the proposition in itself, but the question whether it believes itself compelled to put it on the agenda. Should it refuse, all the primary assemblies of the Republic will be convened to respond to the same question, that is, whether such and such a matter must be taken into consideration. Either the majority of the primary assemblies will support the position of the representatives – in which case the proposition is rejected – or the majority will express an opposite view and the assembly – which as of that moment seems to have lost the confidence of the nation – will be replaced.
>
> (Condorcet, 'The Principles' 420)

Condorcet's meticulous description of this system of a legal mode of resistance reflects the meticulousness of Condorcet's system. Citizens have ways to point out flaws in the law, and thereafter layer upon layer of representatives will, according to Condorcet, make sure that the general will is administered in a rational and deliberative way by professional administrators. This will further ensure that 'a fraction of the people can ever be liberated from the dominion of the general will' and that '[a]ny conspiracy that would not be embraced by the entire Republic would have no hope of success' (ibid.). In this way, resistance will be subsumed under the rule of law, while integrating popular forms of politics and dissent into the modus operandi of the state.

Consequently, it appears that Robespierre is completely justified, when he attacks Condorcet's proposal on the grounds that it confuses 'two absolutely different things: the right to resist oppression on the one side, and the right to reclamation on the other' (*Archives parlementaires LXIII* 114). However, according to Condorcet, there is in fact one instance, and one instance only, in which (violent) resistance – as opposed to the simple right to petition (what Robespierre rightly calls reclamation) – may be legitimate:

> If the majority wants a Convention [to change the constitution, that is], the assembly of representatives has no choice but to agree. A refusal on their part to convene the primary assemblies constitutes the only instance where the right of insurrection may legitimately be put to use.
>
> (Condorcet, 'The Principles' 420)

Thus, once the constitution is implemented, we are in what Condorcet calls a 'free nation', and the only legitimate reason one may have to resist is when those governing refuse to be called back if, after a long deliberative process, as delineated above, they are compelled to do so. In other words, when first the natural rights of man are declared – liberty, equality, security, property, social guarantee, and resistance – the only conceivable form of oppression for Condorcet is that of unjust laws or application of laws, in which case resistance would have to be put up according to the *mode légal*, as described above.

If we turn to Robespierre, things look quite different. As we have already seen, in contradistinction to Condorcet, Robespierre defines the legitimate right to resist as belonging not only to the people *in toto*, but also to '*each part* of the people' (*art. 34*; my emphasis). We will return to this below, but for now we focus on reconstructing Robespierre's definition of oppression, which is crucial to understanding why a 'part' of the people may have a right to resist.

The first thing to note is that, unlike for Condorcet, Robespierre declares the right to resist oppression not as a right in itself, but rather a logical consequence of the other rights of man. According to Robespierre, there are only two such rights: liberty, and the right to exist. Essentially, 'liberty' should be understood as the right to not be a slave. Here, Robespierre is in perfect agreement with Condorcet. However, the right to exist is more complex, and not found in Condorcet's proposal.

Ideas similar to the right to exist were already found in the early parts of the Revolution, as in Jean-Paul Marat's *Proposed Declaration* of 1789, and La Rouchefoucauld-Liancourt's proposal of 1790, to add the 'right to subsistence' to the rights of man (quoted in Gross, 'Saint-Just' 181). As Florence Gauthier has shown, ideas of the right to exist or the right to subsistence were integral parts of the popular movement on the French countryside, in 1789 (Gauthier 67), and also earlier (Gauthier and Ikni). However, in the 1793 debates on the Declaration, it was Robespierre who, based on his speeches of the preceding year or so, once again took it up, and gave it more political substance. What did Robespierre mean by 'the right to exist'? The idea is perhaps best expressed in Robespierre's speech 'On Subsistence' presented before the Convention on 2 December 1792:

> It is not necessary that I be able to purchase brilliant fabrics; but I do need to be rich enough to buy bread, for myself and my children. The merchant is welcome to retain goods coveted by wealth and vanity in his shops, until he finds the moment to sell them at the highest possible price; but no man has the right to amass piles of wheat, when his neighbour is dying of hunger.
>
> What is the first object of society? It is to maintain the imprescriptible rights of man. What is the first of those rights? *The right to exist.* The first social law is therefore the one that guarantees all members of society the means to live; all others are subordinate to that one.
>
> (Robespierre, *Virtue and Terror* 51; my emphasis; translation modified)

According to Robespierre, the right to exist is the most essential of rights, and it must be guaranteed to all members of society by the political order instituted. Thus, it follows that whenever the political system does not guarantee the right to exist to all its members – 'either by procuring work for them, or by ensuring the means to exist for those who are not fit to work' (*art. 10*)[4] – the political system is oppressive and illegitimate, while the right to resist such oppression and ensure one's right to exist becomes legitimate.

Unlike Condorcet, Robespierre is able to imagine forms of oppression other than those of arbitrary or unequal application of laws. It is perfectly possible for a regime to act in accordance with the rule of law, *and* for it to be oppressive. In fact, this is precisely the case in economic oppression. Trade and property rights are perfectly legal, and yet when the means of subsistence do not circulate among the poorest members of the body politic, their right to exist is denied them, and they are, according to Robespierre's logic, oppressed.

When article 33 of the 1793 Declaration holds that 'resistance to oppression is a consequence of the other rights of man', we should keep in mind that these rights are liberty and the right to exist. Here, oppression is to be understood as either slavery – direct economic oppression – or lack of means of subsistence

4 This became article 21 of the 1793 Declaration.

(primarily foodstuffs, but also education[5] and healthcare),[6] that is, indirect economic oppression. Whenever oppression, understood in this way, is a fact, resistance becomes legitimate, irrespective of state regulations, and irrespective of existing law.

The social body

> There is oppression against the social body when a single one of its members is oppressed. There is oppression against each member when the social body is oppressed.
>
> (*art. 34*)

Condorcet and Robespierre perceived insurrections and their political role in two very different ways. For Condorcet, resistance by particular groups in ways not regulated by a *mode légal*, such as the one he himself had proposed, was paramount to 'internal war, a veritable dissolution of society' (Condorcet, *Œuvres complètes de Condorcet: Tome XVI* 124). Condorcet acknowledged that in oppressive states, where such a mode was not given, other forms of resistance might, of course, be necessary to institute what he called a 'free nation'. But under no circumstances could they be perceived as a political form proper, or as in any way legitimate once a *mode légal* of resistance was instituted. In this way, he eventually came to legitimize the popular violence of the second revolution of 10 August 1792 on the grounds that the citizens were 'forced to act by themselves' after the King had broken the original contract, and tried to make the people his slaves (Condorcet *Œuvres complètes de Condorcet: Tome XVIII* 65, 74). But in a free nation, in which the rule of law reigns, there can be no such thing as legitimate resistance beyond the law. As we have seen, Robespierre's position is quite different, in that he insists that once there is oppression (also economically) of even a single member of the social body, 'insurrection is, for the people and for each part of the people, the most sacred of rights and the most indispensible of duties' (*art. 35*). Why this difference? Why does Robespierre accept the legitimacy of resistance by only part of the social body, while Condorcet does not? The answer is found in their respective conceptions of the social body.

In a text of 1793, Condorcet tries to show, as its title indicates, *That All Classes of Society Have but One and the Same Interest.* Condorcet argues that in every society, there are naturally a number of different classes: proprietors, cultivators, financiers, traders, small producers, workers, and so on (ibid. 43). According to Condorcet, society's division into classes is a result of the division of labour,

5 Article 13 of Robespierre's *Projet.*

6 For the Jacobin programme of a welfare state *avant la lettre,* in theory and in practice, see Gross, *Fair Shares.*

which in turn is a result of the differences in natural capacities, or 'talents', as Condorcet labels them elsewhere (Condorcet, *Œuvres complètes de Condorcet: Tome XVI* 130). Natural inequalities in faculties and talents create, in the state of nature, differences in the ability to obtain capital, and, as a consequence, some accumulate more capital than others.[7] These capitals[8] are redistributed when the rich purchase the labour power of the poor. As a happy result of this division of labour, the rich obtain more time to manage production and distribution, and to reflect on how to make these processes more efficient. Consequently, all this is for the benefit of all. 'Do you wish agriculture to progress [*progrès*]? It is necessary to allow cultivators or proprietors be in a position to make great *avances* [advances/profit]' (Condorcet, *Œuvres complètes de Condorcet: Tome XVIII* 49). Thus, capitalist farmers in particular – the 'productive' class in the political economy of François Quesnay and Turgot, to whom Condorcet is deeply indebted – must be given free rein to improve production, including free time to think about how to do this. In this way, these proprietors are the ones who 'essentially make up society', as Condorcet puts it in his text on Turgot (Condorcet, *Vie de M. Turgot* 221).

Thanks to capitalists, an increasingly sophisticated division of labour emerges, with increasingly efficient production, and thus with more and better goods for all. And thanks to free trade, 'fortune does not stay with a certain number of families, with one class of men, but circulates among the masses' (Condorcet, *Œuvres complètes de Condorcet: Tome XVIII* 50). Thus, Condorcet believes to have proven what he set out to prove, namely that the 'pretended oppositions of interests do not exist' (ibid. 45). All classes, by doing their part, work towards a common goal: progress, and the infinite perfection of man and society – which is also the argument of Condorcet's famous *Sketch on the Progression of Mankind* (Condorcet, 'The Principles' 528). Accordingly, all classes of society have but one and the same interest.

When it comes to the right to resist in a free nation, it would therefore make no sense for a certain portion of the people to have a particular interest in resisting. *Either all are oppressed* – which is the case when the representatives refuse to be called back after the long deliberative process of the general will, as we have seen – *and all should be resisting the political system, or none are oppressed, and resistance will, by definition, be destructive to society, hamper progress, and thus be illegitimate.*

Robespierre would have none of this. Though he, like all French revolutionaries, including Condorcet, warned and fought against factions, and believed

7 This is the fantasy of so-called 'original accumulation', conceived of by classical political economists, and forcefully criticized by Karl Marx in Chapter 24, 'The So-Called Primitive Accumulation', of *Capital*.

8 In the eighteenth century, capital was used in the plural. Only later did it become a mass noun.

in the common interest of the republic, Robespierre argued that the actual social body contained different classes with more than one and the same interest.

Already in some of his early speeches, particularly 'On the Silver Mark', of April 1791, Robespierre attacks what he perceives to be a new aristocracy seizing power through the fall of the old one, namely the aristocracy of the rich (Robespierre, *Virtue and Terror* 7). In 'On Subsistence' (December 1792), Robespierre again attacks the aristocracy of the rich, which, he argues, is not to be seen as an entirely new class, but rather as a continuation of the ancient dominant orders of the *ancien régime*: 'noble, ecclesiastical, or bourgeois aristocracy' (ibid. 50). After the fall of the two other orders – the nobility and the clergy, the noble and the ecclesiastical aristocracy – bourgeois aristocracy was, according to Robespierre, the last of the three ancient orders remaining, and thereby the only class obstructing true republicanism – in which all citizens are free and equal – from becoming reality. How do the bourgeois aristocracy do this? By oppressing the people economically through enforcement of unjust laws: 'unlimited freedom of trade, and bayonets to calm fears and appease hunger' (ibid.).

According to Robespierre, the new ruling class was primarily concerned with taking care of their specific class interests. That is, they had, as Robespierre put it, 'far more to say about the grain trade than about the subsistence of the people': 'They counted for much the profits of merchants or landowners, and the lives of men for almost nothing. And why? It was great men, ministers, the rich who were writing, who governed' (Robespierre, *Virtue and Terror* 51).

Thus, it is against the interests of the rich, who are opposed to the interests of the people, that Robespierre introduces the right to exist. This right to exist was part of an entire 'popular political economy',[9] which included a reconceptualization of property, and criminalization of some forms of trade:

> The foods necessary to man are as sacred as life itself. Everything essential to conserve life is property common to the whole of society. Only the surplus can be individual property and left subject to the enterprise of merchants. Any mercantile speculation I make at the expense of my fellow's life is not trade at all, it is brigandage and fratricide.
>
> (Robespierre, *Virtue and Terror* 51)

Ownership, at least of the things necessary to survive – but to some extent also those things needed for being a good republican, that is, education, healthcare, and the time and opportunity to participate actively in political decision-making[10] – are to be understood as property belonging not to private

9 See Robespierre's discourse of 10 May 1793, in Robespierre, *Œuvres: Tome IX*. For Robespierre's 'popular political economy', see Bosc; Gauthier (87–118); Labica (105–114).

10 Cf. Robespierre's 'popular political economy' (see footnote above).

individuals, but to the social body in its entirety. Each act that, in the last instance, threatens the well-being of other members of the social body, whether lawful or not, is an act of oppression equal to fratricide, and thus may be legitimately resisted. As Robespierre puts it in the *Projet*: 'The support essential to those who lack what is necessary is a *debt* owed by those possessing superfluous means' (*art. 11*; my emphasis). However, this does not mean that the poor are simply entitled to take back what the rich owe them, or that they may set up their own organizations for doing so. As article 11 continues: 'it is for the law to determine the way this debt should be acquitted', which is to say that resistance must always be somehow directed at the state, and aim to bring a new political administration to power – one that will ensure that the right to exist is recognized, and that the debt owed to the poor is paid.

As we can see, there are interests at work in society that are not compatible with that of the social body, although this does not mean that all members of society do not have, in the final analysis, a unitary interest (ibid. 55). The strict, egoistic, economic interests may not be the same for the rich and the rest of the people, but, according to Robespierre, the political, republican interest in creating a social body of members, free and equal, is common to both groups. In contrast to many political economists of the eighteenth century, who argued that private vices would lead to public benefits,[11] Robespierre, following Rousseau, distinguishes between self-interest and virtue.[12] Self-interest is taking care of one's private and particular interests, whereas virtue is doing what is in the interest of the social body: acting for the common good, *le salut public*. According to Robespierre (and Rousseau), private vices lead to nothing but private vices, and therefore what a republic needs are virtuous citizens performing their tasks with the *salut public* in mind, which, in Robespierre's version, cannot be separated from democracy and equality. As Robespierre puts it in his (in)famous speech of 18 Pluviôse II, virtue is 'none other than the love of the *patrie* [homeland] and its laws. But as the essence of the republic or of democracy is equality, it follows that love of the *patrie* necessarily embraces love of equality' (ibid. 111). Thus, the interests of the people – free and equal and united in a democracy – are but one, and virtuous actions are directed at the general welfare, rather than particular interests. '[I]n aristocratic states the word *patrie* means something only for the *patricians*', whereas in a democratic republic the particular interest of the patricians, the bourgeois aristocracy, must be brought into line with the interests of the people in its entirety (ibid. 111–112). However, if the rich are

11 Bernard Mandeville in particular, but this is a general trait of the Scottish Enlightenment (see von Eggers, 'Roots of Political Economy').

12 For instance, see the way in which Rousseau counterposes morals and virtue with commerce and money, and his commendation of sumptuary laws in the 'First Discourse' (Rousseau 18), or his discussion of Hobbes' and Mandeville's doctrines of the relation between self-interest and the public good, in the 'Second Discourse' (Rousseau 150–154).

proper republicans, they will see that laws redistributing the goods among the people are also in their own republican interests. Whenever they do not act accordingly, whenever they turn the state into a bourgeois aristocracy in which their own particular interests are served, the right to exist is threatened, and resistance becomes for the people, and each part of the people, the most sacred of rights and the most indispensable of duties.

The relation between the people and the government

> When the government violates the rights of the people, insurrection is, for the people and for each part of the people, the most sacred of rights and the most indispensible of duties.
>
> (*art. 35*)

The question of resistance becomes a question of virtue: Who is virtuous? Where does virtue reside? This is one of the most debated issues concerning the French Revolution, and Robespierre particularly, but if for a moment we look past the moralistic interpretations of Robespierre's alleged moralization of politics, we will see that the question of virtue is also, and I would argue primarily, a political question separating Condorcet's and Robespierre's conceptions of legitimate republican rule in a free nation.[13]

For Condorcet, it is reason rather than virtue that ensures a legitimate political system, which means that the reasonable, the educated, and economic elite must lead the way towards the true equality of republicanism. 'If the mass of the representatives and functionaries are composed of men animated by the public spirit, enlightened, *honnêtes*,[14] the vices of the constitutional forms cannot be a dangerous influence' (Condorcet, *Œuvres complètes de Condorcet: Tome XVIII* 29). In other words, what matters to Condorcet is that enlightened gentleman are brought to power. Though Condorcet finds the people able to 'judge sanely', they only judge with immediate outcomes in mind, and are therefore unable to fathom a long-term strategy that will procure liberty and equality

13 Here, I follow Carl Schmitt, who argued that the political questions of each epoch take place within a certain central area [*Zentralgebiet*], with its specific vocabulary (Schmitt). In the eighteenth century, Schmitt argues, the central political questions and struggles were discussed and fought out in the moral-educational sphere. Thus, struggles over moral and educational problems, and problems phrased in a seemingly moralistic vocabulary – as was the case in the French Revolution – may still be read as having a profoundly political character.

14 *Honnête homme* or *honnêteté* was a French, upper bourgeois culture, similar to that of the English *gentleman*, which entailed a way of behaving, speaking, thinking, and acting, going back to the seventeenth century. The *honnêtes hommes* are the ones, according to Condorcet, fit for government.

(ibid.). In other words, virtue in the form of reason resides with republican government. When first the way has been cleared for a republican rule of a free nation through resistance to oppression, resistance may be subsumed under, and regulated by the wise rule of enlightened men, the 'sweet despotism of reason' (Condorcet quoted in Baker 282). Thus, resistance should be given a *mode légal*, and thereby regulated by the reasonable, and therefore virtuous, republican government.

According to Robespierre, virtue resides not with government, but with the people. As he puts it: '[V]irtue is natural to the people' (Robespierre, *Virtue and Terror* 113). But that virtue is natural does not mean that it cannot die out, letting the people become corrupt. It has to be nurtured by good laws and a good government in order to thrive. Thus, there is a relation between the virtue of the people and the government, where government feeds on the virtuous actions of the people, which in turn feeds on good governance (good governance being, for the Jacobins, essentially a welfare state, securing education, healthcare, and access to public offices) (Gross, *Fair Shares*). A virtuous people and a virtuous government feed on each other, but in an asymmetrical way:

> Republican virtue can be considered in relation to the people, and in relation to the government: it is necessary in both cases. When the government alone is deprived of it, there remains a reservoir in the people; but when the people itself is corrupt, liberty is already lost.
>
> (Robespierre, *Virtue and Terror* 113)

Virtue is natural to the people, and therefore should be sustained and not restrained, whereas government must be restrained, in order to prevent it from becoming corrupt, and thus becoming oppressive. The virtue of the people is natural, and must be left largely to itself, whereas the virtue of government is artificial, and must be constantly recreated. Thus, it is not difficult to see why popular resistance is a continuous necessity, and something that cannot and must not be regulated by the government.

As we can see, there is, according to Robespierre, an inherent logic or inertia of government resulting in those in power becoming increasingly focused on their own specific class interests, rather than the interests of the people as a whole. Thus, whereas virtue is natural to the people, corruption is natural to those governing. Or, in Robespierre's own words: 'Any institution that does not assume the people to be good, and the magistrate corruptible, is itself depraved' (*art. 19*). Therefore, the people must remain vigilant, and be willing and allowed to resist, whenever they feel oppressed. Governors have a natural blindness to oppression, to when they themselves become oppressive, and this is why they cannot be trusted with regulating the means of resistance. As Robespierre put it in the debate on the right to resist, in the National Convention: 'The legislator can never determine the cases in which the people subjected to his laws will find them wicked [*mauvaises*]' (*Archives parlementaires LXIII* 114).

In order to counterbalance the inherent vice of government, it is necessary that the people be vigilant, active, and aware of their rights. Thus, declaring that the right to resist is the most sacred of rights and the most indispensible of duties is to remind the people of their role in preventing the government from becoming corrupt, and revitalizing it with their own virtuous energy, possibly through resistance. In this way, the right to resist becomes a sort of separation of powers, not between different governmental institutions run by *honnêtes hommes*, but between the people and its government, in which the people are encouraged by the rights declaration to act as a check on their corruptible government.

Conclusion

The differences between Condorcet and Robespierre, and their conceptions of the right to resist oppression, reflect a broader division not only of the French revolutionaries, but also of the republican and democratic conceptions following in their wake.

The first difference between Condorcet and Robespierre concerns the way to establish a political system that ensures the people's liberty. According to Condorcet, this was practically – though not formally – achieved in February 1793, when he put forward his Declaration, and the only thing left to do was implement a version of the kind of political administration, dictated by natural reason, that he himself proposed. If political powers were to interfere in economic matters, it would be only to ensure freedom of trade, since such freedom would benefit all. On the other hand, according to Robespierre, republicanism would not be a social reality until the particular and fratricidal interests of the bourgeois aristocracy were either expelled from the social body, or made to work for the people in its entirety.

The second difference, following from the first one, is much more important, and concerns giving, or not giving, the right to resist a legal form. According to Condorcet, when the republic was first established, it would not be necessary or legitimate to have unregulated forms of resistance. The rational rule of law would ensure that the political and social system was not only just, but also on its way towards perfection, whereas all acts of unregulated resistance could therefore be seen only as ways of obstructing or destroying a legitimate political system. 'Any conspiracy that would not be embraced by the entire Republic would have no hope of success', and the state would be regarded as having a monopoly on legitimate violence (Condorcet, 'The Principles' 420).

For Robespierre, even when the republic was established – and he appears confident that the time would come – *resistance must remain unregulated by the state, by law, yet for that reason it is nonetheless legitimate.* Quite the opposite. As we have seen, Robespierre believed that government has a natural tendency to become oppressive, because those governing will tend to form an elite, a ruling class, that will become increasingly focused on their own particular interests at the expense of the interests of the people. For this reason, resistance cannot be regulated by the state. This would be 'the ultimate refinement of tyranny' (Robespierre, *Virtue and Terror* 71). Robespierre articulated the credo of his version of republican rule: 'Any institution that does not assume the people to be good, and the magistrate corruptible, is itself depraved' (*art. 19*). This indicates a conception of a dual power structure, a model in which the state does not have a monopoly on legitimate violence – in fact, state violence must always be viewed with suspicion – and in which popular violence is legitimate, whenever it seeks to address oppression. Thus, defining oppression becomes of utmost importance. And, if one is willing to define oppression in terms that go beyond the mere breach of the rule of law – as in economic oppression – then the right to resist is essentially a much more radical version of democracy than one restricted to private property and the rule of law. In this way, the right to resist marks a point of distinction between liberal and more radical forms of democracy. In the facticity of popular politics created by the overthrow of the King, the right to resist became an important and contested part of the conception of human rights. Both Condorcet and Robespierre responded to the sudden legitimacy of violent resistance, and, in different ways, sought to integrate it into political rule, either by subsuming the right to resist under and into the rule of law (Condorcet), or by subsuming the rule of law under the right to resist (Robespierre). In this way, defining the right to resist became a focal point for contestation between different conceptions of popular political rule. Though the Robespierrist conceptions were triumphant in the first instance, as witnessed by the definition of the right to resist in articles 33–35 of the 1793 rights declaration, the declaration was immediately suspended, and disappeared from the declarations of 1795 and 1948. Nonetheless, the 1793 Declaration's right to resist remains an expression of a much more radical, militant, and egalitarian conception of human rights than that which has become dominant since then.

Works cited

Badiou, Alain. *L'être et l'événement.* Paris: Seuil, 1988. Print.

Baker, Keith Michael. *Condorcet: From Natural Philosophy to Social Mathematics.* Chicago: University of Chicago Press, 1975. Print.

Bosc, Yannick. 'Liberté et propriété. Sur l'économie politique et républicanisme de Condorcet'. *Annales historiques de la Révolution française* 4 (2011): 53–82. Print.

Condorcet. *Vie de M. Turgot.* London, 1786. Print.

——. *Œuvres complètes de Condorcet: Tome XVI.* Paris, 1804. Print.

——. *Œuvres complètes de Condorcet: Tome XVIII.* Paris, 1804. Print.

——. 'The Principles of, the Justifications for, the New Constitution'. *Social and Political Thought of the French Revolution.* Ed. Marc Goldstein. New York: Lang Publishing, 2009. 412–421. Print.

——. 'Proposed Declaration of the Natural, Civil and Political Rights of Man'. *Social and Political Thought of the French Revolution.* Ed. Marc Goldstein. New York: Lang Publishing, 2009. 422–425. Print.

——. 'Outline of an Historical View of the Progress of the Human Mind'. *Social and Political Thought of the French Revolution.* Ed. Marc Goldstein. New York: Lang Publishing, 2009. 525–550. Print.

Gauthier, Florence. *Triomphe et mort de la révolution des droits de l'homme et du citoyen.* Paris: Syllepse, 2014. Print.

Gauthier, Florence and Guy Ikni. 'Le mouvement paysan en Picardie'. *La guerre du blé au XVIIIe siècle.* Ed. Florence Gauthier and Guy-Robert Ikni. Paris: Passion, 1988. 187–204. Print.

Gross, Jean-Pierre. 'Saint-Just et la Déclaration des Droits de l'Homme de 1793'. *Actes du colloque de Blérancourt.* Tergnier: Dupuis, 1989. 171–188. Print.

——. *Fair Shares for All.* Cambridge: Cambridge University Press, 1997. Print.

Labica, Georges. *Robespierre: Une politique de la philosophie.* Paris: La fabrique, 1990. Print.

Mouffe, Chantal. *The Paradox of Democracy.* London: Verso, 2000. Print.

Rancière, Jacques. *La mèsentente.* Paris: Gallimard, 1995. Print.

Robespierre, Maximilien. *Œuvres: Tome IX.* 2nd ed. Paris: PUF, 2000. Print.

——. *Virtue and Terror.* London: Verso, 2007. Print.

Rousseau, Jean-Jacques. *The Discourses and Other Early Political Writings.* Cambridge: Cambridge University Press, 1997. Print.

Schmitt, Carl. 'The Age of Neutralizations and Depoliticizations'. *The Concept of the Political.* Chicago: University of Chicago Press, 2007. 80–96. Print.

Soboul, Albert. 'Robespierre and the Popular Movement of 1793–4'. *Past and Present* 5 (1954): 54–70. Print.

von Eggers, Nicolai. 'Reappropriating Sovereignty: A Critique of Giorgio Agamben' Abandonment of Sovereignty'. *Trópos* 8.1 (2015): 155–179. Print.

——. 'Roots of Political Economy'. *Intellectual History of Economic Normativities.* Ed. Mikkel Thorup. Basingstoke: Palgrave Macmillan, forthcoming. Print.

Part II

Negotiating victimhood

The politics of contextual rhetoric

Chapter 5

From utopia to dystopia?

Bukharin and the Soviet Constitution of 1936

Elisa Kriza

When reading about human rights, it is not very common to hear of dictatorships as being their promoters. Law scholar Samuel Moyn writes that human rights historians tend to adopt the genre of hagiography when approaching their subject: those they consider to have advanced the cause of human rights are 'generally treated with uncritical wonderment' (6). But sometimes, governments and revolutionaries who have promoted the cause of human rights stood very far from today's understanding of these rights and how they come about. In part, this has to do with the fact that today's concept of human rights is linked to the changes in world politics and international law that have taken place since the 1970s (Moyn 7), but it also has to do with the fact that the term 'human rights' means many different things. The crucial difference lies in the understanding of their universality, and their relationship to the state. Not only democratic states, but authoritarian states have also included and include human rights as part of their legislation.

Human rights are by nature utopian, and this utopia can be envisioned by the state or by the people (Moyn 1, 20). Yet, the history of human rights has many examples of contradictions between what is promised and what is delivered, between the rhetoric used to promote certain laws, and the programmatic politics of the issuing government. Particularly in post-revolutionary contexts, the rhetoric of human rights may be used to create communities of citizens and redefine 'the enemies', who are deprived of these rights. In this sense, one may speak of the misuse of human rights rhetoric.

The Russian Revolution of 1917, and the subsequent Soviet dictatorship, played a significant role in introducing human rights rhetoric in Russia, although in a highly ambiguous manner (Stearns 114–116). In this chapter, I discuss the introduction of basic human rights in the Soviet Union during the Stalin Era, while the greatest wave of repression was taking place in that country. It is in this period that the Soviet Union experienced the most complex relationship between the 'is' and the 'ought' in its legal system, although this remained a problem throughout the history of this country. In 1990, only months before the dissolution of the Soviet Union as a state, Rein Mullerson, the director of the International Law Section of the Academy of Sciences of the USSR, wrote:

> It must be acknowledged that the reserved attitude of the Soviet Union in the past towards control mechanisms in the area of human rights protection, the neurotic reaction to the slightest criticism, regarding it as, if not a slight on our sovereignty, then at least interference in internal affairs, was not only the result of ideological dogmatism but also testified to the fact that in the area of human rights there are things to hide in our country, that there is a gap between the idea and the reality.
>
> (Mullerson 43)

Rights as ideals

As in most countries, human rights in the Soviet Union were embedded in the constitution. Constitutions are complex texts that summarize a combination of 'ideas, ideals, and ideology' (Frankenberg 440). Ideals expressed in a constitution are often utopian, and express the 'collective goals' the authors believe the country should pursue (Frankenberg 441). I will analyse how the ideals of the Soviet Constitution of 1936 related to the historical reality of the Stalinist repression of the mid-1930s, with a special focus on the fate of the theoretician Nikolai Bukharin, a victim of the Show Trial of 1938, who had been a member of the constitutional committee. Although legal scholar Günter Frankenberg considers the Constitution of 1936, as all other socialist constitutions, to be a 'programme' constitution with a 'strictly symbolic purpose' (453), there is more to the story of this constitution and the parallel history of the purges than meets the eye. By looking at narrative framings of the specific case of Bukharin's trial within the context of the creation of the new constitution in non-fiction and in fiction, I identify different interpretations of victimhood and agency in this crucial historical period. This case study exemplifies how the dichotomy between victims of human rights abuses and agents may become fuzzy, and how the rhetoric of human rights may be used by a repressive government. The contemporary relevance of this case lies in the Soviet Union's desire to appear democratic, while holding on to a very broad definition of 'enemy', which could be easily manipulated to include generally loyal citizens. In the twenty-first century, more states define themselves as democracies than ever before, but the dire state of human rights protection in our century is connected with the way many democracies exclude people from the utopian promises of such a system.

The Soviet Constitution and its promises

The Soviet Union was founded in 1922, when the Russian Federation, Ukraine, Belarus, and other former territories of the Tsarist Empire came together in a unified socialist state. The 'Dictatorship of the Proletariat' was proclaimed, and the Communist Party gained the monopoly of power by repressing opposing parties. The Congress of Soviets became the supreme legislative body of the Soviet Union (not to be confused with the Communist Party Congress, which was the supreme organ of the ruling Party). The Congress of Soviets ratified the Soviet constitutions of 1924 and of 1936, in which the constitution called for its dissolution and replacement as legislative body. Due to the Soviet Union's one-party rule, the General Secretary of the Communist Party was commonly understood to be the leader of the country. Therefore, it is not surprising that the Constitution of 1936, which was ratified by Congress, is often referred to as the 'Stalin Constitution', as Joseph Stalin was the General Secretary at the time.

The story of the Constitution of 1936 began in 1935, when Soviet Premier Viacheslav Molotov gave a speech about democracy during the VII Congress of Soviets, in which he presented the government's proposal to write a new constitution. The Congress voted on expanding constitutional rights to enhance democratic participation and equality in the Soviet Union (Starr 1144). A constitutional commission was appointed by the Central Committee of the Communist Party, and after about a year of work, the commission presented a draft constitution to the Soviet government, and subsequently to the Soviet people.

The draft was published in great numbers, and discussed in several newspapers. Throughout the country, Soviet citizens were encouraged to debate this text and make suggestions, some of which were sent to Moscow. Changes to the constitution did occur as a result of these discussions, making it easy for the Soviet press to describe it as the 'most democratic' in the world (Wimberg 313). Historian Karen Petrone explains that the national conversation about the constitution was part of a government strategy to educate 'the general population about how they should participate in Soviet political life' (Petrone 175). The study of the new constitution and its promotion by the government, which included numerous public celebrations, continued until December 1937.

In late 1936, the new constitution was approved by the VIII Congress of Soviets of the Soviet Union. An article in *Pravda*, the official organ of the Communist Party of the USSR, describes the date of the approval of the constitution as the second foundational moment of the Soviet state: the first foundational moment was the revolution, and this date (5 December 1936) 'marks the achievement of the first phase of communism' ('K novym pobedam' 1). The new constitution abandoned the Marxist idea of the withering away of the state, thus establishing the Soviet state. It also separated legislative, judicial, and executive powers. For the first time in the Soviet era, legislation curtailed some of the state's powers, and introduced the idea of the state as an entity with obligations to its citizens, for example protecting citizens from arbitrary arrest. The new constitution introduced voting rights regardless of class, religion, or origin, in direct elections by secret ballot. This decision was of immense importance, as one of the harshest aspects of previous Soviet legislation had been the declaration of large segments of the population, such as the clergy or members of the former regime, to be class enemies, deprived of these rights from the outset (Towe 1252). With its inclusive definition of citizenship, the new constitution 'destabilized the old conception of "enemy" as one who was already marked and set apart from the community' (Petrone 180–181). Clear-cut definitions of who belonged to the community of peasants and workers, which was the way the Soviet Union defined its society, and who did not, became blurred through the new laws. The duty to defend the fatherland was included as an obligation of all citizens of the USSR, and treason – including espionage – was to be prosecuted as a most heinous crime ('Konstitutsiia' 4).

The new constitution guaranteed equality for men and women, and surprisingly it also granted citizens freedom of the press, of conscience, of religious practice, of speech, and of association. It allowed for more property rights, and it offered a variety of social rights, such as paid vacations and healthcare ('Konstitutsiia' 2–4). Although clearly flawed by today's standards, the Soviet Constitution of 1936 was a benchmark in the introduction of civil and social rights at the time (Alexeiev 472).

Bukharin and the creation of the constitution

Despite being widely nicknamed the 'Stalin Constitution', this was the work of a number of theoreticians and politicians, among them Nikolai Bukharin. Stalin was the chair of the subcommittee that discussed general questions, and Premier Minister Molotov chaired the subcommittee on economic questions. Bukharin chaired the subcommittee on rights, and Karl Radek, the subcommittee on electoral questions. Andrei Vyshinsky, the future judge in Bukharin's and Radek's Show Trials, chaired the subcommittee for judicial organs (for a full list of subcommittee chairs, see Wimberg 314).

Initially, Bukharin and Radek were to study foreign constitutions and review them. Afterwards, they drafted different versions of the text, and both were in charge of discussing the process of writing the new constitution in the press.

Bukharin was arrested for espionage, treason, and counter-revolutionary activity soon after the constitution came into effect. He was executed one year later, in the spring of 1938. The Show Trial in which Bukharin was convicted was not directly related to his activity as a member of the constitutional committee, but another committee member, Karl Radek, had been convicted in a similar trial a year before, in 1937. Their trials were two of three in which prominent members of the Soviet elite were accused, among other things, of trying to overthrow Stalin by carrying out economic sabotage, spying for the Axis Powers, and joining forces with Lev Trotsky, a former leftist revolutionary who had been driven into exile. These charges were fabricated, as Soviet authorities admitted decades later (Junge 25–61, 161–202).

Bukharin's and Radek's arrests were not regarded as arbitrary, as evidence – however shoddy – was presented during the trial, and a case was made against them by associating their alleged deeds with the dire state of the economy, and the looming foreign threat of fascism. The unusual and ideologically incoherent accusation that the defendants of the Show Trials were simultaneously fascists,

Trotskyites, capitalists, and so on was part of the tendency in the 1930s to lump together enemy images that had the effect of blurring individual agency (Brandenberger 152–153; Getty, 'Pre-Election' 231).

Both Bukharin and Radek fell from grace before the constitution came into effect, and their names were dropped from the final list of members of the constitutional committee ('Sostav redaktsionnoi komissii' 1). Like Bukharin, Radek had also been involved in the 'Communist International', and was later part of the editorial board of the Soviet newspaper *Izvestia.* However, Radek was not a theoretician, and he was not involved in policymaking, as Bukharin was. Moreover, he was 'only' sentenced to 10 years in prison, which is why his case has drawn less attention.

Although Bukharin's expertise as a theoretician was mainly in the area of economic policy, he made theoretical contributions in several areas. In general, Bukharin argued for more moderate policies, including a more humane agricultural policy, and more freedom of expression in the arts. Bukharin saw the constitution as a way of promoting democracy and establishing what he understood to be 'socialist humanism', a doctrine that foresaw 'freedom of maximum development for the maximum number of people' (Cohen 363–364).[1] Bukharin saw socialist humanism as an ideology that put people's needs at the centre, and thus stood in opposition to Stalin's use of violence to impose policies such as mass collectivization of agriculture, and rash industrialization (Cohen 362–363). His second priority, in both his articles and his contribution to the constitution, was to counter European fascism by making the Soviet Union a more humane country (Cohen 359–364, 313–332).

Bukharin's contribution to a less radical interpretation of communism, his ideological influence on the constitution, and his dramatic fall are all linked together. The intersection of these aspects becomes more obvious when one compares the narratives that describe Bukharin's fate in the context of the Soviet 1930s.

Understanding the Show Trials

In texts about the history of the 1930s in Russia, the promised civil rights and the democratic nature of the constitution and the repression of the Show Trials are discussed in different ways. The interest in this subject has transcended national borders, and it has resisted the passage of time. In the next sections, I scrutinize early assessments of the contrast between utopian and dystopic developments in this era, and compare them with later appraisals.

In total, there were three Show Trials in Moscow during the mid-1930s. The first began in August 1936, that is, after the first draft of the constitution had been distributed, and the last took place in March 1938, after the constitution

1 Other thinkers have since used the term 'socialist humanism'. In this chapter, I refer only to Bukharin's understanding of this ideology.

had come into effect. These trials were directed at the Soviet political elite, but hundreds of thousands of similarly baseless trials were held, charging common citizens and the military elite with counter-revolutionary activities, espionage, and/or sabotage (cf. Harris, 'General Introduction' 1–8; Thurston).

A very insightful, early analysis of the contradiction between the trials and the constitution is offered by Russian émigré and law scholar Nikolai Alexeiev, who writes, in 1940, about the hope connected to the developments in the mid-1930s:

> These hopes, however, were very soon to be cruelly deceived. It is a striking fact that the period when the new Constitution was being brought into practical use coincided precisely with a wave of ruthless persecutions and executions.
>
> (Alexeiev 473–474)

Alexeiev then makes the interesting observation that: 'It seemed as if the dictator, before the new and more liberal institutions would be put into force, wished to slay all those who were likely to take an active part amidst the future parliamentary opposition' (474). The promises of human rights and the persecution were not necessarily conflicting policies, but rather parallel developments with one goal: the establishment of a stable Soviet state. State terror was carried out with the utopian promises of democratization and greater freedoms in mind, which is one reason so many citizens were willing to take part. While expanding citizen rights, the Soviet state was 'getting rid' of the voters who might support the wrong policy or party (Getty, 'Pre-Election' 229–230). According to Petrone's study, because all citizens were now granted electoral rights, Stalin may have considered it more urgent to be aware of enemies from within (180). The inefficiency of the Soviet intelligence system, which had only a vague notion of who the enemy was, and the paranoid fear of internal and external threats of the state apparatus were the systemic foundations of the mass persecution of the 1930s (Harris, 'Intelligence' 30–31).

This theory seems even more plausible when we look back at the way *Pravda* argues that the Constitution of 1936 could rightfully be called the 'Stalin Constitution' because Stalin, along with Lenin, had continuously protected the country against its enemies ('Konstitutsiia' 1). The idea that his pugnacity underlined his ability to give citizens new rights is awkwardly akin to the more modern term 'human rights militant'. However repulsive the idea of Stalin fighting for the people may be, it is undeniable that he did approve of the constitution, making his role more difficult to understand.

Bukharin as a symbol

Despite the importance of the constitution for the history of the 1930s, many texts about this era decouple the legal developments of the time from the repression. In some cases, this leads to an overemphasis on the responsibility of the victims of the Show Trials, in particular that of Bukharin, who becomes a symbolic figure, instead of an individual. Fiction, non-fiction, and life writing are genres in which these events are discussed. Some texts have been particularly paradigmatic and/or influential in their interpretations, regardless of their historical accuracy or lack thereof, and their discussions of the roles of victimhood and agency need a closer look.

French philosopher Maurice Merleau-Ponty published his thoughts on Bukharin's Show Trial and its reception in his famous book, *Humanism and Terror*, in 1947. Merleau-Ponty's main argument is that due to the circumstances of the time, the outcome of Bukharin's trial was justified. Merleau-Ponty argues that the Moscow Show Trials of the 1930s cannot be understood as normal trials, but rather as 'revolutionary trials' that operate under circumstances of great duress, and thus function by different rules. He argues that the Soviet leadership was under siege by internal and external threats – the weak loyalty of the population, the lack of recognition abroad, and the external menace of Nazi Germany – and therefore it was compelled to assess all forms of opposition or criticism as treason. Merleau-Ponty explains as follows: '[I]n a period of revolutionary tension or external threat there is no clear-cut boundary between political divergences and objective treason. Humanism is suspended and government is terror' (Merleau-Ponty 34).

Because any opposition to the Soviet Union could potentially further weaken the state and endanger its very existence, he considers the Show Trials defensible. Revolutionary justice sees the future, not the past, as its precedent: both the judge and the defendant – whom Merleau-Ponty clearly considers to be an agent responsible for the outcome of the trial – act according to their vision of the future (Merleau-Ponty xxxiii). In Bukharin's case, the French philosopher believes the revolutionary made the wrong decision by having the wrong vision of the future. Regardless of his guilt or innocence of the particular charges brought against him, he was guilty of 'historical treason' by not foreseeing the potential danger of his criticism of the state (Merleau-Ponty 52). Merleau-Ponty sees Bukharin not as an individual, but as a symbol. He argues that the survival of the Soviet government, not only through the 1930s, but also through the brutal war of annihilation waged by the Germans in 1941–1945, is proof that it made the correct choice. Although the philosopher is conscious of the historical context of the Show Trials, and in fact bases most of his argument on the need to put these trials into the greater context of threat and violence in Europe, he neglects to include the Soviet Constitution of 1936 in his analysis. This allows him to consider these trials as part of the revolutionary justice that was supposed to have ended with the approval of the new constitution.

Merleau-Ponty's judgement of Bukharin is severe, but it is made with consistent Marxist arguments. Yet the idea that Bukharin was not an innocent victim, but an agent who 'got what he deserved', is popular among anti-communists, despite their opposing arguments.

A less prominent, but paradigmatic, example is the view of Walter Citrine, the General Secretary of the Trades Union Congress. He writes about the Show Trials in 1938: 'May it not be that the Communist slogan that the "end justifies the means", exploited with Jesuitical thoroughness, may now, like chickens, be coming home to roost?' (Citrine 371). Citrine had been visiting the Soviet Union, and his assessment of the developments there was that critical members of the Soviet elite were being treated with the methods they had previously used on others.

The idea of the Show Trials as a type of divine justice that underlies Citrine's assessment is developed most famously in the novel *Darkness at Noon*, published in the 1940s by the Hungarian-born British author Arthur Koestler. In this book, Koestler fictionalizes Bukharin's last days. The novel reveals the thoughts of Rubashov (Bukharin's alter ego), as he awaits trial in his prison cell, and takes part in his interrogations. Most of the novel portrays Rubashov's memories of people he betrayed in the name of Party loyalty, and his acceptance of his fate as a form of 'payback' for his treachery. Rubashov repeats to himself that the Party is always right and execution is the only logical outcome for those who diverge from the Party line, a premise he passively accepts. The contrast between his agency as a traitor towards other Party members and the inaction towards his own persecution makes his moral bankruptcy seem even greater:

> He felt warm, secure and very tired; he had no objection to dozing straight off into death, there and then, if only one let him remain lying under the warm blanket. 'So they are going to shoot you,' he told himself. He slowly moved his toes in the sock and a verse occurred to him which compared the feet of Christ to a white roebuck in a thorn bush.
>
> (Koestler 13)

Koestler's Rubashov is a ruthless, yet helpless man, who is highly sentimental and vulnerable: he is a man sentenced to death by his own ideology.

Merleau-Ponty strongly disapproves of Koestler's depiction of Bukharin as a weak man who 'simply awaits for [. . .] judgement in fear and trembling' (Merleau-Ponty 19), even if he agrees that Bukharin was responsible for his tragic demise. Merleau-Ponty vehemently rejects the notion suggested in Koestler's work that the revolutionaries somehow lost control of their project, like the sorcerer's apprentice, who causes chaos despite his good intentions (Merleau-Ponty xxxix). The French philosopher considers that such an interpretation robs the revolutionaries of their agency and their intent.

Historian Stephen Cohen describes how the fictionalized Bukharin in Koestler's novel influenced Western observers' image of Bukharin, as someone who had readily confessed to false accusations (Cohen 372). A misreading of Bukharin's *Last Plea* (1938) may also be at the root of this notion (Hellbeck 57). The wording of Bukharin's speech in court is convoluted, but it is not too difficult to understand that it was his way of denying guilt while avoiding a direct confrontation with the court (Medvedev 70; Hellbeck 58):

> But I consider myself responsible for a grave and monstrous crime against the Socialist fatherland and the whole international proletariat. I further consider myself responsible, both politically and legally, for wrecking activities, although I personally do not remember having given directions about wrecking activities. I did not talk about this. I once spoke positively on this subject to Grinko. Even in my testimony I mentioned that I had once told Radek that I considered this method of struggle as not very expedient. Yet Citizen the State Prosecutor makes me out to be a leader of the wrecking activities.
>
> ('Last Plea' 123)

Apart from the question of a possible confession, many observers express dissatisfaction, disappointment, or anger at Bukharin's overall behaviour in court. The lack of empathy towards Bukharin expressed in some texts is based on judgements of his character, and not only of his political deeds. The notion of Bukharin as a coward who got what he deserved, owing to his action or inaction in court, is semantically linked to the idea that justice was served when he was convicted in his Show Trial, as I have shown in the case of Koestler's rendering of Bukharin's trial in his novel. It is worth noting that the new, more progressive legislation, and Bukharin's contribution to it, play little role in this appraisal.

In the 1970s, Soviet dissident Alexander Solzhenitsyn lambasted Bukharin in *The Gulag Archipelago*. This explosive, multi-volume work generally condemns the Soviet prison camp system, but Solzhenitsyn includes a section in which he sizes up the Show Trials. Here, Solzhenitsyn unloads his contempt for the defendants of these trials by presenting them as fearful cowards:

> Dumbfounded, the world watched three plays in a row, three wide-ranging and expensive dramatic productions in which the powerful leaders of the fearless Communist Party, who had turned the entire world upside down and terrified it, now marched forth like doleful, obedient goats and bleated out everything they had been ordered to, vomited all over themselves, cringingly abased themselves and their convictions, and confessed to crimes they could not in any wise have committed.
>
> This was unprecedented in remembered history.
>
> (Solzhenitsyn 408)

Solzhenitsyn then zeroes in on Bukharin, ridiculing his behaviour in prison and in court, belittling his suffering during this and previous imprisonments (409–412). He claims that Stalin chose Bukharin and the other defendants for their weakness: 'They put on trial the most compliant. A selection was made after all. He [Stalin] also knew that on the whole they were weaklings, and he knew, one by one, the particular weakness of each' (412). His portrayal of Bukharin as invertebrate breaks with the stated purpose of his book as an indictment of the Soviet regime (Kriza 92–96), and it creates a dichotomy between the 'good victims' of Stalinist terror and those who deserved their punishment.

Bulgarian émigré philosopher Assen Ignatow describes Bukharin's death sentence as the macabre irony of destiny (5). Basing his judgement on Solzhenitsyn's and Koestler's depictions of Bukharin in prison, he describes with derision how, allegedly, Bukharin willingly gave up his dignity (Ignatow 17). Ignatow's interpretation of the Purges in general is that they were 'ethical racism', by which a generation had to be 'sacrificed' for the sake of the next (Ignatow 19). Just as Merleau-Ponty chooses to see only Bukharin's criticism of the state, Solzhenitsyn and Ignatow choose to see Bukharin purely as a revolutionary who had abstractly contributed to the creation of the state that destroyed him.

The image of Bukharin as a willing victim pops up even in cases in which the political context is not as polarized. In his Stalin biography, historian Walter Laqueur scathingly criticizes Bukharin's behaviour during his persecution as that of a weakling (Laqueur 19–44). Although Laqueur mentions that Bukharin was probably complying with court orders as a result of a threat to his wife and baby, this does not soften his disappointment in what he considers unmanly behaviour.

The narrative that presents Bukharin as being cowardly and getting what he deserved, with or without *Schadenfreude*, is interesting, because of the way it transcends political boundaries. Authors who identify with communism, oppose communism, or take neither stance argue in this black-and-white manner. Yet, a close reading of this narrative reveals its epistemological barrenness. On the one hand, it ignores the complexity of a situation in which a liberal constitution was accompanied by widespread repression, and how both these phenomena are linked. Moreover, it suggests the existence of some form of vengeful justice against revolutionaries who had at some point condoned certain levels of violence during the creation of a new state. But if the Show Trials do represent justice, be it the result of the 'irony of destiny' (Citrine; Ignatow; Solzhenitsyn) or of 'revolutionary justice' (Merleau-Ponty), why was this limited to these particular people, and not applied to Stalin, who was much more violent, and who, more than anyone, one could argue, stood in the path of the creation of a peaceful Soviet state? The contradictory notion that Bukharin and others' alleged weakness of character was at the root of their selection to be executed shows the ramifications of the view of a victim as defenceless yet responsible for his or her fate.

Judging the victim

Judgemental views about Bukharin's behaviour being the result of a particular interpretation of manliness, or as stemming from 'moral bankruptcy', gain a new angle when seen through the prism of law scholar Robert Cover's thoughts on what a trial does to the accused. In his influential essay *Violence and the Word*, published in the 1980s, Cover discusses how 'legal interpretive acts signal and occasion the imposition of violence upon others' (Cover 1601). Although he does not write about the Moscow Show Trials, and in fact refers mostly to US legal procedure, his analysis of the position of the defendant and the power of the judge lends insight to understanding the Soviet case. Cover notes the impossibility of the defendant not complying with the court, if he or she is unwilling to either 'be dragged or beaten into prison', or to use violence against the judge (Cover 1607–1608). The relationship between the defendant and the judge is that of one 'being violently dominated' by the other, no matter what ideology the defendant may adhere to; the court does not 'talk' the defendant into prison (Cover 1608). The accused is not necessarily passive or devoid of will, but his or her options for action in court are limited. Cover explains that the reason the defendant is often compared to a martyr is because such a defendant is committed to resisting this domination, albeit unsuccessfully. Narratives of Bukharin's compliance or sacrifice remind us of the position of weakness of the defendant in any trial, even if they often do not go so far as to recognize the universality of this phenomenon.

Cover's considerations help put Bukharin's court behaviour into perspective, but they are not enough to help fathom how such a trial could take place after Bukharin and others had worked to create a better legal system in the Soviet Union.

One way around the question of how the Show Trials could have taken place with utter disregard of Soviet law is to describe them as theatrical productions, in which certain historical figures – including Bukharin – perform different roles in a play. This is a very popular rhetorical strategy used to explain these trials in general, and Bukharin's in particular (Hellbeck 58). In this metaphor, Stalin is either the playwright or the director. Other historical figures, such as the judge, Bukharin, and his co-defendants, take part in a macabre play that ends with the spectacular execution of the accused. However, texts using the language of the 'theatrical production' narrative do not always agree about Bukharin's moral role in his trial, or about the agents who functioned as the 'directors'. In the 1970s, Soviet dissident Roy Medvedev wrote, in a well-known essay, about the trial in terms of a stage drama, yet he admits that Bukharin's behaviour in court confused the prosecutor and the judge (Medvedev 69–70). Solzhenitsyn uses the same metaphor, but in his view Bukharin fulfilled his role to the letter (Solzhenitsyn 409–412). Western historians such as Joel Carmichael, in *Stalin's Masterpiece*, and Karl Schlögel, in his recent book *Terror and Dream*, describe the trials as plays carefully planned by Stalin.

It is inevitable for trials – especially foundational trials such as these, taking place while the new constitution was coming into existence – to have a dramatic effect, but one should remember that the purpose of these was to establish a new social order, which they did. This would never have worked without mass mobilization in favour of the Soviet government's policies, but it illustrates how the tendency to focus on the defendant as victim often distracts the attention from the legal aspects of what was occurring at the time. A symbolic framing of an all-powerful tyrant who makes everyone act according to his will obscures all others' agency. Historian Robert Thurston warns that this approach may rob Stalin's victims of some of their humanity, of their capacity to act (Thurston 227). However, the examples I mentioned above (Koestler; Solzhenitsyn; Ignatow; Laqueur) show how even the portrayal of passivity is sometimes used to make the victim responsible for the outcome of the trial. For many authors, it seems immensely difficult to recognize a victim's agency, without blaming him or her for actions for which he or she may or may not be responsible. At the same time, excluding other agents' participation in the Great Purges and the Show Trials glosses over the real problem of the misuse of human rights that took place at the time. Bukharin and others were convicted as enemies of a country that was painting society's future in the brightest colours.

Widening our field of observation to include the complex results of the campaign for the constitution of 1936, the utopian promises the constitution presented, and the redefinition of a community and its enemies that it offered, shows us the irritating similarity to current developments in post-revolutionary states. In the twenty-first century, as in the 1930s, drumming up support for a new regime is often accompanied by a new constitution, full of utopian promises. At the same time, this is just as often accompanied by the persecution of real or purported enemies.

Conclusion

Contemporary and later observers often see the Soviet constitution as a deliberate charade, as a 'Potemkin façade' to trick the West about the true nature of the Soviet Union (Petrone 176, 184). Robert Thurston even calls its proclamations 'mostly a vicious farce' (125). Although it would be unfair to suggest that all members of the constitutional commission intended to deceive the West, it is undeniable that this piece of legislation was conceived with the outside world in mind. The Soviet Constitution of 1936 was introduced at a time when Nazi Germany was gaining power and becoming more aggressive. As contemporary sources confirm, and many scholars today suggest, it was important for the Soviet Union of the mid-1930s to be able to clarify the distinction between its dictatorship and the German one (e.g. Patkin 17; Getty, 'State and Society' 19). The constitution was part of a project to reshape the country under the banners of democracy and equality. As mentioned in the introduction, throughout its history the Soviet Union upheld these ideals as much as it failed to make them a reality (Mullerson).

J. Arch Getty sees the shortcomings of applying the democratic principles of the 1936 Constitution to the Soviet election that followed, as illustrating 'the limits of state power in its interaction with a vast, multifaceted society' ('State and Society' 35). As Merleau-Ponty puts it, a sense of threat polarized Soviet society, forcing people to choose between complete loyalty or being declared traitors. Merleau-Ponty argues that in war and revolution, 'which are extreme situations where tolerance amounts to weakness, we find constant overlap between the judicial and the political' (Merleau-Ponty 32).

By attaching the prestige of the new constitution to his name while liquidating and arresting those he considered enemies, Stalin was using a double strategy to consolidate his power. Most likely to reinforce his hold on power and improve his reputation, he gave his name to an astonishingly liberal Bill of Rights, but he was also ruthlessly committed to limiting access to those rights by persecuting those he did not deem worthy of them. His sense of distrust of the Soviet elite and general population was at the root of his violent actions (Rees 49–65). As a result, he had no problem with allowing Nikolai Bukharin to be a part of shaping the constitution, only to rob him of due credit, and later, of his life. At the same time, this dichotomy helps us to fathom why some of Stalin's potential victims, who had had the opportunity to flee, did not: as Walter Laqueur suggests, it is possible they did not deem it probable that things would develop the way they did. The debates leading to the approval of the constitution and its coming into effect in late 1936 certainly misled thousands into believing that real change would take place. This contributed to the making of willing collaborators who believed they were creating something better (Petrone 175–207).

Interpretations of the ambiguous development of human rights in the Soviet Union and the fate of purge victims such as Bukharin are useful for us today. They represent different symbolic framings of victimhood and agency that prompt us to rethink these categories. But they also remind us of how the paranoid pursuit of enemies by a utopian state may get out of hand. As Philip Alston and Ryan Goodman write in their book, *International Human Rights*, one of the greatest challenges in international legislation today is the definition of 'terrorism', and its relationship to the protection of human rights (383–393). The main problem of the Soviet legal system was the excessively abstract definition of 'enemy'. As long as the world continues to struggle to define what 'terrorism' is, and who is a terrorist (Alston and Goodman 387), the danger of the persecution of internal enemies spinning out of control remains possible, and it is here that a look back at the Soviet 1930s may teach us valuable lessons.

Works cited

Alexeiev, N. N. 'The Evolution of Soviet Constitutional Law'. *The Review of Politics* 2.4 (1940): 463–476. Print.

Alston, Philip and Ryan Goodman. *International Human Rights*. Oxford: Oxford University Press, 2013. Print.

Brandenberger, David. 'Ideological Zig-Zag: Official Explanations for the Great Terror, 1936–1938'. Harris 143–157. Print.

Carmichael, Joel. *Stalin's Masterpiece: The Show Trials and Purges of the Thirties, the Consolidation of the Bolshevik Dictatorship*. London: Weidenfeld & Nicolson, 1976. Print.

Citrine, Walter. *I Search for Truth in Russia*. Revised ed. London: Routledge, 1938. Print.
Cohen, Stephen. *Bukharin and the Bolshevik Revolution: A Political Biography 1888–1938*. New York: Knopf, 1973. Print.
Cover, Robert. 'Violence and the Word'. *The Yale Law Journal* 95.8 (1986): 1601–1629. Print.
Frankenberg, Günter. 'Comparing Constitutions: Ideas, Ideals, and Ideology – Toward a Layered Narrative'. *International Journal of Constitutional Law* 4.3 (2006): 439–459. Print.
Getty, J. Arch. 'Pre-Election Fever: The Origins of the 1937 Operations'. Harris 216–235.
——. 'State and Society under Stalin: Constitutions and Elections in the 1930s'. *Slavic Review* 50.1 (1991): 18–35. Print.
Harris, James R., ed. *The Anatomy of Terror: Political Violence under Stalin*. Oxford: Oxford University Press, 2013. Print.
——. 'Intelligence and Threat Perception: Defending the Revolution, 1917–1937'. Harris 29–43. Print.
——. 'General Introduction'. Harris 1–8. Print.
Hellbeck, Jochen. 'With Hegel to Salvation: Bukharin's Other Trial'. *Representations* 107.1 (2009): 56–90. Print.
Ignatow, Assen. 'Das Individuum als Opferlamm auf dem Altar der Geschichte'. *Studies in Soviet Thought* 32.1 (1986): 1–22. Print.
Junge, Marc. *Bucharins Rehabilitierung: Historisches Gedächtnis in der Sowjetunion 1953–1991*. Berlin: BasisDruck, 1999. Print.
'K novym pobedam kommunizma'. *Pravda* 5 December 1936: 1. Print.
Koestler, Arthur. *Darkness at Noon*. Trans. Daphne Hardy. New York: Macmillan, 1946. Print.
'Konstitutsiia sotsializma utverzhdena!'. *Pravda* 6 December 1936: 1. Print.
Kriza, Elisa. *Alexander Solzhenitsyn: Cold War Icon, Gulag Author, Russian Nationalist? A Study of His Western Reception*. Stuttgart: Ibidem Press, 2014. Soviet and Post-Soviet Politics and Society. Print.
Laqueur, Walter. *Stalin: The Glasnost Revelations*. New York: Scribner's, 1990. Print.
'Last Plea of Bukharin'. *The Slavonic and East European Review* 17.49 (1938): 121–134. Print.
Medvedev, Roy. 'Bukharin's Last Years'. *New Left Review* May–June 1978: 49–73. Print.
Merleau-Ponty, Maurice. *Humanism and Terror*. Trans. John O'Neill. Boston: Beacon, 2001 (1947). Print.
Moyn, Samuel. *The Last Utopia: Human Rights in History*. Cambridge: Belknap Press of Harvard University Press, 2010. Print.
Mullerson, Rein A. 'Human Rights and the Individual as Subject of International Law: A Soviet View'. *European Journal of International Law* 1.1 (1990): 33–43. Print.
Patkin, A. 'The New Stalinist Constitution and Democracy'. *The Australian Quarterly* 9.1 (1937): 15–29. Print.
Petrone, Karen. *Life Has Become More Joyous, Comrades: Celebrations in the Time of Stalin*. Bloomington: Indiana University Press, 2000. Print.
Rees, E. A. 'Stalin: Architect of the Terror'. Harris 49–65. Print.
Schlögel, Karl. *Terror und Traum: Moskau 1937*. Munich: Hanser, 2008. Print.
Solzhenitsyn, Alexander. *The Gulag Archipelago, 1918–1956: An Experiment in Literary Investigation. Vol. 1*. Trans. Thomas P. Whitney. New York: Harper & Row, 1973. Print.
'Sostav redaktsionnoi komissii dlia ustanovleniia okonchatel'nogo teksta Konstitutsii Soiuza SSR'. *Pravda* 2 December 1936: 1. Print.
Starr, Joseph R. 'The New Constitution of the Soviet Union'. *The American Political Science Review* 30.6 (1936): 1143–1152. Print.

Stearns, Peter N. *Human Rights in World History*. London: Routledge, 2012. Print.
Thurston, Robert W. *Life and Terror in Stalin's Russia, 1934–1941*. New Haven: Yale University Press, 1996. Print.
Towe, Thomas E. 'Fundamental Rights in the Soviet Union: A Comparative Approach'. *University of Pennsylvania Law Review* 115.8 (1967): 1251–1274. Print.
Wimberg, Ellen. 'Socialism, Democratism and Criticism: The Soviet Press and the National Discussion of the 1936 Draft Constitution'. *Soviet Studies* 44.2 (1992): 313–332. Print.

Chapter 6

From passive victimhood to committed citizenship

Storytelling by victims of the 'years of lead' in Italy – in search of justice and truth in spite of the state

Marie Andreasen and Leonardo Cecchini

During the Cold War, Italy witnessed an impressive series of acts of violence and subversion, which reached its peak in the 1970s – the so-called *anni di piombo* ('years of lead')[1] that saw approximately 500 deaths, over 1,100 injuries, and about 15,000 violent acts. Bombing attacks on innocent civilians were carried out by extreme right-wing groups in connivance with sectors of the state, starting in December 1969 in Milan, and culminating with the Bologna station massacre of 1980 (85 dead and more than 200 injured).[2] Attempted or threatened 'coups d'état' were carried out by members of the armed forces in the 1970s, supposedly aimed at establishing an authoritarian regime, as in Greece (then a military dictatorship). From the late 1960s to the 1980s, ideologically inspired groups from both the extreme right and the extreme left carried out an 'armed struggle' against the state. This resulted in the wounding, kidnapping, and execution of various representatives of the state (politicians, judges, police officers, journalists, etc.). Perhaps the most well-known episode was the kidnapping and assassination of political leader Aldo Moro by the Red Brigades, in 1978. Although the last significant episodes of organized political violence took place over 20 years ago, terrorism has left an enduring legacy in the country.

Compared to similar phenomena in other Western countries, political violence in Italy in the 1970s presents special features that bring the Italian case nearer to Argentina's 'dirty war' than to occurrences of political violence in other industrialized European countries, such as France and Germany.

1 The term *anni di piombo* to designate the period *c.*1969–1985, taken from the title of Margarethe Von Trotta's film *Die bleierne Zeit* (1981), is inaccurate, because it refers only to the 'lead' (as a metonym) of the bullets of the left wing's armed groups' killings, while it does not include the bombs of the extreme right's massacres. Despite these ideological implications, the term has entered into the Italian imagery, and it is therefore used here. The same may be said of an equally ideological term such as 'terrorism', itself difficult to define scientifically, but which has also come into use. Sometimes, we also use a more ideologically neutral category, equally unsatisfactory because it is too general, such as 'political violence'.

2 Today, the Bologna station massacre is still considered 'the worst single domestic terrorist attack in Western Europe after WW2' (Weinberg 71).

In addition to the exceptionally high number of attacks and victims, and its persistence (in Europe, second only to that of countries such as Spain and Northern Ireland, where the violence was mostly ethnic and nationalistic), we may mention the presence in Italy in those years of both a 'cold' terrorism, and a diffused political violence and mass illegality, with the presence of a great number of terrorist groups (657 acronyms used between 1969 and 1982). But above all, the Italian situation was characterized by the simultaneous presence of two ideologically opposed kinds of terrorism: on the one hand, left-wing terrorism, one of the most internationally relevant ones, and, on the other hand, neo-fascist terrorism, by far the most significant of its kind, able to develop 'the most elaborate strategy of systematic destabilization of the government' (Laqueur 166–167). A further characteristic of the Italian situation in these years was the ambiguity of the state with respect to the neo-fascist terrorism, which was covered, and perhaps even 'guided', by state agencies such as the secret services and anti-democratic organizations, such as the Masonic lodge P2.[3] Finally, a special feature of the Italian situation is the way in which the country overcame political violence, and then approached the difficult problem of re-elaboration and social reconciliation, which is called 'transitional justice', in the field of human rights studies.

As defined by the United Nations, transitional justice is: 'the full range of processes and mechanisms associated with a society's attempt to come to terms with a legacy of large-scale past abuses, in order to ensure accountability, serve justice and achieve reconciliation' (United Nations 8). Emerging as an independent, interdisciplinary field of scholarship as response to the transition from authoritarianism to democracy that occurred in Latin America in the late 1980s and in Eastern Europe in the early 1990s, in the past two decades transitional justice approaches have been increasingly used in contexts where a change in regime has not occurred, to either address civil wars or internal armed conflicts within a country, or to deal with historical injustices that continue to plague established democracies (Bell 15).

Transitional justice actors have sought to define the challenges of addressing past human rights violations in transitional contexts, providing a testing ground for how human rights may be pursued. The central scope of transitional justice includes the promotion of judicial accountability for violations of civil and political rights, such as the right to life, liberty, and the security of the person, and the prohibition of torture. Other important aspects of the scope of transitional justice are ensuring the right to truth about past abuses, and reparation for victims thereby restoring their dignity, but also fostering reconciliation and pacification between the parties in conflict, (re)establishing the rule of law,

3 It is also possible that left-wing terrorism was used by national and international agents to affect the political situation in Italy, and prevent an alliance between the Christian Democratic Party and the Communist Party.

and eventually introducing institutional reforms, and diffusing a more impartial memorialization of past events (van der Merwe and Brankovic 9).

Within transitional justice studies, a debate has arisen about which priority to follow: Should priority be given to the pursuit of perpetrators' accountability, or to allow some degree of impunity, in order to achieve social and political reconciliation? Should one promote 'retributive justice', which prioritizes the punishment of the perpetrators and stresses the fight against impunity, or 'restorative justice', which aims to address the needs of all the parties involved (victims, perpetrators, and broader communities), and tries to promote reconciliation through dialogue (van der Merwe and Brankovic 7–8)?

The way in which Italy defeated terrorism, and then approached the difficult problem of re-elaboration and social reconciliation, illustrates some of the problems inherent to both strategies, if they are pursued inconsistently and with hidden agendas. Today, at a distance of 40 years from the events in question, the result may be said to be opaque; we cannot claim that retributive and restorative justice have not been achieved, but this has only happened incompletely and reluctantly, and, above all, this was due mostly to the active involvement of the victims and their relatives, who underwent a transformation from passive recipients of commiseration, into agents for truth, justice, and political renewal.

With the aim of ending violence, the Italian state introduced controversial legislation fostering disengagement and de-radicalization by offering material inducements to the terrorists, which proved effective in accelerating an end to terrorism, in ways that have often been considered pioneering by the scholarly literature on this argument, thus apparently choosing the path of restorative justice (a concept that had yet to come into being at that time). However, this strategy did not take into account the victims and the relatives of the victims, and their suffering. Furthermore, the state facilitated the end of the 'years of lead' with the knowledge that this would also prevent its own ambiguous behaviour towards terrorism from being exposed and revealed. Many victims accuse the state of disregarding the victims' right to justice, and expose the state's failure in uncovering the truth about perpetrators and masterminds of violent acts, thereby transforming themselves from passive victims into agents for truth and justice, and their experience into a quest for new democratic institutions committed to transparency and accountability. In the following pages, we will investigate the way in which victims, relatives of victims, and victims associations use the human rights discourse to transform victimhood into active and committed citizenship, and into a quest to change society. But first, let us consider how Italy overcame the terrorist threat.

Ending terrorism

In order to defeat terrorism, the Italian state first adopted a strategy based on repression, creating special anti-terrorism units within the police, and introducing anti-terrorism legislation. As we know today, after the experiences of the 'global war on terror' of the past 15 years, anti-terrorism legislation represents one of the most challenging aspects of a democratic society, because, to a greater or lesser degree, it suspends constitutional and human rights by introducing emergency measures or special laws, in order to defeat the threat posed by terrorism to society. Terrorism in Italy in the 1970s was a completely new phenomenon, and legislators were not prepared to face this new challenge. The dilemma of choosing the most effective measures to end the terrorist threat and not suspending constitutional rights was particularly controversial, because the republican Constitution introduced after World War II following the experience of totalitarian fascism contained a number of articles that appeared to preclude the creation of special legislation.

Despite that, a *legislazione d'emergenza* was actually created, in part – paradoxically – by recovering and tightening some articles of the Criminal Code introduced by Minister of Justice Alfredo Rocco during the fascist regime,[4] in part through a series of laws that withdrew or drastically restricted constitutional rights.[5] Finally, high-security prisons and a hard prison regime were created for prisoners accused of terrorism.

The introduction of emergency legislation that altered and suspended rights encompassed by the Constitution triggered doubts and protests in Italian society. Furthermore, the ways in which the fight against terrorism was carried out, with actions that, at times, seemed more inspired by the principle of 'take no prisoners' than by the will to secure the terrorists to justice, troubled the conscience of many Italians. In addition, the first charges started to appear in the press, regarding the use of torture on the part of the law enforcement agencies: initially episodic, but later systematic and somehow authorized.[6] In opposition to those who demanded the introduction of the state of exception and the suspension of the Constitution, others pointed out that counter-terrorism carried out in this way threatened the very democratic values in the name of which the anti-terrorism strategy was fought.

At the beginning of the 1980s, a broad debate developed between the political forces and the public opinion,[7] regarding what would come to be termed

4 Article 270, which introduced the crime of 'subversive association' (whoever promoted, constituted, organized, or directed associations aimed at violently subverting the state); article 306, which punished those who formed an 'armed band' against the state; article 284, which defined the crime of 'armed insurrection' against the state.

5 Law 152, 1975 (*Legge Reale*), which extended the length of time an individual could be detained without being charged; Law 191, 1978, which introduced a new article in the penal code (298bis) covering the crime of kidnapping for terrorism or subversive purposes; Law 15, 1980 (*Legge Cossiga*), which introduced additional punishments for 'common' crimes related to terrorism, extended preventive detention, and facilitated house searches.

6 On the use of torture, see Galfré (69–74); Progetto Memoria.

7 For an analysis of this debate, see Bull and Cooke; Galfré.

'*legislazione premiale*' (reward legislation), that is, the possibility of supporting the repressive approach with a strategy aimed at increasing disengagement from the armed struggle, and de-radicalization. From a judicial point of view, three laws were decisive. Law 304, 1982, also called *legge sui pentiti*, 'law on the repentant offenders' (an interesting religious terminology for the equivalent of a crown witness), exempted from, or reduced, punishment for those who facilitated the disbandment of a terrorist organization, and actively collaborated with the legal system. Law 34, 1987 (also called *legge sui dissociati*, 'law on the dissociated offenders'), attributed these measures also to those who recognized their individual penal responsibility and, although they did not denounce their companions, declared that they abandoned the struggle against the state, and dissociated themselves from terrorism. Finally, Law 663, 1986 (the so-called *Legge Gozzini*), introduced a series of reforms to the hard prison regime, creating the possibility of house arrest and semi-liberty after serving part of a sentence, thereby meeting the wishes of many political prisoners, who wanted to rebuild their lives outside of prison, but had to serve long sentences following the extension of the punishment owing to the emergency legislation.

Through the foregoing legislation, the focus was moved from repression to a strategy aimed at facilitating the abandonment of the armed struggle by many young people, and their reintroduction to society (the rehabilitation of the offender is inscribed in the Italian Constitution). Catholic clergy and Catholic politicians and intellectuals played an important role in this process, especially priests and nuns who performed their roles in the prisons, and who were familiar with the explosive situation inside high-security prisons (Galfré 196–208). The *legislazione premiale* and the introduction of a less severe prison regime for political prisoners, together with the possibility of studying, working, marrying, and starting a family while detained, put an end to violence over the course of a few years, and brought about a sort of pacification between the state and the ex-terrorists, as well as the reintegration into society of a large number of young people (Galfré 174–182). The *legislazione premiale* undoubtedly played a crucial role in the defeat of terrorism, without completely suspending human rights and the rule of the law, and the Italian way of ending terrorism is usually considered an example of good practice by international scholars in the field.[8] However, there were some prices to be paid.

The shift from the simple repression of terrorism to an approach that focused on the reintegration of the ex-perpetrators into society, and therefore privileged a kind of restorative justice, was carried out only through the *legislazione premiale*. No equivalent steps to meet the needs of the victims and their relatives were taken; they were also neither involved in, nor consulted on this legislation. No legislation providing material and symbolic reparation for the victims and their

8 See Bull and Cooke (48–50) for a review of positions among scholars of terrorism.

families was taken into consideration by government agencies. Only much later, and under pressure from the victims' associations – as we will see – did the state carry out a policy of economic and symbolic compensation towards the victims and their relatives. No wholehearted attempts were made to introduce other quasi-judicial measures to achieve truth and justice, such as truth commissions.[9]

The legislation, which attributed great discretionary powers to the judge, who could use the Criminal Code as an instrument of barter and reward, was criticized for putting political considerations before justice. The release of those responsible for many murders because they were *pentiti* (whereas mere sympathizers with little of importance to reveal were given long sentences) was felt as an injustice by the relatives of those who were murdered. Finally, by reducing the length of the sentences served by those who dissociated themselves from the violence without contributing to the clarification of past terrorist events, the search for the truth, and in the end justice, was obstructed. This happened principally, but not exclusively, in the case of the neo-fascist bombing massacres. This fact was worsened by the ambiguity of the state and the politicians (at that time, and still today) concerning their responsibilities in the covering up of the attacks and massacres carried out by the neo-fascists. Paradoxically, legislation introduced with the purpose of 'ending the emergency', or at least diminishing the negative consequences of the emergency legislation in the field of human rights, and with the political aim of reaching a sort of pacification between the parties (but also, less nobly, of concealing the responsibilities of the politicians), in turn revealed itself as a source of the denial of rights – to truth and justice – to those who had paid the highest price: the victims and their relatives.

The outcomes of the *legislazione premiale* highlight the dilemma between retributive and restorative justice, especially in the case where the latter is carried out by the state or other institutional actors, who are themselves, at least in part, involved and/or responsible for some of the human rights violations of the past, and emphasize some of the inherent risks of transitional justice. We can say that the Italian case shows the danger of reaching neither complete accountability nor complete political reconciliation. Only if transitional justice critically addresses the relationship between the state and its citizens, and facilitates bottom-up transitional processes that build up active citizenship, or introduce new forms of citizen participation, may this risk be overcome.

9 A Parliamentary Commission on Terrorism in Italy was set up by law in 1988. However, in 2001, the commission folded with the rejection of its final report by its political representatives, who instead generated a total of 18 different reports, a testament to the many internal disputes and differences within the commission. A subsequent commission, which was set up in 2002, with the scope of investigating the alleged ties between the KGB and representatives of the leftist parties during the Cold War, also folded in 2006, with an inconclusive result due to political disagreements (Bull and Cooke 113–114).

Forgotten victims

During the 1980s and 1990s, the widespread wish of the political institutions, the media, and the population in general to close with terrorism and to forget resulted in a more or less deliberate policy of amnesia towards the victims of political violence and their relatives. This contributed to their isolation in society, and consequently they were more or less reduced to silence.

A testimonial to this situation may be found in the book by the architect Sergio Lenci, *Colpo alla nuca. Memorie di una vittima del terrorismo* (*Shot in the Neck: Memories of a Victim of Terrorism*, 1988, 2009), one of the very few accounts by victims that was published in those years, in contrast to a huge amount of autobiographical writing published by ex-terrorists. Troubled by the lack of interest by the institutions to search for truth and justice, paired with a tendency to reabsorb the ex-terrorists in society 'through amnesties, pardons, dissociation, de-penalization' (62), Lenci, who, in 1980, miraculously survived an attack by a terrorist squad of left-wing group Prima Linea and lived with a bullet in his head for the following 21 years until his death in 2001, decided to write his memoir. However, this initiative faced great difficulties since many editors refused to publish it. Lenci remembers that it was as if they told him: 'Why do you write these things? Why do you bother?' (91). He felt silenced by society:

> This dialogue with my contemporaries that I felt the need to have, in reality, I could not have with anybody. I had no interlocutor who was interested in the reasons of the victim. On the contrary, I observed how official culture and mass media continued to use terrorism for various purposes, and to misinform.
>
> (39)[10]

The lack of interest in the point of view of the victims emerges in the television programme *La Notte della Repubblica* (*The Night of the Republic*). Designed and conducted by journalist Sergio Zavoli, it was transmitted on the Italian national TV station Rai Due from December 1989 until April 1990, and later published as a book. The programme consisted of interviews with a wide array of people involved in the 'years of lead', such as judges, politicians, journalists, and the perpetrators of the violent acts. The programme was the first and, so far, the only one of its kind, and thus occupies an important position as one of the only public attempts to bring clarity to this painful period in Italy's history, and to start a process of reconciliation at a national level, both of which seem to be

10 Questo dialogo con i miei contemporanei, che io sentivo il bisogno di fare, in realtà non potevo farlo con nessuno. Non avevo nessun interlocutore che si interessasse alle ragioni della vittima. Al contrario, constatavo come la cultura ufficiale e l'informazione di massa continuavano a usare il terrorismo per scopi vari e a disinformare (all translations from Italian are ours).

within the scope of the broadcast. All the more remarkable, considering the scope of the programme, is the disproportionate level of representation between the perpetrators and victims of violence.[11]

Because of the silence on the part of the state, the society, and the media, the victims and their relatives feel victimized twice: first, as victims of the terrorist attacks; and second, because of the abandonment of the state and the forgetfulness of society. As Maurizio Puddu, who survived a terrorist attack by the Red Brigades, and founder of the victims association AIVITER (*Associazione Italiana Vittime del Terrorismo*), states: 'The victim is therefore a victim twice, and feels disillusioned, vilified, abandoned. The victim is sacrificed' (Specchia and Canteri 356). This process of re-victimization – very well described by scholars (Bloomberg, Barnes, and Huyse; Hackett and Rolston; Bull and Cooke) – is characterized by anger, indignation, exclusion, and social stigmatization, and especially frustration with the political system and its institutions, which are accused of denying the victims access to the public sphere and the media:

> We victims and relatives of victims do not have the same strength as they do [*the perpetrators*]. Because they have precluded us from the possibility of speaking, of expressing our point of view. We have no voice. They open a microphone to us, sometimes, only to have us say what is convenient to them, small sentences that are extrapolated from their context in order to make us seem insensitive to forgiveness.
>
> (Giovanni Berardi in Fasanella and Grippo 111)[12]

Benedetta Tobagi, who was only three years old when her father, Walter, a 33-year-old journalist, was killed by a left-wing group on 28 May 1980, refers to the early release of her father's killer (*pentito*) as a *sfregio* (*Come mi batte* 238), an Italian term that can mean both a scar (a physical wound) and an insult (a disembodied injury), thus expressing in one word the emotional complexity of the re-victimization process (Glynn 382). As a response to this re-victimization, in the 1980s and immediately after, the victims began to establish victims' associations, in order to help sustain and promote the memory of their loved ones and of the years of violence, and to offer support in the fight to obtain

11 While Zavoli interviewed a large number of perpetrators of both left- and right-wing violence in the studio, there is only one studio interview with a victim, to represent the point of view of the victims. In November 2014, in an interview carried out by Marie Andreasen with a survivor of an armed attack, it emerged that this victim was actually interviewed for the programme, but the testimony was never included in the final broadcast.

12 Noi vittime e familiari di vittime non abbiamo la loro stessa forza [dei carnefici]. Perché ci hanno precluso la possibilità di parlare, di esprimere il nostro punto di vista. Noi non abbiamo voce. Ci aprono un microfono, a volte, soltanto per farci dire quello che a loro fa comodo, piccole frasi estrapolate dal loro contesto per farci apparire insensibili al perdono.

truth and justice. Until recently, these associations were not supported by the state, either financially or politically. Owing to the dual nature of the Italian terrorism, victims' associations were, and still are, divided into two subgroups: associations for victims of armed violence, and associations for victims of bombing massacres, that is, a division based on ideological persuasions ('red' versus 'black' terrorism), a fact that contributed to maintaining a partisan memory of the 'years of lead'. On the other hand, the fact that the victims established these associations while the state pursued a policy of forgetting and amnesia regarding the 'years of lead' testifies to how they underwent a process from passive, isolated, silenced, and traumatized victims, to active citizens struggling to find truth, justice, and political visibility. They reject a victim's identity, to assume that of citizens aware of their rights in a democracy, a democracy that denies them the right to know what really happened during those years, and fails to identify and punish the culprits. The fact that these associations exist more than 40 years after the first act of terrorism testifies to both their continuous commitment, and to the ongoing difficulties in the struggle to obtain truth and justice. Only much later did the state begin to produce legislation in favour of the victims of political violence, providing economic compensation for the families of those who were killed, and for those permanently disabled. However, it is important to keep in mind that this legislation has been obtained only through the pressure of the victims and their associations.[13]

The 'turn to the victim'

Since the start of the new millennium, a new consciousness of the marginalization of the victims of the 'years of lead' has emerged in Italian culture and the public sphere. The media are giving more visibility and attention to the victims and their relatives. A wave of autobiographical accounts, mostly by the children of victims of terrorism, saw publication in the last 15 years,[14] and television broadcast documentaries on both high-profile and more anonymous victims and interviews with their relatives.

It is difficult to precisely identify the origin of the 'turn to the victim' in the Italian public sphere. Glynn explains it by a number of both international and domestic factors, such as the victim-centred response in Western culture to the 9/11 attack in the US, and public dismay at the anachronistic return of domestic terrorism, with the New Red Brigades' murders of Massimo D'Antona in 1999, and Marco Biagi in 2002, combined with a more general fatigue with the cultural

13 Finally, in 2007, after extended pressure from the victims, a national commemoration day for the victims of terrorism was established by the Parliament on 9 May, the date on which the body of the politician Aldo Moro was found, after he had been held hostage and killed by the Red Brigades.

14 A thorough assessment of these publications is given by Glynn.

dominance of the perpetrators of the *anni di piombo* (374). These are plausible reasons, but in our opinion the rise of this victim-centred response should be understood in light of the new global political developments after the end of the Cold War, and the emergence of an international human rights movement seeking to promote human rights accountability in post-authoritarian contexts. The breakdown of the Soviet Union, the decline of left-wing politics with its focus on class struggle, and the ascendancy of political and economic liberalism contributed to this new human rights focus. Within this broader framework, a new form of transnational memory emerged around the new millennium, which Levy and Sznaider have called 'cosmopolitan memory'. They tie this mode of remembering to globalization, on the one hand, and, on the other, to the way memories of the Holocaust have developed in the past 50 years, transcending national and ethnic boundaries, and facilitating the formation of a transnational memory culture or mode to remember conflicts, which, in their opinion, has the potential to become the cultural foundation for global human rights politics. Cosmopolitanism involves a shift from ideology to ethics, and it is related to the need for a moral standard in an age of uncertainty, and in the absence of master ideological narratives. Cosmopolitanism, as a mode of remembering, focuses on victimhood, emphasizes the human suffering of past atrocities and human rights violations, represents good and evil as abstract categories stressing regret and mourning, reaffirms humanity's common aspiration for mutual understanding, and promotes dialogue based on the perspective of the victims.

The arrival of this transnational discourse in Italy affected the way the *anni di piombo* were remembered, and contributed to new visibility for the victims' situation. Meanwhile, a few committed magistrates made attempts to reach retributive justice in trials, even a long time after the events.[15]

In Italy, this 'turn to the victim' or *paradigma vittimario* ('victim's paradigm', De Luna) has not been without critics. De Luna, in his study, criticized it both in general terms as 'a comprehensive privatization of memory' (14), but particularly in connection with the legacy of the *anni di piombo*. According to De Luna, the exclusive focus on victimhood and the abstract and universalistic mode of remembering good and evil tend to construct history as something done to people, negating individual agency, and to conceal the role of the perpetrators and the motivations of the violence, which, during the 'years of lead', as we have seen, had its origins in quite opposite world views and ideologies. Inherent to the victim's paradigm is the danger of a too general ecumenism:

15 For example, in July 2015, 41 years after the event, and after three different investigations and four trials at three levels of justice, two life sentences were handed down to two of the neo-fascist instigators of the bombing massacre in Brescia on 28 May 1974 (eight dead and 103 wounded), thus establishing the only judicial truth of all the neo-fascist bombing attacks so far.

during the 'years of lead', there were many innocent victims; we honour the victims of any colour, and forget the executioners and also the ambiguities of the state. Furthermore, in constituting the victims as passive, unable to fight for their rights, agency is transferred to 'professional specialists' and the public sphere (Giesen 67), acting as mediators for the victims.

It seems to us that De Luna and others' criticism may refer more to the social construction of collective identities of belonging, through a supposed common victim's condition, than to the victims of terrorism. If we look at the autobiographical accounts of the victims of the last 15 years, we can find examples of narratives edited by 'professional specialists' (mostly journalists), who act as intermediaries and advocates on the part of the testifying subjects and speak for them, but much more present are first-person narrators who prioritize their identities as 'citizens', rather than as 'victims', and set forth their claims on behalf of, and for the benefit of, a national community of belonging. Although memory and the condition of being a victim seem to unite the one with the other, in reality it is a matter of phenomena that must be kept well distinct.

Agents for truth

A common theme in the publications by victims and relatives of victims from the turn of the millennium is that of re-victimization, both regarding what the victims see as neglect, and even rejection and betrayal on behalf of the state, and the dominant role granted to the perpetrators of violence by the media and society, which the victims feel have often been presented at the expense of their perspective. Also, many victims reject the common expectation of society that they should forgive the perpetrators, since many do not even know the identity of the people responsible for the death of their loved ones, owing to the failure of the courts to identify the culprits of the killings. Likewise, the victims and their relatives do not feel that 'reconciliation', of which there has been much talk, in relation to the 'years of lead', is the right term to use, since they refuse that the violence committed was part of a war, as opposed to the perpetrators, who often seek to justify their violent deeds as acts performed within the frame of a 'Civil War'.[16] Similarly, but to a varying degree, the works all seek to spread the awareness of the situation and suffering of the victims, and to 'call to account those who have evaded responsibility for the tragic consequences of their violence' (Glynn 377).

There is, however, a conflict between the stories of grief and lament told by some victims, and those told by victims who turn their victimhood into a quest for change in society (Bull and Cooke 198). The victims are divided on issues

16 On the narrative templates of left-wing perpetrators, see Andreasen; Bull; Bull and Cooke.

such as the attitude towards the term 'reconciliation', the perpetrators, and how the past should be remembered. We will now present some examples of victims that have chosen the path of dialogue and social action.

Over the years, some of the victims have turned into what may be termed, 'agents for truth and justice' or 'civic heroes', who embark on a 'survivor mission', and thus take on a more active role, as opposed to other victims and relatives, who remain more silent (Bull 88; Bull and Cooke 153–154). When becoming 'agents for truth and justice', the victims consciously choose an active and politicized role as somebody who can cause change and social action (Hackett and Rolston 2009; Herman 1997 in Bull and Cooke 198). To them, truth:

> takes on transformative meaning in the conviction that the recovery of the truth must lead to its wider public acknowledgement and consequently to new types of state and political institutions where the principles of transparency, legitimacy and accountability are openly upheld and cherished.
>
> (Bull and Cooke 204)

Manlio Milani is a survivor of the bombing massacre at the Piazza della Loggia in Brescia, in which his wife, Livia Bottardi Milani, was killed. In the beginning, he blindly trusted the institutions to do their job, but soon discovered that he would have to fight the simplifications, *depistaggi* (the creation of false trails), and the silence of these institutions, in order to reach the truth about the massacre (Fasanella and Grippo 18–21). Ever since, he has been engaged in the fight to obtain truth and justice, following the trials closely, and assuming the role of president of the victims' association of the Brescia bombing. Milani may be said to be an 'agent for truth and justice', since to him, the active involvement in the struggle for truth and justice is not to be seen as a private matter, but takes on a social dimension:

> I became immediately aware that mine was not a private but a public tragedy, because it had happened during a public antifascist demonstration. The private and the political became the fundamental cornerstones of my existence which from that moment on transformed itself into a testimony.
>
> (Fasanella and Grippo 16)[17]

To Milani, the fight for the truth is a fight for the common good, since it is also a means of improving the democratic system:

17 Immediatamente presi coscienza del fatto che la mia non era una tragedia privata, ma pubblica, perché si era consumata durante una pubblica manifestazione antifascista. Il privato e il politico divennero i cardini essenziali della mia vicenda che da quel momento in poi si è trasformata in una testimonianza.

> I ask it not only due to the 'right to know', but because without the unveiling of that story, of its 'unspeakabilities', it will not be possible to overcome that rancour, that sense of historical revenge that weighs on the present of our democratic system. That is why I insist that every political authority should find the courage to look inside and to tell that past without being influenced by the silence of the others. I am certain that whoever does it will find us attentive and sympathetic.
>
> (Fasanella and Grippo 21)[18]

Some other central figures in this fight to change society, and who are therefore committed agents for truth and justice, are the Dendena family. Francesca Dendena, daughter of Pietro Dendena, who was killed at the bombing massacre in the Banca Nazionale dell'Agricoltura in Piazza Fontana in Milan, on 12 December 1969 (17 dead and 88 wounded), was 17 years old at the time of the massacre, and she describes how the tragedy had great implications for her family: 'Since that tragic afternoon, the life of my family has been dedicated to one ideal only, we want justice to be done and the perpetrators on all levels to be punished' (Dendena 48).[19]

Francesca Dendena devoted her life to obtaining truth and justice, and she founded and has directed the victims' association dedicated to this massacre with great determination:

> We want every effort to be made to ensure that justice is done; only in this way will we be able to speak of democracy and perhaps forget the word massacre. [. . .] We will continue to inquire, because we are not ashamed of our past and we should not have to ask that it be forgotten in the future. We want to be able to tell the generations to come in 10, 20, 50 years that we have done everything possible to restore a sense of justice to the whole society, not only to ourselves.
>
> (Dendena 48, 52)[20]

18 Lo chiedo non solo per il 'diritto a sapere', ma perché senza il disvelamento di quella storia, delle sue 'indicibilità', non sarà possibile uscire da quella rancorosità, da quel senso di rivalsa storica che pesa sul presente del nostro sistema democratico. Ecco perché insisto che ogni forza politica trovi il coraggio di guardare dentro di sé e di raccontare quel passato senza farsi condizionare dal silenzio degli altri. Sono certo che, chi lo farà, in noi troverà ascolto e comprensione.

19 Da quel tragico pomeriggio la vita della mia famiglia è votata ad un unico ideale, vogliamo che giustizia sia fatta e che vengano colpite le responsabilità a tutti i livelli.

20 Vogliamo che ci si adoperi affinché giustizia sia fatta; solo così potremo parlare di democrazia e forse dimenticare la parola strage. [. . .] Noi continueremo a chiedere, perché non ci vergogniamo del nostro passato e non dovremmo chiedere in futuro di dimenticarlo. Vogliamo poter dire alle generazioni che verranno fra 10, 20, 50 anni, che noi abbiamo fatto tutto il possibile per restituire alla società intera, non solo a noi stessi, il senso della giustizia.

Since the premature death of Francesca Dendena in 2012, her niece and nephew, Federica and Matteo, together with their father, Paolo, have picked up the family baton, and committed themselves to the ongoing fight for the memory of the 'years of lead', Federica, as vice-president of the victims' association, and Matteo by publishing a book on the memory of his aunt.

The fight for the truth is of great personal significance to the relatives of the victims, because it is difficult for them to move on when the truth about the past is still unknown. This circumstance affects the possibility of social engagement. Manlio Milani explains:

> Investigating, analysing and understanding the historical truth is the means to leaving behind a blocked memory that acts on the public history of the country and captures the victims inside 'their' story, transforming the fact itself from public to private. In substance, prisoners of the past.
>
> (Milani 125)[21]

Milani is very open to dialogue, and presents himself as a *militante della verità* (Fasanella and Grippo 20). As he states: 'To reach the historical truth is required, firstly, the will of everyone to be able to look sincerely at their past' (Rodella 2011).[22] In March 2011, he participated in a meeting with some representatives of *CasaPound*, an Italian political movement regarded as belonging to the radical right, and was highly criticized for this by his own association, which demanded his resignation as the head of the association. In his explanation of his reasons for participating, he demonstrates a willingness to look beyond the immediate evil, and to instead understand the reasons and motivations of political adversaries, in an attempt to improve both the present and the future:

> I accepted because in this distracted memory of Italy that prefers to eliminate the 70s, it is necessary to go beyond our differences and meet, without limiting ourselves to observing horror as such, but in the attempt to find in the elaborated memory some useful lessons regarding the present and the future.
>
> (Rodella 2011)[23]

21 Ricercare, elaborare, comprendere la verità storica è la strada per uscire da una memoria bloccata che agisce sulla storia pubblica del Paese e tiene ferme le vittime dentro la 'loro' storia, trasformando il fatto stesso da pubblico a privato. In sostanza, prigionieri del passato.

22 Per arrivare alla verità storica occorre prima la volontà di saper guardare ognuno al proprio passato con sincerità.

23 Ho accettato perché in questa memoria distratta dell'Italia che preferisce rimuovere gli anni '70, è necessario andare oltre le nostre diversità e incontrarci, senza limitarci ad osservare l'orrore in quanto tale, ma nel tentativo di trovare nella memoria elaborata degli insegnamenti utili rispetto al presente e al domani.

Postmemory

Since the majority of the autobiographical publications of the last 15 years have been written by the children of the victims of the 'years of lead', they may be read in the perspective of what Marianne Hirsch terms 'postmemory'. Postmemory:

> describes the relationship that the generation after those who witnessed cultural or collective trauma bears to the experiences of those who came before, experiences that they 'remember' only by means of the stories, images, and behaviours among which they grew up. [. . .] Postmemory is not mediated by recollection but by imaginative investment, projection, and creation.
>
> (106–107)

So, the 'events happened in the past, but their effect continues in the present' (107). According to Anna Bull and Philip Cooke, second-generation victims feel the need to counteract the loss of memory caused by both trauma, and by the wider social and political reaction to it, but whereas first-generation writers tend to seek justice with their works, second-generation writers are more likely to be in a search of truth, owing to the difficulty in obtaining justice many years after the event, and since postmemory relates to broader society, and to the transformative value of truth, in relation to democracy. Therefore, second-generation victims are more likely to present themselves as active citizens rather than victims, and engage in activities that reach the public sphere (218–219).

Some of the most interesting victim accounts from the last 15 years are good examples of the above-mentioned category, in which the decision to tell one's story and assume a testimonial role is presented as a conscious rejection of the identity of victim. Silvia Giralucci was only three years old when her father, Graziano Giralucci, was killed by the Red Brigades. She has written an autobiographical account: *L'inferno sono gli altri. Cercando mio padre vittima delle BR nella memoria divisa degli anni Settanta* (*Hell Is the Others: The Search for My Father, Victim of the Red Brigades, in the Divided Memory of the Seventies*, 2011), and made a documentary, *Sfiorando il muro* (*Brushing against the Wall*, 2013), in which she attempts to reconstruct the climate of those years in Padua, a daily theatre of violence between young people of the extreme left and right. Therefore, memory becomes: 'the answer to a profound need to search, in history, for the reasons of my suffering [. . .] to understand the spirit of the period in which it was worthwhile to die or risk ruining one's life for politics' (Giralucci 5). The personal trauma is merely the starting point for a historical reconstruction of the period and, not unlike Manlio Milani, she is also open to hearing the reasons of others. As she affirms, in commenting on the question of one of her father's old enemies, who asks about her political standpoint: 'It was difficult to make him understand that a "position" is something that you find at the end of a journey, not a predetermined idea to be fed by interviews, and that I prefer the grey scales to black and white' (160).[24]

In her first book, *Come mi batte forte il tuo cuore. Storia di mio padre* (*How Strongly I Feel Your Heart Beat: The Story of My Father*, 2009), Benedetta Tobagi deals with the trauma of her life: the murder of her father when she was three years old, and the consequences this had for her future. However, her trauma and pain are only a starting point for a recollection that attempts to understand the events in the sociopolitical context of the time. In addition to declaring her love for the figure of a father she never knew, and whom she remembers only 'by imaginative investment', she also retrieves his public dimension, and recalls the political context in which he operated, thus making the operation of 'remembering' also an act of understanding.

In her second book, *Una stella incoronata di buio. Storia di una strage impunita* (*A Star Surrounded by Darkness: The Story of an Unpunished Massacre*, 2013), Benedetta Tobagi writes about the bombing massacre at the Piazza della Loggia in Brescia that occurred on the same month and day as the assassination of her father, six years earlier. The book begins by remembering every single victim of the massacre, with the help of the testimonies of family and friends, consulting diaries, letters, photographs, and then, gradually, it moves on to the victims' engagement and political stances. In this way, she is able to remember the political activism of the victims, and their civic and democratic commitment. Moreover, in the second part of the book, she analyses the judiciary material of the many criminal trials, reconstructs the political dynamics that led to the attack, and throws light on the unpunished perpetrators, including the involvement of sectors of the state.

Both books are formal and thematic hybrids, combining autobiographical account, essayistic narration, and third-person, sometimes fictive, narration. As in Giralucci and others' postmemory accounts, the connection to the past is mediated by documentary material (photographs, newspaper articles, diaries, letters, interviews, etc.), in an attempt to know the past through its traces.

Benedetta Tobagi is a good example of a victim who has also become an 'agent for truth and justice'. To her, giving up the fight would be the same as becoming an accomplice to the perpetrators. Below, she expresses a not insignificant amount of optimism and fighting spirit, despite her obvious indignation at, and distrust of, the authorities:

> We still do not know everything, it is true. But we know a lot, and we should no longer allow anyone to say the opposite, like too many of the right-wing descendants of the seventies did after they came into government in 1994.

24 Difficile fargli capire che per me una 'posizione' è qualcosa che si trova alla fine di un percorso, non un'idea preconcetta da alimentare con interviste, e che a me piacciono più le scale dei grigi che il bianco e nero.

> Nor should we slip into the fatal temptation of cynicism which is strengthened every time a new wave of scandals rises: we can never know the truth, they got away with it, what is the use? It is the same old mysterious Italy, there is no point in trying to understand, remember, distinguish, recompose the incomplete and patchy list of responsibilities, and so on. Surrendering to these thoughts would be the same as becoming accomplices to the depistatori (those who create false trails). If we consider how vast and harsh the deployment of the authorities was, in their various guises, to distort the truth, create false culprits, hide the perpetrators, it is almost astonishing how much we know, thanks to the commitment of many women and men of good will who have continued, obstinately, to investigate, often in solitude, despite the threats and obstacles. And let us continue to work to ensure that the story can be told, ever more frequently and more effectively, about what really took place in this country.
>
> (Tobagi, 'Ciò che sappiamo')[25]

Tobagi's statement highlights the lights and shadows of the way the country came to terms with terrorism and political violence. Largely owing to the active mobilization of the victims and their associations, we now have a tentative knowledge of what happened in those years (but with significant limitations), whereas the achievements of restorative justice have been largely disappointing.

Conclusion

The experts on processes of transitional justice and reconciliation are divided on the role of the victims and their testimonies. For the purpose of national cohesion, many consider it necessary to emphasize human suffering and mourning by uniting the suffering of the ex-perpetrators with that of the victims, renouncing the achievement of the historical truth on behalf of an abstract ethical ecumenism. It seems to us that this is a reductive perception of the process of

25 Non sappiamo ancora tutto, è vero. Ma sappiamo moltissimo e non bisogna lasciare più che qualcuno s'azzardi a dire il contrario, come hanno fatto troppi epigoni della destra degli anni Settanta dopo essere andati al governo nel '94. Né dobbiamo scivolare nella fatale tentazione del cinismo, che si fa più forte ogni volta che si alza una nuova ondata di scandali: non potremo mai sapere la verità, l'hanno fatta franca, a che serve? È la solita Italia dei misteri, non vale la pena di provare a capire, ricordare, distinguere, rimettere in fila l'elenco, incompleto e lacunoso, delle responsabilità, e via dicendo. Arrendersi a questi pensieri sarebbe come diventare complici dei depistatori. Se consideriamo quanto vasto e feroce è stato il dispiegamento di forze del Potere, nelle sue varie articolazioni, per mistificare il vero, creare falsi colpevoli, nascondere i responsabili, è quasi stupefacente quanto sappiamo, grazie all'impegno di molte donne e uomini di buona volontà che hanno continuato, ostinati, a indagare, spesso in solitudine, a dispetto delle minacce e degli ostacoli. Teniamocelo ben stretto. E continuiamo a lavorare perché si possa raccontare sempre più e sempre meglio cosa è accaduto, davvero, in questo Paese.

reconciliation; a solution that can suit the state well because it covers its ambiguities, but which turns out to be a superficial and short-term approach to reconciliation. The risk of hate continuing to smoulder beneath the ashes of the general ecumenism, and of the conflicts being revived, is strong and real. Restorative justice cannot be implemented without a genuine search for historical truth.

The long struggle for truth and justice, carried out by the Italian victims of terrorism, reveals another important lesson about human rights and agency. Human rights may be understood as something that the state and society develop and introduce from above for the protection and security of their citizens. In Italy, during the 'years of lead', at first the state was not able to secure the right to life and security for many innocent citizens, victims of the bombing massacres of the right, and of the assassinations of the left. Thereafter, the state did not hesitate to suspend and restrict everybody's constitutional rights (and also the rights of the culprits to a humane treatment), in order to repress and defeat the terrorism. Finally, once the problem had been eliminated, the state tried to forget those years of violence (and its own ambiguous role), removing and consigning to obscurity the ones that had paid the highest price: the victims and their relatives, who were denied truth and justice.

Human rights may be conceived as pertaining not only to the institutional and juridical spheres, but as conjoining sociopolitical agency and bottom-up mobilization from the citizens. Human rights must be reached on the initiative of the citizens. In turn, human rights subjects may be conceived not as simple victims or passive recipients who need protection and security, but as active subjects capable of acting politically, and of constituting, delimiting, and determining the character of a political community. Human rights need not only a political system of institutions to implement them, but also collective agency: that is, actions of individual citizens. Without agency, 'not only is there no implementation of human rights, but there is also no "right" within these "rights"'. If there is no implementation of human rights, they lose their meaning and content. Thus, human rights emerge from the 'immanent claims of emancipation of the citizens themselves' in a process of 'invention of democracy' (Balibar 18–19). In this way, it is possible to transform the experience of victimhood into agency.

As we have seen, the experience of the victims of the 'years of lead' in Italy, despite the variety of positions regarding the perpetrators of past crimes, and how the past should be remembered, demonstrates how it is possible to transform an experience of victimhood into agency, and into a path of dialogue and social action, and in this way reaffirm the 'right' to have 'rights'.

Through the creation of associations and the assumption of a testimonial role, the victims and their relatives have rejected the identity of victims, to assume that of citizens aware of their rights in a democracy struggling to achieve truth, justice, and political visibility. Some of them – the Dendena family, Manlio Milani, Benedetta Tobagi, and others – have consciously chosen the role of agents for political change, and have turned victimhood into a quest to change society, and to achieve a new kind of democratic institution, committed to transparency and accountability.

Works cited

Andreasen, Marie. 'Narrazioni autobiografiche degli anni di piombo. La violenza politica di sinistra'. *Conflictos de la memoria/Memoria de los conflictos. Modelos narrativo de la memoria intergenaracional en España e Italia.* Ed. Leonardo Cecchini and Hans Lauge Hansen. *Etudes Romanes* 62. Copenhagen: Museum Tusculanum Forlag, 2015. 349–362. Print.

Balibar, Etienne. 'On the Politics of Human Rights'. *Constellations* 20.1 (2013): 18–26. Print.

Bell, Christine. 'Transitional Justice, Interdisciplinarity and the State of the "Field" or "Not-Field"'. *The International Journal of Transitional Justice* 3 (2009): 5–27. Print.

Bloomberg, David, Teresa Barnes, and Luc Huyse, eds. *Reconciliation after Violent Conflict: A Handbook.* Stockholm: International Institute for Democracy and Electoral Assistance (IDEA), 2003. Print.

Bull, Anna Cento. 'Sfidando l'oblio. Narrazioni di vittime e carnefici dopo un conflitto armato. Un confronto tra Italia, Irlanda del Nord e Spagna'. *Conflictos de la memoria/Memoria de los conflictos. Modelos narrativo de la memoria intergenaracional en España e Italia.* Ed. Leonardo Cecchini and Hans Lauge Hansen. *Etudes Romanes* 62. Copenhagen: Museum Tusculanum Forlag, 2015. 75–96. Print.

Bull, Anna Cento and Philip Cooke. *Ending Terrorism in Italy.* Routledge Studies in Extremism and Democracy. London/New York: Routledge, 2013. Print.

De Luna, Giovanni. *La repubblica del dolore. Le memorie di un'Italia divisa.* Milan: Feltrinelli, 2011. Print.

Dendena, Matteo. *Ora che ricordo ancora. Francesca Dendena: storia di un eroe civile.* Bresso: Maingraf Edizioni, 2012. Print.

Fasanella, Giovanni and Antonella Grippo. *I silenzi degli innocenti.* Milan: BUR, 2006. Print.

Galfré, Monica. *La Guerra è finita. L'Italia e l'uscita dal terrorismo 1980–1987.* Rome-Bari: Laterza, 2014. Print.

Giesen, Bernard. *Triumph and Trauma,* New Haven: Paradigm Publishers, 2004. Print.

Giralucci, Silvia. *L'inferno sono gli altri. Cercando mio padre vittima delle BR nella memoria divisa degli anni Settanta.* Milan: Mondadori, 2011. Print.

Glynn, Ruth. 'The "Turn to the Victim" in Italian Culture: Victim-Centred Narratives of the anni di piombo'. *Modern Italy* 18.4 (2013): 373–390. Print.

Hackett, Claire and Bill Rolston. 'The Burden of Memory: Victims, Storytelling and Resistance in Northern Ireland'. *Memory Studies* 2.3 (2009): 355–376. Print.

Hirsch, Marianne. 'The Generation of Postmemory'. *Poetics Today* 29.1 (2008): 103–128. Print.

Laqueur, Walter. *No End to War: Terrorism in the Twenty-First Century.* New York: Continuum, 2004. Print.

Lenci, Sergio. *Colpo alla nuca. Memorie di una vittima del terrorismo.* 1988. Rome: Editori Riuniti, 2009. Print.

Levy, Daniel and Natan Sznaider. 'Memory Unbound: The Holocaust and the Formation of Cosmopolitan Memory'. *European Journal of Social Theory* 5.1 (2002): 87–106. Print.

Milani, Manlio. 'A-Memoria di sentenza'. *Brescia: Piazza della Loggia.* Ed. Carlo Ghezzi. Rome: Ediesse, 2012. 119–125. Print.

Progetto Memoria. *Le torture affiorate*. Tivoli: Sensibili alle foglie, 1998. Print.

Rodella, Mara. 'Milani a Casa Pound innesca la protesta antifascista'. Brescia oggi, 27 Mar. 2011. Web. 6 Aug. 2015. <www.bresciaoggi.it/stories/Home/238660__strage_milani_a_casa_pound_innesca_la_protesta_antifascista/?refresh_ce#scroll=800>.

Specchia, Francesco and Raffaello Canteri. *Terrorismo. L'altra storia*. Reggio Emilia: Aliberti, 2007. Print.

Tobagi, Benedetta. *Come mi batte forte il tuo cuore. Storia di mio padre*. Turin: Einaudi, 2009. Print.

——. 'Ciò che sappiamo di Piazza Fontana'. *La Repubblica* 12 Dec. 2012. Web. 6 Aug. 2015. <http://ricerca.repubblica.it/repubblica/archivio/repubblica/2014/12/12/cio-che-sappiamo-di-piazza-fontana43.html?ref=search>.

——. *Una stella incoronata di buio. Storia di una strage impunita*. Turin: Einaudi, 2013. Print.

United Nations. 'The Rule of Law and Transitional Justice in Conflict and Post-Conflict Societies'. Report to the Secretary-General. UN Doc. S/2004/616. New York: United Nations, 2004. Print.

van der Merwe, Hugo and Jasmina Brankovic. ' Transitional Justice and Human Rights'. *The Sage Handbook of Human Rights*. Ed. Anja Mihr and Mark Gibney. London: Sage, 2014. 895–908. Print.

Weinberg, Leonard. *Global Terrorism: A Beginner's Guide*. Oxford: Oneworld, 2005. Print.

Zavoli, Sergio. *La notte della repubblica*. Milan: Mondadori, 1992. Print.

Chapter 7

Exemplary victims and opaque agents

Remembering Algeria's Black Decade

Madeleine Dobie

Efforts to portray and thereby oppose violence confront challenges in which ethical and political aims intersect with questions of form. Representing violence involves processes of selection and exclusion by means of which certain acts are censured while others are legitimized, and certain victims are sanctified while other lives are discounted. As Judith Butler observes in her essay *Frames of War*, representations of conflict often reinscribe the social and political relations that made violence possible in the first place. Before we commit our moral energy to protesting or defending violence, it is therefore important to subject this framing to a critical appraisal. Depictions of the violence that ravaged Algeria in the 1990s could certainly benefit from this kind of examination. This decade-long conflict that claimed as many as 200,000 lives has generally been portrayed as a civil war pitting Islamist militias intent on imposing a restrictive code of Islamic law against both the state and figures of secular modernity such as journalists, intellectuals, doctors, and teachers. While this account is not a pure fiction – Islamist guerrillas did take up arms against the state, targeting, in the process, writers and educators – it is a selective narrative that neglects crucial aspects of the conflict. With a growing number of novels and films now being devoted to the bloodshed of the 'décennie noire', or 'Black Decade', this chapter considers how works of literature and cinema have positioned themselves in relation to this painful past. It considers if and how they challenge official discourses, and on what terms they try to heal old traumas and repair fractures within the community.

From crisis to amnesty

Violence erupted in Algeria in 1991, after the country's first democratic elections were suspended to prevent the Islamist party, the Front islamique du salut, or FIS, which had prevailed in the first round of voting, from taking power. For the previous two and a half years, Algeria had seemed to be on course for a democratic transition. Following protests in several cities in the fall of 1988, the ruling Front de libération national, or FLN, which had held a monopoly on power since its historic victory over France in 1962, promised a political opening and a transition to a multiparty system. In the face of the electoral successes of the FIS, however, a cohort of powerbrokers stepped in, suspending the elections and establishing a provisional ruling body, the Haut conseil de l'état (HCE). To cement the shutdown, the FIS was declared illegal and its leaders imprisoned.

The suspension of the political process and suppression of the Islamist opposition led to what Carl von Clausewitz might have called the 'continuation of politics by other means' or what the political scientist Jean-Pierre Filiu has more recently called the 'jihadization of politics'.[1] Deprived of a political outlet, many FIS supporters took up arms, forming militias such as the Groupes islamiques armées, or GIA, and the rival Armée islamique du salut, or AIS.[2] By 1993, violence had become a daily reality, with militias targeting the police, the army, and those whom they perceived to be hostile to their vision of Algeria, notably journalists, intellectuals known for their secular attitudes or for writing in French, and figures of public authority such as judges and teachers.

The assassination of intellectuals, including prominent writers such as the novelist Tahar Djaout, and the dramatist Abdelkader Alloula, soon began to garner international attention. Journalists, academics, and writers were issued emergency visas and offered short-term residencies at North American universities. Their plight was the catalyst for the foundation, in 1994, of the International Parliament of Writers (IPW), and the basis of a project to establish a network of 'cities of refuge' that would shelter persecuted writers.[3] The IPW's first president was Salman Rushdie, who had had his own famous clash with Islamist politics a few years earlier.[4] Other prominent supporters included Hélène Cixous and Jacques Derrida, who had both grown up in Algeria.[5]

But while Algeria's Black Decade became synonymous abroad with the persecution of intellectuals at the hands of Islamists, there were many other less well-publicized victims. While militias targeted the intelligentsia, state security forces arrested suspected supporters of the FIS, often with little concern for their

1 In his classic treatise *On War* (1832), Clausewitz famously described war as 'policy by other means'. In *From Deep State to Islamic State: The Arab Counter-Revolution and Its Jihadi Legacy*, Jean-Pierre Filiu describes a course of events by which nations' 'deep states' (i.e. the network of political powerbrokers and security apparatuses) used the rise of an Islamist party to lock down the status quo, leading to the 'jihadization' of politics. Filiu argues that this scenario played out first in Algeria and has subsequently been repeated in Egypt and Syria.

2 Often treated as a single, unified movement, the GIA were in fact a loose confederation of militias operating under local commanders known, in a somewhat orientalizing fashion, as 'emirs'.

3 The IPW, or in French PIE (Parlement international des écrivains), was founded in 1994 and dissolved in 2004.

4 Rushdie also introduced the 2007 BBC documentary *Shooting the Writer*, devoted to the life and assassination of Tahar Djaout.

5 The initiative to create cities of asylum is central to Derrida's thinking on cosmopolitanism in *Cosmopolites de tous les pays, encore un effort!*

actual sympathies and with scant regard for their civil rights. Many of these detainees, who have become known as the 'disparus' (the disappeared), never returned home, and their fate remains a subject of activism.[6] The pinnacle of violence, however, occurred in 1996 and 1997, when civilian massacres, rather than the targeted killing of individuals, became the order of the day. In the Mitidja Plain to the south of Algiers, a former hub of colonial farming that came to be known as the 'Triangle of Death', entire communities were wiped out in brutal night-time attacks. Though the massacres perpetrated in localities such as Raïs and Bentalha were officially attributed to the GIA, doubts were quickly raised about what really happened there.[7] Survivors of the Benthala massacre, along with several external observers, asked why the military personnel who were stationed all around the village never intervened to stop the carnage. Some claimed that the attackers were not GIA fighters at all, but rather army personnel in disguise. Others asserted that the army had infiltrated the militia and instigated extreme acts of violence.[8] In either case, the narrative by which the state was defending civil society against the onslaught of the Islamists was subject to serious doubts.

Though this spiralling conflict has often been characterized as a civil war, this label is misleading, both in what it implies and for what it fails to communicate. As a concept, civil war suggests one or more deep ideological/political rifts within the nation and the taking up of arms on all sides. In Algeria, despite a high level of violence, only a small number of actors were directly involved, and the population was never neatly divided into pro-FIS and pro-government camps. It would be more accurate to characterize what happened

6 In 2005, Farouk Ksentini, President of the Commission nationale consultative pour la promotion et la protection des droits de l'homme (CNCPPDH), Algeria's official human rights watchdog, acknowledged 6,146 cases of disappearance, but claimed that these were due to the actions of individual state agents rather than a concerted government policy, and that as such the state should be considered 'responsible' for, but not 'guilty' of, the disappearances. By contrast, the Collectif des familles de disparu(e)s en Algérie (CFDA), an organization formed in 1998 by mothers of *disparus* has compiled over 8,000 files, and believes that there are many more undocumented cases. Highly critical of the state's role during the Black Decade, the CFDA opposes the principle of amnesty without truth, and has accused the CNCPPDH of helping to cover up the evidence (see www.algerie-disparus.org/index.php?view=details&id=3%3Ala-verite-en-algerie-bilan-et-perspectives-un-an-apres-les-recommandations-onusiennes&option=com_eventlist&Itemid=154).

7 The string of massacres that occurred over the course of just a few months in the late summer of 1997 included Raïs (29 August), Beni-Messous (5 September), and Bentalha (22 September). The death toll in each case is debated, but Human Rights Watch estimates that at least 600 people died in these three attacks alone (see www.hrw.org/legacy/wr2k/Mena-01.htm).

8 In *Qui a tué à Bentalha?*, Yous Nasroullah, a survivor of the massacre, claims that the GIA units involved in the attack had been infiltrated by the army. His claims have been found persuasive by a number of historians, including Hugh Roberts, who discusses Bentalha in *The Battlefield: Algeria 1988–2002, Studies in a Broken Polity*, 308–310.

in Algeria as a failed revolution in which the 'deep state' thwarted a political transition, then exploited the resulting violence to restore its own legitimacy. Viewed in this light, the bloodshed that occurred in Algeria was not simply pathological – the symptom of a profound identity crisis – but rather also a perverse instrument of political control. If, in the 1990s, the notion that a country's security appatus would catalyse or even simulate Islamist violence in order to strengthen its own hold on power registered as a conspiracy theory, today, in light of events in Egypt and Syria, it seems all too plausible. No wonder that Algerians have the feeling of having lived through dynamics of the 'Arab Spring' two decades before neighbouring countries.

By the end of the 1990s, the acute violence of the preceding years was beginning to subside. This cooling off was due to a number of factors, including the army's gradual victory over its by then bitterly divided opponents, and the policy of clemency towards former militia members pursued by President Lamine Zeroual and, to an even greater extent, his successor, Abdelaziz Bouteflika.[9] A canny political veteran who came out of exile to assume the presidency, Bouteflika implemented two major amnesty decrees – the Civil Concord of 1999 and the Charter for Peace and National Reconciliation of 2005. The second law, in particular, was a sweeping piece of legislation that covered all but the most extreme acts of terrorism, while also stating that any crimes comitted by agents of the state had already been punished. It was first aired in a public address delivered on the anniversary of the outbreak of the war of independence, in which Bouteflika characterized the violence of the previous decade as a 'civil war' in which Algerians had fought against fellow Algerians: a deep social fracture that was in need of repair. Flanked by Ahmed Ben Bella and Chadli Benjedid, both former presidents who had been removed from office and, in the case of Ben Bella, forced into exile, Bouteflika seemed to be practising the very reconciliation that he was preaching.[10]

As I discuss in greater detail below, the Charter for Peace and Reconciliation has been the cornerstone of an official culture of silence with respect to the events of the 1990s. In spite of its provisions, however, questions about the nature of the conflict and the attribution of guilt have continued to emerge. They were aired most publicly in a rather remarkable trial held in Paris in 2000 after a former Algerian special forces officer named Habib Souaïdia published a book titled *La sale guerre: 1992–2000* [The Dirty War], which effectively compares Algeria to Argentina, laying much of the blame for the carnage at the feet of the state. Souaïdia alleged that military personnel had shot suspects in cold

9 Bouteflika left Algeria to escape corruption charges but also, perhaps more importantly, because he fell out of favour after the death of his patron, Houari Boumediene, and the appointment of Chadli Benjedid as his successor.

10 'If today the people is torn apart ["déchiré"]', Bouteflika intoned, 'it is because Algerians have fought other Algerians'. Speech of 31 October 2004 (see www.djazairess.com/fr/liberte/30550).

blood, tortured prisoners to death and, most chillingly, perpetrated massacres while disguised as Islamist guerrillas. These provocative accusations did not go unanswered; General Khaled Nezzar, a former powerbroker who had been central to the cancellation of the elections in 1992, brought a defamation suit against Souaïdia.[11] The resulting trial unfolded as a post-mortem on the Black Decade in which the actions taken by the state were weighed against the threat represented by the Islamists. For several days, witnesses on either side supported or condemned the shutdown of the elections and defended or attacked the military's record.[12]

Witnesses for the defence evoked the regime's tendency to manipulate situations in order to achieve its own ends, highlighting its deep anti-democratic tendencies, propensity for opaque political manoeuvring, and repeated recourse to military authority. Several speakers flagged the FLN's habit of displacing blame onto external enemies: France in the 1950s and 1960s, the FIS in the 1990s.

Nezzar and his supporters, on the other hand, told a story animated by the defence of secularism and human rights in the face of a party bent on the 'Afghanization' of Algeria.[13] The historian and former FLN lawyer Ali Haroun, who had briefly been a member of the Haut conseil d'état, painted a conflict between two sectors of society, one embodying the values of modernity and tolerance, the other composed of religious fanatics, with the army firmly on the side of the former: 'From the moment that all of the democrats, women, workers, intellectuals, and artists became the victims of these religious fanatics [fous de dieu], the Algerian army was, objectively, the ally of the democrats and the republicans', Haroun stated (120). Another prominent witness, the avant-garde writer Rachid Boudjedra, who, after receiving several death threats, had authored a polemical tract titled *FIS de la haine* (FIS (son) of Hate), emphasized the threat that the Islamist movement posed to literary culture. Interestingly, and somewhat to the surprise of the defence, he drew attention to his credentials as a writer published in *France*.[14] The intended message was, presumably, that the FIS was bent on eliminating the values of a modernity firmly established in France but

11 Nezzar was the prime mover in the HCE, which took power following the suspension of the elctoral process.

12 The transcript of the trial was published by La Découverte under the title *Le procès de la sale guerre* [The Dirty War on Trial], cited in the text below. Nezzar accused La Découverte's editor, François Gèze, of having a commercial interest in the judicial process, and proceeded to present his own account of the trial under the title *Un procès pour la vérité* [A Trial for Truth].

13 In 'Un procès pour la vérité', Nezzar characterizes the movement as 'A retrograde and medieval order', stating that 'For democrats, workers, intellectuals, trade unionists, former militants, for women's associations, for the army and the security services, the fundamentalist [intégriste] Islamic state is the negation of democracy' (156–157).

14 Rachid Boudjedra, *FIS de la haine* (Paris: Gallimard, 1994). In a play on words, the title implies that the FIS party is the 'fils', or 'son', of hatred. In his testimony, Boudjedra called attention

menaced in Algeria by the rise of Islamism.

Since it illustrates the reverberation of political questions in the domain of culture, the Nezzar-Souaïdia trial is a useful vantage point for considering the corpus of films and novels that have undertaken to depict Algeria in the 1990s. Like the prosecution's side of the case, many of these works mount a defence of values such as gender equality, freedom of expression, and multilingualism, in the face of the threat represented by the FIS. Others undertake a thicker description of the political situation, gesturing to the devious role of the regime or to enduring uncertainties about what really happened. Below, I consider the ethical and political stakes of these different framings and how they are translated into aesthetic choices. As a point of departure, I explore the implications of focusing on the suffering of the victims and the countervailing strategy of imagining the viewpoint of the perpetrators.

Exemplary victims

If a single episode of violence committed in Algeria in the 1990s has captured the imagination more than any other, it is the story of the seven French monks kidnapped from the Trappist monastery of Tibhirine in March 1996. The abduction of the monks initially seemed to be the work of an Islamist commando, and in the days following their disappearance, demands were issued for the release of a GIA leader, creating the hope of a possible prisoner exchange. A few weeks later, however, the monks' decapitated heads were discovered by the side of a road. Questions quickly arose about the circumstances of their death. A French general claimed to have learned that the monks were killed accidentally during a helicopter attack on a GIA base. He conjectured that the Algerian military had tried to conceal the misstep by destroying the physical evidence. Other sources claimed that units from the Département du reseignement et de la sécurité (DRS) had infiltrated a GIA commando and that the whole incident had been orchestrated from Algiers. The motive, according to this version of events, would have been to dispose of the monks, who had been providing humanitarian aid to guerrillas, while at the same time further demonizing the Islamists in the eyes of the world.

Almost two decades after the events, the fate of the monks continues to be a topic of debate. Following a stream of books and documentaries, an autopsy was conducted in 2014.[15] In addition to these forensic studies, there have been

to the fact that he is published by two prominent French presses, Gallimard and Grasset, that he is a lover of Proust and Flaubert, and that his work, like that of these famous forbears, explores the human psyche and emotions. This self-presentation is striking when we consider that, unlike many other francophone Algerian writers, Boudjedra has written and published in Arabic.

15 Books on the Tibhirine monks include: Mireille Duteil, *Les Martyrs de Tibhirine* (1996); René Guitton, *Si nous nous taisons . . . Le martyre des moines de Tibhirine* (2001); Mohamed Balhi, *Tibhirine,*

works that effectively eulogize the monks, remembering them for their strong Christian faith, simple lifestyle, and service to the local community. Catholic presses, in particular, have portrayed the monks as modern martyrs and sought to bring the story of Tibhirine to a global readership.[16] A small handful of works, finally, has been guided by more aesthetic concerns. These include *Les Sept dormants*, a seven-volume book illustrated by the Algerian artist Rachid Koraïchi, with texts by prominent writers, including John Berger, Michel Butor, Hélène Cixous, and Leila Sebbar, and the elegiac feature film *Des Dieux et des hommes* [Of Gods and Men], winner of the Grand Prix at the Cannes Film Festival in 2010, as well as a BAFTA (British Academy for Film and Television Arts) award for best film not in the English language.

Beautifully filmed and psychologically insightful, *Of Gods and Men* examines the challenge that violence poses both to personal faith and to the fabric of a community. It depicts the monks as men, not saints, registering their personal foibles as well as their resilience and courage. Where the film falls short is the manner in which it situates the monks' story within the broader context of 1990s Algeria. One issue is that the film focuses almost exclusively on the monks, neglecting the fact that the villagers with whom they interacted were confronted by similar threats. Another is that the focus on the monks' psychology and inner life isn't complemented by any reflection on the political context. Though the monks' tense encounters with both militia fighters and army personnel are evoked in several scenes, nothing is ventured on the question of what ultimately happened to them or who was responsible. Though I imagine that the film's director, Xavier Beauvois, wanted to steer clear of political controversy, this silence effectively endorses the official line that the culprits were Islamist terrorists.[17]

l'enlèvement des moines (2002); Christophe Henning, *Petite vie des moines de Tibhirine* (2006); Jean-Marie Lassausse and Christophe Henning, *Le jardinier de Tibhirine* (2010); Henry Quinson, *Secret des hommes, secret des dieux* (2011); and Jean-Baptiste Rivoire, *Le crime de Tibhirine: Révélation sur les responsables* (2011). Documentary films and television programs include: *Frère Luc, moine de Tibhirine* (France 2, 2003); *Le crime de Tibhirine* (Canal Plus, 2011); and *Le Testament de Tibhirine* (France 3, April 2006). On the 2014 autopsy and its conclusions, see the analysis published in *Le Monde* on 2 July 2015: www.lemonde.fr/police-justice/article/2015/07/02/moines-de-tibehirine-la-these-d-une-decapitation-post-mortem-est privilegiee_4667711_1653578.html.

16 Though most of the literature on the monks has appeared in French, there are also English-language publications and translations. See, for example, John Kiser, *The Monks of Tibhirine: Faith, Love, and Terror in Algeria* (2002); Christian Salenson, *Christian de Cherge: A Theology of Hope* (2012); Freddy Derwahl and Bruno Zanzoterra, *The Last Monk of Tibhirine: A True Story of Martyrdom, Faith, and Survival* (2013); and Christophe Lebreton, *Born from the Gaze of God: The Tibhirine Journal of a Martyr Monk (1993–1996)* (2014).

17 Towards the end of the film, for example, there is a poignant visual tableau evoking the Last Supper.

While the monks of Tibhirine are the most prominent victims of the Black Decade, they're not the only group to have garnered the attention of writers and filmmakers in and beyond Algeria. As the Souaïdia trial illustrates, the class of 'exemplary victims' also includes writers, journalists, and especially women. As the journalist Ghania Mouffok has observed, so much media attention has been devoted to the subject of women and violence in Algeria that 'the expression "Algerian women" almost immediately evokes rivers of blood'.[18] The victimization of women at the hands of the FIS or the GIA has been the subject of dozens of newspaper articles, as well as literary works such as Malika Mokkedem's novels *L'Interdite* [The Forbidden Woman] (1993) and *Des rêves et des assassins* [Of Dreams and Assassins] (2000), Leila Aslaoui's *Les jumeaux de la nuit* (2002), Arezki Mellal's *Maintenant ils peuvent venir* [Let Them Come] (2002), and Wahiba Khiari's *Nos silences* [Our Silences] (2009).[19] It also provided the impetus of several films, including *Barakat!* [Enough!] (2006) and *Yema* (2013), both directed by Djamila Sahraoui, and a recently released film adaptation of *Let Them Come*.[20] The main narrative elements of these different works are gathered in the 2002 film *Rachida*, directed by Yamina Bachir Chouikh, a cinema veteran with many writing and editing credits to her name. Screened at the Cannes Film Festival, *Rachida* has enjoyed a comparatively wide international distribution, and is one of only a handful of Algerian films to have been subtitled in English.

The film's opening scenes introduce Rachida, a young elementary school teacher living with her divorced mother in a pleasant neighbourhood of Algiers. We see her walking between the school where she teaches and the family apartment, wearing headphones and listening to the popular raï music of the period. This modern urban lifestyle is brutally interrupted when a group of young men corners her in the street and instruct her to set a bomb at the school where she teaches. When she refuses, they shoot her. Rachida miraculously survives this attack, but fearing that her life may still be in danger, her mother and the female principal of her school whisk her off to what they hope will be a safer environment: a village a few hours' drive from the capital.

The depiction of Rachida's convalescence is heavily indebted to the concept of trauma. Paralysed by fear, Rachida at first can barely leave her house. When she tells a sympathetic doctor that while her body may have healed, 'the scars in

18 Mouffok (71–98).

19 Leila Aslaoui, op. cit.; Malika Mokkedem, *L'Interdite* (1993), *Des rêves et des assassins* (2000); Wahiba Khiari, *Nos silences* (2009); and Arezki Mellal, *Maintenant ils peuvent venir* (2002).

20 *Maintenant ils peuvent venir* (2015), directed by Salem Brahimi, son of the diplomat Lakhdar Brahimi, and produced by the legendary Greek film-maker Costa Gavras, features Rachida Brakni, who played the female lead in *Barakat!*, and the singer Amazigh Kateb, son of the iconic writer Kateb Yacine.

my mind won't', he understandably ventures a diagnosis of post-traumatic stress disorder. Just when she is beginning to recover and has taken up a new job as a teacher in the school in the village in which she has taken refuge, the nightmare begins all over again. The village becomes the target of a group of terrorists and the film ends with the depiction of a night-time massacre similar to those perpetrated in Raïs and Bentalha. In the closing scene, we see a dazed Rachida and the village's surviving children mechanically returning to the schoolroom.

If *Rachida* accomplishes something important in its depiction of the durable effects of violence and its homage to the courage of the many Algerians, including young female teachers, who died defending their convictions, its depiction of violence is, nonetheless, somewhat misleading. The narrative, for one thing, telescopes different moments, juxtaposing the assassination of intellectuals and public figures in 1993 and 1994 with the indiscriminate massacres of 1996 and 1997, while at the same time skipping over the likely involvement of the state in these later incidents. (Interestingly, the film includes an episode in which Rachida and her mother watch a television report on the funeral of the Tibhirine monks, situating the action in the spring of 1996.) In the few scenes in which the security forces appear, they are shown in a fairly positive light, ushering civilians away from a bomb or into an ambulance. The terrorists get more screen time, but remain nebulous figures whose motivations are never really addressed. Since there is no suggestion that they are acting out of religious or political convictions, they basically come off as bloodthirsty thugs intent on victimizing their neighbours, and in particular the women.

Rachida treats violence and gender as being fundamentally interwoven. As we've seen, the film derives much of its pathos from its depiction of the suffering of its young and attractive female protagonist. Most of the other victims portrayed in the story are also women, while the perpetrators are primarily men. Resting on the convention that 'women and children' constitute a privileged class of victims, this distribution neglects both the suffering of men and the significant participation of women in Islamist networks. It also undrpins a sweeping and rather predictable survey of gender inequality in Algeria.[21] In one dramatic episode, a young woman who has been kidnapped and raped by the terrorists manages to escape and make her way back to her village, only to be disowned by her father, who believes that the family's honour has been stained. Only the women of the village come to her aid, gathering round her in a show of female solidarity. In this and other episodes, patriarchy, polygamy, and honour codes – practices that viewers in France and English-speaking countries are likely to apprehend as features of a traditional Muslim society – are thrown into the mix with terrorism in a dubious amalgamation of different social issues.

21 As Ghania Mouffok notes, many women supported Islamist parties, and some played an active role in aiding the militias. Op. cit.

In this conflation, the role of the state is, once again, neglected. Someone unfamiliar with Algerian politics would probably be inclined to conclude that the state was the ally of modern, secular women in their struggle against the patriarchal terrorists. The film gives no sense that throughout the 1980s, Algerian women were at loggerheads with the ruling regime, which in 1984 implemented a new Family Code that severely curtailed their marital and property rights, justifying this new dispensation with allusions to Islamic law.[22]

The forms of critical thinking currently being formulated with regard to the politics of human rights and trauma can be usefully applied to works such as *Of Gods and Men* and *Rachida*, which focus on the suffering of the victims during and in the aftermath of violence. As scholars including Samuel Moyn, Didier Fassin, and Richard Rechtman have argued, the proliferation of legal protections, international agencies, and NGOs focused on the protection of individual rights and the treatment of war-related traumas that has characterized the last 30 years has had some problematic effects as well as some salutary ones. Both human rights discourses and theories of trauma (which are often deployed to demonstrate human rights abuses) attend to the personal suffering of (certain) victims at the expense of the wider social and political context in which violence occurs.[23] Depending on the situation, this bracketing can have wide-ranging implications. In the works of film and literature discussed above, it generates a partial and in many ways polarizing version of what happened in the 1990s: an account of violence that largely ignores the role of the state as well as macro-structural issues such as economic inequality, the absence of social justice, and the lack of democratic process.

The opacity of violence

What happens when, instead of focusing on exemplary victims, works make the counter-intuitive move of exploring the perspective of the perpetrator? Such is the strategy of several recent commemorations of Algeria's Black Decade. In his novels *Tuez-les tous* [Kill Them All] (2006) and *Moi, Khaled Kelkal* [I, Khaled Kelkal] (2012), Salim Bachi tests the elasticity of the first-person narrative by writing from the point of view of, in the first case, one of the 9/11 terrorists, and, in the second, the young Frenchman of Algerian origin who, after becoming a GIA militant, carried out a bombing campaign in France. In *L'Attentat* [The Attack] (2005), a provocative bestseller in which political dynamics in Algeria are refracted through the lens of the more familiar Palestinian conflict, Yasmina Khadra portrays an assimilated Israeli Palestinian who has to absorb the

22 On gender and law in 1980s Algeria, see Marnia Lazreg, *The Eloquence of Silence: Algerian Women in Question* and Mounira M. Charrad, *States and Women's Rights: The Making of Postcolonial Tunisia, Algeria, and Morocco*.

23 Samuel Moyn, *The Last Utopia: Human Rights in History* (2010); Didier Fassin and Richard Rechtman, *The Empire of Trauma: An Inquiry into the Condition of Victimhood* (2009).

discovery that his wife has committed a suicide bombing.[24] And in his fictional memoir, *Fantôme: quatre ans de maquis* [Ghost-Life: Four Years in the *Maquis*] (2009), Youssef Oumli narrates from the perspective of a former militia member remembering his years in a guerrilla band.[25] What is striking about these various narratives is that none of them attempts to fully elucidate the mindset or motives of the perpetrator. Rather, in different ways, each elaborates what, following Édouard Glissant, I would characterize as an ethics and poetics of opacity (Glissant 190). In the following paragraphs, I explore this poetics, focusing on a film that distils several of the currents represented in this group of works.

Le repenti/al-ta'ib [The Penitent] (2012), by the veteran director Merzak Allouache, explores questions of guilt, repentance, and reparation in a context shaped by the politics of amnesty. The judicial immunities implemented in Algeria at the end of the 1990s were couched in a language of 'peace' and 'reconciliation'. The first amnesty, instituted under the Presidency of Lamine Zeroual, was known as the *Rahmah*, the Islamic concept of mercy, while combatants who laid down their arms came to be known as *ta'ib*, a term derived from *tawbah*, meaning to return to God's commands.[26] Yet it is hard to see a correlation between these spiritual concepts and the phenomena to which they are applied. If anything, amnesty in Algeria has signified impunity without repentance, a deviation registered in the fact that the French term 'repenti', which is widely used to designate the amnestied *maquisards*, is associated in people's minds not with Islamic or Christian doctrines of repentence, but with tales of Italian mafiosi who escaped prison sentences by testifying against their former associates.[27] Algeria's 'penitents' are thus effectively viewed as violent criminals whose surrender was a matter of pure self-interest.[28]

If, in South Africa and more recently in Tunisia, amnesty was tied to the public admission of crimes and misdeeds, in Algeria reconciliation has not

24 Yasmina Khadra, *L'Attentat* (2005). A filmed version, directed by Ziad Doueiri, was released in 2012. Khadra also explores the viewpoint of a young man recruited to an Islamist militia in *A quoi rêvent les loups?* (2009).

25 Youssef Oumli, *Fantôme: quatre as de maquis* (2009). The French term *maquis*, literally meaning 'scrubland', became synonymous in the Second World War with the French Resistance. In the Algerian context, it was used to designate FLN guerrillas during the War of Independence, and later to designate AIS and GIA units operating during the 1990s.

26 In the Qur'an, *tawbah* signifies leaving what Allah has prohibited and returning to what he commands. See, for example, 24:31, 25:70–71, 66:08.

27 Allouache has said that he belongs to a generation 'that heard about "penitents" in the context of the USA, in the mafia and so on. And suddenly in 1999 this word appeared in Algeria'. Interview with Jean-Louis Cadet, Radio France International, 4 December 2013.

28 The advantages accrued by former militants is a recurrent topic of discussion in both the Algerian and the French press. See, for example: www.liberation.fr/monde/2005/09/28/la-conscience-tranquille-des-terroristes-repentis-en-algerie_533848, www.siwel.info/Les-repentis-de-Bouteflika-impunite-et-passe-droits-a-la-gare-de-Tizi-Ouzou_a4699.html, and www.jeuneafrique.com/134367/politique/alg-rie-la-vie-apr-s-le-jihad/. The rumour has long circulated

only been independent of such avowals, but indeed has contributed to the suppression of truth and the censorship of further examination of the past. The Civil Concord of 2000 and the Charter of Peace and Reconciliation of 2006 conferred judicial immunity on many former combatants and provided financial assistance to the families of men killed while fighting for Islamist militias. But while people whose loved ones figured among the 'disappeared' were also declared eligible for compensation, accepting reparations meant renouncing any further pursuit of truth or justice.[29]

The state too benefited from the amnesties in various ways, one of which was a blanket amnesty for any transgressions committed in the course of anti-terrorist operations. The Charter states that officers guilty of misdemeanours have already been punished, without, however, providing any details. The 2006 decree also provides the regime with a powerful mechanism of censorship, since anyone who contests the immunity of the agents of the state is subject to a three- to five-year prison term and/or a fine.[30] The language used to formulate this threat is worthy of attention. The law censors anyone who:

> by his declarations, writings or any other act utilizes or instrumentalizes the wounds of the national tragedy to injure the institutions of the democratic and popular republic of Algeria, weaken the state, sully the honor of its agents, who have served it with dignity, or tarnish the image of Algeria on the international scene'.[31]

that Madani Mezrag, former 'Emir' of the AIS, is now the owner of the Texanna bottled water company. While this story is probably untrue, Mezrag has carved out a role for himself as a local notable and television news personality.

29 In January 2000, some 6,000 fighters from the Armée islamique du salut converged on the town of Jijel to lay down their arms. On this episode, see Farid Ailat, 'Algérie après le Jihad', *Jeune Afrique*, 10 March 2014. The only group to decline the amnesty was the Groupe salafiste pour la prédication et le combat (GSPC), a dissident wing of the GIA, formed in 1998, which subsequently affiliated with Al-Qaeda to form Al-Qaeda in the Islamic Maghreb (AQMI). The 2006 Charter expanded the terms of the Civil Concord, granting immunity to combatants who gave up arms within six months of the decree, as long as they had not been implicated in extreme forms of violence such as rape, mass killings, or bombings. Those who were brought to trial were shielded from life imprisonment and the death penalty, while many who had already been tried had their sentences reduced.

30 The fine is set at 250,000–500,000 dinars (roughly 2,500–5,000 US dollars). The UN Committee on Human Rights has called for the abrogation of article 46 of the National Charter on the grounds that it violates freedom of speech and Algerians' right to pursue enquires into the circumstances in which atrocities were committed.

31 'Est puni d'un emprisonnement de trois ans à cinq ans et d'une amende de 250.000 DA à 500.000 DA, quiconque qui, par ses déclarations, écrits ou tout autre acte, utilise ou instrumentalise les blessures de la tragédie nationale, pour porter atteinte aux institutions de la République algérienne démocratique et populaire, fragiliser l'Etat, nuire à l'honorabilité de ses agents qui l'ont dignement servie, ou ternir l'image de l'Algérie sur le plan international', www.interieur.gov.dz/Dynamics/frmItem.aspx?html=1&s=3.

In a remarkable rhetorical contortion, the pathos of tragedy is deployed as a counterweight to potential criticism, while retrospection is denounced as the instrumentalization of the past. The crime of dwelling on the tragic past has not been widely prosecuted. Consistent with the broader workings of censorship in Algeria, the threat operates primarily as a form of discouragement from taking criticism too far. It was, however, the pretext for the banning of a seminar entitled 'For truth, peace and reconciliation' that family members of the 'disappeared' planned to hold in Algiers in 2007. The seminar was relocated to Brussels, where it took place amid calls for the revocation of the National Charter and its replacement with a national truth commission.[32]

Questions of amnesty, amnesia, and lack of closure with respect to the fate of the 'disappeared' form the narrative context of *The Penitent*, whose focal character, Rachid, is a former jihadist or *maquisard* who has taken the opportunity offered by the Civil Concord to leave his militia and return to the social mainstream. Rejected in his native village, he settles in Oran, a city where his past activities are unknown. With help from the police, who hope to use him as an informant, Rachid finds work in a café, yet his situation remains precarious, and he is on the lookout for a way out of Algeria. An occasion presents itself when he recognizes a local pharmacist as the father of a young girl who has been kidnapped and killed by his militia. In what amounts to a form of reverse blackmail, Rachid offers to show the pharmacist, Lakhdar, and his wife, Djamila, whose marriage has fallen apart as a result of the tragedy, where their daughter is buried. In return, they will pay him and he will have a chance to escape.

This plot line channels several themes of post-1990s discourse, notably the combat waged by families of the 'disappeared' to discover what happened to their loved ones. It also picks up on anecdotes and rumours that appear intermittently in the Algerian press, including disgruntled claims that former militia members have profited from the amnesty, using government handouts to start small businesses. Allouache often works from news stories that he develops as fictions. In the case of *The Penitent*, the storyline was apparently inspired by a letter that a bereaved and outraged father sent to a newspaper in 1998.[33] The depiction of Rachid as a blackmailer who seems less concerneed with atoning for whatever misdeeds he has committed than with capitalizing on them to secure a better future is broadly consistent with Allouache's earlier films, particularly *Bab el oued City* (1993), a critical portrait of the rise of the FIS in a working-class

32 See Adlène Meddi, 'Projet pour une Commission pour la vérité, la paix et la conciliation', *El Watan*, 20 March 2007.

33 In an interview with the magazine *Jeune Afrique*, Allouache explains that he 'rework(s) as fictions stories that have a factual basis, that have been reported to me, that I've seen' (11 May 2015). In an interview with *Le Monde*, he says that *Le repenti* was inspired by a letter from a bereaved father that he read in an Algerian newspaper in 1999: www.lemonde.fr/festival-de cannes/video/2012/05/24/merzak-allouache-je-suis-contre-l-amnesie_1706920_766360.html.

neighborhood of Algiers.[34] But while the term 'penitent' is clearly being used ironically, I don't think that the film's main concern lies in showing that immunity doesn't signify remorse.[35]

Rachid's efforts to silence his past, or more precisely to manipulate it to his advantage, emblematize the wider context of post-1990s Algeria: a situation in which the official policy of amnesty has supported a self-serving but ultimately destructive amnesia. In this respect, the film is less an examination of the unpunished guilt of an ex-jihadist than an observation of the psychological and political implications of the repression of memory.[36] There is, of course, a big difference between the deliberate cultivation of amnesia at the level of the state and individual inability to remember and speak about a traumatic past. The film, however, establishes a deep connection between official policy and social dynamics, notably by highlighting the fact that many Algerians still don't know what happened to their loved ones. But if Allouache, like Yamina Bachir-Chouikh, approaches Algeria as a country afflicted with something akin to post-traumatic stress, the handling of this concept is quite different in the two films. Whereas in *Rachida* the examination of individual suffering largely eclipses the wider social and political context, *The Penitent* traces the effects of repression from the personal to the political.

The narrative revolves around the unreachable centre of a buried child whose death represents a rupture with the past and whose whereabouts remain unknown to her parents. It does not, however, progress towards the substitution of knowledge for ignorance. While the film makes a powerful case against the amnesia fostered by the political framework of amnesty, it steers clear of some of the assumptions that can accompany thinking about trauma, for example the idea that restored memory confers closure and lucidity with regard to the past. *The Penitent*, if anything, connects memory with opacity, rather than with clarity.

34 Since *Bab-el-oued* depicts Islamist politics as a blend of fanaticism and cynicism, Allouache would almost certainly have been assassinated had he not left Algeria for France in 1994.

35 In his 2000 film *L'Autre monde*, Allouache depicts the journey of Yasmine, a young French woman of Algerian origin, as she makes her way through Algeria in search of her fiancé, Rachid, navigating the perils of army roadblocks and terrorist ambushes. The film portrays Islamist guerrillas in a somewhat dichotomous way. Though, for the most part, they come off as homicidal gangsters, the story also includes a more sympathetic figure whose path to violence is explained as a reaction to the death of his brothers during the government's crackdown on protestors in October 1988. Though for various reasons the film narrative doesn't add up, *L'Autre monde* can be seen as a first attempt on Allouache's part to imagine the viewpoint of an Islamist while, at the same time, maintaining an overall disdain for the guerrillas.

36 Allouache has emphasized that he is not opposed to the amnesties, but rather to the amnesia that they have fostered. See his interview with *Le Monde*: www.lemonde.fr/festival-de-cannes/video/2012/05/24/merzak-allouache-je-suis-contre-l-amnesie_1706920_766360.html.

The selection of Rachid as focal character reflects this concern with the unknown/unknowable. Though we are given little reason to feel sympathy for the former *maquisard*, he is not portrayed as a monster either. 'There are lots of caricatures about Islamists, who are now often called jihadists', Allouache has observed. 'For me, these young people who joined the militias are not just caricatures. They are young people who could have been policemen or soldiers, who got caught up in the whirlwind of violence' (Interview with Jean-François Cadet, Radio France International, 4 December 2013). Rachid comes across as young and vulnerable, and at times we get a fleeting sense that he is remorseful for his (unspecified) actions, even as he tries to cash in on them. But perhaps more than anything else, he is opaque. Rather than trying to translate the 'mind of the terrorist', the film conveys a sense of the limits of any knowledge of the other. It does not, for example, clarify Rachid's relation to Islam. Though in one scene he is shown shaving his beard in order to avoid signalling his past affiliation, it is unclear whether he is or ever was a pious Muslim, or whether his relation to religion is more instrumental.

A patchwork of silences and ellipses in which almost nothing is spelled out, the film leaves us struggling to understand what's happening and how the various characters are connected to each other. For much of the story, communication between Rachid and Lahkdar occurs only through phone calls, and since we hear only one side of the conversation, the precise nature of their dealings remains unclear. This elliptical narrative evokes both the silence that weighs on the violence of the 1990s and the atomization of a traumatized society. As Thomas Sotinel eloquently summarizes in his review for *Le Monde*: 'This is a very dry film, formed from gaps in the narrative, silences, and roughly drawn gestures that nonetheless convey an unbearable sense of violence. The film exudes an almost total feeling of despair that is only exacerbated by its lucidity' (Sotinel, '"*Le Repenti*": un film sec . . .').

The intent of these readings is not to suggest that works that explore the suffering of victims always fall short of their oppositional aims, while those that take the less conventional step of imagining the viewpoint of perpetrators hit the mark. Rather, I'm arguing in a more general sense that depictions of violence in creative works frequently reinscribe significant elements of the situations that they seek to redress. Dichotomous constructions of victim and perpetraror, for example, tend to bracket the conditions in which the latter turned to violence, while depictions of suffering and trauma omit the thick description of the social and political context. In the case of Algeria, where the state has clearly expended a significant effort to frame conflict to its own advantage, the need for critical reflection is particularly great. In this context in which amnesty has betokened amnesia and the defense of the rights of one group has been used to sanction the violation of those of others, what I have described as a poetics of opacity may be the best recourse.

Works cited

Ailat, Fairid. 'Algérie après le Jihad', *Jeune Afrique*, 10 Mar. 2014.

Allouache, Merzak. Interview with *Le Monde*. Web. <www.lemonde.fr/festival-de-cannes/video/2012/05/24/merzak-allouache-je-suis-contre-l-amnesie_1706920_766360.html>.

Bachi, Salim. *Tuez les tous*. Paris: Gallimard, 2006. Print.

——. *Moi, Khaled Kelkal*. Paris: Grasset, 2012. Print.

Balhi, Mohamed. *Tibhirine, l'enlèvement des moines*. Lebanon: Dar El Farabi, 2002. Print.

Boudjedra, Rachid. *FIS de la haine*. Paris: Gallimard, 1994. Print.

Butler, Judith. *Frames of War. When Is Life Grievable?* London: Verso, 2010. Print.

Cadet, Jean-Louis. Interview with Merzak Allouache, *Radio France International*, 4 December 2013. Web. <www.rfi.fr/afrique/20130412-le-repenti-merzak-allouache-filme-contre-amnesie-algerie/>.

Charrad, Mounira M. *States and Women's Rights: The Making of Postcolonial Tunisia, Algeria, and Morocco*. Berkeley: University of California Press, 2002. Print.

Clausewitz, Carl Philipp Gottlieb von. *On War*. 1832. London: C. Hurst, 2015. Print.

Derrida, Jacques. *Cosmopolites de tous les pays, encore un effort!* Paris: Galilée, 1997. Print.

Derwahl, Freddy and Bruno Zanzoterra. *The Last Monk of Tibhirine: A True Story of Martyrdom, Faith, and Survival*. Brewster: Paraclete Press, 2013. Print.

Duteil, Mireille. *Les Martyrs de Tibhirine*, Paris: Brepols, 1996. Print.

Fassin, Didier and Richard Rechtman. *The Empire of Trauma: An Inquiry into the Condition of Victimhood*. Princeton: Princeton University Press, 2009. Print.

Filiu, Jean-Pierre. *From Deep State to Islamic State: The Arab Counter-Revolution and Its Jihadi Legacy*. London: C. Hurst, 2015. Print.

Glissant, Édouard. *The Poetics of Opacity*. Trans. Betsy Wing. Ann Arbor: University of Michigan Press, 1997. Print.

Guitton, René. *Si nous nous taisons . . . Le martyre des moines de Tibhirine*. Paris: Calmann-Lévy, 2001.

Henning, Christophe. *Petite vie des moines de Tibhirine*. Paris: Desclée de Brouwer, 2006. Print.

Khadra, Yasmina. *L'Attentat*. Paris: Julliard, 2005. Trans. John Cullen as *The Attack*. New York: Anchor, 2007. Print.

——. *A quoi rêvent les loups?* Paris: Pocket. 1999. Trans. Linda Black as *Wolf Dreams*. New Milford: The Toby Press, 2007. Print.

Khiari, Wahiba. *Nos silences*. Tunis: Elyzad, 2009. Print.

Kiser, John. *The Monks of Tibhirine: Faith, Love, and Terror in Algeria*. London: St. Martin's Press, 2002. Print.

Koraïchi, Rachid, ed. *Les Sept dormants*. Arles: Actes sud, 2004. Print.

Lassausse, Jean-Marie and Christophe Henning. *Le jardinier de Tibhirine*. Paris: Bayard, 2010. Print.

Lazreg, Marnia. *The Eloquence of Silence: Algerian Women in Question*. New York: Routledge, 1994. Print.

Lebreton, Christophe. *Born from the Gaze of God: The Tibhirine Journal of a Martyr Monk (1993–1996)*. Trans. Mette Louise Nygard and Edith Scholl. Collegeville: Cistercian Publications, 2014. Print.

Meddi, Adlène. 'Projet pour une Commission pour la vérité, la paix et la conciliation', *El Watan*, 20 Mar. 2007.

Mellal, Arezki. *Maintenant ils peuvent venir*. Arles: Actes Sud, 2002. Print.

Mokkedem, Malika. *L'Interdite*. Paris: Grasset, 1993. Trans. K. Melissa Marcus as *The Forbidden Woman*. Lincoln: University of Nebraska Press, 1998. Print.

——. *Des rêves et des assassins.* Paris: Grasset, 2000. Trans. K. Melissa Marcus as *Of Dreams and Assassins.* Charlottesville: University of Virginia Press, 2000. Print.

Mouffok, Ghania. 'Les Femmes algériennes dans la presse écrite. Entre conscient et inconscient, petite revue de détail'. *L'Image de la femme au Maghreb.* Ed. Khadija Mohesn-Finan. Algiers: Barzakh & Arles: Actes Sud, 2008. 71–98. Print.

Moyn, Samuel. *The Last Utopia: Human Rights in History.* Cambridge: Harvard University Press, 2010. Print.

Nasroullah, Yous. *Qui a tué à Bentalha?* Paris: La Découverte, 2000. Print.

Nezzar, Khaled. 'Un procès pour la vérité' [A Trial for Truth]. *Le procès de la sale guerre* [The Dirty War on Trial]. Algiers: Éditions Anep, 2002. Print.

Oumli, Youssef. *Fantôme: quatre ans de maquis.* Algiers: Union des écrivains, 2009. Print.

Quinson, Henry. *Secret des hommes, secret des dieux.* Paris: Presses de la Renaissance, 2011. Print.

Rivoire, Jean-Baptiste. *Le crime de Tibhirine: Révélation sur les responsables.* Paris: La Découverte, 2011. Print.

Roberts, Hugh. *The Battlefield: Algeria 1988–2002, Studies in a Broken Polity.* London: Verso, 2003. Print.

Salenson, Christian. *Christian de Cherge: A Theology of Hope.* Trans. Nadia Conic. Collegeville: Cistercian Publications, 2012. Print.

Sotinel, Thomas. '"*Le Repenti*": un film sec et violent sur la guerre civile algérienne'. *Le Monde,* 4 Sept. 2013. Print.

Souaïdia, Habib. *La sale guerre: 1992–2000.* Paris: La Découverte, 2001. Print.

Chapter 8

On Gothic romance and the happy ending

Legislating the human rights of transnational migrant workers and their families

Gale Coskan-Johnson

> In the postcolonial context of a constant flux of peoples, affiliation with the nation-state becomes highly partial and contingent.
>
> (Shohat 195)

We are on a tomato farm in Leamington, Ontario. Representatives of the Mexican consulate have been called to the farm to address some 'trouble' with Mexican workers employed on the farm. A supervisor, a young Canadian man in a T-shirt and with rumpled hair, explains, 'last weekend we had a problem where four guys got really drunk. Um, they came back around four or five o'clock in the morning, ah, they caused a little bit of trouble here, did a little bit of damage'. One consulate representative, a youngish man in a neat button-down shirt, takes notes as he listens to the complaint. Another, an older man in a suit, nods intently. Both men are serious, and their behaviour is formal in front of the camera. The supervisor adds, grudgingly, 'mnn, basically, I know, I know they're human, and they're gonna do this, but, like where do you . . . , where do you draw the line, you know?' Through the camera lens, viewers (and evidently the consulate representatives) do not learn the specifics of the complaint – some workers got drunk, they caused a 'little bit of trouble', and they did 'a little bit of damage'. The supervisor calls the workers in from the greenhouses to gather inside a warehouse so that the consulate representatives can speak to them. The workers are in jeans, shorts, and baseball caps. Their respective clothing marks a deep division between the two groups of Mexican nationals. The consulate representative explains, '[the boss] would like some moderation with alcohol'. A second representative, perhaps attempting to bridge the class division with the inclusive language of a national imaginary, adds: 'Look, we're all far from our country. Each one of us is an ambassador of the country. Because they will judge all of us. "How are the Mexicans?" "Well, I know one and he's this and that"'.

The first representative then asks, 'What do you think?' and the second adds, 'If you don't agree, say so'. The camera focuses in closely on the unsmiling faces of the workers as they are being chastised, and it lingers over the group as the workers begin to list some troubles of their own. The first one says,

'The . . . the . . . about the doctor. We need for them to see us when we need it.' Another adds, 'There was a guy . . . and his foot got infected from the chemicals.' The consulate representatives shift and nod uncomfortably. A third worker asserts, 'We've heard of workers who've had accidents, and the boss sends them back to Mexico.' The faces of the workers are intent. Finally, with a question that seems to break the rising tension, one of the workers says, 'We'd also like to see a more organized kitchen. Like, we don't have chairs.'

This chapter asks how subjects might negotiate human rights in a context of work in which one's supervisor might only grudgingly admit that one is 'human'. In order to investigate the relationship between transnational migrant workers and international legislation that aims to protect their rights, I critically examine the (2003) United Nations International Convention Protecting the Human Rights of Transnational Migrant Workers and their Families (CMW).[1] I work to scrutinize the gap that exists between migrant workers (such as those who articulate their interests in the scene above) and representatives of nation states (such as those who chastise the workers' alcohol consumption in the scene above). It is, at least, ironic that a body composed of a collection of nation states is made responsible, through the CMW, for producing a piece of international legislation that aims to protect the rights of transnational migrant workers from the dangers posed by nation states. Of course, this state of affairs is so deeply and historically normalized as to appear obvious to most contemporary observers. Democratic theory teaches us that 'the problem of democratic theory is how to find the right match between a people and its law, a state and its institutions' (Honig 109) – in this case, perhaps, the match is between transnational migrant workers and institutions of international law. Many scholars have determined that the CMW has failed, and they present various arguments about why it failed, and how it might have succeeded (Hennebry; Pécoud; Ruhs; Vucetic). I propose a way of reading the CMW and the scholarship that surrounds it by taking a rhetorical perspective and moving beyond the question of whether or not this is a *successful* piece of international legislation. The strength of a rhetorical perspective, at this point and in this case, is that it is less concerned with judging the success or failure of a text – a decision necessarily (and interestingly) bound up in the subject position from which the judgment is made. Rather, my reading is interested in questions of what this text might *do* in the world, how it is situated as a text, and how it participates at the level of discourse, irrespective of its perceived or authorized desires.

The working group that produced the CMW in the UN Assembly included state delegates from both immigrant-sending and immigrant-receiving nations. The CMW makes certain that it is not necessary or desirable for migrants to

1 The CMW is referred to as the ICMW in some quoted material. In my own work, I use CMW exclusively.

mobilize and demand their rights. It establishes, rather, that the mechanism of the state-to-state system will appropriate migrant agency and mobilize for them. However, while the CMW might have been put to work to normalize state desires, I would argue that it also, like any widely circulated text, enters discourse 'much like a virus' (Edbauer 13), produces novel links, and has the ability to make common cause with unintended audiences, like actual migrant workers. From within the logics of the treaty as a legal document, the particularity of any one migrant worker's story would endanger the orderly structures of its measured discourse. However, while the treaty presents a reductive image of the migrant worker, it also puts on a performance that makes visible the desires and anxieties of contemporary nation states – it is a textual space in which states publicly commit to their desires and their material aims. In other words, when read from a rhetorical perspective, the CMW makes visible the desires of contemporary nation states who seek advantage in a neo-liberal global economic system. Readers learn about what states want from each other in managing an increasingly globalized workforce. Because the CMW exists (given that it might easily not have), it makes discursive interventions in spite of itself, it circulates in unexpected digital space, and it joins the struggle to shape transnational immigration discourses. If the CMW 'is significantly constrained by its overriding commitment to the norms and structures of sovereign statehood' (Bosniak 737), I would ask how it might be read against that grain by audiences that were never targeted by it. I explore the extent to which unintended audiences might learn something useful from the CMW and the scholarship that surrounds it, about ways that the 'international community' imagines itself and its others.

Exploring context: writing and reading the CMW

The idea to produce a convention that aimed to protect transnational migrant workers is attributed to Mexico and Morocco shortly after the International Labour Organization (ILO) adopted the Convention Concerning Migrations in Abusive Conditions and the Promotion of Equality of Opportunity and Treatment of Migrant Workers in 1975 (Pécoud 336). The process leading to the CMW also followed 'lurid reports of abuses against North African immigrants in Europe' (Lyon 406). Pécoud suggests 'these countries were reluctant to leave the issue to the ILO because of its tripartite organization, which, for many governments, grants unions too important a role' (336). In other words, immigrant-sending states sought a treaty to protect migrant workers from extreme forms of abuse, but they sought to do so in a context that would pre-empt the possibility that workers would organize to protect themselves. Mexico and Morocco joined together with other members of a block of states called the Group of Seventy-Seven (G77), including Algeria, Barbados, Egypt, Mexico, Pakistan, Turkey, Yugoslavia, India, and Morocco (Bicocchi 1). Seven states from G77 produced a first draft of the convention (Ruhs, 'The Human Rights of Migrant Workers' 1283).

UNESCO's 'Information Kit: The United Nations Convention on Migrants' Rights' explains that the CMW was 'the outcome of a long process' (8). Delegates from about half of all nation state members of the UN formed the core of the collaborative working group that met over 10 years, each June and October, from 1980 to 1990. The idea for a convention was conceived in 1975, the working group was convened in 1980, and the committee completed the final draft in 1990. At that point, the text was open to ratification by member states, and it took over 10 years to acquire the 20 signatures the Convention required to 'enter into force', which happened in 2003. Today, over 12 years after coming into force, 25 years after being completed, and 35 years after being initiated, the CMW has less than 50 signatures, none of which include a major, wealthy, immigrant-receiving state.[2] Thus, the CMW is 'the least ratified convention among all the major international human rights treaties' (Ruhs, 'The Rights' 1). 'Reportedly', Italy was 'on the verge of signing the ICMW before it was pressurized by other migrant-receiving democracies to do otherwise' (Vucetic 421). Vucetic's loosely cited international community gossip may not be definitive, but it does suggest that 'migrant-receiving democracies' may fear the potential of the CMW to exert or disrupt normalizing pressures, and they may be willing to act on those fears.

A mix of hopefulness and scepticism characterized early responses to the CMW. Lönnroth, delegate from Finland and eventual vice chair of the working group, concludes, 'with all its deficiencies and complexities, the Convention is a major achievement' (734). He insists, perhaps presciently, 'Irrespective of the number of ratifications, the Convention will become a standard norm among the major human rights instruments' (743). Ansay examines the CMW from the perspective of Turkey as a country of origin and Germany as a country of destination, and is particularly concerned by the vagaries of state-based legislation, as evidenced by the experience of Turkish migrant workers in Germany. He views international legislation, or 'world public opinion' (844), as an arena in which such vagaries might be avoided, and he argues, 'the solution should therefore correctly be found outside the involved states; that is, in supranational regulations' (852). Ansay is optimistic when he describes the preparation of the CMW as 'a very encouraging development', and he concludes by saying, 'in spite of its shortcoming, one should hope that the present Convention document will be signed and ratified by the majority of the labor-receiving states, including the Republic of Germany' (831). What Ansay appears to avoid confronting are the state-to-state relations that characterize international legislation at the UN – that it is generally accepted that delegates in the assembly represent their states' interests rather than those of a transnational 'public'. Linda Bosniak echoes Ansay and Lönnroth when she describes the CMW as 'the most-

2 Forty-seven largely migrant-sending nations had signed by September 2013 (Hennebry 374).

ambitious statement to date of international concern for the problematic condition of undocumented migrants' (740). However, in recognition of the state-to-state relations that Ansay ignores, she argues, 'its provision protecting states' sovereign prerogatives to control immigration will often effectively undermine or defeat the rights it provides to those migrants' (759). What each of these scholars has in common is their interest in exploring the question of whether or not the CMW will successfully mediate relations between transnational migrant workers and the international community. Ansay and Lönnroth are guardedly optimistic about the effect the Convention will have on the human rights of transnational migrant workers, while Bosniak's analysis is more bleak, and she suspects that such desirable effects will be defeated by the interests of state sovereignty.

Echoing early observers, Antoine Pécoud recognized, in 2012, that the CMW 'is the most comprehensive international human rights treaty in the field of migration' (333). He claims that migrant-sending nations 'view the Convention as part of a strategy to protect their emigrants' (338); however, he also points out that 'the convention is largely ignored' by global actors, such as the EU, working under the 'migration management umbrella' (344). Martin Ruhs of the Centre on Migration, Policy and Society (COMPAS) concedes, 'the CMW in particular has become a cornerstone of the right-based approach to migration advocated by many international organizations and non-governmental organizations (NGOs) concerned with the protection of migrant workers' ('The Human Rights of Migrant Workers' 1279), yet, with his title, 'The Human Rights of Migrant Workers: Why Do So Few Countries Care?', he makes it clear that this cornerstone does not have the support of receiving-state actors. There is some consensus, then, that the treaty works to protect the rights of transnational migrant workers. However, since no wealthy, immigrant-receiving state has signed the CMW, the countries that are centrally responsible for the conditions of the highest number of migrant workers do not participate in any systematic way in the rights that the treaty extends to them. Hence, the assumption that warrants most arguments about the success or failure of the CMW is that the 'international community', as a collection of nation states, ought to understand, and possibly fix, what went wrong with the treaty, so that they can get it right. In other words, the human rights of transnational migrant workers lie in the hands of collective state entities.

Ideological assumptions about state-to-state relations that circulated among delegates throughout the drafting of the CMW also emerge in scholarship. For example, Lönnroth describes the initial G77 draft version of the convention as 'political', and as a draft 'marked by an antagonism between sending (mostly developing) and receiving (mostly industrialized Western) countries' (718). He reports, 'some delegates even expressed the hypothesis' that the G77 draft:

> was an effort to focus the world's attention on the 'discriminatory' policies in some industrial states (notably Germany, France and the United States)

> in order to have them politically condemned at the UN rather than a serious effort to create a well-functioning human rights instrument.
>
> (718)

Evidently, Lönnroth does not imagine that 'some delegates' might have similarly 'political' reasons for attacking the draft, and neither does he consider, based on evidence, whether or not an attack might have been warranted as a rational strategy produced in response to an unjust situation. He tellingly mentions, 'there was a rather widespread belief that the United States would not sign and ratify the Convention in the immediate future' even though 'their delegation participated actively in the deliberations' (734). This active US participation is characterized as a chaste US desire 'to prevent the instrument from becoming a mere political device' (734). Granted, Lönnroth does begin his article by avowing his personal writerly position as a participating delegate reflecting upon his own experience. He says, 'I recognize that my approach is essentially European, more specifically Nordic', and that 'the truth offered is, therefore, only one of many possible' (713). Given the reflective nature of this piece of writing, personal impressions or even gossip about other delegations are not necessarily out of place. However, Lönnroth's carefully qualified, if profoundly Eurocentric, claims are taken up by other scholars who are less careful.

For example, Lönnroth repeats the claim cited above later in his article, again with hedging, when he writes, 'As previously mentioned, *there may also have been* a political interest among delegations of Group 77 to use the negotiations and the draft Convention as an instrument to achieve a moral condemnation of some of the states of employment' (732, my emphasis). Lönnroth's reflections are picked up by Vucetic in 2007, who transforms the qualified claim into the straightforward declaration that 'This block [G77] *wanted to use* "the negotiations and the drafting of the IMCW as a tool to condemn some states of employment and their discriminatory use of migrant labour"' (418, my emphasis). Vucetic then characterizes the CMW as having been written 'by developing states, for developing states' (418), and he claims, 'the numerically superior G-77 dominated the negotiation process' (418), which is a claim that is not supported by Lönnroth, whom Vucetic evidently relies on to describe the proceedings of the CMW. In fact, Vucetic feels so strongly about pushing his point that he takes quotes from Lönnroth out of context. He writes that the deliberative proceedings of the CMW were 'marked by "mistrust and hostility"' (418), evidently as a result of irrational and disruptive G77 politics. However, Lönnroth's actual claim was that the effect of 'time' on the negotiations was that 'it enabled the group to develop from a state of antagonism and mistrust – which characterized the first years – into a state of consensus in the end' (715). Vucetic's position resurfaces in Ruhs in 2012. Ruhs repeats Vucetic's description of the CMW as a Convention written 'by developing states, for developing states' ('The Human Rights of Migrant Workers' 1285). However, what Vucetic had left out, and Ruhs leaves as an aside, is that the G77 draft was rejected early in the proceedings by other members of the working group, and it was replaced by a draft produced by the MESCA Group (Finland, Greece, Italy, Norway, Portugal, Spain, Sweden, and France), which became 'the basis of negotiations' (Lönnroth 715). In other words, the CMW was not produced from a draft by the G77; rather, it was produced from a draft written by the MESCA group. While it stands as the product of a long and complex deliberative process, the CMW is a European product as much as anything. Literature that examines the CMW suggests that: (1) state-to-state relations are privileged over the human rights of migrant workers; and (2) in general, immigrant-receiving states (the Global North) are viewed as rational actors while sending states (the Global South) are depicted as emotional, vindictive, and 'political'.

Min Sook Lee's documentary *El Contrato*, a scene of which is depicted at the beginning of this chapter, does a different kind of work than the scholarship I have examined above. Though it never mentions the CMW, it materializes the structures that shape relations between transnational migrant workers and the nation states to which they are linked, both sending and receiving. In this documentary, cameras follow a group of Mexican migrant workers through a season picking tomatoes in Leamington, Ontario. These Temporary Foreign Workers (TFWs) are evidently present and working inside Canada as part of the Seasonal Agricultural Worker Program (SAWP), which 'operates according to bilateral agreements between Canada and the participating countries' ('Hiring Seasonal'). Mexico has signed the CMW and Canada has not. Hennebry points out that Canada is among the countries that 'some might argue . . . already provide adequate protection to migrants within their borders' (Hennebry 375). Canada 'is often pointed to as a best practice model on labour migration management' (Hennebry 376). Hennebry's analysis of the Canadian SAWP system finds, however, that 'despite the vital contributions that migrant workers make to the economies of their host and home countries, they are among the most excluded from even basic social protection coverage', and 'within such programs, control over workers' daily lives is nearly complete' (371). *El Contrato*, then, substantiates Hennebry's contention that even the best state-to-state policies fail to provide basic rights, protection, or avenues through which workers can exert agency over their material conditions.

Much like the migrant workers who appear in the scene from *El Contrato* described at the beginning of this chapter, Hennebry concludes that workers 'are left feeling unprotected and angry' (378). What is more, at the end of that scene, *El Contrato*'s narrator adds, 'the Council General's visit to Leamington is not wasted'. The representatives 'attend a meeting with a group of farmers to discuss investment options in Mexico'. Before the camera turns away, the farmer says, 'We have some fairly serious links with Mexico, and as you know we have Mexican workers, so we need the support and the linkage'. To which the Mexican consulate replies, 'That's what globalization's all about'. In the careful juxtaposition that organizes this series of frames, Lee's documentary complicates the position that sending countries have signed the CMW, because it is a 'strategy to protect their emigrants' (Pécoud 338). It also illuminates Ansay's claim that 'it is doubtful that the interests of the sending states regularly coincide with the interests of migrant workers' (832). The Mexican consulate representatives, in this case, exhibit little interest in the substance or complexity of the Mexican workers' complaints in Leamington, and instead they make a veiled threat ('you have to evaluate if it is worth you to come') that alludes to the precarity of the lived experiences of these TFWs, these transnational migrant workers for whom 'clandestine migration fits into the picture of neoliberalism, privatization, and the proliferation of insecure jobs' (Karakayali and Rigo 131). What I have attempted to make clear so far is that the purpose of the CMW to organize state-to-state relations appears to take precedence over its stated aims to mobilize an international community to protect the human rights of transnational migrant workers and their families. In the following section, I turn to the text of the CMW.

A rhetorical reading of the CMW

From my position as a scholar of cultural rhetoric, committed to the decolonizing project of transnational feminism, I am interested in what this carefully controlled piece of international legislation *does*, as a (hegemonic) text, given its entrance into discourse *like a virus*, and its potentially unruly participation in rhetorics of sovereignty and transnational mobility. In other words, signed or not signed, binding or not binding, this text has entered the field, and it takes up and thus performs the desires and the conflicting interests of the nation states that spent 10 years producing it. As a collective textual performance of state sovereignty by UN member states, the CMW constructs transnational migrant workers as victims in need of rescue, and it poses states as prepared to rescue them. Of course, neither transnational migrant workers nor their advocates have been waiting for the 'international community' or supranational institutions to solve the problem of human rights in labour mobility. We can point to activism such as *No One Is Illegal* in Canada (see 'No One Is Illegal'), The Day Without Immigrants protests in the US (see Glaister and MacAskill), and migrant worker strikes in France (see Wirsig). It is in solidarity with such activism and protest that I write this chapter. In effect, I offer a decolonizing reading of the CMW in the genre from which Honig urges citizens to read the nation state – as a female Gothic novel, in which the hero is an undecidable figure that may protect the heroine in one minute and in the next be poised to cut her throat. In other words, while the CMW certainly works to produce a legal framework to protect the human rights of transnational migrant workers and their families, at the same time it couches that framework in rhetorics of sovereign power that reify state-to-state relations, and thus positions the interests of states over and above the human right of transnational migrant workers and their families.

In *Democracy and the Foreigner*, Bonnie Honig explains that 'implicated in violences that could delegitimate them', democratic regimes seek a 'happy ending'. They 'may risk their democratic power in order to restore or preserve its innocence' (108). To this end, they tell 'stories about themselves in which a scapegoat-like foreign-founder takes the people's violence upon himself' (108). Honig demonstrates the persistence of this frame in popular culture (*Shane*, *Dirty Dancing*, and *The Wizard of Oz*) and in classical political theory (Hobbes, Freud, and Rousseau). She claims that '*how should we solve the problem of foreignness?*' is a question that 'has dominated political theory for centuries' (1, original emphasis). She inverts that question and asks, instead, '*What problems does foreignness solve for us?*' (4, original emphasis). Scholarship around the CMW repeatedly asks how the convention could solve (or fail to solve) the problem of the transnational migrant worker (a foreigner wherever he or she goes). I ask, instead, what work the figure of the migrant worker does in and through this text for the state-parties involved. To what extent does this international legislation bring into being a transnational imaginary that preserves what is often perceived today as a waning sovereignty?

The CMW is, at least in its inception, a print text, and as a legal document its ethos relies on the fixity and unchangeableness of its language and its identity as a legal document; to alter its language is to invalidate its claims to legitimacy in the context of international law. Hence, the signatures and stamps in the back matter of each treaty, which lists the languages in which the Convention is 'official', carry performative weight. A UN Convention can be altered by state parties only by initiating a bureaucratic, deliberative process, which is slow and laborious, and which produces additional protocols, amendments, or reservations, which are in turn made official through signatures, ratifications, and stamps. The authoritative ethos of an international treaty depends on this very resistance to change over time. In fact, only an 'official' hard copy that includes stamps and signatures fully performs the document's function, as a proper speech act in its original official context.

From within an awareness of the importance of stability to convention discourse, then, I make three key moves that work to disrupt the fixity of this text: (1) I examine ways that the Convention begins by building a sense of its intertextual links to international institutions and documents, and I demonstrate that the CMW is even more extensively and unpredictably networked; (2) I describe how the CMW defines the problem of transnational migration, and how it solves the problem by producing a circular, ahistorical frame around transnational mobility; and (3) I interrogate a series of three binaries or lexical pairs that circulate in the CMW: (a) home/away; (b) family/nation; and (c) regular/irregular. I suggest that the first two pairs work to remove agency from the migrant in order to construct an international imaginary of harmonious cooperation between beneficent state parties. However, the third pair works quite differently.

The CMW is composed of a preamble and 93 articles divided into nine parts. The bulk of the convention, including Parts III and IV, outlines specific rights. Part III includes rights granted to all migrant workers and their families while Part IV outlines rights reserved for workers in a 'regular situation'. The Preamble of the CMW mobilizes a self-reflexive and controlled intertextuality that places the text within a network of other UN and ILO treaties. It lists six UN instruments, seven ILO instruments, and it alludes to four additional treaties on torture, crime, and slavery. It 'recalls' the objectives of the ILO, 'recognizes' work done on migrant workers in more than five of the 'various organs' of the UN, and it recognizes 'regional and bilateral' progress made to protect workers. The preamble, in this way, invokes an intertextual international community that stands behind the convention and grants it credibility. This ethos suggests that the CMW is simply the continuation of previous, widely accepted work on human rights.

However, I would suggest that in order to make sense of the profoundly embedded and networked nature of the CMW, one might need to make use of 'a model of public rhetoric that sets its sights across a wider social field of distribution' (Edbauer 13). In 'Transnational Feminist Rhetorics in a Digital World', Mary Queen uses the term *global fields of rhetorical action* in order to account for the 'cyberspaces through which an element (images, words, texts, websites, etc.) passes as it circulates' (474). She makes a distinction between print and digital texts by stating, 'it seems illogical as well as ineffective to analyse electronic texts as static artifacts'. While I suggest that it is equally illogical to treat a print text as static, I agree that a written text is necessarily transformed beyond the physical and discursive limits of its deliberative and bureaucratic locations by its move into cyberspace. The full title of the CMW in a Google search today calls up over 200,000 sites ('Google'). A cursory examination reveals that the list includes sites internal to the UN, international human rights organizations, local human rights organizations, regional organizations, local news publications, immigrant support organizations, unions, NGOs, and weblogs. While there is not enough space in this chapter to fully analyse the digital circulation of the CMW, it is clear that this UN Multilateral Convention currently finds itself in novel and surprising virtual spaces, and so it is open to discovery by wide-ranging audiences. There is an element of serendipity here – because it is so heavily hyperlinked, the text of the CMW can be discovered, encountered, and appropriated by readers who are neither looking for it nor versed in UN multilateral treaty protocol. Thus, such readings may produce unruly and surprising encounters with this text. Though no immigrant-receiving states have signed the CMW, and, as Vucetic suggests, some may have even pressured states such as Italy to refrain from signing, the text is clearly circulating widely in public discourses that cannot be contained by the bureaucracy of a self-styled 'international community'. In other words, immigrant-receiving states may wish to control the circulation of the CMW by exerting state-to-state pressures;

however, the CMW is already circulating beyond those networks, and so it is already having an impact, in the very least, at the level of discourse.

When readers come to the text of the CMW, what might they find? The CMW works to bring order to the disorder that characterizes transnational immigration by placing it into a reductive circular frame and by describing the 'problem' of migration in abstract terms as 'flows of migrant workers'. The Preamble states:

> Aware of the impact of the flows of migrant workers on States and people concerned, and desiring to establish norms which may contribute to the harmonization of the attitudes of States through the acceptance of basic principles concerning the treatment of migrant workers and members of their families.

The cause of the problem of transnational labour is attributed to 'flows of migrant workers', such that the worker, the person whose perceived lack of human rights inspired the Convention and who is the object of the treaty, is submerged by these flows. The migrant worker is not introduced as an agent here. The problem in the text of the CMW is not that workers are caught up in particular political and economic systems that proliferate precarity, but rather that the flow of migrants acts as an agent that puts pressure on states. States then act to defend themselves against these flows. Constructing the migrant as agentless is important within the logics of this treaty, because once the migrant is removed from a position of responsibility as an actor, his or her disruptive historical particularity can be replaced by a figure of speech. The solution, then, is to 'establish norms' that will bring state 'attitudes' into 'harmonization' by persuading them to accept 'basic principles'. In other words, a framework of basic principles shared between states will lead states into a normative *harmony*. This harmony, it is assumed, will ensure the protection of the rights of migrant workers and their families even as they remain a homogenous group submerged by a flow. Thus, it would be a mistake to equate the scene of writing in the CMW to Honig's description of the classical model of democratic action. Rather than staging relations between transnational migrant workers and the institutions of an international community, the CMW involves states collaborating with other states to find their own inter-state *happy ending*.

The treaty positions the migrant, or the flows of migrants, in orderly paths when the Convention describes the migrant workers' trajectory. Part II, Article 1, describes the migration process in circular terms such that:

> the entire migration process of migrant workers and members of their families . . . comprises preparation for migration, departure, transit and the entire period of stay and remunerated activity in the State of employment as well as return to the State of origin or the State of habitual residence.

Mobility here is inscribed as a smooth circular path that marks the 'state of origin' as a stable point from which the migrant leaves and eventually returns. The migrant worker and his or her family are 'in a situation of vulnerability', specifically because of 'their absence from their State of origin' (Preamble). Thus, the treaty calls for the 'adoption of measures regarding the *orderly return* of migrant workers and members of their families *to the State of origin*' (my emphasis). It directs states to cooperate 'with a view to promoting adequate economic conditions for resettlement and to facilitate their durable social and cultural reintegration in the State of origin' (Part VI, Article 67). Rhetorically, then, this framework adheres to a geography that identifies *home* as safe and *away* as unsafe, and it explicitly establishes that home, or 'nation of origin', is a place of safety from which the migrant originates and to which the migrant will be, ideally, returned.

This circular frame produces a rhetorical fiction in which transnational migration, through international legislation, will be able to proceed in an orderly fashion in which workers in economically depressed areas of the globe will move smoothly into areas in need of employment until the need is filled, and then the workers will return to the safety of their state of origin. One might argue that this frame simply enacts a pragmatic truth, and that rights are simply more strongly protected inside one's own nation state. However, I would argue that in the context of transnational migration, our pragmatic truths are the ones most in need of rethinking. Two interesting implications of this position that might give us pause are that, first, employers in the country of work (e.g. in the Global North) are released from 'the problem of the reproduction of labour power', given that 'labour is reproduced elsewhere [e.g. in the Global South]' (Mitchell 567). Second, and related, it suggests that migrant workers should enter receiving countries, give nothing but their labour and receive nothing but their wages, and that they will leave in the end without mixing socially, culturally, or biologically with those who claim that state as home through status citizenship.

In the text of the CMW, movement of the migrant body outside the state of origin precipitates a disorderliness that threatens culture and society and requires state-based measures to assure a return to stability. In this way, the convention embeds itself in a 'common sense' binary that has also worked, historically, to control women's free movement outside the home by invoking 'the street' as a dangerous place. Yet, it has also become common knowledge that the violence women face most often takes place inside the home, if not the college dormitory. Here, in the Convention to Protect the Transnational Migrant Worker and Their Family, the transnational migrant worker remains a body out of place, and he or she will be not be safe until he or she returns home, notwithstanding the economic precarity, the poverty, and the decimated welfare state that generally constitutes immigrant-sending states' responses to the demands of neo-liberal globalization.

To push this point further, the binary of home and away in the CMW maps onto a lexical pair, namely that of family/nation. As the title of this treaty suggests, the CMW asserts the primacy of family and attaches to it the quality of 'unity'.

The CMW's definition of family was evidently contentious during deliberations, but ultimately it was 'based on the nuclear family concept' (Lönnroth 730). Both family and nation of origin, then, are bound syntactically with the notions of flow, unity, and harmony. The preamble asserts that migration causes problems for workers because of the 'scattering' of the family. The scattering of the family is constructed in the CMW as a central cause of precarity. It is a problem for the family to be scattered because 'the family *is the natural and fundamental group unit of society* and is entitled to protection by society and the State' (Part IV, Article 44, Paragraph 1, my emphasis). In other words, in the same way that the family is safe, so is the 'state of origin', and similar to the danger caused by the scattering of the family, the 'state' as foreign place of employment is dangerous. In other words, states are safe for bodies that originate within them, as families are safe for the bodies that they originate. By juxtaposing the family as 'natural' alongside the mechanism of the state, the state is granted an organic quality.

Such a construction, especially given the words 'natural and fundamental', works to elide violent histories that underlie both institutions. Both acquire a romantic, heroic quality – to keep individuals together with both their familial and their national origins will bring us closer to a happy ending in the story about the universal protection of human rights. I would not suggest the opposite, that instead, states and families are *unnatural* or fundamentally hostile to their members. Returning to Honig's discussion of the Gothic romance, I would keep in mind that the Gothic romance does not offer happy endings; rather, it produces 'ambivalences' (111). The question is, what rhetorical work do the tropes of family and nation of origin do in the text of the CMW, and how might we read them Gothically? Honig explains:

> Gothic readers know that we may passionately support certain heroes (or principles or institutions) in political life while also knowing that we ought not take our eyes off them for fear of what they might do to us if we did. They know that one can be passionately attached to something – a nation, a people, a principle – and be deeply and justifiably (and even therefore!) afraid of it at the same time.
>
> (120)

The CMW offers the family and the nation of origin as institutions that 'we may passionately support', and it asks that readers view them as fundamental to the protection of the human rights of migrant workers and their families; however, there are many reasons to be deeply and justifiably afraid. In my own (Gothic?) reading of the CMW, I find that it works to simplify and reduce the plurality of the migrant worker's experience, and produce an apparatus of control by mobilizing romantic visions of the family and the state of origin; however, doesn't it also enact what is a vital and current global struggle over the criminalization of the immigrant who lacks status?

The CMW divides transnational migrant workers into two groups. The first group is 'documented or in a regular situation if they are authorized to enter, to stay and to engage in a remunerated activity' (Part I, Article 5.a). The second group is 'non-documented or in an irregular situation if they do not comply with the conditions provided for in subparagraph (a) (Part I, Article 5.b). The desire to include irregular migrants *and* not to name them 'illegal' was a major point of contention during the deliberative process between the G77 and the major immigrant-receiving states. This move is important, because it means that the CMW, at least, participates in the disruption of a process of normalization in which immigrants are increasingly criminalized in contemporary public discourses of the Global North. The rejection of 'illegal' resists national legislation that increasingly defines the irregular migrant as criminal in receiving nations such as the US, the EU, and Australia. The treaty plays a delicate game here in which it attempts to allay state fears by preserving a lexical structure that separates regular from irregular migrants: migrants in a 'regular situation' get more rights. Nevertheless, the discursive victory is profound in terms of what this text *does*. Bosniak lauds the inclusion of irregular migrants as bearers of rights in the CMW, but describes the treaty's treatment of irregular immigrants as 'deeply ambivalent' (741). The CMW is, ultimately, a 'staunch manifesto in support of state territorial sovereignty' (Bosniak 742). In other words, Bosniak's decidedly Gothic reading finds that the text is a fickle lover who includes irregular migrants in the Convention, but gives states the power to exclude them from their territories by asserting their sovereign prerogative. Vucetic insists that the inclusion of irregular workers was a 'fundamental deal breaker', that the G77 'ignored' receiving nations' concerns, and that 'at least four migrant-importing democracies – Australia, Germany, Japan, and the USA – implicitly stated that they were "unlikely to ratify" the convention because of the inclusion of "illegals" in the treaty language' (419). Thus, the term 'illegal' appears to have marked an intense struggle within the working group that parallels similar struggles in national discourses across the globe. The inclusion of 'irregular migrants' in the text of the CMW, and its refusal to adopt the term 'illegal', makes the text of the CMW available, perhaps in spite of itself, to activists who work to eradicate the criminalization of migrants across the globe.

Concluding thoughts

If we consider its framing, the CMW seems to be constructed to assuage the fears of states in a Eurocentric postcolonial context in which the direction of transnational migration is generally from 'south' to 'north' or one-third world to two-thirds world (Mohanty 227). It supports the development of circular migration programs such as that depicted in *El Contrato*; however, it also gives rights to such workers that are not included, for example, in the Canadian SAWP program (Hennebry). A contextualized reading of the CMW suggests the contemporary existence of an inter-state imaginary in which poor, racialized bodies enter wealthy nations in order to provide labour, but then return to their 'home' countries when the work is done, leaving the sociocultural context untouched. The performative power of the CMW as an official document depends, then, on physical and historical discursive structures to lend it legitimacy. It relies on a Western rational tradition that privileges binary thinking and that is deeply invested in rescue narrative structures in which the victim is agentless and irrational about his or her own situation. This structure invests state-parties with the power to save 'others' from victimization and, in doing so, it elides alternative histories of anti-capitalist, anti-imperialist struggle initiated by those others; for example, by migrant workers in Leamington who articulate their needs with intelligence and dignity to Mexican consulate representatives seemingly more motivated by the potential of Canadian foreign investment opportunities than human rights. The irony that is elided in this construction and by this discourse, in general, is that what the migrant worker is being protected from is the tendency of state-parties to withdraw rights from migrant workers. In other words, the international community is a place where the wolves protect the 'lambs'.

In another scene from *El Contrato*, the migrant workers sit on chairs in the kitchen and discuss their responses to the lecture they received from the consulate representatives. One worker says:

> It was very bad of the Consul to tell us that. I mean, we're looking for viable solutions, and all he says is: 'This is your wage, this is how they'll treat you, and if you like it great. And if not, then don't come'. And that is not a viable answer.

Another of the workers adds, 'Well, maybe a union would be good'. The workers in this scene, charged with fury as they clearly are, articulate their complaints with intelligence and dignity. They are keenly aware that the representatives of the Mexican consulate are not motivated to take their problems seriously, and they understand the precarity of their relations to their state of origin. As I have demonstrated, particular power relations structure scholarly descriptions of the working group of the CMW such that sending countries are depicted as rational actors making sensible demands while receiving states are depicted as making irrational, unreasonable, and 'political' demands. A similar frame works to structure the conversation between the Mexican consulate representatives and the migrant workers in *El Contrato*. The workers are drunkards, they break things, they need to be taught how to behave like proper Mexican ambassadors. However, the documentary facilitates the workers' disruption of that established pattern. The CMW reproduces an inter-state scene and organizes state-to-state relations. What is more, it does not, itself, recognize the agency of these workers or protect them from the precarious situation of current global economic and political policies and practices; however, having entered the discursive field, the Convention provides tools for transnational immigrants and their advocates to disrupt discourses that criminalize immigrants and normalize global inequalities.

Works cited

Ansay, Tugrul. 'The New UN Convention in Light of the German and Turkish Experience'. *International Migration Review* 25.4 (1991): 831–847. Print.

Bicocchi, Luca. 'Rights of All Migrant Workers (Part III of the Convention) Travaux Preparatoires'. Intern Report, Office of the High Commissioner of Human Rights (OHCHR), n.d. Web. 19 May 2016. <www2.ohchr.org/english/issues/migration/taskforce/docs/draftinghistoryrev1.doc>.

Bosniak, Linda S. 'Human Rights, State Sovereignty and the Protection of Undocumented Migrants under the International Migrant Workers Convention'. *International Migration Review* 25.4 (1991): 737–770. Print.

Edbauer, Jenny. 'Unframing Models of Public Distribution: From Rhetorical Situation to Rhetorical Ecologies'. *Rhetoric Society Quarterly* 35.4 (2005): 5–24. Print.

Glaister, Dan and Ewen MacAskill. 'US Counts Cost of Day without Immigrants'. *The Guardian* 2 May 2006. Web. 20 Apr. 2015. <www.theguardian.com/world/2006/may/02/usa.topstories3>.

'Google'. *Google.* 19 Apr. 2015. Web. 19 Apr. 2015. <www.google.ca/?gfe_rd=cr&ei=hhk0VciXFoeN8QecwIGoAg&gws_rd=ssl#q=International Convention Protecting the Human Rights of Transnational Migrant Workers and their Families&start=20>.

Hennebry, Jenna. 'Falling Through the Cracks? Migrant Workers and the Global Social Protection Floor'. *Global Social Policy* 14.3 (2014): 369–388. Print.

'Hiring Seasonal Agricultural Workers'. *Government of Canada, Employment and Social Development Canada.* 13 Mar. 2015. Web. 14 Apr. 2015. <www.esdc.gc.ca/eng/jobs/foreign_workers/agriculture/seasonal/index.shtml>.

Honig, Bonnie. *Democracy and the Foreigner.* Princeton/Oxford: Princeton University Press, 2001. Print.

'Information Kit: United Nations Convention on Migrants' Rights'. United Nations Education, Scientific and Cultural Organization (UNESCO). Paris, France. 2005. Print

Karakayali, Serhat and Enrico Rigo. 'Mapping the European Space of Circulation'. *The Deportation Regime: Sovereignty, Space, and the Freedom of Movement.* Ed. Nicholas Genova and Nathalie Peutz. Durham: Duke University Press, 2010. 123–144. Print.

Lönnroth, Juhani. 'The International Convention on the Rights of All Migrant Workers and Members of Their Families in the Context of International Migration Policies: An Analysis of Ten Years of Negotiation'. *International Migration Review* 25.4 (1991): 710–736. Print.

Lyon, Beth. 'The Unsigned United Nations Migrant Worker Rights Convention: An Overlooked Opportunity to Change the Brown Collar Migration Paradigm'. *School of Law Working Paper Series* 14 (2010): 1–500. Print.

Mitchell, Don. 'Work, Struggle, Death, and Geographies of Justice: The Transformation of Landscape in and beyond California's Imperial Valley'. *Landscape Research* 32.5 (2007): 559-577. Web.

Mohanty, Chandra Talpade. *Feminism without Borders: Decolonizing Theory, Practicing Solidarity.* Durham: Duke University Press, 2000. Print.

'No One Is Illegal' – Toronto. n.p. n.d. Web. 20 Apr. 2015. <http://toronto.nooneisillegal.org>

Pécoud, Antoine. 'The UN Convention on Migrant Workers' Rights and International Migration Management'. *Global Society* 23.3 (2009): 333–350. Print.

Queen, Mary. 'Transnational Feminist Rhetorics in a Digital World'. *College English* 70.5 (2008): 47–51. Print.

Ruhs, Martin. 'The Human Rights of Migrant Workers: Why Do So Few Countries Care?' *American Behavioral Scientist* 56.9 (2012): 1277–1293. Print.

Ruhs, Martin. 'The Rights of Migrant Workers: Reframing the Debate'. *The Price of Rights: Regulating International Labor Migration.* Princeton: Princeton University Press, 2013. 1–12. Print.

Shohat, Ella. 'Post-Third-Worldist Culture: Gender, Nation, and the Cinema'. *Feminist Genealogies, Colonial Legacies, Democratic Futures.* Ed. M. Jacquie Alexander and Chandra Talpade Mohanty. New York/London: Routledge, 1997. 183–209. Print.

Vucetic, Srdjan. 'Democracies and International Human Rights: Why Is There No Place for Migrant Workers?' *The International Journal of Human Rights* 11.4 (2007): 403–428. Print.

Wirsig, Karen. 'Workers without Status in France Emerge as a Social Force'. *Global Research.* 19 Oct. 2010. Web. 20 Apr. 2015. <www.globalresearch.ca/workers-without-status-in-france-emerge-as-a-social-force/21509>.

Chapter 9

Willful targets of rights[1]

Hanna Musiol

> Willfulness as a style of politics might involve not only being willing not to go with the flow, but being willing to cause its obstructions.
>
> (Ahmed)

> [When the active political process disappears,] rights appear actually empty. They seem to be of no use. And when they are of no use, you do the same as charitable persons do with their old clothes. You give them to the poor. Those rights that appear to be useless in their place are sent abroad, along with medicine and clothes, to people deprived of medicine, clothes, and rights. It is in this way, as the result of this process, that [they] become the rights of those who have no rights . . . They become humanitarian rights, the rights of those who cannot enact them, the victims of the absolute denial of right.
>
> (Rancière)

> When we say Black Lives Matter, we are broadening the conversation around state violence to include all of the ways in which Black people are intentionally left powerless at the hands of the state. We are talking about the ways in which Black lives are deprived of our basic human rights and dignity.
>
> (*Black Lives Matter*, 'About Us')

'Genocide doesn't only mean bombs/at high noon and the cameras/panning in on the ruptured stomach/of somebody else's pubescent daughter', writes Audre Lorde, a Caribbean-American writer, theorist, and activist, in her 1974 poem 'Viet-nam Addenda' (46). Genocide also means the systemic, silent terror

1 I am indebted to Sara Ahmed's work on willfulness and queerness in the contexts of rights and social emancipation debates, and I use the term 'willful' as she does, to denote political disobedience and resistance. My use of the term 'target' is inspired by its use in *City as Target* (Bishop, Clancey, and Phillips), to invoke its constructive and destructive meanings in the economic and military senses.

that grips New York's Harlem and every other inner city in the United States in the mid-twentieth century.[2] While '[a] small difference in time and space/ names that [Vietnam] war' as genocidal, this other 'domestic' war waged against the United States' citizens or residents has no name, is unaccounted for. And so, 'we live/117th street at high noon', she mourns, 'powerlessly familiar', yet unknown, 'with all the time in the world/for the nightmare of idleness/to turn their hands/against us'. Lorde's 'Viet-nam Addenda' captures the violence of the at-one-time supposedly humanitarian Vietnam War and the limits of human rights and humanitarianism within US borders. Stephen Hopgood calls this paradox 'the tension between Human Rights and human rights' (96), that is, the hegemonic international regime and the actual rights of the people on the ground, so to speak.[3]

Yet, Lorde does not just challenge the logic of 'military humanitarianism' abroad (Weizman) while exposing simultaneous 'unseen' violence at home. Neither does she simply reveal the incompatibility of international Human Rights and grassroots social justice struggles, or its poor record of enactment on behalf of victims of atrocities, either. When she laments that 'We are raped of our children/in silence', and calls systemic violence a form of genocide, Lorde shows that fundamentally different understandings of violence, humanity, and rights across time and geopolitical spaces define the limits of our perception of violence and genocide, and that these, in turn, shape our political and legal responses to such human rights crises.[4] While mass exterminations that demand humanitarian intervention underwrite hegemonic Human Rights, other kinds of brutality – acts of retribution for acts of decolonial, economic, and political disobedience; and violence, which is often systemic, 'quiet' (Lorde), or 'slow' (Rob Nixon),[5] but still brutal in its targeting of queer communities, of people

2 For a poignant meditation on blackness and genocide, see contributions to the 2015 'Dossier: On Race and Innovation' in *boundary 2* (Harney and Moten; Martin).

3 I preserve Hopgood's distinction throughout this paper. Capitalized 'Human Rights' refers to the international, UN-backed regime, and hegemonic and 'official' human rights in the United States; lower-case 'human rights' refers to their grass-roots articulation.

4 I thank Andrew Hersher ('Regarding the Genocide of Others' lecture delivered at NTNU Trondheim on October 19, 2015) for pointing out that the legal definition of 'genocide' that undergirds the 1948 Convention on the Prevention of the Crime of Genocide, and much of the official understanding of what genocide is, is a radically narrowed version of Raphaël Lemkin's original, and much broader, concept (Lemkin, *Axis* 79–95). In his pre-1948 writing, Lemkin, who coined the term genocide, observed that mass-scale murder of social groups was the end result of multiple techniques or 'philosophies' of genocide: economic, political, moral, and social ('Genocide'). The limitation of the 1948 Convention's definition of genocide to mass destruction of human bodies, but less to culture and economy, for instance, is telling in the context of decolonial struggles.

5 Rob Nixon defines 'slow violence' as violence that is often cognitively unobservable, invisible, because it unravels slowly over time and 'outside of our flickering attention spans . . . and outside the purview of the spectacle-driven corporate media' (3, 5, 6, 8).

of colour, or of the poor – are not seen as violence at all, and thus not acknowledged as needing a remedy through international legal instruments.

What violence means in different geopolitical and cultural contexts, therefore, and the conceptual and geospatial reasons why some violence remains unheard and unseen,[6] is a key question for marginalized communities around the globe.[7] Particularly vulnerable are those excluded from the political process, and limited in their access to the legal instruments of domestic and international law by the many jurisdictional restrictions on who can become a justice claimant under its auspices,[8] and where, and by the political pressures that spotlight selectively some sites of violence but not others.[9] But even when Human and Humanitarian Rights[10] are invoked, imposed, or 'performed' with military precision on such victims of 'the absolute denial of right' to protect them (Rancière 307),

6 Ta-Nehisi Coates highlights the way discourse obscures violence when he argues that 'All of our phrasing – race relations, racial chasm, racial justice, racial profiling, white privilege, even white supremacy – serves to obscure that racism is a visceral experience, that dislodges brains, blocks airwaves, rips muscle, extracts organs, cracks bones, breaks teeth' (10). Harney and Moten go further and argue that such violence is empirically perceivable but is not registered because it cannot be *imagined* (84), pointing out the crucial role innovative and creative practices play in the social justice projects.

7 In their reflection on blackness and state violence, Stefano Harney and Fred Moten say, for example, that 'The state can't live with us and it can't live without us. Its violence is a reaction to that condition. The state is nothing other than a war against its own condition' (83). Patrisse Cullors, Opal Tometi, and Alicia Garza, the founders of #BlackLivesMatter, include a radical visual-textual dictionary of violence on their website. In their powerful infographics section, simple signs – a gun, a wheelchair, a ribbon – are transformed by textual incantations that name targets of violence with great precision, and describe and indict the types of violence that are unnarratad in the official discourse of the state (*Black Lives Matter*, 'About')

8 Laws function within spatial and legal jurisdictions, and although International Law offers a chance to reterritorialize legal subjects by placing them in a new transnational framework and jurisdiction, in the context of marginalized, indigenous, LGBT, and migrant communities of color, such legal reterritorialization may itself become problematic, given the long history of colonization, slavery, forced removal, racial or gender segregation, and these oppressive practices' dependence on spatial violence and forced mobility and the legal apparati for achieving such variously conceived 'civilizing' or humanizing missions.

9 The strikingly different global responses to terrorist attacks in Nigeria, France, Syria, and Mali in the fall of 2015 exemplify how differently violence is interpreted and understood. Spectacular violence committed in a European safe space such as Paris on 13 November 2015 prompted an immediate international political and cultural reaction, from states and cities declaring states of emergency, to military action, to global mourning on social media, to even changes to the safety check and free calling features provided by Facebook and Google. Similar violence committed in Beirut (12 November 2015) or Bamako (20 November 2015), mere days from the Paris attacks, did not generate a comparable response (Crowell) and was not seen or mourned as a global human rights tragedy.

10 Throughout the text, I consciously conflate the two concepts humanitarianism and human rights, which are not the same in legal terminology. While International Humanitarian Law applies to armed conflict contexts, and Human Rights primarily to peacetime (but also

such subjects of rights also become targets of a legal regime that, at least since the Cold War, has been a tool of a '*foreign* policy for non-Americans' (Hopgood 97, original emphasis).

However, even victims of such humanitarian targeting do have what Stefano Harney and Fred Moten call the 'jurisgenerative . . . capacity to make (and break) the law' (81, 83), and often become 'willful' agents of radical reformulations of rights (Ahmed). In her work on 'willful subjects', Sara Ahmed reinterprets a Brothers Grimm story in which a child is punished for her willfulness with illness and death, but who then refuses to be completely buried (1). Rather than glossing over this act of post-mortem disobedience – the girl's hand sticks defiantly out of her grave, even after the burial – Ahmed sees this gesture of willfulness as an important 'style of politics' (1, 133). A similar theme appears in Kendrick Lamar, Flying Lotus, and Hiro Murai's collaboration, 'Never Catch Me', released soon after the accounts of police killings of unarmed men of color in the US began to multiply online in 2014. In the music video, two dead teenagers, a black boy and girl, resting in coffins during the sleepy funeral proceedings, suddenly awaken and escape from the church, to the frenetic tempo of Flying Lotus's music and Lamar's lyrics. The teenagers are not ready to be buried, and, in defiance, they dance their way out into the hearse, and out into the world.

These stories of willfulness focus on defiance and ingenuity in the aftermath of violence and death, and they lend the vocabulary to and frame my project invested in looking at contemporary acts of 'jurisgenerative' willfulness in the US. This chapter, therefore, not only reflects on the precarious nature of 'humanitarian targeting', which often makes some human subjects more visible and vulnerable at the same time,[11] but also examines specifically how in the contemporary US context, such subjects – targets of rights and their advocates, from the creators of #BlackLivesMatter, Alicia Garza, Patrice Cullors, Opal Tometi, and activists affiliated with the US-wide grass-roots Black Lives Matter movement, to American human rights scholars – redefine 'violence', reclaim the legacies of queer and grass-roots human right activism, and obstruct the violent targeting of existing legal habits.[12] And how they make Human Rights *theirs* by engaging with them through feats of aesthetic, intellectual and political willfulness and creativity (Ahmed).

occasionally wartime) situations, here I focus on how they may target and victimize marginalized communities in similar ways. As such, I also allude to Harney and Moten's conflation of the categories of American 'state' and 'war' into 'state of war' (85). For a post-1980s militarization of domestic policy in the US, see also Mauer; Alexander; Passavant.

11 For a more extensive discussion on visibility and violence, see Harney and Moten; Coates; Bishop and Phillips; Azoulay; Musiol, 'Museums of Human Bodies'.

12 It is also not a coincidence that the willful #BlackLivesMatter creators acknowledge an explicit debt to queer intellectual history and activism, which is central to Ahmed's *Willful Subjects* (*Black Lives Matter*, 'A HerStory', section 'The Theft of Black Queer Women's Work').

Human Rights and violence

Contemporary Human Rights genealogy is, of course, knotty. The origin of Human Rights may be traced back to the Ancient Greeks (Douzinas; Hall), the European Enlightenment ideals, the French Declaration of the Rights of Man and the Citizen, or the Holocaust and 1948 UDHR. Other accounts of modern Human Rights point to the foundational role of the US Constitution, referenced in many manifestos and documents of legal enfranchisement. Katherine C. Hall cites pre-twentieth-century international ethnic and religious minorities treaties, such as the 1856 and 1898 Treaties of Paris, the 1878 Treaty of Berlin (3), and the pre- and post-1900s international slave trade bans (5), as other pre-1948 antecedents to the Human Rights regime. Other scholars take a *longue durée* and postcolonial approach, and point to the colonial roots of contemporary Human Rights law, and recover complex entanglements of Human Rights and violence (Mignolo; Santos; Fregoso; Esmeir). Their research links modern Human Rights discourse to the troubling Euro-American, colonial, civilizing missions imposed on non-white global subjects before 1948, and later, to often violent foreign policy used to support overt or covert foreign humanitarian interventions in, for example, the Philippines, Iran, South Korea, the Dominican Republic, Vietnam, Indonesia, Cambodia, East Timor, British Guyana, Congo, and Chile after 1900 (Arias 327; Ignatieff 2).[13] While strategic deployment of Human Rights law to support global legal subjects excluded from the political process is laudable, no less important in that story are the violent uses of Human Rights as well as the neglected histories of grass-roots and global human rights theories, activism, and norms (Wynter in McKittrick; Esmeir; Martha F. Davis in Soohoo *et al.* xvii) in different media, genres, and narrative styles (Harney and Moten; Musiol, 'Sites'; Palumbo Liu; Powell).

Interestingly, the US has both supported the UN Human Rights order and, at the same time, resisted the ratification of its key legal instruments (Condé; Hall; Anderson, *Eyes off the Prize*; Wronka; Lewis).[14] Moreover, the country has long celebrated itself as both a universal Human Rights champion and an inherently violent and 'exceptional' nation at the same time (Pease; Ignatieff).[15]

13 Given the ways in which Human Rights and Humanitarian Law are routinely invoked in military operations, Hopgood's view that Cold War humanitarianism plays a much more central role than the 1948 UDHR in the consolidation of Human Rights on the international arena is an important observation. However, it is also crucial to keep in mind the settler colonial antecedents to the modern Human Rights regime.

14 The US has not ratified the 1981 Convention on the Elimination of All Forms of Discrimination against Women, or the 1990 Convention on the Rights of the Child, or the 1976 International Covenant on Economic, Social and Cultural Rights. It also has not signed the 2003 International Convention on the Protection of the Rights of All Migrant Workers and Members of their Families ('Status of Ratification').

15 Note that the country's foundational legal text contains the Second Amendment to the US Constitution, which anticipates state violence and a violent resistance to it, and the US's unsettling colonial origins are reflected in its legal codes.

Thus, while 'human rights' and 'peace' may have become buzzwords of political speech at least since Jimmy Carter's presidency, de facto US foreign policy has often contradicted their meaningful usage, and American global interventions consistently reveal the US's and the UN's complicity in, if not propensity for, violent military action to resolve humanitarian crises (Hopgood 119–141).

The relationship between international Human Rights and American domestic policies is often equally inconsistent. In their award-winning collection, Cynthia Soohoo, Catherine Albisa, and Martha F. Davis demonstrate the great challenges of 'bringing human rights home' to the US, to stamp out spectacular and quiet, 'uneventful' violence against racial and ethnic minorities, LGBT communities, women, and the poor, despite this nation's championing international Human Rights abroad (Rob Nixon 8). Contributors to their project record historical attempts by US victims of local human rights abuses to 'go global', that is, to seek redress for domestic human rights violation through international Human Rights institutions, rather than through federal and state institutions only (Huang 105).[16] They also remind us that modern Human Rights were from the very onset not intended to be an all-encompassing category open to all human bodies, and non-white or non-Anglo Americans were actively discouraged from applying international Human Rights to themselves (Soohoo *et al.*; Anderson, *Eyes off the Prize* 58–112).[17]

Although domestic and international laws are never meant to smoothly complement one another, it is important to note that they often produce *targets* of rights in similar ways. Instead of leading to political enfranchisement, in the post-World War II landscape, international *and* domestic (US) legal frameworks often construct target-subjects through militaristic humanitarianism, providing them mainly with '"the right to humanitarian interference" – a right that some nations [and even domestic institutions] assume to the supposed benefit of victimized populations, and very often against the advice of the humanitarian organizations themselves' (Rancière 308). This often violent 'humanitarian interference' regularly destroys the potential of the law to create political subjects

16 Such acts of disobedience and resistance included, for instance, National Negro Congress and NAACP efforts to seek UN protection against lynchings and the brutality of Jim Crow segregatory laws in the 1940s. Their efforts met with a stern rebuke from their domestic supporters such as Eleanor Roosevelt and the UN. Other scholars have also exposed different types of violence that go uncounted for; for instance, economic and spatial segregation in the US (Davis, *City of Quartz*) and worldwide (Davis, *Planet of Slums*); neo-liberal funds redistribution and de-investment in public facilities in New York (Katz, Klein); the forced Europeanization/Westernization and gendering of indigenous populations subject to US law (Rifkin); and the domestic carceral regime (Alexander; Mauer).

17 It may be even more difficult to turn the Human Rights apparatus on itself, so to speak, not only because internal 'slow' and state-supported violence is often not seen as violence to which Human Rights law might apply, but also because this violence is committed domestically by the international hegemon, which also happens to be an arbiter of what the Human Rights it routinely violates are (Rob Nixon).

of rights, who engage in politics and 'dissensus' (304), that is, who engage actively in negotiating the rights they have, but cannot exercise, or the ones they exercise, but do not have (302).

In the domestic US context, immigrants and citizens of color, especially poor and LGBT citizens[18] of color, who are citizen-noncitizens,[19] or 'citizen-exiles', in Martin Luther King Jr.'s words, become targets or '*absolute* victims' of rights (Rancière 309, original emphasis). Yet, this is also a designation such targets of rights have resisted, as much at the time of the establishment of the UN Human Rights system (Anderson, *Eyes off the Prize*; Soohoo *et al.*) as now, through acts of political, intellectual, and cultural willfulness and 'innovation' (Ahmed; Harney and Moten).[20]

American targets of rights

Those who see Human Rights as a continuation of either colonialism or the Cold War, and as a politically disempowering, and often violently militaristic system, may, in other words, be justified in their criticism of this paradoxically humanitarian and violent character of rights targeting, evident in some domestic social programs and policies of the post-Civil Rights era in the US.

The most obvious example of this is the infamous War on Drugs,[21] supposedly established to protect the security, public health, and overall well-being of American citizens. This domestic 'humanitarian-military project' (Douzinas 225) led to the mass incarceration of men of color, increasing the US prison population from 300,000 to over 2 million by the end of the century (Alexander 6; Mauer 33). It also legalized racial profiling, and literally trapped and reproduced the poor and racialized American underclass, or 'caste', making some scholars call it the 'new Jim Crow' system of racial segregation and disenfranchisement (Alexander 13). Many subject-targets of such 'humanitarian' methods are sceptical of their international, outside of Europe and North America, but also

18 The 2015 *Obergefell et al. v. Hodges, Director, Ohio Department of Health, et al.* Supreme Court decision legalizing same-sex marriage in the United States is likely to dramatically improve the human rights experience of non-white LGBT persons in the United States, especially in states that did not recognize same-sex marriage.

19 The rights of actual non-citizens, undocumented and documented immigrants, and legal residents comprise another crucial area of domestic human rights violations, but that topic exceeds the scope of this article. For more on the subject, consult Molina, Plascencia, Asbed, and Lyon.

20 Also consult the important work of domestic human rights organizations such as the Human Rights Campaign (HRC), the Human Rights Network (HRN), and the National Economic and Social Rights Initiative (NESRI).

21 See Alexander. For a genealogy of the War on Drugs and the role of the administrations of Richard Nixon, Ronald Reagan, and Bill Clinton in the development of its racialized discourses and policies specifically, consult Mauer; Alexander (1–98).

intranational, in the US, uses for internal social emancipation projects. While some US state and federal legal programmes that, at least in theory, aim to protect urban residents' rights, they are themselves conceived through the military-style tactics applied selectively to already marginalized populations, mimicking the ways in which international interventions supposedly support human rights of certain global citizens through military operation.

Paradoxically, recent instances of violence against unarmed American citizens of color in the US demonstrate that not only 'slow' systemic violence, but even the most visible, spectacular, physical brutality, when inflicted on non-white communities, does not count as violence (Rob Nixon). In fact, most of the homicides committed by the police literally do not count and are not included in the FBI statistics as '[o]nly 224 of 18,000 law enforcement agencies reported fatal shootings in 2014' (Swaine and Laughland). Exposed in 2014 and 2015, violent deaths and abuse of such American subjects-targets of rights at the hands of the police and the justice and political systems, accounts of which were often recorded and circulated on the Internet, highlighted that for an African American or a poor person to be the target of the criminal justice system often means to be the target of the law in the most literal and physically violent sense. Stefano Harney and Fred Moten refer to this as 'dead citizenship' (86), citizenship 'confer[red by] the state war machine . . . upon its subjects [not] at birth, but rather, at death' (84).

The often deadly confrontations with police that did not warrant the use of lethal force and that nevertheless ended in civilian deaths galvanized some Americans to question the US model of policing, in part because those deaths' spectacular, outrageous character was magnified by countless online reshares. It also prompted calls to at least finally recognize, to 'say the names' of the unaccounted-for victims of police brutality (Monáe and Wondaland). Yet, instead of epitaphs mourning and imagining the lives that existed and ceased, the public sphere was saturated with 'ghoulish' reinscriptions of 'dead citizenship' such as the ones below (Harney and Moten 85).

On 17 July 2014, Eric Garner was stopped for selling untaxed cigarettes in New York City, and placed in a deadly and illegal chokehold. He could hardly breathe – his pleas caught on camera – and was left to die of asphyxiation shortly after. On 9 August 2014, another 'black life . . . got caught walking – with jurisgenerative fecundity – down the middle of the street' (Harney and Moten 85; Hennessy-Fiske). It was an unarmed Michael Brown who died of multiple gunshot wounds in Ferguson, Missouri, shortly after he encountered the police (Bosman and Goldstein). On 11 August 2014, Ezell Ford was shot during an 'investigative stop' and interrogation in Los Angeles (Sieczkowski). On 20 November 2014, Akai Gurley was shot *by accident* as he was exiting his girlfriend's apartment in Brooklyn. Tamir Rice, just 12, was shot and killed on a Cleveland playground where he was playing with a toy pellet gun on 22 November 2014 ('Tamir Rice Video'). Horrifying videos of new police brutality and killings emerged in 2015, as well. On 2 April, in Tulsa, Oklahoma, Eric Harris was shot in the back by a white volunteer reserve sheriff deputy, who falsified his weapons training records with the help of the police department he donated to. On 7 April 2015, Walter Scott was stopped for driving with a broken taillight in North Charleston, South Carolina, and shot eight times in the back as he was running away from his car to avoid getting tasered (Schmidt and Apuzzo). His shooter, a white police officer, did not administer CPR and left him to die, and then made up a false report on the cause of Scott's death, a fact made apparent thanks to a video of the fatal encounter taken by a bystander, who after publicizing his recording feared for his own life. Another 2015 case involved the inexplicable suicide death in state custody of Sandra Bland, a vocal critic of police brutality, following a traffic stop and arrest in Prairie View, Texas, conducted in what many felt was violation of her constitutional rights (Lartey).[22] Unrelated acts of violence against young females of color in Texas and South Carolina (Hemmer) made visible the amount of police violence a teenage black could be subject to at a local pool and at a public school (Izadi and Brown).

Yet despite the brutal nature of these acts of violence, discussion fora on key national media – *The New York Times*, *The Washington Post*, the *Los Angeles Times*, *The Huffington Post*, the *Chicago Tribune* – public and commercial radio stations, and diverse online sites revealed a complex picture of the public response to such acts of state violence. Although many commenters saw the authorities' arbitrary use of lethal weapons as unwarranted, some accepted, and even commended, the police officers' killing of unarmed men or 'disciplining' disobedient teenage girls.[23] Death in many accounts was accepted as a logical consequence of, and a fair punishment for, 'failing to comply' with even the most trivial, arbitrary, and often unconstitutional police orders (Ahmed 1). Not surprisingly, then, even protesting such an obvious perversion of justice, from brutalizing teenage kids to killing of unarmed people, turned out to be a daunting and willful political task. It involved not only revealing, but 'imagining what exists' (Harney and Moten 81). Black Lives Matter activism was an indispensable part of this process.

The afterlife of violence

The 2014 Ferguson protests, in the aftermath of Michael Brown's death, featured now-iconic images of not only demonstrators with 'hands up, don't shoot' signs, but also mine-resistant, ambush-protected vehicles (MRAPs) and police in camouflage gear bearing semiautomatic rifles, tasers, tear gas, and smoke bombs, and using dogs. All this was deployed in response to the demonstrators

22 As this article goes to print, the death toll for racially motivated violent crimes without police involvement also continues to climb. The most notorious one, the 15 June 2015 massacre at the Emanuel A.M.E. Church, in Charleston, South Carolina, left nine African Americans dead at this historic site of civil rights.

23 It is important to note that it was not just conservative outlets and their consumers who represented police officers as victims, not perpetrators, of aggression.

exercising their constitutional First Amendment rights to free speech and assembly (Konnikova; 'MRAPs and Bayonets'). The Missouri National Guards, called in on August 2014 to quell the unrest, referred to protesters as 'adversaries' and as '*enemy forces*' (my emphasis) in internal briefings, and certainly treated them as such (Starr and Bruer).[24] If the Ferguson footage seemed both real and unreal, commentators were quick to point out that it seemed out of place because it reminded viewers more of international 'humanitarian' interventions that should be happening *elsewhere* (Batuman; Carter). But it was twenty-first-century America, one that many Americans still refuse to acknowledge, where protesters, including members of the press, faced a military response, where they were also intimidated, harassed, beaten, or arrested for demanding justice for all the domestic victims of systemic and state-supported violence in the US, and for arguing publicly that black lives, too, are human lives.

In the months after Michael Brown's death, and after the first series of Ferguson demonstrations in the fall of 2014, protesters staged demonstrations in cities across the US despite great risks. The hashtag #BlackLivesMatter – created after the 2012 shooting of another unarmed African American man, Trayvon Martin – by Alicia Garza, Patrisse Cullors, and Opal Tometi,[25] has become not only a recognizable slogan in the Twittersphere, but the *sound* and *look* of the post-Ferguson protests, so to speak.[26] In addition to circulating news about police brutality and protests organizing, #BlackLivesMatter articulated core concerns for the most important American movement for racial and economic justice in the twenty-first century, and gave them new now-iconic aesthetics in black and yellow, public gestures, community rituals, music, T-shirt slogans, poetry, and so on (*Black Lives Matter*, 'Instagram'; *Black Lives Matter*, 'tumblr'; Monáe and Wondaland). The hashtag transformed into an online platform, a network, and soon into Black Lives Matter, a powerful cultural and political movement.

For the creators of the #BlackLivesMatter hashtag and platform, Garza, Cullors, and Tometi, Black Lives Matter was 'a call to action and a response to the virulent anti-Black racism that permeates our society', but also to the heterosexism and ableism that dominates militaristic Human Rights discourse and domestic social justice struggles. Their mission was to 'affirm the lives of Black queer and trans folks, disabled folks, black-undocumented folks, folks with

24 The violent escalation of the military police response in Ferguson was so outrageous that Senator Claire McCaskill (D–Missouri) spearheaded an effort to demilitarize domestic police forces, in order to ensure that 'the images that we saw where there was a red pinpoint of laser in the chest of a young woman who [is] protesting' is not something we 'see . . . in America again' ('MRAPs and Bayonets').

25 For a genealogy of Black Lives Matter, consult *Black Lives Matter*, 'A HerStory'; for the violence of aesthetic evaluation in Trayvon Martin's case, see Musiol ('Museums' 160–161).

26 The role of Twitter in reporting police abuse in Ferguson has been widely commented on (Christiansen), but its role in both mobilizing activists and transforming the discourse of social justice claims cannot be underestimated.

records, women and all Black lives along the gender spectrum' (*Black Lives Matter*, 'About Us'). Borrowing as much from international Human Rights as from transnational, queer, and pan-ethnic human rights vocabulary, they described the movement as 'rooted in the experiences of Black people in this country who actively resist [their] de-humanization' (*Black Lives Matter*, 'A HerStory'; *Black Lives Matter*, 'About Us'). Garza, Cullors, and Tometi, and thousands of Black Lives Matter supporters not only framed Ferguson in human rights and queer terms, to confront racial profiling, the militarization of policing, and the economic and cultural exploitation of non-white, poor, LGBT, disabled persons within the US; they also activated public and official debates about police brutality.

What is more important, they moved such debates out of the communities most afflicted by police abuse, to the sports stadiums, white suburbs, the Capitol, and MTV, public spaces in which such conversations should have been taking place but did not.[27] In the process, they also sought to transform rights' targets into subjects. Instead of resigning themselves to the human rights modelled after the 'hand-me-downs' of the violent humanitarianism in international interventions (Rancière 307), Black Lives Matter activists focused on people's potential to actively and creatively participate in politics, and specifically in political 'dissensus' practices in order to change how domestic human rights are defined and applied (304). They emphasized that human rights belong to their subjects and must be articulated, demanded, reclaimed by victims of human rights violations. This was a particularly important intervention, given that in 'surviving police encounters' workshops, American participants of color are taught to *avoid* 'asserting [the human] rights' they *do* have, as the mere assertion of their rights may prove lethal (Marquez Claxton, qtd. in Lartey).

If demanding 'an End to all Forms of Discrimination and the Full Recognition of our Human Rights' in their manifesto, 'Our Vision for a New America' (*Black Lives Matter*, 'Ferguson') meant also demanding accountability on the part of criminal justice institutions, their acts of political willfulness led to long overdue, perhaps small, but also tangible victories. While some of the police shooters walked free, others were indicted, but most important, the nationwide grass-roots protests led to the launching of civil and criminal investigations,[28] new

27 On 11 December 2014, black congressional staffers staged a public walkout with their hands up, a tribute to the 'hands up don't shoot' slogan. On 19 January 2015, MTV ran its programming in black and white to encourage people to have 'the talk' about race. On 21 January 2015, people of different faiths staged a five-minute die-in at the Capitol; since late 2014, many athletes and sports fans across the US have displayed Black Lives Matter signs, in support of victims of police brutality. In 2015, Black Lives Matter supporters forced contenders for the Democratic and Republican 2016 presidential election nominations, Bernie Sanders, Jeb Bush, and Hillary Clinton, to address their demands in speeches, interviews, and even personal meetings ('Exclusive'; Madhani; Seitz-Wald).

28 The criminal investigation by the St. Louis County Prosecutor's Office, and a civil rights investigation by the Federal Bureau of Investigation and the U.S. Department of Justice Civil Rights Division (Amnesty International 3).

research and the publicizing of research results (Amnesty International; U.S. Department of Justice; Krieger *et al.*), the reorganization of the Ferguson Police Department, and the launching of several initiatives to demilitarize domestic police, and to hold them accountable for the crimes they commit.[29] Thanks to their activism, in Ferguson, as the American and global public learned, the county system depended ideologically and economically on discriminating against poor and African American local residents for revenue (U.S. Department of Justice 9–49).

Two official reports, one by Amnesty International and the other by the U.S. Department of Justice, which revealed the systemic abuse of African Americans, state clearly that such practices violated international and domestic human rights norms. *On the Streets of America: Human Rights Abuses in Ferguson* (Amnesty International 6) explicitly states that the domestic urban violence carried out by county and state actors – excessive use of lethal force, restrictions placed on the right to protest, intimidation of protesters, and obstruction of media and human rights observers' reporting – qualify as human rights violations according to the UDHR, the US Constitution, and Missouri state laws.

Particularly disturbing findings about the institutionalization of racialized economic oppression were revealed in the *Investigation of the Ferguson Police Department* (U.S. Department of Justice), a report that gave domestic human rights new cadence but also inserted 'economic' and 'spatial justice' in the popular rhetoric of human rights. Although the report did not focus on Michael Brown's death explicitly, it exposed the widespread 'slow violence' of institutionalized racial and economic discrimination, of which Brown's death was a culmination, carried out by the city institutions in violation of the First, Fourth, and Fourteenth Amendments in Ferguson, which victimized Brown and other Ferguson residents (U.S. Department of Justice 15–41, 62–79; Rob Nixon). The report documented that the primary function of the Ferguson police and municipal court – located unsurprisingly in the police department – was to generate revenue (U.S. Department of Justice 8). To achieve that, the city expanded the list of code violations that could lead to fines levied against, and/or to the arrest of, a resident, including, for example, not mowing one's lawn ('High Grass and Weeds'), letting one's dog bark too loudly or run free ('Barking Dog' and 'Dog Running at Large'), playing loud music in one's car ('Peace Disturbance'), and not walking on the sidewalk ('Manner of Walking in Roadway' 7, 18). Municipal codes and state laws were designed to increase the court's and the Ferguson Police Department's

29 President Barack Obama, for example, ordered a review of the Pentagon's controversial 1033 program channelling unwanted military equipment to police departments across the country between 2006 and 2014. Such 'unwanted equipment' included MRAPs and '79,288 assault rifles, 205 grenade launchers, 11,959 bayonets, 3,972 combat knives, $124 million worth of night-vision equipment, including night-vision sniper scopes, 479 bomb-detonator robots, 50 airplanes, including 27 cargo transport airplanes, 422 helicopters, and more than $3.6 million worth of camouflage gear and other "deception equipment"' ('MRAPs and Bayonets').

(FPD) fees in 2013 by 7.5 per cent and 10 per cent, respectively, per the suggestions of the city finance director, and in violation of residents' constitutional rights (13). Citations, fines, and arrests for non-payment placed a huge economic burden on Ferguson residents, 25 per cent of whom live below the federal poverty level and cannot afford fines, let alone excessive ones (6, 16).

Militarizing public spaces and extorting revenue through criminalization of practically every aspect of life, humiliated, and economically, culturally, and physically terrorized, the African American community to which these guidelines were disproportionately applied (5). Ninety per cent of the FPD's use of force, which often included the administration of electronic control weapons (ECWs)/tasers, involved African Americans (5, 18, 29–30). *All* reports of dog bites – canines were used on Ferguson residents by the FPD – involved African Americans. Excessive force was also used against mentally disabled persons (35–37) and underage students (37–38). The complicity of the court system in this process is perhaps the most disturbing aspect of the long-term racial and economic discrimination embedded in the city's governance. Instead of being the 'neutral arbiter' of justice, the court relied on arrest warrants to extort payments from poor residents, the report concluded, demonstrating that it 'primarily uses its judicial authority as the means to compel the payment of fines and fees that advance the City's financial interests' (3, 55–58). Meanwhile, police misconduct and brutality went unaccounted for.

Beyond

At a time when 'violent humanitarianism' (Weizman) is a discursive and logistical model for both foreign military interventions and often abusive domestic policies, it is crucial to understand the violence of such conceived or executed (pun intended) international and domestic Human Rights, but also the violence it fails to identify and respond to: legalized racial profiling that restricts access to the law by racial minorities, immigrants, and other disenfranchised social subjects (Alexander; Gonzales; Plascencia); zoning and tax policies that underfund public schools in poor neighbourhoods and that force cities to seek tax revenue by criminalizing innocuous activities such as walking in public, and on the wrong side of the sidewalk (U.S. Department of Justice 4–5); domestic labor exploitation of low-wage earners resulting from overseas labour outsourcing, which forces many urban residents to resort to employment in illegal, shadow economies, and so on (Alexander 50–51; Klein; Katz). If systemic violence continues, and is unspoken and unaccounted for, there is no aftermath. There is no beyond, no recognition and remediation.[30] And no emancipatory American human rights.

30 Unlike victims of the 9/11 attack or the Boston Marathon bombing, 1980–1990 LGBT AIDS victims, men of color incarcerated in the last three decades, and the poor victimized by the police violence are still rarely recognized as bodies worth public mourning or protections.

The Black Lives Matter human rights activism that shaped the post-Ferguson movement for racial and economic justice enabled a debate about intranational human rights violence of the 'spectacular' and the 'silent' kind (Lorde), but also added new practices to the ongoing project of the 'innovation of survival' (Harney and Moten). American scholars, activists, theorists, and artists (from Audre Lorde, to the NAACP activists, to scholars who contributed to Soohoo *et al.*'s collection, to the #BlackLivesMatter creators) have long worked in diverse cultural forms – in poetry, songs, and digital worlds; on Twitter; in the classroom, in the courtroom, and in the streets – to innovatively rearticulate the concept of violence, and to 'bring human rights home' (Soohoo *et al.*). Their 'dissensus' practices have challenged the 'violent humanitarianism' of international and domestic policies, and have been instrumental to organizing publics around concrete, local human rights claims (Weizman; Rancière 304) invoking Human Rights actively, and, as a result, changing the usage practices of international Human Rights in the US. More importantly, when 'affirmati[ng] Black folks' contributions to this society, our humanity, and our resilience' (*Black Lives Matter*, 'A HerStory'), Black Lives Matter organizers have tied these contributions to a long history of domestic and international human rights activism and queer intellectual history and politics, which are nearly erased from official and popular accounts of civil and human rights struggles.[31] Theirs and others' acts of political and intellectual willfulness and innovation point to neglected archives, revealing both tense resistance to hegemonic Human Rights, and their strategic and creative invocations. They also remind us of the persistence of and the role that marginalized domestic communities, the willful, disobedient targets of rights, play, in creating new aesthetic and political possibilities for heterogeneous, disobedient human rights, envisioned against the framework of their other, foreign aid and 'state of war' model (Harney and Moten).

Acknowledgements

I thank the Program on Human Rights and the Global Economy (PHRGE) at the Northeastern University School of Law for supporting my research with a Visiting Research Scholar fellowship in 2015; Lester Spence and Paul Passavant for organizing the Race, Space, and Policing panel at the 2015 ASLCH conference; Jonas Ross Kjærgård, Karen-Margrethe Simonsen, and anonymous peer reviewers for their thoughtful feedback on an earlier version of this chapter; and Kristen Ebert-Wagner for her editorial help.

31 Note that even researchers who work on Black Lives Matter gloss over its female creators and the movement's indebtedness to queer activism (Passavant).

Works cited

Ahmed, Sara. *Willful Subjects*. Durham: Duke University Press, 2014. Print.

Alexander, Michelle. *The New Jim Crow: Mass Incarceration in the Age of Colorblindness*. New York: New Press, 2012. Print.

Amnesty International. *In the Streets of America: Human Rights Abuses in Ferguson*. New York: Amnesty International USA, 2014. Print.

Anderson, Carol. *Eyes off the Prize: The United Nations and the African American Struggle for Human Rights, 1944–1955*. Cambridge/New York: Cambridge University Press, 2003. Print.

——. 'A "Hollow Mockery": African Americans, White Supremacy, and the Development of Human Rights in the United States'. Soohoo *et al.* 1: 75–101.

Arias, Arturo. 'Violence, Indigeneities and Human Rights'. McClennen and Moore 326–332.

Asbed, Greg. 'Coalition of Immokalee Workers: "Golpear a Uno Es Golpear a Todos!" To Beat One of Us Is to Beat Us All!' Soohoo *et al.* 3: 1–24.

Azoulay, Ariella. 'Ending World War II: Visual Literacy Class in Human Rights'. McClennen and Moore 159–172.

Batuman, Elif. 'What Does It Mean to Compare Ferguson to Iraq?' *New Yorker* 22 Aug. 2014. Web. 16 Aug. 2015. <www.newyorker.com/news/daily-comment/comparing-ferguson-iraq>.

Bill of Rights. *The Charters of Freedom*. n.d. Web. 17 Apr. 2015. <www.archives.gov/exhibits/charters/bill_of_rights_transcript.html>.

Bishop, Ryan, Gregory K. Clancey, and John Phillips, eds. *The City as Target*. London/New York: Routledge, 2012. Print.

Bishop, Ryan and John Phillips. 'Sighted Weapons and Modernist Opacity: Aesthetics, Poetics, Prosthetics'. *boundary 2* 29.2 (2002): 157–179.

Black Lives Matter. 'About Us'. n.d. Web. 1 Dec. 2015. <http://blacklivesmatter.com/about/>.

——. 'Ferguson, 1 Year Later: Why Protesters Were Right to Fight for Mike Brown Jr.'. n.d. Web. 1 Dec. 2015. <http://blacklivesmatter.com/ferguson-1-year-later-why-protesters-were-right-to-fight-for-mike-brown-jr//>.

——. 'A HerStory of the #BlackLivesMatter Movement'. 6 Dec. 2014. Web. 1 Dec. 2015. <http://blacklivesmatter.com/herstory/>.

——. 'Instagram'. n.d. Web. 1 Dec. 2015. <www.instagram.com/blklivesmatter/>.

——. 'tumblr'. n.d. Web. 1 Dec. 2015. <http://blacklivesmatter.tumblr.com/>.

Bosman, Julie and Joseph Goldstein. 'Timeline for a Body: 4 Hours in the Middle of a Ferguson Street'. *New York Times* 23 Aug. 2014. Web. 16 Aug. 2015. <www.nytimes.com/2014/08/24/us/michael-brown-a-bodys-timeline-4-hours-on-a-ferguson-street.html?_r=0>.

Carter, Phillip. 'Ferguson's Cops Are Armed Like I Was in Iraq'. *The Daily Beast* 14 Aug. 2014. Web. 16 Aug. 2015. <www.thedailybeast.com/articles/2014/08/14/ferguson-s-cops-are-armed-like-i-was-in-iraq.html>.

Christiansen, Anna. 'Social Media and Instant News in #Ferguson'. *PBS Newshour* 27 Aug. 2014. Web. 17 Apr. 2015. <www.pbs.org/newshour/extra/2014/08/social-media-and-instant-news-in-ferguson/>.

Coates, Ta-Nehisi. *Between the World and Me*. New York: Spiegel and Grau, 2015. Print.

Condé, H. Victor. *An Encyclopedia of Human Rights in the United States*. 2nd ed. Amenia: Grey House, 2011. Print.

Convention on the Prevention of the Crime of Genocide 1948. Web. 29 Nov. 2015. <https://treaties.un.org/doc/Publication/UNTS/Volume%2078/volume-78-I-1021-English.pdf>.

Crowell, Maddy. 'Paris vs. Beirut: Why Didn't Facebook Offer Safety Check for Both Attacks?' *Christian Science Monitor* 14 Nov. 2015. Web. 29 Nov. 2015. <www.csmonitor.com/World/Global-News/2015/1114/Paris-vs.-Beirut-Why-didn-t-Facebook-offer-Safety-Check-for-both-attacks>.

Davis, Martha F. 'Introduction to Volume 1'. Soohoo *et al.* 1: xv–xix.

Davis, Mike. *City of Quartz: Excavating the Future in Los Angeles.* London/New York: Verso, 1990. Print.

——. *Planet of Slums.* London/New York: Verso, 2006. Print.

Douzinas, C. *Human Rights and Empire: The Political Philosophy of Cosmopolitanism.* London: Routledge-Cavendish, 2007. Print.

Esmeir, Samera. *Juridical Humanity a Colonial History.* Stanford: Stanford University Press, 2012. Print.

'Exclusive: When Hillary Clinton Met Black Lives Matter'. *The Rachel Maddow Show* 17 Aug. 2015. Web. 19 Aug. 2015. <www.msnbc.com/rachel-maddow-show/watch/when-hillary-clinton-met-black-lives-matter-507155523571>.

Federal Bureau of Investigation. *Crime Trends by Population Group, 2009–2010.* 2010. Web. 9 Apr. 2015. <www.fbi.gov/about-us/cjis/ucr/crime-in-the-u.s/2010/crime-in-the-u.s.-2010/tables/10tbl14.xls>.

Fregoso, Rosa-Linda. 'For a Pluriversal Declaration of Human Rights'. *American Quarterly* 66.3 (2014): 583–608. Print.

Gonzales, Roberto G. 'Learning to Be Illegal: Undocumented Youth and Shifting Legal Contexts in the Transition to Adulthood'. *American Sociological Review* 76.4 (2011): 602–619. Print.

Grimm, Jacob and Wilhelm Grimm. 'The Wilful Child'. *Household Tales.* Trans. Margaret Hunt. Vol. 2. London: George Bell & Sons. 117–118. Print.

Hall, Katherine C. *International Human Rights Law: A Resource Guide.* Queenstown: Aspen Institute Justice and Society Program, 1993. Print.

Harney, Stefano and Fred Moten. 'Michael Brown'. *boundary 2* 42.4 (2015): 81–87, Print.

Hemmer, Nicole. 'Texas Pool Party Police Brutality Footage More Fuel for Black Lives Matter'. *US News & World Report* 15 Jun. 2015. Web. 20 Dec. 2015. <www.usnews.com/opinion/blogs/nicole-hemmer/2015/06/09/texas-pool-party-police-brutality-footage-more-fuel-for-black-lives-matter>.

Hennessy-Fiske, Molly. 'Walking in Ferguson: If You're Black, It's Often Against the Law'. *Los Angeles Times* 4 Mar. 2015. Web. 4 Mar. 2015. <www.latimes.com/nation/la-na-walking-black-ferguson-police-justice-report-20150305-story.html#page=1>.

Hopgood, Stephen. *The Endtimes of Human Rights.* Ithaca: Cornell University Press, 2013. Print.

Huang, Margaret. '"Going Global": Appeals to International and Regional Human Rights Bodies'. Soohoo *et al.* 2: 105–126.

The Human Rights Campaign. 'About Us'. Web. <www.hrc.org/the-hrc-story/about-us>.

Ignatieff, Michael, ed. *American Exceptionalism and Human Rights.* Princeton: Princeton University Press, 2005. Print.

Izadi, Elahe and Emma Brown. 'FBI, Justice Department Investigating S.C. Police Officer Who Threw Student across Classroom'. *Washington Post* 27 Oct. 2015. Web. 20 Dec. 2015. <www.washingtonpost.com/news/education/wp/2015/10/26/authorities-investigate-<video-of-police-officer-throwing-student-across-classroom/>.

Katz, Cindi. *Growing Up Global: Economic Restructuring and Children's Everyday Lives*. Minneapolis: University of Minnesota Press, 2004. Print.

King, Martin Luther Jr. 'I have a dream . . .' (Speech by the Rev. Martin Luther King at the 'March on Washington') [Transcript]. 1963. Web. 15 Apr. 2014. <www.archives.gov/press/exhibits/dream-speech.pdf>.

Klein, Naomi. *No Space, No Choice, No Jobs, No Logo*. 2nd ed. New York: Picador, 2002. Print.

Konnikova, Maria. 'Dressed to Suppress'. *New Yorker* 3 Dec. 2014. Web. 10 Feb. 2015. <www.newyorker.com/science/maria-konnikova/will-decreasing-police-use-military-gear-prevent-another-ferguson>.

Krieger, Nancy, Mathew V. Kiang, Jarvis T. Chen, and Pamela D. Waterman. 'Trends in US Deaths Due to Legal Intervention among Black and White Men, Age 15–34 Years, by County Income Level: 1960–2010'. *Harvard Public Health Review* 3 (January 2015): 1–5. Web. 15 Aug. 2015. <http://harvardpublichealthreview.org/190/>.

Lamar, Kendrick, Flying Lotus, and Hiro Murai. 'Never Catch Me'. 2014. Web. 17 Apr. 2015. <http://hiromurai.com/>.

Lartey, Jamiles. 'Sandra Bland Dashcam Video Raises Doubts About Officer's Basis for Arrest'. *The Guardian* 23 July 2015. Web. 16 Aug. 2015. <www.theguardian.com/us-news/2015/jul/23/sandra-bland-dashcam-video-analysis>.

Lemkin, Raphaël. *Axis Rule in Occupied Europe: Laws of Analysis of Government, Proposals for Redress*. Washington, DC: Carnegie Endowment for International Peace, 1944. Print.

——. 'Genocide: A Modern Crime'. Apr. 1945. Web. 29 Nov. 2015. <www.prevent genocide.org/lemkin/freeworld1945.htm>. Orig. pub. in *Free World* 4 (Apr. 1945): 39–43.

Lewis, Hope. '"New" Human Rights: U.S. Ambivalence Toward the International Economic and Social Rights Framework'. Soohoo *et al.* 1: 103–144.

Lorde, Audre. 'Viet-Nam Addenda'. *New York Head Shop and Museum*. Detroit: Broadside, 1974. 46. Print.

Lyon, Beth. 'From Sanctuary to Shaping International Law: How Unauthorized Immigrant Workers in America Are Advocating Beyond U.S. Borders'. Soohoo *et al.* 3: 25–54.

McClennen, Sophia and Alexandra Schultheis Moore, eds. *Routledge Companion to Human Rights and Literature*. London/New York: Routledge, 2015. Print.

McKittrick, Katherine, ed. *Sylvia Wynter: On Being Human as Praxis*. Durham: Duke University Press, 2015. Print.

Madhani, Aamer. 'Voices: Coming to Grips with Black Lives Matter'. *USA Today* 11:58 a.m. EDT 18 Aug. 2015. Web. 19 Aug. 2015. <www.usatoday.com/story/news/politics/2015/08/18/voices-coming-grips-black-lives-matter/31813319/>.

Martin, Dawn Lundy. 'The Rules of the Game: An Editor's Note'. *boundary 2* 42.4 (2015): 1–4. Print.

Mauer, Marc. *Race to Incarcerate*. 2nd ed. New York: New Press, 2006. Print.

Mignolo, Walter. 'Who Speaks for the "Human" in Human Rights?' *Hispanic Issues Online* 5.1 (2009): 22. Print.

Molina, Natalia. *How Race Is Made in America: Immigration, Citizenship, and the Historical Power of Racial Scripts*. Berkeley: University of California Press, 2014. Print.

Monáe, Janelle and Wondaland. 'Hell You Talmbout'. 2015. Web. 18 Aug. 2015. <https://soundcloud.com/wondalandarts/hell-you-talmbout>.

'MRAPs and Bayonets: What We Know about the Pentagon's 1033 Program'. *National Public Radio* 2 Sep. 2014. Web. 2 Mar. 2015. <www.npr.org/2014/09/02/342494225/mraps-and-bayonets-what-we-know-about-the-pentagons-1033-program>.

Musiol, Hanna. 'Museums of Human Bodies'. *College Literature* 40.3 (2013): 156–175. Print.

——. 'Sites of Human Rights Theory'. *Routledge Companion to Human Rights and Literature.* McClennen and Moore 389–397.

National Economic and Social Rights Initiative. 'About NESRI | NESRI | National Economic & Social Rights Initiative'. Web. 21 Aug. 2015. <www.nesri.org>.

Nixon, Rob. *Slow Violence and the Environmentalism of the Poor.* Cambridge: Harvard University Press, 2011. Print.

Obergefell v. Hodges, 576 U.S. Supreme Court (26 June 2015).

Palumbo Liu, David. 'Fragmented Forms and Shifting Contexts: How Can Social Media Work for Human Rights?' McClennen and Moore 233–242.

Passavant, Paul A. 'I Can't Breathe: Heeding the Call of Justice'. *Law Culture and the Humanities* 11.3 (2015): 330–339. Print.

Pease, Donald E. *The New American Exceptionalism.* Minneapolis: University of Minnesota Press, 2009. Print.

Plascencia, Luis F. B. *Disenchanting Citizenship: Mexican Migrants and the Boundaries of Belonging.* New Brunswick: Rutgers University Press, 2012. Print.

Powell, Catherine. 'Louis Henking and Human Rights: A New Deal at Home' . Soohoo et al. 1: 57–101. Print.

Rancière, Jacques. 'Who Is the Subject of the Rights of Man?' *South Atlantic Quarterly* 103.2/3 (2004): 297–310. Print.

Rifkin, Mark. *When Did Indians Become Straight? Kinship, the History of Sexuality, and Native Sovereignty.* New York: Oxford University Press, 2011. Print.

Santos, Boaventura de Sousa, ed. *Another Knowledge Is Possible: Beyond Northern Epistemologies.* London: Verso, 2007. Print.

——. *Epistemologies of the South: Justice against Epistemicide.* Boulder/London: Paradigm, 2014. Print.

Schmidt, Michael S. and Matt Apuzzo. 'South Carolina Officer Is Charged with Murder of Walter Scott'. *New York Times* 7 Apr. 2015. Web. 8 Apr. 2015. <www.nytimes.com/2015/04/08/us/south-carolina-officer-is-charged-with-murder-in-black-mans-death.html?ref=topics>.

Seitz-Wald, Alex. 'Bernie Sanders Event Shut Down by Black Lives Matter Activists'. *MSNBC* 09:17 p.m. 8 Aug. 2015; updated 02:48 p.m. 9 Aug. 2015. <www.msnbc.com/msnbc/bernie-sanders-event-shut-down-black-lives-matter-activists>.

Sieczkowski, Cavan. 'LAPD Shoots, Kills Black Man during "Investigative Stop"'. *Huffington Post* 13 Aug. 2014. Web. 13 Apr. 2015. <www.huffingtonpost.com/2014/08/13/lapd-shoot-kill-ezell-ford_n_5674679.html>.

Soohoo, Cynthia, Catherine Albisa, and Martha F. Davis, eds. *A History of Human Rights in the United States. Vol. 1 of Bringing Human Rights Home.* Westport: Praeger, 2008. Print.

——. *From Civil Rights to Human Rights. Vol. 2 of Bringing Human Rights Home.* Westport: Praeger, 2008. Print.

——. *Portraits of the Movement. Vol. 3 of Bringing Human Rights Home.* Westport: Praeger, 2008. Print.

Starr, Barbara and Wesley Bruer. 'Missouri National Guard's Term for Ferguson Protesters: "Enemy Forces"'. *CNN* 17 Apr. 2015. Web. 17 Apr. 2015. <http://edition.cnn.com/2015/04/17/politics/missouri-national-guard-ferguson-protesters/>.

'Status of Ratification Interactive Dashboard'. 2014. Web. 1 Dec. 2015. <http://indicators.ohchr.org/>.

Swaine, Jon and Oliver Laughland. 'Eric Garner and Tamir Rice among Those Missing from FBI Record of Police Killings'. *The Guardian* 15 Oct. 2015. Web. 1 Dec. 2015. <www.theguardian.com/us-news/2015/oct/15/fbi-record-police-killings-tamir-rice-eric-garner>.

'Tamir Rice Video Shows Cop Opening Fire on 12-Year-Old'. *Huffington Post* 26 Nov. 2014. Web. 8 Apr. 2015. <www.huffingtonpost.com/2014/11/26/tamir-rice-video-shows-co_n_6227552.html>.

United States Constitution. Web. 18 Aug. 2015. <www.law.cornell.edu/constitution>.

The Universal Declaration of Human Rights. 1948. Web. 23 Mar. 2014. <http://www.un.org/en/documents/udhr/resources.shtml>.

U.S. Department of Justice. *Investigation of the Ferguson Police Department*. 4 Mar. 2015. Web. 8 Apr. 2015. <www.justice.gov/sites/default/files/opa/press-releases/attachments/2015/03/04/ferguson_police_department_report.pdf>.

The US Human Rights Network. 'US Human Rights Network | Building a People-Centered Movement'. Web. 21 Aug. 2015. <www.ushrnetwork.org/>.

Weizman, Eyal. *The Least of All Possible Evils: Humanitarian Violence from Arendt to Gaza*. London: Verso, 2012. Print.

Wronka, Joseph. 'A Little Humility, Please: Human Rights and Social Policy in the United States'. *Harvard International Review* 20.3 (1998): 72–75. Print.

Wynter, Sylvia. 'Unsettling the Coloniality of Being/Power/Truth/Freedom: Towards the Human, After Man, Its Overrepresentation – An Argument'. *New Centennial Review* 3.3 (2003): 257–337. Print.

Part III

Responding to human suffering

Affective space and aesthetic response

Chapter 10

Drawing the line

Zombies and citizens in Heinrich von Kleist's 'The Earthquake in Chile'

Isak Winkel Holm

'Behavioural note – an infected male exposed himself to sunlight today. Now it's possible decreased function or growing scarcity of food is causing them to . . . ignore their basic survival instincts. Social de-evolution appears complete. Typical human behaviour is now entirely absent'. In Francis Lawrence's 2007 movie *I Am Legend*, Robert Neville, played by Will Smith, passes judgement on a so-called 'Darkseeker' whom he observed earlier the same day. Darkseekers are speechless mutants, vulnerable to daylight, an athletic variety of zombie created by a cancer cure gone awry. Three years after its introduction, a genetically re-engineered measles virus has wiped out 90 per cent of the human race, and turned the rest into Darkseekers. The virologist Neville seems to be the last uninfected human being on earth, an updated, biopolitical omega man surviving in a deserted New York City where grass has begun to sprout in the streets.

Neville's behavioural note draws a line between humans and non-humans, between members and non-members of the community of the 'human race'. Since social de-evolution now appears complete, and typical human behaviour is now entirely absent, the humans infected by the fatal measles virus may no longer be judged human. Based on this judgement, Neville hunts down the Darkseekers, in order to use them as test animals in his basement laboratory, before killing them with impunity.

While Neville is recording his behavioural note, he is sitting in his basement laboratory dressed in the white coat of a scientist, so at first glance his judgement about the Darkseekers' legal status appears to be based on their objective features. However, a closer look reveals that there is something weirdly unscientific about it. It is, to say the least, surprising that Neville uses 'basic survival instincts', a feature common to all living beings, as the sole criterion for 'typical human behaviour'. It is also disturbing that he seems to pass judgement even before pointing out the Darkseekers' non-human lack of survival instincts. The first words of Neville's behavioural note – 'an infected male', as opposed to 'an infected man' – implies his perception of the Darkseeker as a different species rather than as a fellow human being. Neville's use of language, rather than objective science alone, excludes the Darkseeker from the human race.

According to Neville, the Darkseekers do not count as rights-bearers: to use Hannah Arendt's famous description of the political refugees in the years preceding World War II, they experience 'the calamity of the rightless' (Arendt 295). By highlighting the interpretation process that draws a line between rights-bearers and rightless, between members and non-members of the political community, *I Am Legend* shifts the focus of justice from the *application* of the laws to a given community, to the *constitution* of the community to which the laws are applied. In political philosopher Nancy Fraser's terminology, built on Arendt's chapter on the political refugees, the question of drawing the line between humans and non-humans is not a 'what' question, but a 'who' question of justice:

> At issue here is the scope of justice, the frame within which it applies: who counts as a subject of justice in a given matter? Whose interests and needs deserve consideration? Who belongs to the circle of those entitled to equal concern?
>
> (Fraser 123)

In the contemporary avalanche of zombie movies, to which Lawrence's movie is related through their common descent from Richard Matheson's classical vampire novel *I Am Legend*, of 1954, this 'who' question of justice is routinely answered by the traditional headshot with which you put down zombies.

The shift in focus from the application of legal norms to the constitution of a political community is a recurrent feature in disaster fiction, not just in zombie movies and related movies, such as Lawrence's *I Am Legend*. In this chapter, I leave the zombies behind, and explore the 'who' question of justice in Heinrich von Kleist's short story 'The Earthquake in Chile', of 1806, one of the foundational texts of modern disaster fiction that emerged from the rubble of the Lisbon earthquake, in 1755.

First, I explore what may be called the *thematics* of judging someone human or non-human. My intent is to show that Kleist's earthquake story – like Lawrence's disaster movie, and like a large number of zombie movies – depicts an act of judgement that distinguishes between the inside and outside of a political community, between citizens and zombies.

Second, I focus on the *stylistics* of judging someone human or non-human. Here, I argue that the distinction between members and non-members of the political community seems to be connected to a certain rhetorical style, which I suggest be called 'prophetic' speech. In Kleist's short story, the language that draws the line between rights-bearers and rightless echoes the language of the Old Testament prophets, and this stylistic intertextuality is important to understanding the question of justice in the story.

Third, and last, I discuss the *aesthetics* of judging someone human or non-human. By this, I mean the relationship between the reader's aesthetic experience of Kleist's story, and the political act of judgement represented in the story: in other words, the relationship between the 'how' question of literary form, and the 'who' question of justice.

Here are those godless humans!

In Kleist's short story, the earthquake that hit Santiago de Chile in 1647 does not just interrupt the normal run of things; it also interrupts the normal run of things legal. Josefa, the daughter of a prosperous family, and Jeronimo, her Spanish tutor, have fallen in love, against the wishes of Josefa's father, and conceived a child in the garden of the convent. In seventeenth-century Chile, this is a crime, so the two young lovers are subjected to a strict penalty according to the law. However, the very moment Josefa is on her way to the scaffold to be beheaded, and Jeronimo is on the verge of hanging himself from a pillar in his prison cell, the earthquake strikes, and wipes out the Chilean government and legal system. The viceroy's palace collapses, the archbishop's mangled body is found, the courthouse is in flames, and in place of the main character's father's house, 'there was now a seething lake from which reddish vapors were rising' (Kleist, *The Marquise* 56). Josefa and Jeronimo manage to escape from the crumbling city, and in the second part of the story the young family reunite in an idyllic valley outside the city, where they make friends with the family of the nobleman Don Fernando Ormez.

In the third and final part of the story, legal proceedings against Josefa and Jeronimo continue, but this time in a different mode. This modified process takes place in a Dominican cathedral, the only church still standing in the city. The day after the quake, the citizens of Santiago gather in the cathedral where a fanatical canon, a *Chorherr*, interprets the earthquake as a divine punishment, and singles out Josefa and Jeronimo as the godless sinners who have called down the wrath of God.

Suddenly, the *Chorherr*'s sermon is interrupted by a loud voice that identifies Josefa and Jeronimo in the crowd. This triggers a release of brutal violence in the cathedral, and after a series of random misunderstandings, the young couple is killed, along with Juan, the infant child of their new friend, Don Fernando.

In most of the older interpretations of the story, the killings in the cathedral are described as an outburst of uncivilized violence, a sudden regression into a primal state of nature. René Girard, in an important essay from 1985, suggests seeing the killings not as naked violence, but as ritual violence. According to Girard's interpretation, the congregation gathered in the cathedral directs its violence against the scapegoated Josefa and Jeronimo, in order to re-establish the social order (Girard). Today, researchers tend to interpret the killings in the cathedral as a primitive version of either a legal process (Kaul 108) or a political process (Howe 68).

I side with the political interpretation of the killings. The violence is neither 'raw' nor 'ritualistic', but rather 'ethnogenetic', to use a concept of Peter

Sloterdijk's: the kind of violence that goes into the constitution of a political community (Sloterdijk). It is important to note that the voice from the crowd identifying Josefa and Jeronimo starts up with an invocation of the citizens of Santiago: 'Keep well away from them, citizens of Santiago, here are those godless humans' (*Weichet fern hinweg, ihr Bürger von St. Jago, hier stehen diese gottlosen Menschen!*) (64, my translation (m.t.)). While describing the young couple as *gottlosen Menschen*, the voice simultaneously urges fellow citizens to keep their distance from them. And indeed, the drawing of a line between members and non-members of the political community takes place as a kind of 'ethnogenetic' choreography in the overcrowded cathedral: 'a wide circle of people backed away in horror' (. . . *indessen sich ein weiter Kreis des Entsetzens um sie bildete*) (64).

Following the first voice from the frenzied crowd, the cobbler, Master Pedrillo, the leader of the crowd, tries to ascertain Jeronimo's identity: 'Citizens [*ihr Bürger*], which of you knows this young man?' (65). Moments later, Jeronimo's own father identifies his son in a similar way: 'This is Jeronimo Rugera, Citizens [*ihr Bürger*]' (66). In the end, Don Fernando's frightened son, Juan, carried at this moment by Josefa, reaches out to his father, and thus seems to identify him as Jeronimo. Once again, the identification is followed by an invocation to the citizens of Santiago: 'At once a voice yelled: He is the father! and another: He is Jeronimo Rugera! and a third: These are the blasphemers! And: Stone them! Stone them! The whole congregation of Christians in the temple of Jesus!' (*die ganze im Tempel Jesu versammelte Christenheit!*) (65, m.t.).

Whereas the legal process in the courthouse drew a line between guilty and not guilty, the political process in the cathedral draws a line between members and non-members of the political community, between Christians and 'godless humans'. A guilty/non-guilty judgement in the first part of the story is succeeded by a judgement of human/non-human in the third part.

It is important to note that the judgement that creates an empty space between members and monsters is not based on the objective features of the human beings present in the cathedral, nor is it determined by the legal norms of Chilean society. Instead, judging someone human or non-human is supported by a network of rhetorical tropes and figures. The identification of the *gottlosen Menschen* is characterized by tropes, most often by metaphors: Josefa is a 'convent whore', her child is a 'bastard'. Jeronimo uses the same kind of dehumanizing rhetoric when he finally identifies himself, in order to save the falsely identified Don Fernando: 'At this Jeronimo now cried out: Stop! You monsters! If you are looking for Jeronimo Rugera, he is here! Set free that man, who is innocent!' Here, Jeronimo describes the angry crowd as 'monsters' or, literally, 'inhuman' (*Halt! Ihr Unmenschlichen*). In the last pages of the story, this dehumanizing metaphorics is picked up by the narrator, who describes the crowd as 'bloodthirsty tigers' and 'Satanic rabble' (66, 67).

The invocation of political community is fuelled not by rhetorical tropes, but by rhetorical figures, in this case by apostrophe. The original Greek meaning of 'apostrophe' is 'turning away': the speaker turns away from his human addressee, in order to direct his speech to an inanimate object, a deceased person or an abstract concept. In this case, the voices in the crowd turn away from Josefa and Jeronimo, and address the political community. As Jonathan Culler elegantly writes, 'the apostrophe makes its point by troping not on the meaning of a word but on the circuit or situation of the communication itself' (Culler 135).

In other words, Josefa and Jeronimo's legal standing is determined by a *mode of address*, as well as by a *mode of seeing*. When the voices from the crowd are 'troping' (as Culler writes) on the meaning of words, the result is the exclusion of the young couple as *gottlosen Menschen*; when the voices are 'troping' on the situation of the communication, the outcome is a constitution of the political community of Santiago.

My claim is that Kleist's cathedral scene may be read as an early precursor of the zombie movie, where non-members of the human community are put down with a violent headshot. Kleist's version of 'ethnogenetic' violence hardly contains less gore than Lawrence's and Romero's. The outbreak of violence in the cathedral ends when Master Pedrillo drags the little Juan from Don Fernando's grasp, whirls the infant round in the air above the head and dashes him against the edge of one of the stone pillars of the cathedral. Josefa's, Jeronimo's, and Juan's legal standing is analogous to that of the zombies in George A. Romero's classical zombie movies, and of the Darkseekers in Lawrence's *I Am Legend*: they are politically, although not yet biologically, dead.

In Kleist's short story, as well as in the zombie movie, the judgement drawing the line between humans and non-humans is based on rhetorical tropes and figures. In his basement laboratory, Robert Neville describes the Darkseeker as an 'infected male', even before he notes the lack of 'typical human behaviour'. In the Dominican cathedral, the *Chorherr* and the voices from the crowd refer to similar social imaginary: a network of metaphors and apostrophes supporting the fatal identification of non-members, and invocations to members of the citizenry of Santiago.

Your hurt is incurable

The shift in focus from the application of the laws to a given community to the constitution of the community to which the laws are applied may be found not only in zombie movies and in Kleist's earthquake story, but also in the prophetic books of the Bible, some of the earliest contributions to Western disaster culture. The Old Testament prophets – Isaiah, Jeremiah, Ezekiel, and Daniel, as well as the so-called lesser prophets – lived in catastrophic times, before the fall of Israel in 722 BC, and Judaea in 586 BC. They were, understandably, obsessed with future disasters, such as Babylonian invasions, plagues, earthquakes, and insect attacks.

One hundred years ago, the sociologist Max Weber, in his work *Ancient Judaism*, described the Jewish prophets as 'world-political demagogues and publicists'

(Weber 275). Since Weber, this interpretation of the prophets, highlighting their political and social roles, has been taken up by a number of scholars, including Abraham Joshua Heschel, André Neher, Martin Buber, and, most recently, the American philosopher Michael Walzer, who, in his book *In God's Shadow*, of 2012, characterizes the prophets as 'the first social critics in the recorded history of the West' (Walzer 86).

According to the political interpretation of the prophets, the important thing about the Old Testament prophets is not that they predicted future disasters, but rather that they interpreted the existing social and political situation. Prophetic speech is diagnostic rather than prognostic: the prophets speak of the two Jewish kingdoms of Israel and Judaea, in light of future disasters. 'The prophet's eye is directed to the contemporary scene', Heschel writes, 'the society and its conduct are the main theme of his speeches' (Heschel 25). Or, in Walzer's words, 'what makes prophecy truly significant is not the oracle, the military forecast, but the moral admonition [. . .] The prophet is less foreteller than censor' (78). In fact, the Greek word *prophetes* (of *pro* and *phanau*, 'to say, to talk') refers to someone uttering the truth – not necessarily someone speaking of the future.

When the prophets direct their eyes to the contemporary scene, what they see is injustice. They never tire of charging the rich and mighty with not protecting the oppressed, the fatherless, and the widows. According to Jeremiah, to quote but one example of many, the Lord is made furious by the unjust ways of his people: 'Your hurt is incurable, / and your wound is grievous. / There is none to uphold your cause, / no medicine for your wound, / no healing for you' (Jer. 30:12).

According to the prophets, the injustice is a hurt to the very structure of the societies of Israel and Judaea. The prophets do not teach the individual subject how to live an ethical life; neither do they make metaphysical claims about the structure of the universe. Instead, they focus on the Jewish people as a political community, a people tied together by the covenant into which they entered at Mount Sinai when they were still wandering through the desert. In other words, they rely on political and social ideas of justice. The unjust 'you' that God addresses in the quotation from the book of Jeremiah is not an individual person, but Israel and Jacob, that is, the Jewish people as a body politic.

But what kind of injustice do the prophets see at the level of the political community? How are we to understand an incurable hurt to the body politic? At this point, the political interpretation of the prophets runs into a philosophical problem. As Weber notes, the prophets' strong sense of injustice does not make them dream about a reformed version of justice. They rarely refer to the positive laws of the two Jewish kingdoms, and never suggest new laws or changes to old laws. They are radicals and extremists, to be sure, but not revolutionaries or reformists: they do not create political or social movements, they do not make any effort to organize their audience, they do not counsel their kings – basically, they do not ask the generic politic question, 'What ought to be done?' (Walzer 85).

Thus, the philosophical problem is how to understand a strong sense of injustice that has very little to do with the substance of justice. To solve this problem, I suggest distinguishing between the application of the laws to a given community, on the one hand, and, on the other, the constitution of the political community to which the laws are applied. In Nancy Fraser's terminology, the prophets are concerned not with the 'what' question, but with the 'who' question of justice concerning the membership of the Jewish political community defined by the covenant. As Weber writes, the prophets were generally obsessed by the need for die jüdische *Gemeindebildung*, 'the organization of the Jewish congregation' (Weber 360), a need which urged them to emphasize the establishment of 'the decisive ritualistic barriers against the outside, in organizing the internal affairs of the community' (357). In the words of the contemporary Egyptologist Jan Assmann, the prophets perceive law as a tool with which to erect 'a high wall around the chosen people, a cordon sanitaire that prevents any contamination by, or assimilation of, the ideas and customs of the environment' (Assmann 17).

It is due to their 'ethnogenetic' point of view that the prophets disregard the normal, run-of-the-mill discussions of justice in the legal systems of the two Jewish kingdoms. To them, justice is a problem only because the high wall between members and non-members of the political community has begun to crumble. As God says of his people, through Jeremiah, 'They have turned to me their back and not their face' (Jer. 32:33). Having reached the fat and fertile Canaan, the Jewish people have begun forgetting what it means to constitute a political community. They are gradually abandoning the historical moment in the desert when they first entered into their covenant with God. Instead, they worship Baal and the idols of the neighbouring tribes, they sleep with Canaanite temple prostitutes, they sacrifice their children, and they make burnt offerings on the tops of the mountains. Seen from a prophetic point of view, the body politic is a body on the verge of dissolution. In a situation such as this, an unjust act is not a criminal or an immoral act, but an act of apostasy. In Luther's translation of the prophetic books, the word *gottlos*, 'godless', is used as a German equivalent of the Hebrew word *rasha'*, meaning unjust, wicked, criminal, and hostile to God. Being *gottlos* is being unjust at the level of the constitution of the political community. It is not so much that the *gottlos* person is a fellow citizen who happens to be in conflict with a specific law, as that he or she is a kind of internal enemy, a human being incompatible with the very principles of law. In other words, *Gottlosigkeit* is 'alegality' rather than illegality. The synonyms and metaphors for *rasha'*, much cherished by the prophets, are impudent, hypocritical, stubborn, corrupt, and stone-hearted.

What ought to be done, according to the prophets, is not a political reformation of the positive laws, but rather a 'turning back', a *teshuvah*, a return to the well-known laws of the covenant. When the prophets talk about a new law, the crucial question is not *what* should be written in this new law; it is *where* the law should be written: in the heart of the Jewish people, and not just on stone tablets (Jer. 31:33).

A flood of priestly eloquence

After Josefa and Jeronimo and their new friends have arrived at the Dominican cathedral, Kleist offers a lengthy summary of the *Chorherr*'s sermon:

> The service began with a sermon delivered from the pulpit by one of the oldest canons, vested in ceremonial robes. Raising his trembling hands high up to heaven, with the wide folds of his surplice flowing around them, he began at once to give praise and glory and thanks that there should still be, in this part of the world that was crumbling to ruins, men and women able to raise up their faltering voices to God; he described how, at the will of the Almighty, an event had taken place that must scarcely be less terrible than the Last Judgement; and when, nevertheless, pointing to a crack in the wall of the cathedral, he called yesterday's earthquake a mere foretaste of that day of doom, a shudder ran through the whole congregation. From this point his flood of priestly eloquence bore him on to the subject of the city's moral depravity: he castigated it for abominations such as Sodom and Gomorrah had not known, and ascribed it only to God's infinite forbearance that Santiago had not been totally obliterated from the face of the earth. (63)

This 'flood of priestly eloquence' is a flood of prophetic rhetoric based on some of the recurring tropes and figures of the prophetic books. Disaster is punishment: it does not happen by accident, but at the will of the Almighty, because of the city's moral depravity. And disaster is upcoming: it is not a past traumatic event from which the city should try to recover, but a future calamity that the city must work to prevent by showing moral repentance, and a 'turning back' to the old laws. According to the *Chorherr*, the crack in the wall of the cathedral is an omen, 'a mere foretaste of that day of doom'. Moreover, like the Old Testament prophets, he draws an analogy between his own city, and the cities of Sodom and Gomorrah (e.g. in the book of Ezekiel: 'As I live, says the Lord GOD, your sister Sodom and her daughters have not done as you and your daughters have done' (Ez. 16:48)). And, like the Old Testament prophets in Martin Luther's translation, the canon claims that it is only thanks to God's infinite forbearance that the city has not been totally obliterated, *vertilgt*, from the face of the earth (e.g. in the book of Amos: 'the eyes of the Lord GOD are upon the sinful kingdom, / and I will destroy it [*vertilge*] from the surface of the ground; / except that I will not utterly destroy [*vertilgen*] the house of Jacob' (Am. 9:8)).

To sum up, the *Schauder*, the shudder running through the whole congregation during the sermon, is the affective atmosphere created by prophetic speech. It is important to note that this example of prophetic speech is not just a piece of efficient rhetoric creating a certain affective response in the audience. The rhetoric comes with its own point of view on the question of justice. If we follow

Weber's political interpretation of the prophets, we must see the *Chorherr* as a political demagogue and publicist who uses the disaster-as-punishment trope to propagate his views on social and sexual order.

In his flood of priestly eloquence, the *Chorherr* recycles the word *gottlos* from Luther's translation of the prophetic books: 'He condemned as impious [*gottlos*] the indulgence with which it had been treated by society' (64). Here, the word *gottlos* does not describe Josefa and Jeronimo as individual human beings, as *gottlosen Menchen*, even if the canon goes into great detail when describing the outrage that was perpetrated in the garden of the Carmelite convent. Rather, *gottlos* indicates the 'indulgence' (*die Schonung*) with which the whole city purportedly treated this crime. Injustice, according to the *Chorherr*, is an incurable hurt to the very structure of the society. A *gottlos* city is a city in which the social contract is out of order. In his sermon, the canon denounces the 'moral depravity' of the Chilean society (*das Sittenverderbnis*), literally translated as 'the corruption of the norms'. The covenant has lost its force; it is engraved on crumbling stone tablets, not written in the hearts of the people. Like the Old Testament prophets, the *Chorherr* has shifted the focus from the application of the legal norms to the constitution of the political community.

The focus on the constitution of the political community is not only to be found in the cathedral scene. Before the killings, in the second part of the story, the citizens of Santiago gather in the valley outside Santiago in Rousseau-ian, post-disaster harmony:

> And indeed, in the midst of this horrifying time in which all the earthly possessions of men were perishing and all nature was in danger of being engulfed, the human spirit itself seemed to unfold like the fairest of flowers. In the fields, as far as the eye could see, men and women of every social station could be seen lying side by side, princes and beggars, ladies and peasant women, government officials and day labourers, friars and nuns: pitying one another, helping one another, gladly sharing anything they had saved to keep themselves alive, as if the general disaster had united all its survivors into a single family.
>
> (60)

To be sure, this image of 'a paradise built in hell', to use a phrase from contemporary disaster research (Solnit), is the complete opposite of the *Chorherr*'s denunciation of 'moral depravation', and of the short story's depiction of the frenzied crowd in the cathedral. The narrator praises 'the human spirit itself' (*der menschliche Geist selbst*), a natural, flower-like precondition for social order. Half a page later, Jeronimo speaks to Josefa about the benign nature of 'the public mood' (*die Stimmung der Gemüter*). In contrast, the canon rages against the 'indulgence' and the 'moral depravity' (*Sittenverderbnis*) of the Chilean society. While the young couple sees the resilience of the human community, the *Chorherr* sees the cracks in the social order.

Regardless of the conflicting valorizations, all the above-mentioned concepts – *menschliche Geist, Stimmung der Gemüter, Sittenverderbnis* – describe the constitution of the political community. The *Menschlichkeit* in the valley collides with the *Unmenschlichkeit* in the cathedral, but both concepts refer to the *Mensch* as a bearer of rights. In other words, the second and the third parts of the story concur, in shifting the focus from the application of legal norms to the constitution of the political community.

As John Ellis was the first to notice more than half a century ago, 'the point of the story lies less in the meaning of the events than in the attempts of the characters involved [. . .] to make sense of them' (Ellis 14). What I want to add to this discussion is that the point of the story lies in offering two conflicting interpretations of the 'who' question of justice. Three conflicting interpretations, in fact, for the second part of the story juxtaposes two different images of the utopian political community. The human spirit seems to unfold like the fairest of flowers, but the story contains two versions of this unfolding. On the one hand is an interpretation according to which the human spirit expresses itself through acts of nursing, feeding, and bodily care. As we saw, the disaster survivors in the valley are 'pitying one another, helping one another, gladly sharing everything they had saved to keep themselves alive'. According to this interpretation, the pre-legal community is constituted as 'one single family'. Kleist's word for the normative value organizing this community is goodness, *Güte*, and the recipients of the normative orientation are, first of all, the newborn child and the injured victim. In modern terms, one could describe the paradisical valley outside Santiago as the aid worker's utopia of a well-functioning humanitarian camp. The second part of the story presents a different interpretation according to which the human spirit expresses itself in heroic deeds:

> Instead of the usual trivial tea-table gossip about the ways of the world, everyone was now telling stories of extraordinary heroic deeds. Persons hitherto held to be of little consequence in society had shown a Roman greatness [*Römergröße*] of character.
>
> (60)

Römergröße is presumably some kind of republican civic virtue that motivates heroic deeds for the common good, a word that recalls the cult of the Roman republic during the French Revolution (Howe 70). In this passage, then, a *Mensch* is not a vulnerable, pre-political body, but a Roman citizen. According to this interpretation, the human community in the valley is based on *Würde*, indeed, a very Kantian notion of dignity that permeates the story.

Emotional learning?

In *Human Rights in Camera*, of 2011, political theorist Sharon Sliwinski describes the famous 1755 Lisbon earthquake as 'one of the first great mass media events' (Sliwinski 38):

> The circulation of eyewitness reports and images produced an intense emotional climate that provided fertile ground for the notion of a singular humanity, a notion that took shape in the minds of distant spectators. Indeed, the 1755 disaster marks one of the first instances in which subjects became world spectators faced with a barrage of representations of distant suffering, 'snapshots' that elicited an imaginative and affective engagement with strangers at a distance.
>
> (45)

According to Sliwinski, these aesthetic representations of distant suffering preceded the formal articulation of the 'Rights of Man'. At later historical moments, images from Belgian Congo and Auschwitz played a similar role, training our ability to recognize distant victims as fellow humans: 'Our membership within the political community we call humanity is granted by others. One must be *judged* human – and thus be endowed with "a legal personality" – in order to enjoy the benefits of the title' (46, original emphasis).

Sliwinski develops an argument presented by historian Lynn Hunt. In *The Invention of Human Rights* (2007), Hunt asserts that Rousseau's *Julie* and Richardson's *Pamela* and *Clarissa* had an indisputable cultural impact, because they prompted a 'new learning of empathy in operation' (Hunt 42). Through the highly charged identification with a fictional character such as Julie, for instance, the eighteenth-century novel 'enabled readers to empathize across class, sex, and national lines' (38). In this sense, the aesthetic experience opens the path to human rights. According to Hunt and Sliwinski, the reading of novels and the viewing of graphic representations function as 'a kind of hothouse of emotional learning' (Hunt 55).

While I find the thesis positing the relationship between the 'how' question of aesthetic experience and the 'who' question of justice convincing and intriguing, I doubt that it applies to a work of literature such as 'The Earthquake in Chile'. To be sure, Kleist's short story is a part of the barrage of representations set in motion by the Lisbon earthquake. In fact, the fictional earthquake in Santiago is strikingly similar to the factual earthquake in Lisbon; in both cases, a major city is destroyed by three elements of nature: trembling earth, rising water, and fire (Bourke). But the proto-zombie story in the Dominican cathedral may hardly be described as a series of 'snapshots' that elicits the reader's imaginative and affective engagement with the *Chorherr*, with Master Pedrillo, or even with the wretched Josefa, Jeronimo, and Juan. What is at stake here is the *aesthetics* of judging someone human or non-human. Kleist's prose, with its violent and jarring style, is anything but a hothouse of emotional learning. The same goes for a number of Kleist's fellow writers struggling with questions of human rights in disastrous situations, from Dostoevsky's Siberian prison camp, to Kafka's penal colony.

The claim I make could be put in this way: in Kleist's earthquake story, the relation between aesthetic experience and human rights is a matter of reflection, rather than education. The story elicits affective disengagement, not affective engagement. The multitude of fictional characters that judge one another as either human or non-human, either Christian *Bürger* or *gottlosen Menchen*, forces the reader to step back from judging someone human or non-human, and instead to question the presuppositions underlying our capacity to determine the 'who' question of justice. As we have seen, these presuppositions happen to be a network of metaphors and apostrophes fuelling the identification of 'godless humans'. In the aesthetic experience, the act of judgement that draws a line between humans and non-humans becomes reflexive: it stops up, turns back, and makes palpable its own way of judging.

Conclusion

The morning after the quake, as Josefa and Jeronimo leave the idyllic valley in the company of their new friends, they all start discussing whether it is a good idea to participate in the mass at the Dominican cathedral: 'Someone in Don Fernando's party raised the question of whether they too should not participate in this solemnity and join the general procession' (61). Here, precisely at the junction between the second and the third part of the story, the narrative slows. On one side of the debate is Don Fernando's sister-in-law, Doña Isabel, who fears the future events in the cathedral. The other side is taken by Don Fernando and the other members of the two families, who are all a little euphoric because of the social harmony in the valley. They trust the benign public mood, and have no fears regarding joining 'the general procession'.

This reflective slowing of the plot is due to a vacillation between two opposing interpretations of the political community, a moment of indecisiveness between judging the citizens human and judging them non-human: is the Chilean community, after all, characterized by *Menschlichkeit* or by *Unmenschlichkeit*?

We find a similar slowing down in deleted scenes of *I Am Legend*, now available as extra material on the Two-Disc Special Edition. As we have seen, Neville categorizes the Darkseekers as non-human. 'Social de-evolution appears complete. Typical human behaviour is now entirely absent', he dictates, in his behavioural notes. In accordance with this judgement, he is compelled to deny the possibility that it was the Darkseekers who set a snare trap for him. 'They have no higher brain function, they don't plan', he argues in a deleted scene. In another deleted scene, closer to the end, however, he starts to vacillate: 'Could they be evolving?' Is the community of Darkseekers characterized by *Menschlichkeit* or by *Unmenschlichkeit*?

It is my contention that the two families' baffled lingering *in* Kleist's story may be read as an image of the readers' aesthetic experience *of* Kleist's story. The same goes for Neville's hesitation in *I Am Legend*. Like Doña Isabel, Don Fernando, Josefa and Jeronimo, and like Neville in the deleted scenes, the reader cannot help but slow down and linger between two different interpretations of the political community, thereby not learning to perceive someone as human, but instead reflecting on the act of judging someone human or non-human.

Works cited

Arendt, Hannah. *The Origins of Totalitarianism.* San Diego: Harcourt Brace Jovanovich, 1979. Print.

Assmann, Jan. *The Price of Monotheism.* Stanford: Stanford University Press, 2010. Print.

Bourke, T. E. ' Vorsehung und Katastrophe. Voltaire's Poème sur Le Désastre de Lisbonne und Kleists Erdbeben in Chili'. *Klassik und Moderne: Die Weimarer Klassik als Historisches Ereignis und Herausforderung im Kulturgeschichtlichen Prozess*: Walter Müller-Seidel zum 65. Geburtstag. Ed. Walter Müller-Seidel, Karl Richter, and Jörg Schönert. Stuttgart: Metzler, 1983. Print.

Culler, Jonathan. *The Pursuit of Signs: Semiotics, Literature, Destruction.* Ithaca: Cornell University Press, 1981. Print.

Ellis, John M. 'Kleist's Das Erdbeben in Chili'. *PEGS* (Publications of the English Goethe Society) 33 (1963): 10–55. Print.

Fraser, Nancy. 'Abnormal Justice'. *Justice, Governance, Cosmopolitanism, and the Politics of Difference.* Ed. Kwame Anthony Appiah, Seyla Benhabib, Iris Marion Young, and Nancy Fraser Berlin: Der Präsident der Humboldt-Universität zu Berlin, 2007. 117–147. Print.

Girard, René. 'Mythos und Gegenmythos: Zu Kleists Das Erdbeben in Chili'. *Positionen der Literaturwissenschaft: Acht Modellanalysen am Beispiel von Kleists* Das Erdbeben in Chili. Ed. David E. Wellbery. Munich: Beck, 1985. 130–148. Print.

Heschel, Abraham Joshua. *The Prophets.* New York: Harper & Row, 1962. Print.

Howe, Steven. *Heinrich Von Kleist and Jean-Jacques Rousseau: Violence, Identity, Nation.* Rochester: Camden House, 2012. Print.

Hunt, Lynn. *Inventing Human Rights: A History.* New York: W. W. Norton, 2007. Print.

Kaul, Susanne. *Poetik der Gerechtigkeit: Shakespeare-Kleist.* Munich: Fink, 2008. Print.

Kleist, Heinrich von. 'Das Erdbeben in Chili'. *Sämtliche Werke und Briefe.* 4 vols. Ed. Ilse-Marie Barth, Klaus Müller-Salget, Stefan Ormanns, and Hinrich C. Seebad. Frankfurt am Main: Deutscher Klassiker Verlag, 1987–1997, vol. 3. Print.

——. *The Marquise of O-, and Other Stories.* Trans. David Luke and Nigel Reeves. Harmondsworth: Penguin, 1978. Print.

Sliwinski, Sharon. *Human Rights in Camera.* Chicago: University of Chicago Press, 2011. Print.

Sloterdijk, Peter. *Im Schatten des Sinai: Fussnote über Ursprünge und Wandlungen Totaler Mitgliedschaft.* Frankfurt am Main: Suhrkamp, 2013. Print.

Solnit, Rebecca. *A Paradise Built in Hell: The Extraordinary Communities That Arise in Disasters.* New York: Viking, 2009. Print.

Walzer, Michael. *In God's Shadow: Politics in the Hebrew Bible.* New Haven: Yale University Press, 2012. Print.

Weber, Max. *Ancient Judaism.* Glencoe: Free Press, 1952. Print.

Chapter 11

Recoding *The Look of Silence*

Alexandra Schultheis Moore

In his short experimental film *MUZAK: A Tool of Management* (2003, 3 min.), Joshua Oppenheimer interviews a former leader of one of Indonesia's 1965–1966 death squads, which killed hundreds of thousands of people in the anti-communist purges that brought President Suharto's government to power. Sharman Sinaga is initially reluctant to recount his actions, exclaiming 'he [Oppenheimer] might tell people' and 'it's a secret!' – disingenuous statements, to be sure, given that Oppenheimer is witness to the scene as a film-maker. Indeed, Sinaga soon follows his wife's urging to 'tell him again how you killed the communists', as their granddaughter looks on: 'I'd just cut their throats [. . .] cut off their heads. Sometimes I'd rip their throats out like this. Mostly, I'd hold them upside down like this and crush their skull with my foot'. One of the first of 41 interviews with perpetrators that Oppenheimer conducted over a two-year period displays what would become a pattern of willing, oftentimes boastful mock demonstration of the physical movements and psychological gymnastics required to kill Communist Party of Indonesia (PKI) members, suspected sympathizers, unionists, students, intellectuals, landless farmers, and ethnic Chinese at the behest of the state. These interviews provided the seeds for Oppenheimer's two recent films, Academy Award nominees for best documentary, *The Act of Killing* (2012) and *The Look of Silence* (2014). The two films interrupt the legacy of silence around the mass murders that is imposed by an oligarchy founded on corruption and fear. By rendering apparent the violent underbelly of Suharto's New Order government (1965–1998) and the continued impunity and privilege of those who have retained power since his ouster, the films create the conditions for the emergence of human rights discourse where none has existed over the 50-plus years since the murder campaign occurred.

In this chapter, I examine how *The Look of Silence* recodes silence at first by manifesting and then by dismantling the conventions that undergird victims' silence as appropriate and necessary for national unity. Those conventions, I argue, rest in part on the presumption among perpetrators of their own inviolability – inviolability rooted in neo-liberal and biosecurity ideologies that the film exposes and denaturalizes. Whereas the perpetrators describe the violence they committed as necessary to immunize the state against the disease of communism, the film reveals this logic as little more than propaganda used to decimate potential political opposition and maintain power. Oppenheimer's film-making method meets the illusion of inviolability with his protagonist Adi Rukun's strategic display of vulnerability. In doing so, the film undermines the foundations of the regime's legitimacy and its claims to be democratic. Rather than counter official history through a documentary that is driven by expert testimony, historical footage, and the suffering of victims, Oppenheimer and Adi stage confrontations with perpetrators that are grounded in physical, psychological, and social vulnerability. The performativity of Adi's vulnerability – when he courageously reveals himself as a survivor to perpetrators who still hold power and threaten to wield it – in relation to the egregious crimes of the perpetrators therefore plays a key role in dismantling the official narrative of the mass murders that explains them as the result of the spontaneous uprising of the people against communism. Vulnerability becomes a foundation upon which the past must be acknowledged and the future negotiated and imagined, rather than precisely what national unity, impunity, and inviolability sought to secure. Adi's willingness to exercise vulnerability in the face of boasting also recodes the film's titular silence. The film develops a complex register of silences that refers, of course, to victims' exclusion from the public sphere, but also comes to include moments of discursive impasse, as well as those long pauses in which listening can occur, culpability might be acknowledged, and from which negotiation might begin.

In recoding silence, the film explores new modes of human rights storytelling and documentary film. As the title of this volume indicates, human rights narratives wrestle with the twinned expectation that they will represent the process by which victims become agents (a process usually marked by the transformation of silence into speech), or, when that fails, mourn those who have suffered (e.g. Chowdhury xiii–xix; Nance 137–156). Readings from 'celebration to mourning' (Nance) locate culture's work in the messy dialectic between instrumentality and sentimentality most often rooted in identification. Such approaches depend upon the legibility of victimhood and emphasize a text's ability to raise awareness and generate ostensibly universal feelings of sympathy, despair, or outrage. *The Look of Silence* reworks these expectations in crucial ways. It engages viewers through a noble protagonist, evidence of atrocity, and the need for mourning; however, it does not respond to the representation of vulnerability with a positivist human rights discourse that would assuage it. Instead of showing silence and vulnerability as that which the juridico-political framework can mend, the film manipulates the conventions surrounding both conditions in order to generate what might be called a new human rights ethos. This ethos emerges from the recoding of silence and vulnerability as sources of rights claims that must be acknowledged.

Although *The Look of Silence* includes the long takes, spare equipment, and sparce direction of direct cinema, it regularly discloses the layers of performativity it documents and employs careful visual and aural storytelling cues. The emphasis on performativity illuminates the ways in which both the mass murders of 1965–1966 and the contemporary encounters on screen are rooted in the ideologies that sustained Suharto's regime and continue to hold sway, and it insists on the possibility of other narratives of past and future. By rendering the atmosphere and discourses of violent nationalism as politically constructed rather than naturalized, in other words, the film insists that other performances are possible. Here, too, the film emphasizes narrative potential through a quiet soundtrack that shifts attention from the fearful imposition of silence to the necessity of careful listening and the moral responsiveness that listening demands.

A brief contextual overview

A failed coup attempt on 30 September 1965, in which six army generals were killed, provided an opportunity for Army General Suharto to assert military control ostensibly in defence of President Sukarno, Indonesia's national independence hero. As historian John Roosa writes, for Suharto, the 'claim that the PKI organized [the coup attempt] was [. . .] not just any ordinary fact, it was *the* supreme fact of history from which the very legitimacy of the regime was derived' (7, original emphasis). This fact was no less powerful for being false, and Suharto worked strenuously to demonize the PKI through control of news media, the construction of the Museum of PKI Treason, and sponsoring the production in 1984 of a four-hour film, *The Treason of the September 30th Movement/PKI*, which became mandatory viewing every year until 1998. That film worked retrospectively to legitimate the state-sponsored mass murders of 1965–1966, fuelling the propaganda that depicted 'communists' as cruel, sadistic, sexually perverse, and unreligious. Such depictions, in turn, polished the lens through which the state's foundational ideology was reimagined to condone Suharto's carefully engineered path to the presidency and his 32-year military dictatorship.

Upon Indonesia's independence from Dutch rule in 1945, Sukarno articulated his government's commitment to nationalism, religion, and communism (commonly referred to through the acronym Nasakom) – which guaranteed the PKI (the largest Communist Party in the world in 1965) legitimate political power – as well as the nationalist principles of Pancasila: national unity, social justice, belief in God, humanitarianism, and democracy (Simpson, *Economists with Guns* 14–15). Suharto used the manufactured 'fact' of communist sadism and disloyalty in the September 30th Movement to discredit Nasakom while elevating Pancasila to what Roosa calls a 'sacred covenant' and the 'official state ideology' (Roosa 10). The paramiltary Pancasila Youth Movement (Pemuda Pancasila) and other, similar parastatal institutions were thereby empowered to attack suspected communists and sympathizers. Although the army clearly organized the violence, outsourcing it to such groups in concert with fabricating news stories of communist atrocities and censoring coverage of the massacres furthered the state's claim that the purge resulted from the people's spontaneous uprising in national defence. This storyline also masked the implicit and explicit support of the US for Suharto's rise to power, support that included tacit approval, supplying lists of names of suspected communists to be targeted, the suppression of human rights reporting on the atrocities, and a decades-long alliance with Suharto based on shared neo-liberal economic interests.[1]

The US alliance with Suharto, which encouraged 'foreign investment and oriented the country's economy around export production for Western markets' (Roosa 197), deteriorated with the Asian financial crisis of 1997 and the imposition by the International Monetary Fund of structural adjustment programmes that notoriously shrank social services and favoured private investment. Aihwa Ong describes how after the decline of the rupiah at that time:

> millions of Indonesian workers laid off from their jobs returned to poverty-stricken neighborhoods and villages. A picture of Suharto signing away his power, with the stern IMF chief standing over him, his arms crossed, had been a widely publicized image of national humiliation.
>
> (53)

Facing mass protests – many of which targeted ethnic Chinese in a reprisal of the 1965–1966 identification of enemies of the state, as well as because of the ties between wealthy Chinese families and the Suharto regime – and the withdrawal of US support, Suharto resigned in 1998. Ong describes this period in terms of a 'clash of neoliberal strategies'. On the one hand, Suharto's New Order government was founded upon a purge that killed an estimated 1 million people and was maintained through military control and an extensive prison system. Even since Suharto's resignation, the army has continued to 'wor[k] hand in hand with factories to maintain social order among the labor force' in industrial zones, and 'Indonesians think it is normal for the army to keep industrial cities secure for factories, and factory bosses to routinely make "donations" to local commanders', while workers themselves are 'constantly vulnerable to the state's repressive apparatus' (Ong 85–86). These policies have kept Indonesian industries such as rubber and oil open to US and other foreign investment and have favoured the accumulation of private wealth among the oligarchy. On the other hand, when the financial collapse occurred, the IMF stepped in to ensure what Ong (borrowing from Stephen Gill) calls the 'strategic aspect of "disciplinary neoliberalism," whereby emerging states are subjected

1 See, for instance, Simpson's analysis of the US's 'enthusiastic' support of the mass murders (*Economists with Guns* 189) and his discussion of the Carter Administration's complicity in suppressing Indonesian human rights in '"The First Right": The Carter Administration, Indonesia, and the Transnational Human Rights Politics of the 1970s'. Roosa also discusses the various forms of material aid the US supplied during the time (194–197).

to rules that intensify their subordination to global market forces' (93). After 1998, Indonesia continued to be ruled by Suharto's associates, at least until the election in 2014 of President Joko Widodo, which was seen as a break from decades of corrupt rule (although how much of a break is debated).[2] Indeed, as *The Look of Silence* makes clear, local elites and officials (including the Speaker of the regional legislature) in northern Sumatra where the film takes place have retained the privileged positions they assumed through the Komando Aksi death squad during the purges.

Oppenheimer has described how the possibility of making *The Look of Silence* emerged in the time between filming and releasing *The Act of Killing*, when local commanders who had cooperated and appeared in the first film had not yet seen the results. The perpetrator interviews that subtend both films and were conducted just a few years after the 1997 collapse may also have been facilitated by the 'clash of neoliberal strategies' that Ong describes, in that economic failures of the state and resurgence of international monetary controls both put pressure on the ideology of nationalism. Patricia Spyer, for example, analyses the political changes wrought by the economic crisis, including in 2000 more decentralized political control and regional autonomy:

> Following KRISMON (Krisis Moneter, or Monetary Crisis) and even KRISTAL (Krisis Total, or Total Crisis), Reformasi, the battle cry of protesting students in the heady spring of 1998, arrived with a slew of terms that were drawn equally from the language of democracy, good governance, and human rights – *demokrasi*, *transparan* (transparency), and *masyarakat sipil* (civil society) – along with their alleged opposites, *korupsi*, *kolusi* (collusion), *nepotisme* (KKN).
>
> (191)

For Spyer, attention to the social climate that such discourses respond to and influence evinces the deep roots of structural violence without imposing a teleology of historical change (e.g. transition to democracy or uni-linear capital accumulation). I follow Spyer's lead in examining the '"climate," "ambiance," "atmospherics," and "milieu," often invoked in descriptions of social and political violence,' in order to focus on 'the role of the anticipated, the barely sensed, the possible, and the conditional in the structuring of ordinary people's

2 A recent editorial in the *Jakarta Globe* condemns the President and his Attorney General H. M. Prasetyo for instituting a reconciliation commission with only 'non-judiciary' resolutions to address the 1960s violence. The editorial points out the hypocrisy of the recent very public executions of drug dealers, which the government describes as simply following the letter of the law, with the lack of strong legal response to the purge, and concludes that any reconciliation process will fail without 'the moral leaders in our government to make it work' ('Joko's Reconciliation Commission').

perceptions and actions in extraordinary times of acute duress and chronic violence' (Spyer 190, 191). *The Look of Silence* invites viewers and participants into the persistent climate of impunity and fear, and it does so by exploiting the tension between the boasting of perpetrators and the layers of silence and silencing. These layers include the false demonization of the PKI, the complicity of the US and related global financial institutions, and the enforced silence of victims and survivors whose suffering cannot be publicly acknowledged or mourned. Benedict Anderson notes, 'impunity is nothing without repetitive, boastful demonstration before different audiences' ('Impunity and Reenactment'); however, the film demonstrates ways in which shifts in discursive conventions can turn boasting into self-incrimination, certainty into doubt, and inviolability into vulnerability, as well as transform silence and vulnerability into sources of social and political agency.

On *MUZAK* and *Silence*: soundtracks of violence and impunity

In *MUZAK: A tool of Management*, Oppenheimer has taken footage from an early (2002) perpetrator interview and transformed it into a three-minute film that simultaneously links thematically with his short films about biopolitical and neo-liberal violence in the US and his feature films about Indonesia.[3] The common thread among these films is the violence implicit in claims to bio-political exceptionalism that are fuelled by neo-liberal predations. I draw my concept of biopolitical exceptionalism here from Jasbir Puar's work in *Terrorist Assemblages* in that exceptionalism 'paradoxically signals distinction from (to be unlike, dissimilar) as well as excellence (imminence, superiority), suggesting a departure from yet mastery of linear teleologies of progress' (3). Although Puar discusses exceptionalism primarily in the context of US nationalism, my use of exceptionalism is tied less to a singular national identity than to transnational neo-liberal ideology that validates particular distributions of privilege and expendability. Those distributions are locally specific, but rooted in a shared dedication to private accumulation at the expense of social welfare.[4] What *MUZAK: A Tool for Management* and *The Look of Silence* depict is how discourses

3 See, for instance, *Postcard from Sun City, Arizona* (2003, 3 min.), in which Oppenheimer overlays a radio-show interview with 'Bridget' about her rewarding work on the chain gang and how it keeps her fit with a television advertisement for the Sun City retirement community, an unincorporated town first opened in 1960. As residents gush about their fitness facilities and sense of retirement as the permanent luxury vacation they have earned, the talk show interview and other radio spots that provide the soundtrack draw attention to violent labour practices coded in discourses of health and profit.

4 Puar uses the term 'bio-necro collaboration' to describe the interdependencies of bio- and necro-politics (35).

of health, virility, and impunity, which signal fantasies of everlasting inviolability, attempt to mask the roots of neo-liberal privilege in structural violence in Indonesia.

In *MUZAK*, Sinaga is filmed from the side and below and appears shirtless, ageing, and smoking in his kitchen, his voice only audible (though not directly intelligible to anglophone audiences) when he describes mud filling the mouths of his victims as he stomped on their skulls, such that at that moment, his voice substitutes directly for those of his victims. The film presents his visual testimony – smoking, smiling awkwardly, demonstrating the work of his hands and knees – both forward and then running backward, intercut periodically with stills taken from various perspectives of his granddaughter's face as she silently bears witness to her grandfather's boasts. In place of his voice (with the exception of the one moment cited above), the viewer learns of Sinaga's actions through subtitles against a cheerful soundtrack. Once he has told how mass murder was routinized ('It happened every day at 2 pm'), directed by the state ('Finish them off!'), and easy ('If it was 2 or 3 at a time, it was a piece of cake!'), the subtitles switch to information about MUZAK: a 'non-entertainment medium' that programmes its product in 15-minute intervals in order to enhance 'employee attitude, efficiency and productivity'. Thus, MUZAK functions at once as a non-diegetic voice-over that substitutes for direct perpetrator testimony, and MUZAK metaphorically connects the means and ends of the violence Sinaga describes. MUZAK as 'a tool of management' cultivates the employee and the customer in service of corporate profits, and Sinaga recounts his labour installing a neo-liberal oligarchy.

Initially developed in 1922 and commercialized in 1934, MUZAK was most influential in the US in the 1960s, although it has continued to develop and supply 'scientifically engineered sound' that 'is there to be heard but not listened to' ('Muzak and Background Art'). MUZAK was designed according to a theory of stimulus progression, such that each interval would be comprised of six songs of gradually increasing tempo (on a scale of one to six), followed by an equal interval of silence; and it was programmable to different times of day 'to achieve predetermined effects' in terms of labour and customer management. In today's corporate-speak, MUZAK's 'audio architects' code these effects to match the client's brand culture – what David Owen writing in *The New Yorker* reports as a song's '"topology," the cultural and temporal associations that it carries with it, like a hidden refrain' ('The Soundtrack of Your Life'). In the short film, the 'non-entertainment medium's' coding of the milieu of labour and consumption and its constitutive use of silence (mud filling victims' mouths) set the stage for *The Look of Silence*.

It is commonplace to counterpose victims' voicelessness with their testimony as the goal of human rights representations; however, *The Look of Silence* provides a much more complex rendering of the ambience of silence. While silence registers as absence, the victims' silence and silencing function in familiar ways to denote their exclusion from the public sphere. That designation, in turn, reinforces the conception of 'the public as normatively locutionary' (54). In 'Silence: A Politics', Kennan Ferguson argues for an understanding of silence not as lack, marginalization, exclusion, or even resistance, but as potentially constitutive of 'selves and even communities' (49). Noting that silence can also be employed to 'provoke discursive subjectivity' (57), as in the case of the professor or therapist's silence designed to elicit a response, he demonstrates that such multivalent uses point to a further possibility: that of the communal and politically open-ended role of silence. Rather than lead to a definitive 'politics of silence' as in the case of reading silence as exclusion or resistance, this possibility renders silence disruptive, if unfixed (62). It 'disturbs precisely because the ideal of transparent speech is the presumed mode of participation', and thus invites negotiation as opposed to any singular response, such as a settlement or verdict (63).

The striking achievement of *The Look of Silence* is its representation of the complexity of silence, particularly in relation to perpetrators boasting of their atrocities. Whereas the boasting initially serves to enforce the silence of victims, the film deconstructs that relationship through a dense cinematic language that captures and transforms the social milieu. The film interweaves three main narrative lines. The first, of Adi screening interviews that Oppenheimer conducted with perpetrators a decade earlier, provides historical context in the perpetrators' own words and introduces viewers to the characters (see Figure 11.1). Oppenheimer primarily shows Adi sitting silently and pensively in front

Figure 11.1 Adi rescreening Oppenheimer's early interviews in which perpetrators describe the torture and murder of Adi's brother, Ramli.

Source: Photo by Lars Skree. Reprinted by permission of Final Cut for Real.

of the screen, listening to the perpetrators' shameless recounting of their abhorrent acts, including the grotesque murder of Adi's brother Ramli, with only minimal prompts from the director. On one level, these scenes replicate the status quo of the public performance of impunity and imposed silence. However, the film-making process simultaneously alters the context and conventions that surround that speech and silence: Adi views this footage in an empty room, with only the glare of the screen to illuminate him, so that the testimony is at once decontextualized and at a distance. Without the apparatus of the state to validate perpetrators, boasting becomes self-incrimination and silence reads as Adi's moral stature rather than debilitating fear.

The second storyline focuses on Adi's family – his parents, wife, and two children. In these scenes, Ramli's absence is palpable in his mother's anger and grief and his father's combination of fear and dementia; however, the scenes also depict the family's intimacy, care, and humour. The private discourse of the family provides a powerful counterweight to their public silence. When Adi and his mother, Rohani, talk about Ramli's murder, or Adi corrects the misinformation that his children learn in school, viewers understand the imposition of silence as a failed attempt to mask much more complicated narratives of intergenerational and communal knowledge and responsibility. Scenes in the family are notable, too, for the quiet soundtrack of birds and insects that accompany Rohani in her garden, as well as for presenting the sound of her voice before her image, such that audiences must attend carefully to the work of listening to attribute sound to its source. Whereas scenes of Adi watching perpetrator testimony ask audiences to bear witness alongside him, these familial moments refuse to counter political discourse with a conventional narrative of the opposing side. Instead, they provide a sphere in which mourning Ramli's death can occur while insisting that mourning cannot be the sole objective. In addition to conveying silence as a form of respect for the dead, these scenes suggest that a shared future will necessitate careful listening to quiet voices of survivors and, metaphorically through the sounds and images of insect larvae, to other narratives about to break forth.

The final storyline, discussed in detail below, moves unevenly towards this future through the confrontations Adi stages with perpetrators. These confrontations, which shift from gardens into domestic spaces and up the chain of command for the death squads, map alternative futures from those represented by other characters in the film: Kemat, the sole survivor among the prisoners taken for execution along with Ramli, advises Adi and Rohani to forget the past, focus on the present, and leave judgement to God; Adi's father is trapped in dementia that has erased memory of his son and the source of his lasting fear, but not fear itself; and Rohani persists in love for her family and hate for the perpetrators among whom she lives. For all three of these characters, the past has a kind of stranglehold on the present, whether it is through the extraordinary efforts needed to suppress it or the intractability of emotion it fosters. Adi's confrontations are attempts to found an alternative means not just for persisting, but for what Anna Grear has described as flourishing. Flourishing in this sense refers to the possibility of conviviality, of social coexistence. It is also for Grear rooted in the acknowledgment of embodied vulnerability as constitutive of sociality. Vulnerability becomes revalued in this sense from a temporary condition of weakness one seeks to overcome in the pursuit of inviolability to a differentiated condition 'refracted through the prism of bio-material embodiment and located within the materialities of advanced global capitalism' (Grear 41). Both forms of materiality intersect when Adi meets perpetrators in his role as an optometrist – providing the film's signature image of a perpetrator in red glasses (used to measure vision and test different lenses) and the governing metaphor of how to see clearly. Here, the perpetrators' failing eyesight signifies inviolability as a temporary, political condition (rather than inherent privilege), and underscores the common fragility of embodied existence.

The transformation of perpetrators from terrorizing to physically and socially vulnerable is also visible in scenes where former executioners gently help each other down the bank to the river where they then describe how they dis-emboweled, decapitated, and disposed of their victims. Such moments of layered vulnerability and atrocity underscore the paradox of evil that James Dawes describes: '*Evil is demonic and other; it is also banal and common to us all*' (vii, original emphasis). In depicting perpetrators who want to demonstrate their physical prowess and mental fortitude in ageing bodies and minds, the film demystifies their power and raises the question of how atrocity could become normalized. That atrocity can be common (as in the number of local executioners needed to individually kill hundreds of thousands of fellow Indonesians) does not excuse it to any degree, but calls upon the imagination of shared vulnerability as counter-measure. Thus, the confrontations that Adi stages emphasize that listening carefully and seeing clearly are both necessarily grounded in embodied and social materialities. When that grounding is acknowledged or illuminated, boasting loses its ideological cover; perpetrators' sense of their own invincibility is betrayed by their ageing bodies, failing eyes, and dubious reason; and Adi's willingness to disclose his own vulnerability, to listen to perpetrators, and then to insist that they listen to him models the kind of mutual regard and acknowledged vulner-ability that must augur a shared future.

Seven confrontations: from 'everything is safe now' to 'the wound is open'

Sharman Sinaga of *MUZAK: A Tool of Management* reappears at the beginning of *The Look of Silence* in the first early interview that Adi rescreens. Now fully dressed and in his living room, he sings into a microphone while his grand-daughter plays nearby. Adi watches, as Sinaga sings, 'Why should I remember, if remembering only breaks my heart?' The song functions doubly to signal the need for *communal* memory and mourning: while the lyrics speak of the painful past, Sinaga's singing echoes in the film through both Adi's father and another death squad leader's renditions of love songs from their youth. Whereas MUZAK in the short film provides a soundtrack to neo-liberal violence, in *The Look of Silence* the old men singing conjures an atmosphere of decline and regret. The interview continues when Sinaga segues into descriptions of individual murders. His recounting parallels that from the short film, complete with his gestures and laughter, and the scene ends with Adi, as a member of the next generation, silently watching this display of performative impunity (see Figure 11.1). This opening sequence serves a tutelary function, while also aligning viewers with Adi's desire to understand both the originary violence and the continued boasting. In doing so, the film recodes the fearful silence of victims to an inquisitive one, perhaps made possible by the generational distance from the purge as well as through the mediatized distance (viewers watching Adi and Adi watching Oppenheimer's earlier footage, rather than having been present at the original interviews).

Adi's seven confrontations replace the silence he displays before the older footage with questions and corrective commentary to what he hears. His first meeting investigates the positionality of the bystander. During an optometry exam with a woman who lived in Aceh (the neighbouring province) during the killings, Adi asks her what happened in 1965. She claims there were no killings and 'nothing happened', communists were killed, and 'I know nothing about it'. These contradictions between knowing and not knowing are manifested further in the next shot, when she has on the red spectacles and recounts how victims were blindfolded, taken to the river, and killed. Not only does this scene continue the metaphor of the red glasses (symbolizing Adi's corrective interventions); it also exemplifies Oppenheimer's strategy of dismantling the official propaganda through words and images that should align but that are always either contradictory or askew (e.g. her vision in relation to blindfolded prisoners on their way to execution). The exchange establishes the parameters of propriety and is instructive in defining the bounds of what the 1965–1966 beneficiaries are willing to discuss openly, as well as perpetrators' 'cognitive dissonance – the gap between what we know and we emotionally believe' (Oppenheimer in Moore 485): her comments reflect broad public knowledge of the killings, the ongoing power of anti-communist rhetoric, and moral confusion that comes from the attempt to rationalize mass murder in the name of national security.

Tension increases in the second confrontation, which moves from bystander and beneficiary to perpetrator. Adi meets Inong, a former death squad leader whom Oppenheimer also interviewed a decade earlier. The sequence works assiduously to dissolve the claims of biopolitical exceptionalism that are mobilized to defend the purge. The film comes close to ridicule in showing Inong, ageing with perhaps not many teeth, wearing the red optometry glasses, and maintaining that people still fear him. His claims become more perverse, if still true, when seemingly unprompted he adds, 'If we didn't drink human blood, we'd go crazy', a shocking detail repeated in other perpetrator testimony in the film. Regardless of his claims of invincibility, Inong quickly becomes angry and defensive in the face of further questions. When he relays the rationales for murder – that Indonesian Communist Party members were sexually immoral and unreligious, Adi probes this rationale in relation to Islam's injunction against killing. For Inong, 'Everything is safe now' and, 'Luckily, I drank blood'. However, each attempt to probe beneath these outrageous platitudes leads to anger first directed towards Adi, but then towards Oppenheimer. By including Inong's demand that Oppenheimer stop filming, *The Look of Silence* reveals perpetrators' fear of full disclosure notwithstanding their boastfulness, as well as perpetrators' recognition that both the film and the survivor are altering the discursive conventions that sanction(ed) that boasting.

The third and fourth confrontations build an atmosphere of intimate and imminent danger by moving indoors and further up the chain of command, and they include Adi's first two disclosures of his own relationship to the killings. In Adi's meeting with Amir Siahaan, a leader of the Komando Aksi who earlier demonstrated for the camera how Ramli's murder occurred, there is no pretense of an eye exam. Adding another facet to the film's portrayal of a corrupt and immoral regime, Siahaan attributes his wealth to his work during the purge: 'If you do good, you're rewarded'. Once Adi reveals himself as the brother of one of those killed, Siahaan quickly becomes menacing, asking Adi his name and village. These are not idle questions, and Siahaan reverts to the logic of the past by warning that 'these days subversives are everywhere'. He adds accusingly, 'so, keep going . . . continue with this communist activity'. Adi receives a similar response from the former Secretary General of Komando Aksi, M. Y. Basrun, who has also served as Speaker of the regional legislature since 1971. He initially repeats the propaganda that the 'mass killings were the spontaneous action of the people'; however, when Adi presses the point, reminding the commander that the political prisoners were taken under police escort to the river to be killed, Basrun replies, 'That's politics', and, 'If the victims' children didn't like me – I would never get the most votes'. This self-aggrandizing logic fails to sustain itself, however, once Adi discloses himself as a survivor. Basrun immediately insinuates a threat that reveals the falsity of his earlier statements: 'Do the victims' families want the killings to happen again?' And he warns that to raise the spectre of the past means 'it will definitely happen again'. These two confrontations, interspliced with Adi informing his mother and wife of his meetings and their worried concern that he will be killed in return, make palpable the danger he faces in breaking his silence. Siahaan and Basrun's threats also bespeak a failure of imagination. They strenuously maintain an atmosphere of imposed silence and fear because they can imagine no future politics other than survivors' revenge and retribution.

The fifth confrontation, although its failure is particularly poignant, initiates the film's compulsion to imagine alternatives to silence and fear, revenge and retribution. When Adi visits his uncle under the pretense of another eye exam, he learns that his uncle was a prison guard for those (including his nephew) awaiting execution, who were taken to the river in regularly scheduled truckloads. As in the other confrontations, Adi's uncle both denies and admits knowledge of the murders, ultimately excusing his own culpability by saying, 'I did it to defend the state, so I don't feel that way'. The meeting concludes in another impasse when he answers Adi's charge of complicity with, 'How dare you!' The rhetoric of daring resurfaces in the next sequence when Adi informs Rohani of her brother's role in Ramli's death. 'He never dared tell me', she replies in an emotionally laden scene that at once reveals another, interfamilial layer of silence and the pain of breaking it. Even when the meetings themselves end in what appears to be an ideological dead end and communicative failure, the film, in representing these impasses, performs the daring acts of communication that individuals themselves cannot commit.

The final two confrontations underscore that the film at once makes possible Adi's interactions with perpetrators – building upon the relationships Oppenheimer founded in his earlier interviews, providing some measure of physical protection, and documenting Adi's journey to uncover the circumstances of his brother's brutal death – and tells its own story of the legacy of violence and corruption. Like the fifth, the sixth and seventh meetings also pivot on the trope of the family. Whether these scenes of victim and perpetrator families document betrayal, complicity, or care, or a combination of the three, they have a density of meanings. First, scenes in which members tenderly care for one another provide an alternative model of human flourishing from that offered by Suharto in his self-anointed role as the 'Father of Development' (Nakashima). As Joseph Slaughter has demonstrated, the neo-liberal model of economic development subsumes human flourishing and rights to the logic of choice, commodities, and capabilities (211). Images of Rohani bathing her husband, for example, decouple development and national, paternalistic care, representing the embodied suffering of those targeted by Suharto's New Order as well as the need for mutual support rather than private accumulation. Second, the film's depictions of familial rhetoric and relations seek to reclaim the family as a metaphor for the nation, without the violent trappings of Suharto's 'fatherhood'. As Adi's confrontation with his uncle indicates, the violence of 1965–1966 up through the present has an intimacy to it, from the physical handling of victims as they are tortured and killed, to the drinking of victims' blood, to the boasting that takes place in living rooms and gardens. Scenes within Adi's family provide a counterpoint to intimate violence, while the sequence of confrontations explores the possibility of more extensive, caring kinship networks. The last two confrontations, when Adi meets with perpetrators' families in their homes, emphasize his desire to forge social bonds in the image of the family, and thus dissolve the imposed boundary between private speech and public silence.[5] Third, the family trope emphasizes the need for transgenerational processes of negotiation and deliberation. As both the sixth and seventh confrontations make clear, the future Adi tries to imagine depends less on the responsiveness of perpetrators than of their children – the members of Adi's generation, who have been either beneficiaries or second-order survivors of the New Order government's founding violence.

In his sixth confrontation, Adi meets an ageing death squad leader Samsir and his daughter (who is also married to a perpetrator). The sequence displays many of the characteristics of earlier confrontations; however, the film juxtaposes father and daughter's perspectives in ways that demonstrate that children of perpetrators need not inherit the discursive norms of their parents. Samsir's daughter describes her pride at learning in junior high school about her father's work killing communists. Over the course of their conversation, however, her pride changes first to horror and then to a widening sense of familial responsibility that still includes her father but extends to Adi as well. This transformation takes place through the strategies Adi and Oppenheimer used earlier – of Adi repeating perpetrators' claims, so that the rhetoric is divorced from the designated rhetor and thereby loses its power, and of Adi's willingness to disclose his position as a survivor. 'You brought a woman's head'. 'Was it useful for you to buy the head [to scare Chinese people]?' By paraphrasing perpetrators, Adi takes their testimony out of its heroic context and makes it available for scrutiny. What for perpetrators are boasts to maintain fictions they can live with and enforce the silence of survivors become, in Adi's repetitions, performative speech acts that reveal the horror behind what was formerly acceptable. Although Samsir does not fully recognize the shift that is occurring, his daughter clearly does. When he describes his preferred method for slitting victims' throats to collect the blood he would drink 'to stay strong', his daughter and caretaker is shocked into the quiet admission that this knowledge is 'terrifying'. Here, 'terrifying' becomes radically recoded to refer not to the threat Samsir poses to targeted enemies of the state, but to his effect on his own daughter. What is terrifying is the recognition that one's father committed countless, grotesque atrocities and that his heroism was a lie. Once Adi reveals himself as a survivor, Samsir's daughter provides perhaps the one moment of catharsis in these confrontations: she asks for her father's forgiveness and for Adi to think of them as family. Moreover, her apology is grounded in vulnerability as that which can invite care and co-flourishing as opposed to paternalistic virility and control: 'He's old now. Consider him your own father'.

5 Although the dialogue is not in the film, Oppenheimer has described how Adi begins his final meeting (with Amir Hasan's family) by reminding them that their children go to the same school and could one day marry.

Although the exchange with Samsir and his daughter exemplifies the kind of opening up of communication and social relations that Adi seeks, Oppenheimer productively refuses the closure the daughter's apology might offer. Oppenheimer has suggested that her apology models the kind of reconciliation process needed; however, ending there would gloss the scale of the violence by falling back on the narrative convention that allows one character to stand for many. This is, of course, a device that is central to the work of human rights storytelling, but one that also bears the paradox of individuation and reductionism. On one hand, the compelling, 'narratable self' is crucial to the understanding that '"reconstructing" the thread of a life story [. . .] is above all opposing the destruction that has devoured life itself' (Cavarero 14). On the other hand, the individuation of egregious suffering through characterization and biography, whether fictional or non-fictional, simultaneously masks the differentiated experiences and voices of the suffering it represents. By including as its final confrontation an interview in which Adi and Oppenheimer's projects diverge, *The Look of Silence* insists upon a more radical commitment to narrative openness and negotiation of multiple perspectives than can be satisfied by a single apology.

The sequence is introduced by Adi rescreening an early interview with the death squad leader Amir Hasan, conducted during the months Oppenheimer spent with him and his family. After the earlier footage in which Hasan proudly displays his authored and illustrated account of the murders (a book he wanted to transform into a musical!), the film cuts to Adi meeting with Hasan's widow and two grown sons. Whereas in earlier encounters, Adi kept the details of his own identity secret to protect himself and his family, here, despite Hasan's family's claims of ignorance, the families already know one another: Adi was a student in the school where Hasan's widow worked. Taking Hasan's book as a point of departure (thereby signalling both Oppenheimer's and his own familiarity with the family), Adi tells the gruesome story of his brother's death, while Hasan's widow shakes her head in dismay and his sons grow increasingly angry. When the sons refuse to acknowledge their father's work (in effect, also refusing to acknowledge their relationship with Oppenheimer) and their mother gets up and removes her microphone, Adi and Oppenheimer's projects diverge. Whereas Adi is willing to let stand the refusal of recognition and to end the meeting, Oppenheimer retrieves the earlier footage on his laptop and asks the sons to review it for themselves. In this final sequence, then, Oppenheimer imposes on the sons the position of listener (to Adi as he tells the story of Ramli's death, rather than asks about it) and spectator – the position Adi has occupied (of his own volition) up until this point. Of course, by becoming spectators of their father's boasting, the sons do not occupy the position of victims or survivors; however, the switch negates the logic of their earlier denials and leaves them floundering for new foundations. This adds another layer to the film's title, as the sons quickly refuse to look at the screen, thereby attempting to silence their father from the boasting that is now self-incriminating as well as to silence Oppenheimer for piercing the conventions that contained that boasting. Faced with this refusal, Oppenheimer intervenes more forcefully to say on Adi's behalf that he 'is here to speak openly' and not for revenge. Although Oppenheimer's statement is heartfelt, the sons recognize what perhaps Oppenheimer cannot at that moment – that here it is the film rather than the survivor that most threatens the status quo. As the younger son says angrily, 'Because Joshua makes this film and my father wrote this book – the wound is open', concluding, 'I welcomed you here, Joshua, but I don't like you anymore'.[6]

Whose wound is now open? For survivors, as Adi's family indicates, the wound never healed. Thus, Hasan's son can only be referencing the breach of his own defences, such that the confrontation is no longer between Adi and Hasan's family, but between the sons and their father's legacy. Whereas having drunk their victims' blood may provide ageing perpetrators some bizarre confirmation of their own invincibility, their children have no available antidote to the moral poisoning that accompanies their sociopolitical privilege.

Conclusion: 'That's the true story of Ramli'

The film circles back to the earlier interview by the river, where Inong and Siahaan demonstrate how Ramli was beaten, stabbed, and dismembered, and Siahaan concludes, 'That's the true story of Ramli', before pausing for a photograph of them holding up a 'V' for victory. However, here, too, closure is undone by the multiple narratives of Ramli's death that the film has elicited: these include the perpetrators' re-enactment by the river and Hasan's memoir, as well as Rohani's description of Ramli's abduction and the lasting pain of his death, Kemat's report of their transport to the river, and the story Adi tells to Hasan's family. These multiple tellings do not dispute the 'truth' of Ramli's death, but speak to the common knowledge of atrocity that the imposed silence either tries to suppress or employs to generate fear. That Ramli's death has been narrated many times in the film, by both perpetrators and survivors, fundamentally alters the discursive conventions that had heretofore allowed only their respective boasting and silence. In addition, as the perpetrators note, 'others have similar stories . . . but not the same', an acknowledgement that allows Ramli's death to represent the scripted work of the killers without claiming to represent the individual suffering of each victim.

6 This was also the confrontation in which Adi and the film crew were in the greatest danger. Whereas in earlier interviews, the perpetrators were threatening, here Amir Hasan's son reached for the phone to call for their arrest. Oppenheimer describes putting his hand on the phone to stay the call, saying, you can call the police but not until after we leave (personal interview). For every perpetrator interview conducted in 2012, Oppenheimer used his own small crew, travelled in two unmarked cars, and had Adi's family waiting at the airport to evacuate in case he and the crew were arrested. At each meeting, Adi arrived without carrying the mandatory public identity card and Oppenheimer brought no identification save a clean cell phone containing only the number of the US Embassy in Jakarta.

Finally, in transforming Adi from spectator to interlocutor to narrator of his brother's murder, the film creates a strong protagonist without re-instantiating the liberal subject of human rights. Adi's 'success' within the confines of the film is to assert a vulnerable subject position as that which founds the right to be meditative and silent, to pose questions, and to tell his story at once on screen and in the domestic spaces of still powerful perpetrators.[7] Even in those moments when he is met with threats and lies, the film intervenes both to offer some measure of physical protection as well as to demonstrate that the open wound belongs to perpetrators as well as their victims. Thus, it is Adi and Oppenheimer's entwined and reticulated projects that puncture the bubble of impunity and make way for juridical–political discourses of redress to follow.

Works cited

Anderson, Benedict. 'Impunity and Reenactment: Reflections on the 1965 Massacre in Indonesia and Its Legacy'. *The Asia-Pacific Journal* 11.15 (15 April 2013). Web. 21 May 2015.

Cavarero, Adriana. 'Narrative against Destruction'. *New Literary History* 46 (2015): 1–16. Print.

Chowdhury, Elora Halim. *Transnationalism Reversed: Women Organizing against Gendered Violence in Bangladesh.* Albany: State University of New York Press, 2011. Print.

Dawes, James. *Evil Men.* Cambridge: Harvard University Press, 2013. Print.

Ferguson, Kennan. 'Silence: A Politics'. *Contemporary Political Theory* (2003) 2: 49–65. doi: 10.1057/palgrave.cpt.9300054. Web. 24 May 2015.

Grear, Anna. 'Vulnerability, Advanced Global Capitalism and Co-Symptomatic Injustice: Locating the Vulnerable Subject'. *Vulnerability: Reflections on a New Ethical Foundation for Law and Politics.* Ed. Martha Albertson Fineman and Anna Grear. Burlington/Surrey: Ashgate Publishing, 2013. 41–60. Print.

'Joko's Reconciliation Commission Lacks Moral Weight'. *The Jakarta Globe* 22 May 2015. Web. 24 May 2015.

The Look of Silence. Dir. Joshua Oppenheimer. Final Cut for Real, 2004. Film.

Moore, Alexandra Schultheis. 'Film after Atrocity: An Interview with Joshua Oppenheimer'. *Routledge Companion to Literature and Human Rights.* Ed. Sophia A. McClennen and Alexandra Schultheis Moore. New York/London: Routledge, 2015. 480–498. Print.

MUZAK: A Tool of Management (3 min.). Dir. Joshua Oppenheimer. General Broadcasting Corporation, 2003. Film.

Nakashima, Ellen. 'Indonesia's Despotic "Father of Development"'. Suharto Obituary. *The Washington Post* 25 January 2008. Web. 28 May 2015.

Nance, Kimberly. *Can Literature Promote Justice? Trauma Narrative and Social Action in Latin American Testimonio.* Nashville: Vanderbilt University Press, 2006. Print.

7 Adi Rukun was present at the two large, sold out inaugural screenings of *The Look of Silence* in Jakarta, where he received a standing ovation. Although his family had to be relocated for their safety, he has emerged since the film's release as a powerful advocate for the murdered, the disappeared, and their families.

Ong, Aihwa. *Neoliberalism as Exception: Mutations in Citizenship and Sovereignty*. Durham: Duke University Press, 2006. Print.
Owen, David. 'The Soundtrack of Your Life: Muzak in the Realm of Retail Theatre'. *The New Yorker* 10 April 2006. Web. 5 May 2015.
Postcard from Sun City, Arizona (3 min.). Dir. Joshua Oppenheimer. General Broadcasting Corporation, 2003. Film.
Puar, Jasbir. *Terrorist Assemblages: Homonationalism in Queer Times*. Durham: Duke University Press, 2007. Print.
Roosa, John. *Pretext for Mass Murder: The September 30th Movement and Suharto's Coup d'État in Indonesia*. Madison: University of Wisconsin Press, 2006. Print.
Simpson, Bradley R. *Economists with Guns: Authoritarian Development and US–Indonesian Relations, 1960–1968*. Stanford: Stanford University Press, 2008. Print.
——. '"The First Right": The Carter Administration, Indonesia, and the Transnational Human Rights Politics of the 1970s'. *The Human Rights Revolution: An International History*. Ed. Akira Iriye, Petra Goedde, and William I. Hitchcock. Oxford: Oxford University Press, 2012. 179–200. Print.
Slaughter, Joseph. *Human Rights, Inc.: The World Novel, Narrative Form, and International Law*. New York: Fordham University Press, 2007. Print.
Spyer, Patricia. 'Some Notes on Disorder in the Indonesian Postcolony'. *Law and Disorder in the Postcolony*. Ed. Jean Comaroff and John L. Comaroff. Chicago: University of Chicago Press, 2006. 188–218. Print.

Chapter 12

The problem of empathy

Reading the Wilkomirski Affair in the light of the history of literature

Ingvild Hagen Kjørholt

> The biggest deficit that we have in our society and in the world right now is an empathy deficit. We are in great need of people being able to stand in somebody else's shoes and see the world through their eyes. The great power of books is the capacity to take you out of yourself and to put you somewhere else.
>
> Barack Obama

> After the Holocaust, reading has to be changed.
>
> Robert Eaglestone[1]

There seems to be a common belief today, among book circle readers, scholars, and presidents alike, that human rights and literature are interrelated phenomena. From different points of view, based on more or less qualified analyses and assumptions, it is widely held that the two areas are based on two mutual cornerstones: the individual experiential human being, and the psychological capacity of empathy – of being able to imagine how it is to be another (cf. Goldberg and Moore; Hunt; Keen; Nussbaum). Just think about classic modern novels, such as Samuel Richardson's *Pamela* (1740), or Harriet Beecher Stowe's *Uncle Tom's Cabin* (1852), which foreground the personal experiences and feelings of 'inferior' characters, such as the female servant or the Negro slave, or any Amnesty International campaign that criticizes human rights abuses globally by telling the stories of individuals – of the 600 days of imprisonment of an Egyptian photojournalist, or of the death sentence of the Sudanese woman whose crime was to marry a Christian.[2] The novels, as well as the campaigns, invite their readers to emotionally engage with the personal stories that are being told, as Martha Nussbaum puts it, to 'recognize the other

1 Barack Obama cited in Pavlovich and Krankhe 1; Eaglestone 136.

2 Cf. Amnesty International's official website, www.amnesty.org/en/ (retrieved 7 April 2015).

as a center of experience' (*Political Emotions* 146). Despite the different political, legal, and cultural institutions, discourses, and agencies that structure and validate them, novels and a universalist ethics of human rights thus welcome a similar reaction from its receivers – an empathic response.

Contemporary Western societies display a cultural absorption in the personal story. The aim of this article is to critically examine a part of its genealogy. From the point of view of literary history, I will discuss a particular way of reading such stories, or, more specifically, a certain type of reader – what I call 'the empathic reader'. My point of departure is that the empathic reader, a product of the eighteenth century's rise of the novel, and a still dominant mode of perceiving fiction, has become a fundamental subject position in the modern discourse on human rights. The key questions of this analysis are: Who is the empathic reader? How does this figure incarnate the interconnection of the history of literature and the history of human rights? And, what happens to the empathic reader when confronted with the genre of Holocaust testimony? The discussion will start from a specific case, the so-called 'Wilkomirski Affair', which, I argue, emphasizes the shortcomings of the empathic reader, and thus reveals a need, as Holocaust scholar Robert Eaglestone has put it, to change the way we read (136).

The Wilkomirski Affair

In 1995, Jüdischer Verlag, a division of the large German publishing house Sührkamp, published *Bruchstücke: Aus einer Kindheit 1939–1947*, written by a hitherto anonymous Swiss musician named Binjamin Wilkomirski, and characterized as a memoir or, more specifically, a Holocaust memoir.[3] It is the horrifying narrative of an orphaned Jewish boy who – before he was adopted by Swiss foster parents in 1945 – spent his early childhood alone, in Eastern European orphanages, on the run, and in the Nazi death camps of Majdanek and Auschwitz Birkenau. The memoir was shortly after translated into nine languages, including the English *Fragments: Memories of a Wartime Childhood* (1996), and it soon became a media event. Both in Europe and the US, the book was hailed as a masterpiece, not only by prominent Holocaust scholars such as Daniel Goldhagen and James Young, and survivors such as Elie Wiesel, but also by literary critics. *Bruchstücke* was called a new Holocaust classic, and received several prestigious awards, including the American National Jewish Book Award for autobiography and memoirs, the Jewish Quarterly prize for non-fiction in the UK, and the Prix Mémoire de la Shoah in France. Wilkomirski was compared to authors and Holocaust victims such as Anne Frank, Primo Levi,

3 The following outline of the reception history is based on Maechler's writing.

and Paul Celan. In 1997, the author's wartime biography was the subject of two TV documentaries, Esther van Messel's *Fremd Geboren*, and Eric Bergkraut's *Das gute Leben ist nur eine Falle*. The Fortunoff Video Archive (Yale) and other Holocaust testimony collections interviewed Wilkomirski, and he was also invited to TV shows and memorial ceremonies as a witness and expert on child survivors. Thus, from being an unknown, silenced victim of his traumatic past, he became an important public agent: the mouthpiece for a group of victims that had long been neglected, but had only recently begun to make itself heard in the public sphere – child survivors of the Nazi genocide, or what has been called 'the 1.5 generation' of Holocaust survivors (Suleiman).

However, Wilkomirski's success turned out to be fleeting. In autumn 1998, the journalist Daniel Ganzfried published several articles in *Die Weltwoche*, a conservative Swiss newspaper, which suggested that Wilkomirski had invented his biography. The author was neither a Jew nor a concentration camp victim, Ganzfried claimed, and his real name was not Binjamin Wilkomirski, but Bruno Dösseker. According to Ganzfried, Bruno had not been born into a Jewish family in Riga, but in Biel, Switzerland, in 1941 as the illegitimate son of a Swiss woman named Yvonne Grosjean. Bruno had spent his first years in a Swiss children's home before Mr and Mrs Dösseker adopted him in 1945. As the only child in the family, he grew up in their home in Zürich. Ganzfried, who built his claim on several historical records, suggested that a pathological identification had led the adult adoptee to rewrite his own miserable autobiography by appropriating the ultimate twentieth-century victim identity – the child Holocaust survivor. Ganzfried's delicate revelation was soon picked up by the media, worldwide. In particular, two essays, from the summer of 1999, presented the peculiar history to the Anglo-American audience: Philip Gourevitch's 'The Memory Thief' (*The New Yorker*) and Elena Lappin's 'The Man with Two Heads' (*Granta*). Although Wilkomirski himself kept on insisting that he had told the true story of his life, huge media institutions such as *60 Minutes* and the BBC called *Fragments* a fraud, and the author an identity thief. The revelation of the scandal turned the tide, and the public condemnation of writing fiction masked as testimony proved merciless. The book was withdrawn from the market, and both the author and his defenders soon disappeared from public view.

In 1999, Sührkamp hired the Swiss historian Stefan Maechler to investigate Wilkomirski's identity. After thorough archive studies and interviews, Maechler concluded that the man who called himself Binjamin Wilkomirski was born Bruno Grosjean, and that there existed neither historical documents, credible witness reports, nor DNA analyses to support the autobiographical claims. The official report from Maechler's inquires, *Der Fall Wilkomirski* (2000, *The Wilkomirski Affair*), presents the author's own story, the documentation of his real historical identity, and a thorough outline of *Bruchstücke*'s publication and reception (Maechler). *Bruchstücke* and its peculiar reception have since been referred to as the 'Wilkomirski Affair', and Wilkomirski's memoir has only been reprinted as an appendix to Maechler's report. Consequently, today, it is practically impossible to read the memoir without the associated contextual information.[4]

The history of *Bruchstücke*'s reception reveals that two contradictory ways of reading were activated in the wake of the publication of Wilkomirski's memoir. Empathic readers that read *Fragments* as a Holocaust testimony representing the experiences, feelings, and memories of an innocent child victim dominated the first phase of the reception. The memoir, a first-person narrative representing the fragmented childhood memories of the narrator, touched the public, whose compassionate response motivated political action that led to increased attention to child Holocaust survivors. Thus, the readers became important agents in the affair – they made the book an object of political attention. An essential presupposition for readers' empathy – their vivid imagination of how the poor orphan had suffered both during and after the war – and their subsequent engagement, was a belief in the author's identity. Furthermore, they relied on the autobiographical contract, which guarantees that the author and the narrator are one and the same (cf. Lejeune), and on the historical truth value of the narrative.

When, suddenly, all three conditions (author identity, autobiographical contract, historical truth claim) were questioned, the reader's intuitive recognition of Wilkomirski's story of pain as true and authentic was replaced by a suspicious and critical reader response. The suspicious reader refused to accept the narrator's representation of the little boy as a victim in need of care, and ignored the pain the narrative communicates. Rather, the second phase of the reception was preoccupied with readers' questioning the author's authority, or lack of such, and his right to speak as a Holocaust victim.

The Wilkomirski Affair is frequently mentioned in Holocaust studies and memory studies as an example of the paradigmatic shift from history to memory, and to a representational mode that seems to pervade Western public discourse: the individualization and privatization of historical events. Advocates of this trend argue that the personal story, the testimony, and an empathic (or emotional) approach to history is a prerequisite to understanding what it meant to be a victim of the Nazi genocide in Eastern Europe in the 1930s and 1940s. For instance, Holocaust scholar Allison Landsberg has argued for what she calls 'a radical politics of empathy' – a concept of knowledge that embraces the experiential and emotional processes involved in engaging with history (Landsberg). Historian Dominick LaCapra, who has discussed the need for affectivity in historical writing and understanding of atrocities, asks for an

4 As this article's topic is the reception of the Wilkomirski Affair, a thorough analysis of *Bruchstücke* as an autonomous work is beyond its scope. Nevertheless, it is worth remarking that the text's rhetorical devices establish a certain implied reader position, and thus that the reader response is conditioned by the text itself. For a thorough analysis of the rhetoric of *Bruchstücke*, see Pennington.

'empathic unsettlement' – a responsiveness to the traumatic experiences of others, without appropriating their identity (41). Others have critically questioned the idea that historical truth should be represented from the point of view of individual experience, and in an interpersonal relationship between victim and recipient. They see the trend as a device to decontextualize historical events. As Daniel Levy and Natan Sznaider have claimed: 'The enthusiastic reception of Wilkomirski's book is proof that the Holocaust has become completely decontextualized and turned into a personal trauma with which everyone can identify' (151).[5] Several critics have noted that Bruno Dösseker/Binjamin Wilkomirski himself embodies the ultimate affective response to the Holocaust, as he identifies with its victims, and feels their pain to such a degree that he appropriates their identity. Whether the author himself may be considered some kind of an empathic reader will not be further discussed.[6] In the following pages, I will rather focus on the historical readers' leading part in the Wilkomirski Affair.

The empathic reader

In Maechler's discussion of whether Wilkomirski actually believed in his own memoir, or rather cynically and deliberately invented a false autobiography, he concludes that:

> There is every indication that Wilkomirski found his own narrative true and authentic because it unleashed such stunned silence, such waves of sympathy. Perhaps he did not believe his story, but he did believe his own telling of it. Anything that had such an effect on listeners must be true. The glow in their eyes lent him a living, coherent identity – that of the greatest of all victims – and gave his story overwhelming authenticity. Without an audience, there would be no Wilkomirski.
>
> (273)

Maechler pinpoints what I suggest is of basic importance when it comes to the discussion of *Bruchstücke*'s veracity and generic status. Namely, that its truth value is not primarily produced in the narrative. It neither depends exclusively on the autobiographical contract nor on the author's authority, but is principally

5 Another well-known example that illustrates this trend is the Holocaust Museum in Washington, where, at the entrance, visitors are given the identity of an original camp victim (his or her photograph, prisoner number, and biography), and invited to experience the genocide through his or her eyes.

6 It is also worth distinguishing his response from an empathic response. Empathy requires the recognition of the alterity of the other. By appropriating the Holocaust victim identity, Wilkomirski instead becomes the other.

an effect of the public response. The readers' empathy, and the actions that stemmed from imagining the pain of the lonely child, determined the text's production of truth. From such a point of view, the empathic reader is the main agent of the Wilkomirski Affair.

What is an empathic reader? In order to identify the figure, it seems necessary to begin with a definition of empathy. The term 'empathy' is complex, and applies to various phenomena. The English psychologist Edward Titchener first coined the English term in 1909 as a translation of the German *Einfühlung*, literally 'feeling into': 'imaginatively projecting oneself into another's situation' (in Batson 6). In its origins in the English language, empathy belonged to the register of aesthetics, referring to the process by which a writer or a painter imagines what it would be like to be either some specific person or a particular inanimate object. Today, empathy is considered to be the human capacity that 'depends on a biologically based ability to understand the subjectivity of other people and to be able to imagine that their inner experiences are like one's own' (Hunt 39). To empathize with another person is to feel what we believe are his or her emotions (cf. Keen 5). It is a 'virtual experience' (LaCapra 47); it is about being able to feel a stranger's situation.

Although the empathic reader is involved in what narratologists call 'character identification' (i.e. readers identifying with the characters in a narrative), empathy is not about feeling pity for the other. Thus, it is an emotional response similar to, but differentiated from, sympathy. As Allison Landsberg has explained: 'While sympathy [. . .] relies upon an essentialism of identification, empathy recognizes the alterity of identification. Empathy, then, is about the lack of identity between subjects, about negotiating distance' (82). Whereas the empathic reader imagines him or herself to be the other, to experience the world from the other's viewpoint, the sympathetic reader imagines how he or she would feel in the other's situation. Thus, the latter transposes his or her identity onto others. The sympathetic reader and the empathic reader both take part in a process of affective engagement, but nevertheless there is a considerable distinction between the two ways of approaching another person's experience.

Empathy is a widely discussed phenomenon within diverse academic disciplines, from Holocaust studies via the expanding field of affect studies, to neurosciences. It is also of particular interest within literary history. During the eighteenth century, the phenomenon of empathy, or human sensibility in general, constituted an important point of intersection between literature and political history – an intersection in which historians and literary scholars have, in recent years, begun to show interest (cf. among others Anderson; Eagleton; Hunt; Maslan). Despite the different perspectives scholars have revealed, they seem to share the basic idea that human sensibility, both as an important literary subject and as a capacity that developed from reading fiction, became a political matter when a new subject of rights, the man-citizen, became the basis of the emerging political European constitutions (e.g. *La Déclaration des droits de l'homme et du citoyen*), and of the American Constitution.

The new subject of rights, the modern European citizen or the human rights subject, implies a breakdown of the traditional distinction between private and public identities. The new public or political identity was founded in humanity. From that point on, an important citizen virtue found its model in affective bonds between brothers or spouses. Whereas man as a natural or biological creature, defined by his physical sensibilities and vulnerability, traditionally had his place in the private sphere, such qualities were now imagined as belonging to man's political identity. Fellow citizens should act towards one another as affectionate brothers (cf. Maslan 80). Consequently, in the emerging modern society, both private and public life should be anchored in the human being's natural and universal affects.

In her clever thematic analyses of canonical literary works, such as Corneille's *Horace* (1640) or Montesquieu's *Les Lettres Persanes* (1721), literary historian Susan Maslan convincingly reveals how, in seventeenth- and eighteenth-century French fiction, the fusion of man and citizen, humanity and citizenship, takes place at the level of the story, or plot. This man-citizen is a being of emotions; a man who is able to shed tears when confronted with the suffering of a stranger.[7] Maslan suggests that literary representations such as these preceded the founding of modern politics and modern human rights.

Instead of focusing on literary plots, as Maslan does, historian Lynn Hunt, in her influential *The Invention of Human Rights* (2007), approaches the intersection of literary and political history as a question of reading. She argues that, above all, it was the structure of the early modern novel that taught men and women the capacity to empathize with strangers, a required capacity for being able to approach a random fellow citizen as one's brother:

> Novels like [Rousseau's] *Julie* drew their readers into identifying with ordinary characters, who were by definition unknown to the reader personally. Readers empathized with the characters, especially the heroine or the hero, *thanks to the workings of the narrative form itself.* [. . .] novels taught their readers nothing less than a new psychology and in the process laid the foundations for a new social and political order.
>
> (38–39, my emphasis)

A crucial point in Hunt's argument is that it was the literary *form* of the novel that invited its readers to be empathic. In particular, she claims that the epistolary novel enabled such an approach.

The epistolary novel, a genre that foregrounds the interior thoughts and feelings of its characters, has a narrative order (letters sent between different

7 An example is to be found in Voltaire's *Candide* (1759), when the protagonist meets a mutilated Negro slave in the Dutch colony of Suriname, and bursts into tears when the latter tells him the story of his life of slavery. For an analysis of the episode, see Kjørholt.

senders and recipients) that makes the reader aware of a number of different subjective viewpoints simultaneously. Instead of predicting 'truth' as unified and stable, the epistolary novel – through its very form – visualizes truth as subjective, and depends on the individual's specific circumstances and viewpoints. The epistolary novel reader engages emotionally in the fictional characters' lives, and he or she learns that each character experiences the world in his or her own way. In the emerging early modern democracies, this capacity of seeing the world through others' eyes became an important citizen virtue for socializing with fellow citizens.[8] In other words, in order to fulfil his citizen duties, the individual was supposed to apply a particular way of reading fiction. From Hunt's point of view, eighteenth-century novels indirectly, by providing a certain model of, and conditions for, reading, paved the way for a modern idea of sensibility – and empathy, in particular – as an important citizen quality.

In contemporary discourse, the empathic reader is still an ideal of novel reading. The reading method has also been transferred to other media; in particular, the commercial, narrative film relies heavily on emotionally engaged spectators. And today, the idea that 'novel reading cultivates empathy that produces good citizens for the world' has become a 'contemporary truism' (Keen xv), a view politicians often express with wonderful pathos, and which, in the academic world, is perhaps most famously advocated by the American philosopher Martha Nussbaum. Nussbaum has argued that literature (and art in general) helps to cultivate what she calls 'narrative imagination' – the capacity to see the world through another person's eyes. In her view, literature is a tool for developing emotions such as empathy, which is a fundamental citizen quality, and necessary in building and sustaining democratic societies (cf., for instance, *Political Emotions*; *Not for Profit*; *Poetic Justice*).

Holocaust testimony

The Wilkomirski Affair illustrates that the empathic reader is still vital, and no longer reserved for the domain of fiction, but also makes him or herself felt in the reception of documentary Holocaust representations, in particular testimony. The testimony was originally a judicial genre. Its writers assumed the role of an eyewitness to a criminal event. Whereas the novel is regarded an invention of early modern Europe, Holocaust testimony has been seen as the archetypical genre of late modernity.[9] In broad terms, Holocaust testimony is a narrative

8 Benedict Anderson makes a similar argument in *Imagined Communities*: the nation state emerges because its citizens are able to imagine a community of fellow citizens with whom they never meet physically. Anderson claims that newspapers and novels serve as models for this way of imagining, as literary technologies that manage to represent simultaneity and plurality.

9 Cf. Elie Wiesel's well-known dictum: 'if the Greeks invented the tragedy, the Romans the epistle, and the Renaissance the sonnet, our generation invented a new literature, that of testimony' (9).

genre constituted by a certain approach to a certain subject – personal experiences of the historical event known as the Holocaust. It includes various subgenres, such as diaries, memoirs, interviews, and notebooks. In addition to its many subgenres, the location of the writer, the date of writing, and the authority of the writer may vary radically. Some testimonies were written down during or immediately after the Second World War, whereas others were written decades later. There exists a certain transnational canon of Holocaust testimony, which includes writers such as Anne Frank, Primo Levi, Elie Wiesel, and Jorge Semprun, to mention but the best-known, together with a massive corpus of texts and statements authored by less-known witness-authors.

A characteristic feature of Holocaust testimony is that it complicates the border between fiction and historiography. It has been defined as 'a "factually insistent" narrative' (Young 404) and 'a subject's recall of facts from the past' (Vice, 'Questions' 47). An important cause of this intermediate genre status is the concept of 'trauma'. Holocaust testimonies are narratives of trauma, and the genre has been extensively discussed within academic fields such as trauma studies and memory studies.[10] Following Freud, trauma has been defined as the experience of a repressed or forgotten memory. Thus, an experience of trauma is always belated with respect to the event that originally caused it, and the faculty of imagination is necessarily involved in the psychological reconstruction and literary representation of the original experience that precedes a testimonial text. Although Holocaust testimony is authorized by the writer's relationship to the historical event that is described, the Nazi genocide in Europe in the 1930s and 1940s, it is also a narrative of a personal trauma. Consequently, the truth on which Holocaust testimony depends is not only historical truth, but also a kind of psychological truth that is to be found in the unconscious (cf. Caruth; Felman).

Fiction is a precarious concept when it comes to Holocaust representations, as Sue Vice clearly reveals in her *Holocaust Fiction*, where she analyses several well-known literary representations of the Holocaust, such as the novels *Schindler's Ark* (1982, the basis of Steven Spielberg's *Schindler's List*, of 1993) and *Time's Arrow* (1991). Vice concludes, with particular reference to the Wilkomirski Affair, that receptions of Holocaust literature reveal that the relationship between author and narrator, and knowledge of the author's biography, are significant, in terms of reader response (*Holocaust Fiction* 163). This does not mean that we do not read novels about the Holocaust, but rather that knowledge of the narrative's relation to historical and biographical truth is of great importance. But *Bruchstücke* illustrates that the dividing line between fiction and history in Holocaust literature

10 Psychoanalytical concepts such as 'trauma', 'deep memory', or 'transference' are associated with these fields' treatments of the genre, and a thorough presentation of Holocaust testimony would require a discussion of these and other key psychoanalytical terms. Owing to the limits of this article, I give only a brief presentation of the concept of trauma, and do not thoroughly discuss this approach to testimony.

is blurred, and difficult to trace on an immanent level of the text. One aspect that makes it difficult to tell the one from the other is that both fictional and autobiographical testimonies apply the same narrative devices and metaphors. Another reason is that the historical truth of the political event (the Nazi genocide) is supplemented by a notion of psychological truth that accompanies individual traumatic experience, which are often the core of the story. We may also add that, owing to its extensive use of literary devices, Holocaust testimony hinges on the concept of universal truth, to which works of fiction, according to Aristotle, refer. Hence, the testimony makes three different and contradictory truth claims – it depends on historical, psychological, and fictional truth. Its complex ontological and epistemological status makes it perhaps even more important to establish the contract between writer, reader, and subject matter when reading Holocaust literature than when reading in general.[11] Even though such a contract is always at work in the reception of literature, it may be understood as a defining, generic feature of Holocaust representations. Consequently, the contribution of the reader is crucial in the transmission of Holocaust testimony.

Being a narrative of a trauma, Holocaust testimony often presupposes a certain reader response that is historically linked to fiction – an emotional response. In *Holocaust and the American Life* (1999), historian Peter Novick claims that 'we actually read Holocaust testimonies not for their historical insight, but for their emotive power' (in Gross and Hoffmann 33). Similarly, Robert Eaglestone emphasizes that 'one of the most important characteristics of the genre of testimony stems from the reader's experience of identification' (117). Both scholars question emotional identification as an adequate reader response to Holocaust testimonies. Eaglestone is one of the few who has discussed the genre of testimony in light of the history of literature. According to him, Holocaust testimony, owing to its intermediate position between the traditional nineteenth-century novel and historiography, consists of 'a paradoxical "doubleness"': its form leads the reader to identification, as it applies the traditional narrative scheme of the nineteenth-century novel, while its content and context lead away from it (119). He argues that Holocaust testimony ought to be considered on its own terms, and provides a taxonomy of general traits and concrete examples, in order to reveal its generic qualities.[12] Eaglestone insists that although Holocaust testimony asks for the reader's identification, the invitation results in what we might call a 'receptional fallacy': Holocaust testimony per se precludes identification, in the sense that a personal experience of the Holocaust is an extreme viewpoint nearly impossible to imagine, it is inaccessible to most. That is why, he concludes, '[a]fter the Holocaust, reading has to be changed' (136).

11 Inga Clendinnen also emphasizes the importance of the reading contract when it comes to literature about the Holocaust; a work of history establishes a different contract between author and reader, and author and subject, than fiction does (170).

12 These traits are: overidentification, epiphany, interruption, the way of using narrative frames, and the ways of using history (Eaglestone).

Empathy put to the test: from early modern novels to Holocaust testimony

If experiences of the Holocaust are impossible to imagine for someone who was not there, as Eaglestone claims, the empathic approach is theoretically not an available reading point of departure when it comes to Holocaust testimonies. Still, the ideal of the empathic reader is powerful, and persistently called upon in the public discourse of Holocaust memory. The empathic reader at work in the Wilkomirski Affair has a similar way of reading Holocaust testimony as an eighteenth-century citizen, a human rights subject to be, reads novels: his or her chief concern is to emotionally engage in the personal story that is being told – to imagine the world from another centre of experience. But what happens to the empathic reader, understood as a historical product of the early modern novel, when confronted with the genre of Holocaust testimony? What are its effects and functions when it is deployed in a historical context completely different from the context in which this figure emerged?

Eaglestone emphasizes that 'reading testimony is not like reading a novel' (135), and therefore questions the functionality of the empathic reader when confronted with the testimonial genre. However, he does not offer an alternative way of reading Holocaust testimonies. Furthermore, I do not agree with his claim that it is the narrative form of the testimony, and not its subject and surroundings, that lead the reader to identify with the narrator. In light of the Wilkomirski Affair, I suggest the opposite: that the reader's empathic response to Holocaust testimony is a matter of the genre's defining subject – personal experience of the Nazi genocide – and the status of this specific trauma in the context of our contemporary Western culture.

The eighteenth-century reader's empathy was trained by the novel form's ability to represent several subjectivities simultaneously. The ethical response was triggered by certain aesthetics of representation. Thus, we may suggest that the novel's aesthetics taught its readers to empathize. In the case of Holocaust testimony in general, or of Wilkomirski's so-called memoir *Bruchstücke* in particular, I suggest that the reader empathizes with the narrator, not mainly because of the way he represents his traumas, but because of the specific trauma he represents. Thus, I claim that, contrary to Eaglestone's view, the empathic readers of Holocaust testimony instead respond to the narrative's content and historical context.[13] In other words, the cause of the victim's suffering demands

13 On this point, I also disagree with Sally Miller's psychoanalytic analysis of the Wilkomirski Affair. She argues that it is not the content of *Fragments* that engages the reader, but its narrative form, and, more specifically, the implied reader constructed in the narrative: 'I propose that it is not the details of Dössekker's imagined experience of the Holocaust that resonated so strongly with readers but its positioning of the reader as a witness. [. . .] we can see that the narrative of *Fragments* is concerned with staging a very particular encounter between the testimonial speaker and the secondary witness' (51).

the reader's emotional response; it makes him or her capable of feeling the emotions of the traumatized child in Wilkomirski's narrative.

When reading Holocaust testimony, and not (an early modern) novel, not only the cause of the empathic response, but also its effects, differ radically. Even though literature was an important subject of discussion in the eighteenth century's emerging public domain, the typical novel reader was a woman, confined to the private sphere where she read to herself in silence. Her capacity to experience the world through novel characters did not lead to immediate public and political actions. Thus, the effect of the empathic reading became a public matter only indirectly, by providing a model of social bonding that gradually became an ideal in the modern discourse on human rights, as Lynn Hunt has argued. In the Wilkomirski Affair, however, the readers' concrete reactions to the little orphan Binjamin's wartime experiences instantaneously became a public matter. The readers (in the broad sense of the term) were, as I have argued, the main agents of the media event that followed the publication of *Bruchstücke*, and their judgements determined the book's public significance. As Maechler pointed out, the empathic response of *Bruchstücke*'s readers worldwide contributed to its status as an authentic and authorized testimony of the Nazi genocide, and to increase the public attention paid to child victims.[14]

A third difference between the early modern novel readers and the readers of Holocaust testimonies is the object of their empathy. In the first case, the empathy is directed at the novel's fictional characters; in the latter, the author-narrator is the object of empathy. Although empathy with fictional characters is unrestrained, in contrast, empathy with the author of a testimony relies on a certain precondition – the belief that the represented experiences have actually happened. The Wilkomirski Affair reveals the breakdown of the empathic reader when this precondition is falsified. The initial, intuitive, empathic response to *Bruchstücke* as a Holocaust memoir ceased when it turned out that the story was the product of the author's imagination. Quite paradoxically, then, its reception history shows that the reader position that was originally inherent to the fictional novel genre fit Holocaust testimony, but was invalidated as soon as it turned out to be mere fiction.

Although critics have claimed that Wilkomirski's book has novelistic qualities, and, after the revelations of the author's identity, could still be regarded as a valuable work of fiction about the Holocaust, in my view it is impossible to read *Bruchstücke* as a novel. Not only because it was published as a memoir, but also because its reception history has now become inseparable from the work.

14 Marouf Hasian has also discussed how the readers participated in the rhetorical process we know as the Wilkomirski Affair, and he emphasizes the productive 'roles that audiences and critics play in the co-creation of any "authentic" Holocaust witness' (235).

The reception has altered the contract between writer, reader, and subject matter. Today, one reads the Wilkomirski Affair, rather than *Bruchstücke*. Knowledge of the author's falsified biography, and the production context in general, information that now accompanies the narrative as paratexts that the reader need to think of, forces the reader to consider several aspects that fall outside an empathic approach. Thus, the empathic approach, which for most readers is still the most intuitive when reading the story of a traumatized, child victim, is, so to speak, de-automatized, when reading the Wilkomirski Affair.

Empathy – a problem of excess?

'Personal stories are the contemporary currency of human rights projects', states Joseph R. Slaughter (in Goldberg and Moore xiii). Personal stories, narratives of eyewitnesses, help us realize how history and politics concern individual human beings, and condition our experience of the world, and vice versa – the personal story may also have tremendous political impact, to the extent that it changes the world. For instance, the slave narrative, a subgenre of the novel that gained popularity in the nineteenth century, contributed to giving the so-called Negro slaves – who colonial law had reduced to commercial objects – a subjectivity: proper names, identities, and biographies. Thus, the personal story qua slave narrative contributed to humanizing a dehumanized population, and its reader – the empathic reader – was important in developing the modern discourse on human rights. The personal story is also the core of memory culture today, and several scholars agree that it owes its almost hegemonic place to the 'Holocaust discourse'. Similar to the slave narrative, the personal story qua Holocaust testimony is a device of resistance, insofar as it re-establishes names, experiences, and biographies of the Nazi victims. It has clearly helped to change the world, as the public recognition of the Holocaust victims' stories of suffering led to the institution of the Universal Declaration of Human Rights in 1948.

The personal story – whether represented in museums, Amnesty International campaigns, novels, testimonies, or Hollywood blockbusters – remains a powerful aesthetic strategy for narrating human rights, and the idea that reading it fosters empathy and educates future world citizens is widespread. But perhaps the Wilkomirski Affair reveals a dead end to such individualization, and the empathy vogue that follows in its wake. For the eighteenth-century novel reader, novelistic representations of individual suffering were a new phenomenon. In our contemporary world society, such representations are omnipresent. In the wake of the Holocaust, individual suffering and empathically relating to the pain of others have nearly become a cultural cliché (cf. Sontag). Is 'the biggest deficit that we have in our society and in the world right now . . . an empathy deficit', as US President Barack Obama has claimed? Or is the problem perhaps the opposite – too much empathy? Is the empathic reader – who once provided a model of citizen virtue – today at risk of becoming an instrument for obscuring a critical understanding of historical and cultural artefacts?[15]

The Wilkomirski Affair offers an important lesson in revealing the power, as well as the shortcomings, of the empathic reader. It shows us what happens if we automatically read personal stories the way we (used to) read novels – we recognize the other (i.e. the narrator of or the character in a story) as a centre of experience, as Nussbaum puts it, without regard for the story's genre, the concepts of truth to which it refers, or its production context. I hope this analysis has revealed that the contemporary invitation to an empathic reader response runs the danger of foregrounding the receiver's emotions and feelings. Knowledge of the person whose story is being told, as well as of the narrative's contextual circumstances, risks being left in the shadows. In and after Holocaust testimony, the dynamics that interconnect literature, politics, and human rights are of a different character than they were in the early modern era. The question that should be addressed today is not that of the kinds of feelings a personal story such as Wilkomirski's evokes, but rather what body of knowledge it represents. To conclude, I suggest that what our society and the world today suffer from is not an empathy deficit, but rather an excess of empathy. The empathic response falls short of recognizing the complexity of the historical and political conditions that cause personal trauma. The Wilkomirski Affair, from its position between fiction and autobiography, and with its different concepts of truth, reveals the possible impact of literature, and the need to understand the dynamics between text and context. Empathy may block our access to contextual – historical, cultural, political – conditions, and consequently we are in need of readers that are able to recognize reading contracts in which paratexts, such as those that surround the reception of Wilkomirski's memoir, are taken into consideration.

Works cited

Amnesty International. 2015. Web. 7 Apr. 2015. <https://amnesty.org/en>.

Anderson, Benedict. *Imagined Communities: Reflections on the Origins and Spread of Nationalism.* 1983. London: Verso, 2006. Print.

Batson, C. Daniel. 'These Things Called Empathy: Eight Related but Distinct Phenomena'. *Social Neurosciences of Empathy.* Ed. J. Decety and W. Ickes. Cambridge: MIT Press, 2009. 3–15. Print.

Caruth, Cathy. 'Introduction'. *Trauma: Explorations in Memory.* Ed. C. Caruth. Baltimore/London: Johns Hopkins University Press, 1995. 3–12. Print.

15 The argument is in line with Gross and Hoffmann's, which claims that: 'This approach [i.e. to empathize with the victims] preserves the sanctity of individual memory, but at the expense of converting the Holocaust into the sublime, something that can be felt but not understood. [. . .] the result is not history or knowledge but a common – and transcendent – identification with the victims' (40).

Clendinnen, Inga. *Reading the Holocaust.* Cambridge: Cambridge University Press, 1999. Print.

Eaglestone, Robert. 'Identification and the Genre of Testimony'. *Representing the Holocaust.* Ed. Sue Vice. London: Valentine Mitchell, 2003. 117–140. Print.

Eagleton, Terry. *Trouble with Strangers: A Study of Ethics.* Oxford: Wiley-Blackwell, 2009. Print.

Felman, Shoshana. 'Education and Crisis, or the Vicissitudes of Teaching'. *Trauma: Explorations in Memory.* Ed. C. Caruth. Baltimore/London: Johns Hopkins University Press, 1995. 13–60. Print.

Goldberg, Elisabeth Swanson and Alexandra Schultheis Moore, eds. *Theoretical Perspectives on Human Rights and Literature.* New York: Routledge, 2012. Print.

Gross, Andrew S. and Michael J. Hoffman. 'Memory, Authority, and Identity: Holocaust Studies in the Light of the Wilkomirski Debate'. *Biography* 27.1 (2004): 25–47. Print.

Hasian, Marouf, Jr. 'Authenticity, Public Memories, and the Problematics of Post-Holocaust Remembrances: A Rhetorical Analysis of the Wilkomirski Affair'. *Quarterly Journal of Speech* 91.3 (2004): 231–263. Print.

Hunt, Lynn. *Inventing Human Rights: A History.* London/New York: W. W. Norton, 2007. Print.

Keen, Suzanne. *Empathy and the Novel.* New York: Oxford University Press, 2007. Print.

Kjørholt, Ingvild. 'Cosmopolitans, Slaves, and the Global Market in Voltaire's *Candide ou l'optimisme*'. *Eighteenth-Century Fiction* 25.1 (2012): 61–84. Print.

LaCapra, Dominick. *Writing History, Writing Trauma.* Baltimore/London: Johns Hopkins University Press, 2001. Print.

Landsberg, Allison. 'America, the Holocaust, and the Mass Culture of Memory: Toward a Radical Politics of Empathy'. *New German Critique* 71 (1997): 63–86. Print.

Lejeune, Philippe. *Le pacte autobiographique.* Paris: Seuil, 1975. Print.

Levy, Daniel and Natan Sznaider. *The Holocaust and Memory in the Global Age.* 2001. Trans. A. Oksiloff. Philadelphia: Temple University Press, 2006. Print.

Maechler, Stefan. *The Wilkomirski Affair: A Study in Biographical Truth.* Trans. John E. Woods. New York: Schocken Books, 2001. Print.

Maslan, Susan. 'The Dream of the Feeling Citizen: Law and Emotion in Corneille and Montesquieu'. *SubStance* 35.1 (2006): 69–84. Print.

Miller, Sally. 'Fantasy, Empathy, and Desire: Binjamin Wilkomirski's *Fragments* and Bernhard Schlink's *The Reader*'. *MODERNISM/modernity* 21.1 (2013): 45–58. Print.

Nussbaum, Martha. *Political Emotions: Why Love Matters for Justice.* Cambridge/London: Harvard University Press, 2013. Print.

——. *Not for Profit: Why Democracies Need the Humanities.* Princeton: Princeton University Press, 2010. Print.

——. *Poetic Justice: The Literary Imagination and Public Life.* Boston: Beacon Press, 1995. Print.

Pavlovich, Kathryn and Keiko Krahnke, eds. *Organizing through Empathy.* New York: Routledge, 2014. Print.

Pennington, Heidi L. 'Reading for Narrative Truth through the Absence of Narrative Awareness in Wilkomirski's *Fragments*'. *Auto/Biography Studies* 28.1 (2013): 36–63. Print.

Sontag, Susan. *Regarding the Pain of Others.* New York: Picador, 2003. Print.

Suleiman, Susan Rubin. 'The 1.5 Generation: Thinking about Child Survivors and the Holocaust'. *American Imago* 59.3 (2002): 277–295. Print.

Vice, Sue. 'Questions of Truth in Holocaust Memory and Testimony'. *The Bloomsbury Companion to Holocaust Literature.* Ed. Jenni Adams. London: Bloomsbury Academic, 2013. 47–63. Print.

——. *Holocaust Fiction.* London/New York: Routledge, 2000. Print.

Wiesel, Elie. 'The Holocaust as Literary Inspiration'. *Dimensions of the Holocaust.* Evanston: Northwestern University Press, 1977. Print.

Young, James E. 'Interpreting Literary Testimony: A Preface to Rereading Holocaust Diaries and Memoirs'. *New Literary History* 18.2 (1987): 403–423. Print.

Chapter 13

The predicament of spectatorship

Renzo Martens and the humanitarian image

Devika Sharma

My focus in this chapter is the cultural practice of looking at humanitarian images.[1] More specifically, I examine a social disposition of privilege, which I term 'the predicament of spectatorship'. This predicament will be well known to most people living in the Global North, referring as it does to the ways in which we respond, or fail to respond, to distant suffering presented to us by the media. The questions central to the predicament of spectatorship are about how to live with and act on the awareness of the immense suffering of others, and of the global injustices and inequalities, testified to by this suffering. How can we look, and how can we not look? If we look away, we might feel that we are engaging in some kind of escapism, a disavowal of our own situation in the world. If we look, we are likely to experience a kind of impotence, an experience of ourselves as passive voyeurs. Being moved by humanitarian images, how do we come to act, and what might constitute an act in the face of a humanitarian crisis somewhere else? The predicament of being a spectator is closely related to the predicament of being privileged. Being a spectator is itself a function of some kind of privilege.

Photography and digital images are among the most important media for humanitarian governance and culture, and gazing at photographs or moving images depicting precarious, distant others is a cultural practice fundamental to the Western subject.[2] In the first part of this chapter, I examine the current

1 By 'humanitarian images', I refer to images from the Global South shown in a Western context in order to mobilize support or raise awareness about either a given humanitarian crisis, or poverty and vulnerability more generally. Such images are typically presented within a framework designed to help the spectator situate the image in a geographical context, and to act according to the appeal manifested and illustrated by the image.

2 With the term 'humanitarian culture', I wish to designate the cultural production, distribution, and consumption of phenomena such as humanitarian narratives (literary narratives, political narratives, news stories, campaigns, and testimonies), charitable shopping, charitable investment (micro-financing), humanitarian tourism, simulation gaming (experience how it is to be, for instance, a refugee), and humanitarian celebrity culture. This cultural formation can also include forms and genres crucial to the contemporary art institution such as socially committed art and the aesthetic of documentary realism.

critique of humanitarian images, focusing particularly on how this critique purports to deal with the predicament of spectatorship. Recently, we have seen a surge in critical interest in humanitarianism, and decisive work has been done on its genealogies and on its ideological structure.[3] Most often, a critique of humanitarian culture centres on the sentiments of the privileged consumer of humanitarian imagery, either embracing or challenging the moral sentiments crucial to humanitarian practices: empathy, sympathy, compassion, and pity. I argue that the social disposition of spectators typically comprises neither purely honourable emotions nor purely self-satisfied emotions. Looking to Sianne Ngai's study of negative emotionality, and to Raymond Williams' conceptualization of 'structures of feeling', I suggest that the contemporary humanitarian structure of feeling is a highly ambivalent structure, indexing the ambivalent experience of being among the globally privileged. Acknowledging that mixed emotions are central to humanitarian experience has consequences for how we discuss the spectatorship of suffering so crucial to humanitarian governance and culture.

The second part of this chapter looks closely at Dutch video artist Renzo Martens' 2008 film *Episode III: Enjoy Poverty*. With this film, Martens has found ways to ask new and radical questions about humanitarian spectatorship and the image economy that informs it. Usually, we think of the humanitarian relation as one existing between two asymmetrical positions. We know this relation is an unequal relation, because we have, whereas others have not. But this relation is unequal also because, we imagine, some are watching, whereas others are forced to act, in the sense of living vulnerable lives, rather than gazing at vulnerability. The act of gazing is regularly associated with passivity and a sense of impotence. In both popular discourse and scholarly inquiry into the functions of humanitarian images, this seems a standard assumption: we see so much that we cannot seem to find the tools, affective and political tools, for acting. This idea is at the centre of the predicament of spectatorship. As I understand the film, *Enjoy Poverty* speaks to the powerlessness experienced by the First World spectator. But it does so only by placing this powerlessness in close and discomforting conjunction with the power of humanitarian governance and culture also attested to by the film.

Critique of humanitarian imagery

In criticism of photography, it is commonly understood that the *raison d'être* of humanitarian images is to raise awareness, move spectators, and prompt them to act in response to the crisis and suffering in question. Assuming that the suffering of distant others ought to produce a sense of responsibility in the

3 For discussions of the history of humanitarianism, see Moyn; Hunt; Manfredi; Paulmann. For ethnographies of humanitarian emotions and practices, see Feldman and Ticktin; Fassin; Bornstein and Redfield.

spectator, this critical literature examines the ways in which some forms of mediatization produce such a sense of responsibility, whereas other forms of mediatization preclude it (see Sontag; Pollock, 'Not-Forgetting Africa', 'Photographing Atrocity'; Chouliaraki, *The Ironic Spectator*, *The Spectatorship*; Silverstone; Butler).[4] This line of critical inquiry examines the conditions under which we, as privileged spectators, are moved by the mediatized suffering we are witnessing.[5] It asks which kind of framing elicits our humanitarian or political emotions – be they pity, compassion, grief, or outrage – and what the visual, discursive, and political barriers to such responsiveness are. It is commonly acknowledged in this literature that our moral and affective responsiveness are dependent upon the culturally recognizable humanness of the subjects whose suffering we contemplate (Butler). Which hierarchies of human life assert themselves when images of suffering fail to move or mobilize us, this literature asks.[6]

One important type of critique of humanitarian imagery focuses on the choice of motif in the images: the stereotyping typically involved in the humanitarian image repertoire, the preference for depicting starving children, the infantalization of entire regions possibly involved in this kind of imagery, and, more generally, the colonial residues in humanitarian aesthetics. In this vein, political scientist Kate Manzo suggests that the iconography of childhood 'reproduces colonial visions of a superior global north and an inferior south' (638). The risk, Manzo notes, is that this iconography reproduces a colonial, paternalistic logic with regard to the way international development and aid work are carried out today. Media scholar Lilie Chouliaraki has carefully analysed the ways in which the imagery favoured by humanitarian organizations regulates the interactions between the Global South and North. In her book *The Ironic Spectator*, Chouliaraki discusses the affective and ethical implications of both 'negative' and 'positive' humanitarian visual appeals. Negative visual appeals, exemplified by the dramatic photojournalistic capturing of the starving child or the human body on the brink of death, are often criticized for robbing their subjects of dignity, Chouliaraki notes. At the same time, according to a typical argument, such negative images drain the spectator's capacity for empathy, thereby causing

4 For more general introductions to questions about gaze and visual culture, see Mirzoeff; Sturken; Rose.

5 For a recent discussion of photography and political violence that tends to focus less on the moral sentiments of the spectator, see Azoulay.

6 It is important to note that the explicit focus in the critical literature on the affective and moral effects of humanitarian imagery does not necessarily entail the evaluation of such effects taking the individual as its point of reference. On the contrary, much work done on the representation of distant suffering asserts the *social* nature of the norms that regulate our affective response to these images. Thus, it articulates an observation that is also central to the thriving field of affect studies, namely that our emotional repertoire is a socially shared repertoire, and thus culturally and historically contingent.

widespread apathy, rather than engagement. On the other hand, Chouliaraki suggests, positive appeals – we may think of images of poor people smiling at the camera – often render invisible the radical asymmetry of the positions in the humanitarian relation. Such positive images, Chouliaraki holds, focus on the beneficiary's gratitude, and thus fail in terms of producing the wished-for sense of responsibility in the spectator.

A somewhat different critical tradition focuses instead on the sheer number of humanitarian images circulating in the media, and on the commodifying effect on suffering that this 'bombardment' of images may have. Does not the overload of images encourage us to not take seriously what we are being shown? May the result of this bombardment be that we simply lose the energy to look intently at what is right in front of our eyes? Here, we may think of art historian Griselda Pollock's rather typical analysis of the desensitizing effect of the commodification of humanitarian images:

> We want to see, but from elsewhere, and so we send photographers into the most alarming and dangerous places so that we might be able to see everything, the more extreme the better, but at a protected and often aestheticizing second-hand. We hunger for our daily doses of news reports, which must be filled with vivid images that alone make us believe that this is reality.
>
> ('Not-Forgetting Africa' 121)

Pollock concludes that the more we see, 'the less we are able to respond affectively to what we are shown' ('Not-Forgetting Africa' 121). This emptying of meaning through an excess of images is also a central theme in Susan D. Moeller's much-read 1999 book, *Compassion Fatigue: How the Media Sell Disease, Famine, War, and Death.*

The body of work I have presented above often understands itself as critiquing sentimental, humanitarian practices. Yet, we may see the fundamental ethical norms of humanitarianism reflected in this line of work, insofar as it affirms the importance of identifying with, or feeling for the suffering of, distant others. We do not find here a commitment to non-involvement, as in the radical politics of independence, prescribing, for instance, 'African solutions to African problems'. At the same time, we may also contrast this particular line of inquiry with a more radical critique of humanitarianism and its emotional foundations. Such radical critique would stress the asymmetrical nature of humanitarian emotions – as Lauren Berlant has noted, privilege seems to be intrinsic to the structure of compassion (4). It would also stress the ways in which the moral sentiments of humanitarianism allow us to discard the moral burden of being globally privileged, by inviting us to feel solidarity with the poor of the world and victims of disaster, without necessarily questioning the structural causes of the suffering in question (Badiou; Fassin; Demos, 'Poverty Pornography').

The privileged experience

To my mind, the critical work on humanitarian images and the critique of humanitarian emotions are both relevant and necessary frameworks for understanding humanitarian culture today. Yet I wish to suggest that the sensorium of privilege is of a more composite kind than both these perspectives seem to suggest. In the critical literature, the moral and emotional bases of humanitarianism are described as derivates of compassion, sympathy, superiority, or self-righteousness. But I argue that this basis is not so much a basis, as it is a structure in flux. When looking to art and popular culture dealing with relations between the Global North and South, we see that such artefacts in fact often treat the moral and noble feelings of humanitarianism with irony or mistrust.[7] Judging from such works, the prevalent humanitarian structure of feeling is neither purely moral nor purely amoral. And it should not come as a surprise that being hailed as 'globally privileged' usually involves a tense, unsatisfying, and ambivalent evaluation of the humanitarian call, and of our capacity to respond appropriately to that call. Thus, the humanitarian structure of feeling seems built not so much on grand and consistent emotions such as compassion, pity, grief, or cynicism. Rather, it consists of a more ambivalent register of affectivity, indicating an unresolved interpretation of humanitarian reason, and the solutions it calls forth. It seems to me that this confused and unsettled structure is characterized, most significantly, by providing no morally superior position for the privileged subjects whose lives are organized according to it.

In attempting to understand and describe the humanitarian structure of feeling, I suggest we look to Sianne Ngai and her work on negative emotionality. In her 2005 book *Ugly Feelings*, Ngai studied not the grand, transformative, and strategic emotions that Aristotle favoured, but rather a range of petty, amoral, and non-cathartic feelings, such as envy, irritation, and paranoia. Taking her point of departure in Melville's *Bartleby, the Scrivener* and the opacity of Bartleby's dismissive attitude, his perpetual 'I would prefer not to', Ngai asks how we are to comprehend this kind of affective negativity. Ngai then suggests that the negative, ignoble, asocial, dysphoric, ambivalent affects arise when we experience situations of obstructed agency, when we experience an impasse, that is. Therefore, according to Ngai, studying these negative emotions may enhance our understanding of various social experiences of inaction and powerlessness, and of the political implications of those experiences.

7 The common unease with regard to the compassionate impulses and their functions became clear in the wake of the *Kony 2012* campaign by the American charity Invisible Children, for instance. However, as I argue elsewhere, the ambivalent and confused character of our response to the humanitarian call is evident even in formats cherishing and celebrating the compassionate emotions, such as the nationally broadcast humanitarian fundraiser (Sharma).

Along the lines of Ngai's insights into the prevalence of minor feelings in late modernity, I wish to argue that the privileged experience of humanitarian imagery only rarely consists in unmixed affective attitudes such as compassion or cynicism. Therefore, I find one recurrent discussion within the critique of humanitarian images to be imprecise and unproductive, namely the discussion focusing on the desire of the spectator for ever more visceral suffering.[8] For instance, in *Regarding the Pain of Others*, Susan Sontag wrote that '[i]t seems that the appetite for pictures showing bodies in pain is as keen, almost, as the desire for ones that show bodies naked' (41). In the same vein, Griselda Pollock has described 'our apparently insatiable need to be shown the horrors of the world and to be exposed to the suffering of others' ('Not-Forgetting Africa' 121). I think it is worth questioning the apparent consensus in the criticism of photography that we, as a collective of spectators, desire suffering. Everyday reactions to images of suffering are, after all, most often about how terrible and unbearable it is to watch such pictures. To be interpellated as a subject of humanitarian reason – in this case, as a spectator of humanitarian images – is rarely associated with unmixed feelings.

My claim is that both the critique of humanitarian imagery and of humanitarian affectivity would benefit from a more nuanced understanding of the experience of being subject to the humanitarian call. Acknowledging the murky ethical reflections that take place even in situations where the privileged spectator seems simply compassionate, simply cynical, or simply desiring would prompt us to ask different questions about humanitarian imagery and humanitarian emotions. Which convictions, beliefs, and values are conveyed, if only in a negative sense, by the small and ugly feelings of cluelessness, indifference, shame, hopelessness, a bad conscience, and sheer reluctance to let oneself be emotionally engaged, which are all evident in contemporary humanitarian culture? The ugly experiences of the humanitarian self may be derived less from an overload of humanitarian images than from a lack of confidence in the double humanitarian promise of collective goodness and a better world. But the potential criticality of such ugly feelings is not relevant in and of itself. It is relevant because of the specific critical interpretation of humanitarian governance, humanitarian culture, and humanitarian subjectivity that the ugly feelings register. In line with Ngai's theory of negative affectivity, I suggest that we regard the ugly feelings as indicative of the situations in which support for the social, cultural, and political practices validated by compassion begins to fray. As such, they are affective

8 We find an early variant of this assumption in Saint Augustine's *Confessions*, in which Augustine noted that as spectacle, the suffering of others evokes terror and compassion, yet often we simultaneously experience some sort of pleasure – if not in the spectacle itself, then by being moved by our feelings of pity (49; bk. 3).

indications that may help us to comprehend the social conflicts that are often curbed by the optimism of humanitarian reason.

Enjoy Poverty

Renzo Martens' 2008 documentary, *Episode III: Enjoy Poverty*, the second film of a trilogy, seems uninterested in generating those moral sentiments either embraced or challenged by the literature on humanitarianism. Martens' film instead comes across as a piece of self-reflexive and self-reflective, humanitarian visual culture. Here, humanitarian emotions are treated with a cool interest, they appear strangely objectified and anonymized, and thus they are made available for a new kind of reflection. To some extent, the method of *Enjoy Poverty* is to shift its attention to the affective and sensory perception of the people we usually look at as the subjects of the humanitarian gaze, this shift exposing some of the tensions of the predicament of spectatorship, and of our attachment to it. Just as importantly, Martens presents us with a rare materialism in his investigation of the production of humanitarian images, and of the image economy of which they form a part.

Enjoy Poverty is the visual documentation of an artistic and educational project conceived and realized by the artist himself. Over a period of two years, Martens travelled in the Democratic Republic of Congo with the aim of convincing the Congolese that their poverty is, in fact, their most important resource. With his video recorder, often turned on himself, Martens films at an art show in Kinshasa, at a meeting arranged by the World Bank, in refugee camps, and in plantations. In all these places, he talks to high and low about how the Congolese themselves can capitalize on their natural resources, including poverty. He is met with surprised ignorance by Western aid workers and photojournalists alike, whereas the Congolese see his project as a sort of testimony to the situation in Congo.

Photography and the image economy play the main roles in *Enjoy Poverty*. When Martens learns from a Western photojournalist that agencies typically pay approximately 50 USD for a good picture of suffering, he takes it upon himself to re-educate a small group of Congolese photographers, who, until then, had been mostly taking colourful pictures at weddings and other festive occasions. Now, they instead needed to learn about the aesthetics of humanitarian imagery, and its advantageous economy. In other words, humanitarian photojournalism is the means, Martens suggests, by which his Congolese students can finally capitalize on the poverty that is theirs.

In a sense, *Enjoy Poverty* is a classical documentary with a classical documentary aim, the intention being a critical exposé of a blameworthy order. As a documentary, the film includes the elements described by media scholar W. J. T. Mitchell as characterizing the traditional photoessay:

> The 'taking' of human subjects by a photographer [. . .] is a concrete social encounter, often between a damaged, victimized, and powerless individual

> and a relatively *privileged observer*, often acting as the 'eye of power', the agent of some social, political, or journalistic institution.
>
> (288, my emphasis)

On the one hand, *Enjoy Poverty* is a typical documentary, insofar as the film displays the characteristics of the visual documentary. On the other hand, it is atypical, because it is first and foremost a reflection of the production and distribution of exactly the kind of documentary art and journalism to which it itself belongs. The reprehensible order that it so critically displays is not an order external to the production of images; it is instead the production of images itself. Or, put in a different way, to a large extent, the subject of the film is the very asymmetrical relation between privileged observer and the observed, described by Mitchell in the quotation above as a characteristic trait of the photographic documentary.

Art historian T. J. Demos has described this atypical documentary form in Martens' project as 'a kind of reverse photojournalism, or reverse documentarism, one that centers on the documentarian-artist-photojournalist, who is normally hidden in such projects' (Demos, 'Roundtable One' 8). In *Enjoy Poverty*, a reverse documentarism is particularly recognizable in Martens' thorough examination of the status of the photograph. Martens seems primarily interested not in the ontology of the photograph, its more or less privileged relationship to reality, but rather in the economic and legal conditions of the production and circulation of photographs inside and outside of Congo. More generally, Martens is interested in the relationship between visibility and invisibility: Which Western activities in central Africa are made visible, and how come, and which activities are made invisible? When Doctors without Borders withdraw from the hardest hit and most inaccessible parts of the country, is it partly because there is no one around to document the good work they are doing? Why is it apparently impossible for refugees in a UN-run camp to get a tarpaulin without a UN logo on it? Why do aid workers from FIDA, the Finnish development programme, take pictures of all the people they smilingly hand out aid to? And why is there no photo-documentation of the UN aiding, with armed protection, Western companies exporting gold and other raw materials from the Congo? From Martens' seemingly haphazard questions, we understand that not only a production of images, but also an effort to render invisible, organize the management of aid measures in Congo, and thus a part of life there.

Dignity is a common reference point for theoretical discussions of the ethically well-composed humanitarian image. A dignified portrait of poverty and its victims does not, however, seem to be a determining factor for tone and style in *Enjoy Poverty*. Early in the film, an enraged father shows his seven-year-old daughter's anus to Martens' camera. The father holds up his daughter, and spreads her cheeks; the girl has sores all over, presumably because of malnutrition. Later, we see a mother who, confronted with the news of her little daughter's death owing to malnutrition, breaks down. Still, Martens' method does not seem aimed at making the viewers of his film feel compassionate, since there is no coherent story to give weight and tragic meaning to these scenes. Instead, the scenes appear as weirdly flat and snapshot-like statements about a reality that Martens has had no real interest in unfolding and making affectively relevant. In fact, *Enjoy Poverty* seems surprisingly uninterested in my feelings as a spectator. The work does not stare at me, asking me for a specific response. In a way, the film does not even seem addressed to me, the privileged, Western spectator.

This is a truth with modifications, insofar as the film's primary audience is a certain segment in the Western world with an interest in art. But because Martens continuously, and always in a matter-of-fact, non-indignant way, explains to his Congolese apprentices what the Western spectator thinks and feels when confronted with images of suffering, the privileged spectator figures rather as an anonymized and neutralized entity *in* the work, rather than a sensate recipient *of* the work. The film has everything to do with humanitarian aesthetics and humanitarian emotions, but the arousal of such emotions is not a structuring intention of the film. Does this mean that the tone of the film is cynical? A combination of desperation and mischievousness would be more precise. This peculiar affective combination comes across in the absurdity of Martens' entire project, as well as in his self-satirizing pose as the white teacher, and in the film's colonial clichés more generally. At night, black shadows dance bewitched around Martens' tall neon sign with the words *Enjoy Poverty, Please.*

Fair Trade

Two scenes, in particular, exemplify Martens' notable way of critically examining the conditions of humanitarian photojournalistic practice. In the first scene, Martens is tagging along with a small group of Western photojournalists who have received a tip about some bodies, presumably victims of the civil war in the country. The photographers are escorted by what we might suspect are guerrilla soldiers, perhaps even the ones responsible for the killings. When the small group of photographers and soldiers reaches the spot in the jungle, we see two or three lifeless and bloodstained bodies lying on the ground. But Martens chooses, characteristically, not to focus his camera on the bodies, but on the situation of the photo shoot itself. From Martens' video account we get the impression that these masked soldiers wish to put the bodies on display, and that in turn, the photographers are snapping away without considering the possible kinds of complicity that seem to characterize the premise of their work. The scene turns absurd when a photographer's mobile phone rings. Rather than turning off the phone, the photographer answers the call, and Martens films the short, everyday conversation that follows. 'Can I call you later?' the photographer finally asks.

Martens' critical method is to focus on the contrasts between desperate machine gun gravity, and the everyday, journalistic way of dealing with this gravity, between war and the photographer's livelihood. As such, this asymmetry should neither surprise nor scandalize us. Presumably, Martens' aim is to make visible a history of production that most often remains invisible. His framing of the situation raises questions about the implications of photojournalism, and thus of the spectator, in terms of the suffering on display. It is not entirely clear exactly what kind of critique we should deduce from this framing – what critical judgements does Martens invite us to pass, over what, and whom? Nevertheless, it is clear that Martens' discreet turn of his video camera, his reverse documentarism, creates a very different position for us, the viewers of *Enjoy Poverty*, than for the viewers of the photojournalists' pictures. And, I propose, this is central to what the film provides us with: a new place from which to see. As a work of art, the film offers us a new place to imagine from. It does so by introducing a new place from which to see, by letting us see, more specifically, others seeing for us, as it were. In this way, the problems of spectatorship are at once magnified and concretized. By seeing from somewhere new, we become a new kind of spectator. This becomes more evident in a later scene.

The second scene to which I wish to turn our attention is Martens' conversation with the Western photographer who tells him about the photo agencies' standard payment for disaster images. 'I cover Congo', this photographer claims. He introduces Martens and us to the fact that there exists a competitive market for humanitarian images: 'It's a market out there,' as he puts it. Here, we see Martens in a favourite inquisitive role, where he seems to fully accept the situation of the photographer, but at the same time finds a way to ask unconventional questions. 'Who owns the photographs you take?' he asks. The photographer answers that he is indeed the author of his images. 'But who organizes the situations you take pictures of?' Martens asks. The photographer becomes annoyed, and dismisses Martens' unusual questions. There are a thousand situations here, he says. In other words, the photographer affirms that documentary humanitarian photography is rooted in the subjectivity and authority of the photographer.

In criticism of photography, a recurring discussion surrounds whether photography should be celebrated for its function as social documentation, or for its aesthetic and fictional qualities. Yet it seems clear, judging in particular by the major art biennales, that contemporary photojournalistic and documentary genres most often understand themselves as aesthetically autonomous, in the sense that they are not bound by contracts with their 'objects' when it comes to property rights. Conversely, the materialism so central to Martens' interpretation of the humanitarian image economy comes to the fore exactly in the film's interest in contracts. For instance, the man who exposes his daughter's anus to the camera also shows Martens the contracts into which he entered with the owner of the plantation where he works. The owner has in fact cancelled those contracts, the man explains, so now he simply works with no contract, unable to feed his family on the small salary he receives. Martens films the daughter while she skins a mouse and eats its tiny shreds of meat, and we clearly understand that this man and his fellow workers desperately need a radically different contractual relationship with the plantation owner. At the end of the film, it is implied that something like a contractual relationship has been entered, not between the man and the plantation owner, but between the man and the image-producing Martens. Here, Martens serves a meal to the man, who reports that it is the best food he has ever had. Thus, we are invited to understand this meal as a payment for the images made possible by the man and his family, the food appearing as the exchange value of the images, and thus testifying to their inevitable commodification in the humanitarian culture in which they partake. But the scene also indicates Martens' attempt to extend a 'food chain' in which photojournalists and documentary artists have traditionally been at the end of the line.

Several elements of *Enjoy Poverty* support the interpretation of Martens' attempt to establish a kind of *fair trade* for humanitarian images. According to Martens himself, the film is a parable of the activities of the West in the Third World, in the sense that the film not only critiques several examples of exploitation, but at the same time itself exploits in a very similar way. Martens says:

> [The film] doesn't critique by showing something that is bad, it critiques by duplicating what may be bad. On the one hand it gives some critique within the film, oh, media might be bad, it exploits you, take possession of the means of production; on the other hand I, the guy in the film, does exactly the same thing, or maybe not exactly but pretty much exactly the same thing and in the end then just leaves.
>
> (Penney)

If the film is critical, it is so in repeating the logic of exploitation that is the focus of the film, Martens says. Thus, mimicry would be one way of interpreting the strategy of the film. But it is equally clear that the film also works against the possible exploitative aspects of this strategy. In the above-mentioned interview, Martens does not tell us that he, as the film's creator, actually changes the existing conditions for humanitarian image production. Martens enters two contracts with his 'protagonists', local Congolese in Kinshasa and its environs.[9] The first contract echoes current practice in central Africa, and maintains that any profit from a given image will not go to the persons depicted. But later, Martens signs a different contract that guarantees those depicted a share of a profit, if any.[10] In her book *The Civil Contract of Photography*, visual culture scholar

9 These contracts are not a topic of the film, but they were later reprinted in the Belgian art magazine *A Prior Magazine*. See the discussion about these contracts in Els Rolandt's interview with Martens, which may be read here: http://squarevzw.be/picturethis/renzoapm16.htm.

10 Martens has since established the Institute for Human Activities (IHA) in Western Congo, a centre for aesthetic and critical practice, with an aim of channelling the profit of the center into the local communities, rather than back into the capitals of the art world. See www.ucl.ac.uk/art-history/about_us/academic_staff/dr_tj_demos/further_publications/Demos-Martens-IHA.pdf.

Ariella Azoulay discusses the affective-moral contractual relationship between the citizens of what Azoulay terms the 'citizenry of photography'. Martens expands on this juridical vocabulary by highlighting the economic dimensions to such a contractual relationship.

Relating *Enjoy Poverty* to the theoretical discussions about humanitarian images that I sketched out earlier in this chapter, we may summarize the film's way of critiquing images as not about ethically correct motives, or about ethically appropriate emotions on the part of the spectator. Martens' critical method may seem both primitive and radical in its simplicity. At the level of plot, the film is about the redistribution of humanitarian resources from Western hands to Congolese hands, through new contracts for the ownership of images. At the level of the more general terms of production of humanitarian culture and art, Martens' suggestions are exactly the same: to let the world's poorest people receive a fair share of the value they generate for media and art scenes – and research communities, we would have to add – in the West. Thus, one lesson of this film is that ethically responsible images must also always involve the question of economic responsibility, according to some principle of distributive justice. In the following section, I suggest that the politics of images implied by *Enjoy Poverty* also involve a critical examination of the predicament of spectatorship, and our attachment to it.

Lessons

As Thomas Keenan stated in his interpretation of *Enjoy Poverty*, Renzo Martens, the teacher, gives the Congolese pupils and photographers four lessons in all (Demos *et al.* 10), two of which take place in what could be a village school. Martens is at the blackboard; the Congolese people sit on school benches, taking notes. The first lesson is about poverty as a natural resource that may be made profitable. Poverty is a gift, Martens suggests, and he points out that others are stealing the poverty that rightfully belongs to the Congolese people. They need to understand that instead of being mere objects of humanitarian images, they should assume the role of its producers: images of suffering generate money in the form of aid, and the Congolese photographers should learn to see themselves as agents for it, not as passive recipients of aid. The next lesson is about math and rationality. Since wedding photography procures only 1 dollar a month, it is much better, so Martens argues, to focus on suffering, insofar as images of suffering, as we have seen, have a radically higher market value.

The third lesson takes the form of a regular photo school outing in the humanitarian field. Martens and the photographers are in a refugee camp. Here, Martens shows them what constitutes a good subject for their pictures, how close they need to go, and how long they should 'work with' the subject in order to secure the best image. The scene is painful for both the photographers and for us, as the inhabitants of the refugee camp do not realize the futility of begging from the photographers; with cameras in their hands, the photographers are immediately identified as privileged visitors, and they soon have to turn their backs on the begging camp inhabitants and flee the place. The small group of photographers then enters the refugee camp's modest hospital. Martens once again matter-of-factly explains that, as photographers working in the humanitarian field, they will have to aim for the worst cases. Those are the pictures you can sell, he assures them. If the Western viewing public sees pictures like that, they will better understand how bad things are here. The photographers, in other words, are being taught how to co-produce the humanitarian aesthetic: closer, closer, dwell, dwell, this dying little girl will wait for you to finish your photo shoot. A doctor, holding the girl forward for the photographers to better get their pictures, explains that it is indeed customary for the doctors to wait for the foreign photojournalists visiting the hospital to finish taking pictures before continuing their work with the patient. The photographers are visibly ill at ease, awkward and unsure of their assignment and their new status as privileged beings, as onlookers.

The scene at the hospital is unbearable. It is unbearable because of the patience and servility with which the doctor holds out the sick girl, a servility seemingly indicating both hope and trust in the rationality of the humanitarian image. But if we feel discomfort when watching this scene, it is not only, I think, because of what we see, but also because we experience someone else seeing it for us. What we see is the very situation of watching from a privileged distance; we *see* the act of witnessing other people's suffering. The spectator's position is visualized and materialized in an unfamiliar way, and this position becomes the object of a new kind of affective reflection. In a sense, the scene is organized for us to see in it a loss of innocence, one that comes with intense discomfort, but also one that comes with an opportunity to reflect in new ways on our social disposition as global spectators. The people we imagine to be, by default, inherently innocent by virtue of being objects of the humanitarian gaze are here made to participate in what we experience as the guilty act of watching other people's pain through mediating devices. What makes the scene so unbearable is the situation itself, but it is also the fact that the Congolese photographers, the innocent objects of our humanitarian gaze, are experiencing it. Before our eyes, they undergo a transformation. They are initiated as spectators, and thus they become, in a sense, like us.

In the hospital scene, we witness the transformation of the photographers from being objects of the humanitarian gaze to being its manufacturers, exactly the transformation their teacher was hoping for. Taking up the humanitarian means of production, they have succeeded in becoming humanitarian actors, by being humanitarian spectators. On the one hand, their transformation introduces a rare shift, or doubling, in perspective – from the privileged experience to the sensate experience of others. Now, we are not merely seeing African others; we are also seeing *with* African others. On the other hand, their transformation has a tragic feel to it. Now, the Congolese photographers seem like poor fellows, not so much because they *are* poor, but because they have become spectators.[11] This experience of a tragic transformation taking place is likely to generate conflicted feelings in us, the spectators of this scene of spectatorship. What causes this conflict and discomfort is, I think, the degree of moral corruption we usually ascribe to this position of spectatorship. If the scene is painful for us, it is so partly because it is painful to share the predicament of spectatorship. Not because we are fond of this predicament; on the contrary, because it is at the very centre of our paralysing self-understanding as globally privileged beings.

What are the effects of the blurring, in Martens' film, of the distinctions between those who see and those who act? The scene at the hospital, I suggest, invites us to reframe and rethink the concern underlying much discourse on humanitarian visual culture, about how to transform the humanitarian spectator into a humanitarian actor.[12] That is, a subject not merely looking at humanitarian situations, but also acting on them. Martens' project is, specifically, to make humanitarian actors of the photographers by helping them to transform into humanitarian spectators. He has them perform the humanitarian act *par excellence*: they see, they witness, they frame. In other words, what the photographers in the small hospital room make visible is the convergence in humanitarian cultures of seeing and acting.

The question posed by *Enjoy Poverty* is not so much 'How do we come to act?', but rather 'Which kinds of agency, which social forms of actions, may be conceived from within the humanitarian imaginary?' As Ngai reminds us, not having a sense of agency is a reason for having ugly feelings. But perhaps the ugly feelings of humanitarianism are caused not so much by experiencing one's agency as blocked by something or someone, but by not having a sense, an image, of what humanitarian action may be, apart from spectatorship. Today, there is a host of handbooks on humanitarian action, but none addresses the viewer of humanitarian images. For instance, in *The Routledge Companion to Humanitarian Action*, of 2015, there is a section called 'Actors', with a dozen article contributions, none of which addresses the question of the spectator as a First World actor. The reason for this omission is that in the humanitarian culture of the Global North, action appears to be already inscribed, but only unsatisfyingly so, in humanitarian spectatorship. The peculiar project of *Enjoy Poverty* allows us to glimpse how the predicament of spectatorship unfolds, not solely at the level of representation, nor solely at the level of the supply chain

11 The photographers from Kanyabayonga were not suddenly transformed from objects of humanitarianism into its implied subjects, as though they were previously blind to their lived experience. But the film's suggestion that the idea that innocence and moral corruption correlate with positions within the humanitarian relation is central to the predicament of spectatorship, and thus to the humanitarian imagination.

12 I draw here on the deconstructive analysis of the concepts of seeing and acting, famously offered by Jacques Rancière in his book *The Emancipated Spectator* [*Le spectateur émancipé*] (2011).

of humanitarian images. The predicament of spectatorship is, instead, central to humanitarian subjectivation.

After their ordeal at the camp hospital, the photographers from Kanyabayonga had one last lesson in store. In this sequence, the photographers and their teacher show up at the local MSF office and a curious dialogue between a strangely decadent doctor and Martens follows. MSF does not want to use the pictures in their campaigns, the doctor states. The photographs are not good enough, and who do these photographers think they are, showing up with images for sale, as though MSF was some sort of grocery exchange. The small group of dismissed humanitarian entrepreneurs must face the fact that poverty might be a valuable raw material, but that trading it in the form of pictures is a closed circuit reserved for Western actors – just as is the case for many of the continent's other raw materials. In spite of the reputation of photography as a particularly democratic media, being both cheap and easy to access, citizens in Azoulay's 'citizenry of photography' are not, in effect, equal. The mission is a failure, and the only lesson Martens promotes thereafter is the imperative that is too desperate to seem seriously resigned: Enjoy poverty, please.

Works cited

Augustine, Aurelius. *Confessions of St. Augustine.* Auckland: The Floating Press, 2009 (written in the years AD 397–401). Print.

Azoulay, Ariella. *The Civil Contract of Photography.* New York: Zone Books, 2012. Print.

Badiou, Alain. *Ethics: An Essay on the Understanding of Evil.* Trans. Peter Hallward. London/New York: Verso, 2001. Print.

Berlant, Lauren. 'Introduction: Compassion (and Withholding)'. *Compassion: The Culture and Politics of an Emotion.* Ed. Lauren Berlant. New York/London: Routledge, 2004. 1–13. Print.

Bornstein, Erica and Peter Redfield, eds. *Forces of Compassion: Humanitarianism between Ethics and Politics.* Santa Fe: SAR Press, 2010. Print.

Butler, Judith. *Frames of War: When Is Life Grievable?* London/New York: Verso, 2009. Print.

Chouliaraki, Lilie. *The Ironic Spectator: Solidarity in the Age of Post-Humanitarianism.* Cambridge: Polity Press, 2013. Print.

——. *The Spectatorship of Suffering.* London: Sage, 2006. Print.

Demos, T.J. 'Poverty Pornography, Humanitarianism, and Neoliberal Globalization: Notes on Some Paradoxes in Contemporary Art'. *Stedelijk Bureau Newsletter* 121 (2011). Print.

——. *et al.* 'Roundtable One: A Discussion of Renzo Martens' *Episode III (Enjoy Poverty) (2009)*'. *In and out of Brussels.* Ed. T. J. Demos and Hilde Van Gelder. Leuven: Leuven University Press, 2013. 5–22. Print.

Fassin, Didier. *Humanitarian Reason: A Moral History of the Present.* Berkeley/Los Angeles: University of California Press, 2012. Print.

Feldman, Ilana and Miriam Ticktin, eds. *In the Name of Humanity: The Government of Threat and Care.* Durham: Duke University Press, 2010. Print.

Hunt, Lynn. *Inventing Human Rights.* London/New York: W. W. Norton, 2007. Print.

Manfredi, Zachary. 'Recent Histories and Uncertain Futures: Contemporary Critiques of International Human Rights and Humanitarianism'. *Qui Parle* 22.1 (2013): 3–32. Print.

Manzo, Kate. 'Imaging Humanitarianism: NGO Identity and the Iconography of Childhood'. *Antipode* 40.4 (2008): 632–657. Print.

Martens, Renzo. *Episode III: Enjoy Poverty*. 2008. Film. Please refer to Martens' website for more information: www.renzomartens.com/episode3/film.

Mitchell, W. J. T. *Picture Theory*. Chicago/London: University of Chicago Press, 1994. Print.

Mirzoeff, Nicholas, ed. *The Visual Culture Reader*. 1998. London/New York: Routledge, 2012. Print.

Moeller, Susan D. *Compassion Fatigue: How the Media Sell Disease, Famine, War, and Death*. New York: Routledge, 1999.

Moyn, Samuel. *The Last Utopia: Human Rights in History*. Cambridge/London: Harvard University Press, 2010. Print.

Ngai, Sianne. *Ugly Feelings*. Cambridge/London: Harvard University Press, 2005. Print.

Paulmann, Johannes. 'Conjunctures in the History of International Humanitarian Aid during the Twentieth Century'. *Humanity* 4.2 (2013): 215–238. Print.

Penney, Joe. 'The Politics of Helping Others: Interview with Renzo Martens'. *McGill Foreign Affairs Review*, Winter 2010. Web. May 2016. <www.renzomartens.com/articles>.

Pollock, Griselda. 'Not-Forgetting Africa'. *Alfredo Jaar: La Politique des Images*. Lausanne: Ringier, 2008. 113–135. Print.

——. 'Photographing Atrocity: Becoming Iconic?' *Picturing Atrocity: Photography in Crisis*. Ed. Geoffrey Batchen *et al.* London: Reaktion Books, 2012. 65–78. Print.

Rancière, Jacques. *The Emancipated Spectator*. London/New York: Verso, 2011. Print.

Rose, Gilian. *Visual Methodologies: An Introduction to Researching with Visual Materials*. London: Sage, 2012. Print.

Sharma, Devika. 'The Predicament of Privilege: Between Humanitarian and Cynical Reason'. forthcoming. Print.

Silverstone, Roger. *Media and Morality: On the Rise of the Mediapolis*. Cambridge: Polity, 2006. Print.

Sontag, Susan. *Regarding the Pain of Others*. New York: Picador, 2003. Print.

Sturken, Marita. *Practices of Looking: An Introduction to Visual Culture*. London: Oxford University Press, 2009. Print.

Williams, Raymond. *Marxism and Literature*. Oxford: Oxford University Press, 1978. Print.

Chapter 14

Agency from beyond the grave

A case study of the documentary and dramatic aspects of Rabih Mroué's *Pixelated Revolution*

Peter Ole Pedersen

Lebanese artist Rabih Mroué's documentary installation, *Pixelated Revolution*, showcases a frightening and unbelievable phenomenon: civilian victims of snipers documenting their own deaths in the Syrian civil war. This is a complex example of how a prominent member of the professional art world lends agency to the victims of an armed conflict in a country that is notoriously known for its brutal disregard for civil rights. *Pixelated Revolution* poses a number of interesting questions: How can documentary evidence be used to represent victims? Where do we situate the multifaceted use of drama and documentary in contemporary art? How does art meaningfully address the question of human rights suspended between suffering, catastrophe, and historical significance?

Mroué's work is a multifaceted installation that comprises flick books, photographs, and textual quotations, which, combined with a lecture-performance filmed at the Staatstheater in Kassel during *Documenta 13*, confronts the viewer with mobile phone recordings of the sniper killings. Historically, human rights have been poorly upheld in Syria. In the tumultuous aftermath of the Second World War, the country went through a number of military coups, and after the 1963 coup d'état and the ensuing rule of the Ba'ath party, Hafez al-Assad effectively upheld a state of emergency that allowed security forces to circumvent existing laws, and even harass or imprison human rights activists. The situation has not improved under the rule of his son, Bashar al-Assad. Both the mobility and freedom of speech of the population are strictly controlled by the military and secret police. The latter, in particular, has been challenged during the Syrian civil war, where a number of journalists, activists, and regular civilians started recording demonstrations, crackdowns, and daily life. Mobile telephone documentation forms a large part of these recordings, and under the still-extreme situation in Syria, this fairly new phenomenon continues to work as a way for civilians to express themselves, and as a resource for journalists.[1]

1 The use of mobile phones in the documentation of the Syrian civil war has been so comprehensive that a festival dedicated to the medium now exists. *Syria's Mobile Phone Films Festival* screened a number of productions based on this documentation, and took place in Kafranbel, Aleppo, Atareb, Jabal Al-Zawiya, and Deraa in October 2015.

Pixelated Revolution recycles some of the most desperate documentations made by the civil war victims as the raw material for an art installation, which is both dramatized and aestheticized. In this way, Mroué's work writes itself into a long tradition of politically oriented docudrama.

A strained relationship exists between drama and documentary. The fusion of these two genres has produced a number of media phenomena, which, unfortunately, more often than not, result in stereotypical representations of its subjects, or even retellings of historical events that are downright problematic and misleading. One of the most well-known and widespread formats of this genre are the dramatized TV and film documentaries, which have been an integral part of the content on most channels, and have helped shape our expectations and the conventions surrounding the coupling of factual and dramatic elements in audiovisual storytelling.

Like so many other popular cultural phenomena, the mainstream version of the docudrama genre is intertwined with a number of distinctive works, which either break the conventions or help to establish them in challenging ways. Among them may be mentioned such diverse works as British docudrama pioneer Peter Watkins' political criticisms of modern society, and Errol Morris's hyper-stylized, cross-genre hybrids. It is hard to imagine two film-makers who differ more in their stylistic approaches or artistic temperament, and when, by way of introduction, I choose to mention them as notable representatives of the docudrama, it is primarily because this serves to illustrate the range and complexity that characterizes works in this genre.

Thus, the degree of dramatization and the way it is executed as part of, or in addition to, the documentary recordings, needs to be considered, not as the demarcation between fact and fiction within the docudrama genre, but instead in terms of media-specific effects, such as editing, scenography, or lighting. No matter how immediate the documentation, or how comprehensive the dramatization, it is the contextualization of these images and the style of acting that determines how the finished work affects us.

The docudrama genre has its own position within theatre, as well as film history. There are different movements in documentary theatre, with more or less explicit political agendas. The longest and most enduring tradition is found in Germany, with George Büchner's first play, *Danton's Death* (*Dantons Tod*, 1835), being one of the earliest examples of using elements of (contemporary) real-life events as the basis of its story. One hundred years later, Erwin Piscator utilized both film and lectures as part of his Epic theatre (*episches Theater*), whereas Peter Weiss' plays, *Die Ermittlung* and *Vietnam Diskurs*, stand as notable, later docudramatic interpretations of the Frankfurt Auschwitz trials and the Vietnam War, respectively.

Between medium and genre

If one is to identify a consistent development in these artistic treatments of documentation, and the violent and dramatic historical events they sometimes portray, then it is the preoccupation with multimedia aspects either in the artistic expression of the work or the subject matter that is investigated through art.[2] Reflection on this fundamental relationship between form and content produces some interesting questions: What is the intent behind the work? How is the documentary material integrated in the artistic project?

In the context of documentary and human rights that are central to these enquiries, one has to address the way in which cultural expression, such as art, may contribute to a critical reflection, be that in an intellectual, emotional, or proactive way. To come up with useful answers to these important questions, I intend to embark on an interdisciplinary discussion of the role of documentation as the main substance of artistic works, as opposed to the more media-specific theories that have been formulated within this field of research.[3] This focus means a departure from the central preoccupation with verifying the degree of authenticity, an understandable approach to the genre, but also one that risks overshadowing the main potential of the documentary: the capacity to present an alternative, audiovisual take on a factual event. This perspective is not meant to ignore the connection between genre and reality, but rather to address this complicated relationship, and how it animates and revitalizes specific material, to create a certain critical understanding of history and memory.

Pixelated Revolution draws parallels to a number of documentary practices, and various film aesthetic movements as diverse as *Dogme 95* and cinéma-vérité. Another intention of this article is a discussion of the definitions and limitations of the genre. Documentary works are defined by their combination of specific editing strategies, narration, and real-life footage, but an installation such as *Pixelated Revolution* establishes a sensory framework that combines the didactic and traditional presentation of the story with a variety of media, which accentuates the different modes of experience, be it affect or intellectual contemplation. To paraphrase the term used by art historian Rosalind Krauss in her famously provocative text about sculpture, to a great extent, 'the expanded field of documentary' has to do with reconsidering the historic conception of the genre, and asking central questions, such as: How is the use of authenticity distributed in the work? What is the relationship between dramatic and factual

2 As an example of this content-oriented aspect of the double focus, it should be mentioned that Weiss's magnum opus, the novel *Die Ästhetik des Widerstands*, is formed around a discussion of the relationship between politically motivated resistance movements and art, with a pluralistic perspective on literature, painting, and sculpture.

3 The majority of the research and theory concerning documentaries has been focused on the medium of film (e.g. Nichols, *Introduction to Documentary*; Renov, 'Towards a Poetics of Documentary'). Surprisingly, the perspective of the documentary in relation to contemporary art has not been explored that thoroughly. One of the recent and only publications on the subject is Julian Stallabrass's anthology, *Documentary (Documents of Contemporary Art)*, published in 2013.

elements? Where is the difference between filmic, textual, and performed documentarism located?[4]

Rabih Mroué's background is in theatre, and in the years since the Lebanese civil war he has collaborated with his wife, the performance artist Lina Saneh, to develop the avant-garde movement of national theatre. This gradually led to a media-oriented mode of expression, where Mroué uses film projection, photography, and texts as the documentary background and scenic framework for his performances. His international breakthrough came with *How Nancy Wished That Everything Was an April Fool's Joke*, of 2007, an episodic performance wherein representatives from four different militia groups present conflicting recollections of their involvement and affiliations during the war. The setting was a sofa that seats three, whereon four actors sat cramped together, while posters of the 'martyrs' and militias, which, to this day, are a common sight on the streets of Beirut, were projected above each actor's head, like speech bubbles in a comic strip.

Coarse humour is not as apparent in Mroué's *Pixelated Revolution*, although a return to the strategy of portraying actual historical events through diverging points of view still permeates the work. In this case, the ambiguous atmosphere primarily has to do with the material aspect of the installation. Here, mobile telephone recordings published on, and collected from, the Internet are translated into a number of other media formats. The performative framework for this aestheticized documentation consists of a video recording of the artist giving a lecture, which is both a story about his personal motivation for working with this specific material, and an attempt to analyse it. If one looks at *Pixelated Revolution* with the filmic documentary in mind, it seems that Mroué's work has changed genre from a format comparable to the re-enactment of real-life events with which we are familiar from the dramatized documentary, to a form of presentation that is best understood from the perspective of the classic, didactic documentary, and its display of visual evidence and conventional use of the voice-over, classic genre characteristics to which I will return later.

Pixelated moments of death

The orchestration of uncanny evidence through the use of theatre, text, photography, and film is what challenges the viewer's understanding of the relationship between documentation and interpretation, especially concerning the use of the last-mentioned medium. When an audience explores an installation, it often takes place as an examination of a room and the objects it contains. Thus, *Pixelated Revolution* presents an opportunity to use Mroué's recorded lecture as a narrative

4 For a further discussion of the documentary genre, based on Krauss's reflections on the expanded field of art, see my dissertation, *Pixelated Reality – Documentary between Net-distribution, Popular Culture and the Avant-Garde*, Aarhus University 2014.

Figure 14.1 A selection of the enlarged stills made from the mobile phone recordings distributed on the Internet.

Source: © Rabih Mroué 2012.

framework for the physical *mise en scène* that simultaneously functions as both a reconstruction and a deconstruction of events and the media that portray them.[5] As mentioned before, the installation consists of different media variations of original, Net-distributed documentation from victims' mobile phones, pixelated moments of death. One of these modes of presentation features enlarged stills from video recordings, mounted in a row with metal clamps on one of the walls, a presentation that transforms the victims' documentation, and transports it to a setting that is reminiscent of both a darkroom and a crime scene investigation.

5 It is important to point out that in this context, *mise en scène* means the entire combination of sound, objects, and visual presentations. The whole point of this analysis of Mroué's installation is to accentuate how these 'in betweens' affect the conventional understanding of media and genre. As a further note, Mroué himself calls the filmed presentation that is part of the installation 'A non-academic lecture', a subtitle that I am certain he did not choose with the conviction that it would indicate either a subjective or an incontestable approach to the events, but instead a middle discourse, which accentuates just how much the conventions of a genre affect the mode of presentation and the subsequent reception.

Another, more directly engaging format is the collection of flick books, which are also part of the installation. They give the audience the opportunity to activate the digitally recorded and distributed clips found on YouTube and other video sharing websites, and figuratively shoot the victims, while leaving their fingerprints from ink pads mounted on the tables to which the books are attached.[6]

On the whole, there is a rather complex relationship between the use of specific materials, audience participation, and visual evidence in Mroué's work. In addition to the two tangible media transformations of the collected camera recordings, a video projection of the silhouette of a person holding a mobile phone while being shot and falling to the ground is shown in a continuous loop, and in real-life scale. Time after time, he is 'killed' and resurrected by the camera. It is this specific recording that may be considered the pure dramatic element of the installation; paradoxically, it is also the farthest removed from a depiction of real events, or any concrete storytelling. Even so, this short sequence is like a blueprint for the central element of docudrama: re-enactment. The reconstruction of a certain historic moment, no matter how small or seemingly insignificant, is the basis of the genre.

In the foregoing perspective, Mroué's re-enactment strategy may be interpreted as a stylized remake, which is diametrically opposed to the specific desire for realism that cultural theorist Vanessa Agnew identifies as a consistent characteristic across the different media, and one she approaches with skepticism: '[. . .] preoccupations with extremity and authenticity easily slips into a reductio ad absurdum – ever-higher production values for re-enactment events and participants subjected to increasingly dire situations in order to try to narrow the mimetic gap' (Agnew 332).

Agnew's criticism is based on a study of re-enactment as a broad-based historical practice, and one of her central arguments is specifically that this form of presentation is uncomfortably situated between sympathetic insights into historical experience, and the emphasis of the impossibility of ever reaching that privileged access to the past. If one follows this criticism of the genre, then Mroué's performative loop of the moment of death may be interpreted as a minimalist version of the docudrama. It does not include any photographic

6 This consistent interest in the material and materiality has a curious convergence with Morris's oeuvre, as I mentioned in the introduction to this article. In his most canonical work, *The Thin Blue Line*, of 1988, the criminal acts and the detective work (in a more or less metaphorical way) are the focal points, as is the intense preoccupation with the tactility of the evidence. In Mroué's work, this gets a further twist in the various physical versions of the mobile phone recordings. Here, the contrasting perspectives produced by re-enactments and close-ups in Morris's film are created by migrating among various media, an interesting correspondence within the 'expanded' framework of one of the most popular docudrama subgenres: the crime film.

identification of victims, but places the viewer in a disturbing position as witness to the continuous shooting and resurrection of a faceless silhouette that represents all victims of this war crime. We are confronted with a type of re-enactment that draws overwhelming attention to the sensuous physical experience, and thereby tries to establish an effective link between this filmic element and the aforementioned media-transformed documentation, and its pronounced activation of the senses. I argue that with this performativity, Mroué is primarily interested in examining what happens to our experience of documented historical events, when they are included as both convention-affirming and challenging dramatizations. On the one hand, it is just a film sequence that is part of a larger narrative, which binds the abstract stylization of this central event to a more complex meaning and comprehensive significance. On the other hand, we are dealing with a visual distillation, which, through its insistent repetition, signals the impossibility of ever returning to the original event.

Mroué's filmed performance sacrifices conventional authenticity for the benefit of a media-oriented and sensuous exploration of our relationship with dramatic and tragic historical events. We are over-stimulated by current Internet culture, and its distribution of private recordings through video sharing websites and other social media. Even in the title of his work, it is indicated that intelligibility of the image is not the potential, but, on the contrary, its immediate availability. This strategy further becomes illustrative for a central paradox connected to re-enactment that has more to do with changing discourse than the direct connotations derived from Mroué's staging of the events. By way of a thought-provoking quote from anthropologist Gregory Bateson, documentary theoretician Bill Nichols describes the intricacy of this specific element in the genre:

> 'These actions, in which we now engage, do not denote what would be denoted by those actions which these actions denote'. A shift in signification changes the name of the game. The reenacted event introduces a fantasmatic element that an initial representation of the same event lacks. Put simply, history does not repeat itself, except in mediated transformations such as memory, representation, re-enactment, fantasy – categories that coil around each other in complex patterns.
>
> ('Reenactment and the Fantasmatic Subject' 73)

Following this, Mroué's installation, with its variety of documentary forms, no doubt appears to be more of a meta-reflective and very conscious experiment, with the effects produced by migrating the genre among various media. Here, the dramatic re-enactment is turned into an iconic representation of a tragic event, to specifically trigger the imagination of the spectator. By referencing Bateson, Nichols suggests a valid and thought-provoking way of understanding the action and exchange associated with re-enactment. In the original essay, Bateson distinguishes between play and fighting among animals, and points out that, though a 'nip denotes the bite [. . .] it does not denote what would be denoted by the bite' (Bateson 180). The same is evident in the re-enactment, and illustrates its ambiguous character. Mroué is showing us a theatrical and absurd parody of dying, and therefore we are unable to fully invest our emotions in what we are witnessing. This has to be seen as a deliberate strategy, which forces the viewers to contemplate their involvement in the re-enactment, and what they get out of experiencing this version of tragic events. Furthermore, this element of the installation strengthens one of the central interests expressed in *Pixelated Revolution*, namely that depictions of war come with a built-in paradox. They demonstrate current stereotypical behaviour in our use of media, in this case our eagerness to document, even in the face of death, while simultaneously displaying the impossibility of communicating this experience in any meaningful way, without critical reflection or a historical frame of reference. Here, the (over)acted moment of the dying victim functions as the missing piece, which accentuates what was not caught on camera in the original documentation, and through its stylized re-enactment serves to focus our attention on the whole scene of the puzzle.

Addressing the subject of human rights through a Net-based documentary practice

As the previous excursions into the conventions of the documentary genre have, I hope, shown, a work such as Mroué's installation, based on dramatic, real-life events, confronts us with a number of transformations of well-known representations of reality, which forces us to think across different artistic disciplines. On a general level, this has to do with the detective work of discovering the fairly complex connections in the meta-reflective comments concerning visual evidence and the power of social media to alter our behaviour, even in extreme situations. But *Pixelated Revolution* also poses a more fundamental question about how and why we categorize a specific art form as documentary. Since my endeavour here is to challenge the conventions of the genre through an analysis of this work that desperately tries to escape any single reading, both in its migration of visual evidence between various media, and in the conflicted approach to its content, it seems relevant to seek inspiration in a canonical text that questions the conventions connected with the documentary as an art form traditionally associated with the representation of reality and collective memory, that is Linda Williams' critical analysis of postmodern documentary film, *Mirrors without Memories: Truth History and the New Documentary*. Here, Williams specifically discusses the implications of a genre-innovating film, such as Morris's *The Thin Blue Line*, which directly addresses the theme of human rights and the roles of individuals in an extreme situation, where the laws of society are circumvented, and even put to deadly use against them. *The Thin Blue Line* is famous for having had a direct effect on the criminal case it examined, and actually resulted in the release of the wrongfully accused Randall Dale Adams, a man convicted of a murder he did not commit. This documentary engages with what may be seen as a classical theme for the genre: a single criminal case is used to reflect on the highly problematic aspects of the criminal justice system, and illuminate the fragility of human rights in a broader political context.[7] Williams' point is that the film does not do so with the filmic language traditionally associated with the NGO documentary, but through the intricate use of re-enactments, and by including the film-maker/artist in his or her own production:

> Like many of these new documentaries, it is acutely aware that the individuals whose lives are caught up in events are not so much self-coherent and consistent identities as they are actors in competing narratives. [. . .] the documentarian's role in constructing and staging these competing narratives thus becomes paramount. In place of the self-obscuring voyeur of vérité realism, we encounter in this and other films, a new presence in the persona of the documentarian.
>
> (Williams 73–74)

In her analysis, Williams reminds us of the new tendencies in postmodern documentaries to always present truth as part of a strategy, and that reality is a fragment in a negotiation that is facilitated by the director. If we consider Mroué's work in this perspective, we now see a shift from the auteur-driven documentary that deals with aspects of human rights by addressing the viewer through different re-enacted perspectives, to a type of documentary art that also integrates the concrete evidence produced by the witnesses themselves into an expanding field of communication.

Human rights activist Sam Gregory and film professor Patricia R. Zimmermann analyse the new situation in the landscape of documentation of the violation of human rights. Their central point is that human rights documentation has traditionally functioned within a closed, professional space, where a clear identification of the sender-receiver relationship was the primary validation of evidence, and therefore also a type of control mechanism that determined which types of cases and which areas of NGO initiatives got the attention of the public. With the significant growth of Net-based media, this focus on visibility has moved towards circulation, and maybe even more importantly, aggregation. It is specifically this strategy that Gregory and Zimmermann emphasize as both the most important, and also the most problematic, in the

7 Randall Dale Adams was tried and convicted primarily because of political pressure and corruption in the Texas justice system.

wake of new, networked political realities.[8] Four challenging areas exist within the Net-based area of human rights issues: *Connecting the Viral Virtual to the Physical*, *Geopolitical Positioning*, *Middle Class Technologies*, and *Issues Beyond Visuality*. As is apparent, in various ways, the first three areas have directly to do with the logistics of communicating human rights violations. Most of the physical technology and the well-established networks are located in the Global North, whereas the violations most often take place in the Global South (even though they may well originate sociopolitically and culturally in the North). Surprisingly, *Middle Class Technologies* covers the fact that in most countries, there is some access to mobile phones and social media (which probably explains how the recordings that constitute the basis of Mroué's work reached the artist). However, in my examination of the relation between human rights as a documentary subject, and the field of contemporary art, the focus on *Issues Beyond Visuality* may produce the most problematic and interesting challenge. If we look at Mroué's work, he approaches this problem by physically changing and transforming the materiality of the evidence itself, and thereby addressing the very act of seeing. Determining the degree to which this artistic strategy touches the intellect and emotions of the audience is difficult, but *Pixelated Revolution* does successfully remind us that we confront the subject of human rights violations with a preconceived notion of how to react, how to reflect on it, and what to expect. Since it is almost impossible to move beyond the image in documentary practice, which is based on the aggregation and recirculation of audiovisual evidence, it seems like a necessity for the artist to address how and why the material was chosen. This may be done through a number of different techniques, be they audiovisual or textual. In this perspective, Mroué's installation exemplifies how filmic space, as well as documentary space, needs to be re-examined in the context of a viral network culture. Gregory and Zimmermann emphasize this relation between curated and 'viral' space:

> A dialectic has emerged between the curated space, and networked, viral media making. The curated space promotes the media object. The networked, viral space accentuates the vectors between object and users. The curated milieus of long form documentary emphasize space – its exploration, its production, its exhibition. The viral space emphasizes temporality: movement, ability to dissolve in utility, immediacy.
>
> (Gregory and Zimmermann)

8 In their advocacy for a new, critical look at the relation between media representations and human rights issues, Gregory and Zimmermann draw heavily on Henry Jenkins' theory about convergence culture, that is, the understanding of net-based communication, not as a technological development that centralizes our cultural expressions in individual devices, but instead as a constant exchange between participatory tendencies and top-down, corporate media (Jenkins).

The installation space presented in *Pixelated Revolution* shows us that documentary art has the capacity to address the subject of human rights violations, and maybe even to move the subject away from a predictable set of reactions, although to fulfil this potential both the artist and the viewer have to be aware that the subject traverses various fields of media.

The voice of the artist

After reflecting on the media-oriented transformations of documentation that also determines the name of Mroué's work, it seems logical to turn one's attention to the last part of the installation, which is the artist's own comment on the phenomenon. Since this documentation is presented under the subtitle *A non-academic lecture by Rabih Mroué* [*sic*], it is automatically situated in an ambiguous position between a subjective and expressive retelling of events, and an objective account of tragedy. As must be considered common knowledge concerning artistic strategies, pointing out what something is not does not necessarily make it so; on the contrary, it often accentuates that specific aspect. This is also evident in Mroué's speech, where he touches upon the relation of the camera to the human eye, and the impossibility of conveying the tragedies of war through media. His tone is overtly academic, and systematically gives an explanation of the footage with which he has chosen to work. In two segments, called *The Tank* and *Director/Witness*, we are presented with a comparative analysis of one of the victims' recordings of a tank shooting down a side street, where the person in question is hiding, and a scene in the 2009, semi-biographical drama, *The Time That Remains*, by Palestinian director Elia Suleiman, where one of the protagonists is walking the streets of Nazareth, talking on his mobile phone, while the gun turret of a giant tank follows his every move. The absurd scene ends with the turret pointing straight at the audience and actor-director Elia Suleiman, as the astonished witness seeks cover behind a wall. The recordings of reality play out like a bizarre scene in fiction, and the communicative function of the phone has now been changed from that of conversation to that of documentation. Despite this, Mroué argues that the moment of death constantly eludes us in these recordings, and leaves the viewer staring into a silent black screen. It is with this conclusion that he gets closest to the essence and complexity of this documentation, that they are visual evidence, and at the same time a testament to the impossibility of ever conveying those last moments. They are inevitably situated in the category of *not-fiction*, although Mroué's playing with ambiguity, and the overall editing of his filmed lecture, with chapter indicators such as 'prologue' and 'epilogue', with which we are familiar from works of fiction, points this towards what I have chosen to term *Documentary Intervention*.

This meta-analytical part of the installation also functions as a type of voice-over for the other elements, creating a verbalized and intellectual perspective

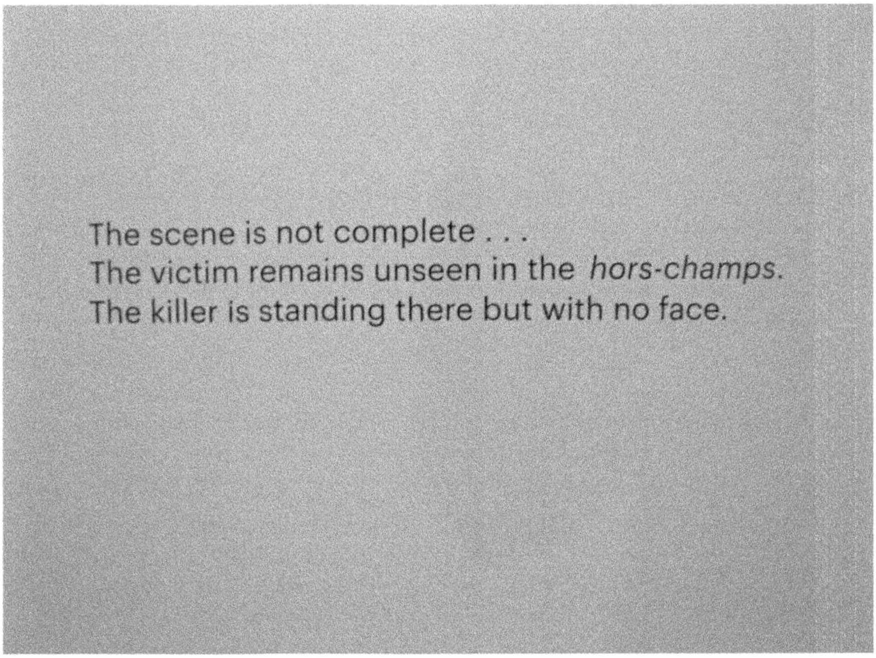

Figure 14.2 Example of the text printed on the wall of Rabih Mroué's documentary installation under the title 'Instructions and Advice How to Shoot Today'. These quotes are taken from the filmed lecture with the artist, which is also part of the work.

Source: © Rabih Mroué 2012.

on the immediate and sensuous experience of the work.[9] As film theoretician Sarah R. Kozloff argues, stylistically, a voice-over is a naturalizing and humanizing device, which narrates and orchestrates the events.[10] The humanizing role of the voice-over has the further effect of transforming the viewer's position from eavesdropper or voyeur (here, strictly the latter), to being a part of an intimate exchange (Kozloff 128–129). The degree to which the audience commits to this exchange can unquestionably be discussed, but since the physical surroundings of the film are the elements of an installation that encompass various media, I would argue that this space, facilitated by Mroué, challenges the viewer

9 Mroué's voice is audible to the viewer throughout the entire work, since it is the only sound in the installation.

10 Kozloff is addressing the effect of the voice-over in fictional film, but since one of my points is that the barrier between fiction and non-fiction is traversed, I find it highly relevant to consider her interpretation of this filmic element.

to regard the artist's commentary as a voice-over for the whole work. This also leads to considering the function of the voice-over in non-fiction film. According to Bill Nichols, here, voice is something more specific than a stylistic feature:

> By 'voice' I mean something narrower than style: that which conveys to us a sense of a text's social point of view, of how it is speaking to us and how it is organizing the materials it is presenting to us. In this sense 'voice' is not restricted to any one code or feature such as dialogue or spoken commentary. Voice is perhaps akin to that intangible, moiré-like pattern formed by the unique interaction of all a film's codes, and it applies to all modes of documentary.
>
> ('The Voice of Documentary' 248–249)

This understanding of the film-maker's voice challenges our conventional conception of the purely technical aspects of a film's voice-over, since these are usually devices for developing parts of the narrative that are too lengthy to show, or persuading the viewer through didactic commentary on the documented events. In the case of *Pixelated Revolution*, Mroué's voice ambiguously shifts between authority and emotion, while it interweaves the additional elements in the installation, both as fragments of sound and writing on the wall.

Renegotiating the aesthetics of human rights

Mroué's work is all about media transformations, which makes it an obvious choice for illustrating many of the points I have been discussing here. I have specifically chosen *Pixelated Revolution* as a case study, because it accentuates how different artistic strategies affect the inclusion of factual evidence in art. The central point is that the multiple changes in the cultural space surrounding a specific art form are also what we are witnessing, through ubiquitous documentary practices, and the artistic responses to which they give rise.

An interesting aspect of Mroué's transformed, video-recorded shootings is as much a revealing reactivation of the inherent dramatic element of the documentary, as it is an examination of how we change our perspective on factuality through specific media and rhetorical discourse. Through a combination of these different approaches and their expression, the audience experiences changing roles as witness and investigator, or symbolically even victim and perpetrator. It could be argued that Mroué's artistic approach brings matters as much to a head as my attempt at devising new, useful categories for understanding a vivid and multifaceted documentary culture.

Professor Sharon Sliwinski has suggested that the act of judgement, and in particular its aspect of participation, is at the centre of thinking about human rights in connection with image production. Sliwinski goes by way of Hannah Arendt's famous critique of human rights, in which attention is directed towards their 'prepolitical foundation'. She locates this potential in both legal and individual, aesthetic judgement:

> The legislation of universal human rights has brought little relief to the world's sufferings. However judgments does imply the *participation* of individuals in the daily strife of existence. It is the action of judgment that galvanizes a polity and enables the recognition of those who have been expelled from the human community. [. . .] Although these aesthetic judgments are not directly political demands, they provide an affective climate, a 'prepolitical foundation' that can give rise to the thought of human rights – or better, to the thought of the 'one human right': a right to the human condition.
>
> (Sliwinski 37, original emphasis)

The multifocal and dramatized display of the ultimate impossibility of *identifying* killers and *identifying with* victims in *Pixelated Revolution* suspends audience participation among a number of different emotions: bewilderment, guilt, sorrow, fear. At the same time, this is framed by a (media) historical resonance and an academic undertone, which make it impossible to stay suspended in this affective state. Mroué's highly self-conscious and meta-analytical work may seem too calculated, but its provocative and unsettling presentation, shifting between the factual and the dramatic image, makes it impossible to crystallize the role of the victim, or, perhaps even more importantly, the role of the spectator.

Works cited

Agnew, Vanessa. 'Introduction: What Is Reenactment?' *Criticism* 46.3 (2005): 327–339. Print.

Bateson, Gregory. 'A Theory of Play and Fantasy'. *Steps to an Ecology of Mind: Collected Essays in Anthropology, Psychiatry, Evolution and Epistemology*. 1972. Cambridge: MIT Press, 2000. 177–193. Print.

Gregory, Sam and Patricia Zimmermann. 'Speculations on the Virtual and the Viral Witness to Human Rights Crises'. *Mediascape*. Winter 2011. Web. 18 May 2016. <www.tft.ucla.edu/mediascape/Winter2011_HumanRights.html>.

Jenkins, Henry. *Convergence Culture*. New York: New York University Press, 2006. Print.

Kozloff, Sarah R. *Invisible Storyteller: Voice-Over Narration in American Fiction Film*. Berkeley: University of California Press, 1988. Print.

Krauss, Rosalind E. 'Sculpture in the Expanded Field'. *The Originality of the Avant-Garde and Other Modernist Myths*. 1978. Cambridge: MIT Press, 1993. 276–291. Print.

Nichols, Bill. 'The Voice of Documentary'. *Film Quarterly: Forty Years – A Selection*. Ed. Brian Henderson and Ann Martin. Berkeley: University of California Press, 1983. 247–266. Print.

——. *Introduction to Documentary*. Bloomington: Indiana University Press, 2001. Print.

——. 'Reenactment and the Fantasmatic Subject'. *Critical Inquiry* 35.1 (Autumn 2008): 72–89. Print.

Pedersen, Peter Ole. *Pixelated Reality: Documentary between Net-Distribution, Popular Culture and the Avant-Garde*. Aarhus University, 2014. Print.

Renov, Michael. 'Towards a Poetics of Documentary'. *Theorizing Documentary*. Ed. Michael Renov. New York/London: Routledge, 1993. 12–36. Print.

Sliwinski, Sharon. 'The Aesthetics of Human Rights'. *Culture, Theory and Critique* 50.1 (2009): 23–39. Print.

Stallabrass, Julian, ed. *Documentary (Documents of Contemporary Art)*. London: Whitechapel Art Gallery, 2013. Print.

Williams, Linda. 'Mirrors without Memories: Truth, History and the New Documentary'. *New Challenges for Documentary*. 1988. Ed. Alan Rosenthal and John Corner. Manchester/New York: Manchester University Press, 2005. 59–79.

Chapter 15

Victimhood, voice, and power in digital media

Lilie Chouliaraki

Digital media have been celebrated for giving voice and attributing agency to the hitherto voiceless victims of disaster or oppression (Meier; Crowley *et al.* 2013; UNOCHA 2013). Taking my point of departure in the key implication of this claim, namely that the vocalization of the suffering of victims facilitates cosmopolitan processes of symbolic recognition that go beyond Western communities of belonging (Silverstone), I explore how voice is distributed in two crucial instances of digital journalism: the Haiti earthquake (2010) and the Egyptian Arab Spring (2011). I conclude that the voicing of victimhood is a precarious process with ambivalent implications: it can both invite recognition of the victim's agency as a catalyst of its own historical destiny (even if, as we shall see, such recognition is itself fragile and contingent) and re-establish the victim's passivity as a powerless subject within the asymmetrical structures of the global order. The potential for cosmopolitan solidarity in convergent journalism, I argue, depends therefore on the positioning of the victim's voice in a broader system of Western journalism and on the degree to which such positioning may guarantee the digital and symbolic resources for such a voice to be heard and recognized as worth listening and responding to.

I first introduce an account of journalism as *performative* practice – a meaning-making practice that construes the communities it addresses at the moment that it claims to represent them.[1] Convergent, digital media-driven journalism differs from traditional, press, or electronic journalism in that it entails a new performativity – one that emphasizes deliberation and witnessing over information – and it is this new emphasis that introduces the victim's voice as a potentially legitimate source of news (in Journalism, performativity, and voice). In order to establish the precise performative mechanism through which convergent journalism regulates the status and scope of such voice, I approach it in terms of three separate but interconnected dimensions of mediation: (i) the *remediation* of the victim's voice in global news networks, such as the BBC;

1 For this view of performativity, see Butler (*Excitable Speech, Frames of War*).

(ii) the *intermediation* of the social media, which structures and groups this voice in distinct types of intervention (say, digital humanitarianism or e-campaigning); and (iii) the potential for *transmediation*, that is the shift of this voice from the symbolic realm onto the realm of physical action (Victimhood and the journalism of witnessing and deliberation). Using the Haiti earthquake and the 2011 Egypt protests as case studies, I show how variations in their remediation mechanism reflects further variations in their mediation of victimhood, and hence in the forms of symbolic recognition each case enables. Differences in the nature of the event granted (disaster vs political conflict context), these variations, I show, reflect systemic asymmetries in the positioning of each country within the sphere of global governance (in The digital voicing of victimhood: Haiti and Egypt). I conclude by drawing attention to the deeply ambiguous character of the voice of victimhood in digital media, both as a reminder of caution vis-à-vis uncritical approaches to convergent journalism and as an invitation for case-driven studies of the role of such journalism in empowering the victim and enabling cosmopolitan connectivities (Victimhood, voice, and power).

Journalism, performativity, and voice

In her *Frames of War* (2009), Judith Butler draws on the Abu Ghraib photographs to contend that journalism is performative in the sense that its stories of the Iraqi prison are not simply offering information, but actually construct the framework within which we are invited to imagine the predicament of those sufferers, as well as think, feel, and act towards them. It is, she continues, this 'field of the perceptible', rather than the concrete imagery of Abu Graib, that calls upon us as ethico-political collectivities, insofar as this field that controls and delineates 'whether and how we respond to the suffering of others, how we formulate moral criticisms, how we articulate political analyses' (Butler, *Frames of War* 64).

Central to this performative construal is the process of symbolic recognition, whereby journalism attributes agency both to those suffering others and to their body of viewers, through defining the boundaries of voice: what the voice of victimhood is and how it addresses its viewers.[2] Recognition is, here, a symbolic act both in the semiotic sense of originating in the linguistic and visual news narratives of victimhood but also, because of this, in the normative sense of contributing to the making and remaking of ethico-political agency and community. Who the victim is and who witnesses his or her suffering, the Abu Ghraib example suggests, demonstrates and recreates existing relations of power between a Western sphere of safety and relative prosperity and a non-Western

2 For the relationship between recognition and performativity, see Butler (*Frames of War*); for key theorizations of recognition, see Taylor; Fraser.

one of suffering and devastating conflict that may (or may not) silence the victim and so exclude him or her from the scope of 'our' recognition (Chouliaraki, *The Spectatorship of Suffering*, 'Ordinary Witnessing'). The key challenge for journalism, here, appears to be formulated as the task to achieve a fairer and broader distribution of the voice of victimhood in the news – of a subject that, by virtue of his or her positioning within the zone of danger, is primarily defined by his or her suffering and consequently by his or her inability to voice the conditions of his or her suffering beyond his or her own local community of belonging.

Convergent journalism is often celebrated as accomplishing this task, in that it complements the singular voice of the journalist with the many voices of local people who now reach the news through mobile phones and social media platforms. In articulating local voice, the argument has it, convergent journalism enhances its own performative function in a crucial way: it renders a range of victims, from citizens of oppressive regimes, to victims of disaster or conflict zones, more audible and visible than ever before. This new audibility of voice not only gives victims an unprecedented sense of agency, but, in so doing, also challenges the power relations of global information flows; as Russell, in her study of the Egypt uprising, puts it, 'the news moves from being mostly journalist-centered, communicated as a monologue, and primarily local, to also being increasingly audience-centered', thereby enabling this audience to '. . . deeply affect the news, in which the margins grow in power to shape the center' (Russell 1239). And it is, indeed, the connectivity of local voice that has often been regarded as powerless and marginal. The digital circuits of global communication, according to Madianou *et al.*, further enable the voice of the natural disaster victims to reverberate beyond their own locale: 'Never before have populations affected by disaster had so many opportunities for making their voices heard' (3021). If there is a cosmopolitanizing potential in this voice, then, such potential lies in the remediation structures of convergent journalism to allow a hitherto voiceless subject of suffering to assert his or her agency and to be heard beyond its own community and across Western contexts. In this spirit, CNN describes its iReport live blogging site as a hub that seeks 'not only to report but also to connect . . . informing the public but also providing them a possibility to connect with the victim and help'.[3] Along similar lines, Richard Sambrook, ex-Director of BBC's Global News, speaks of the news as a 'collaborative product', explaining that, following the 2004 tsunami catastrophe, the BBC has become committed to an interactive form of reporting where 'the public can offer us as much new information as we are able to broadcast to them'.[4]

To summarize, convergent journalism inserts the voice of the victim onto platforms of real-time and global communication, rendering this voice more

3 Quoted in www.guardian.co.uk/media/pda/2010/jan/14/socialnetworking-haiti.

4 'Citizen Journalism and the BBC', Neiman report: www.nieman.harvard.edu/reportsitem.aspx?id=100542.

visible than ever before but also potentially contributing to opening up spaces of cosmopolitan solidarity between distant victims and Western communities of viewers. Given, however, that the institutional and technical infrastructures of convergent journalism are firmly embedded within a broader system of power relations between West and non-West, the question remains as to whether the circulation of voice can, in fact, agentify distant sufferers and facilitate forms of symbolic recognition that may catalyse bonds of solidarity with the West. Which are the conditions under which convergent journalism that render the voice of victimhood legitimately and efficiently heard and seen? It is to this question that I will turn in the analytical part of the paper, but, for now, I focus upon the development of a novel conceptual framework for understanding convergent journalism as a structure of witnessing – that is, as a structure for the voicing of victimhood and its potential recognition.

Victimhood and the journalism of witnessing and deliberation

Drawing on sociological views of practice as performative, journalism can be defined as a structure of communicative acts that both tells stories about the world, ordering the world in meaning (its ideational dimension), and, at the same time, connects us to the world and invites us to interact with it (its interpersonal dimension). While, in the past, the institutional voice of the journalist rendered the news primarily an ideational vehicle that narrated the world events of the day, today the proliferation of digital media and the ensuing pluralisation of voices in the news have shifted the focus to the interpersonal dimension. This means that news journalism now allows for a multiplicity of suffering others to tell various stories about their world and invites Western audiences/users to connect with their predicament in different ways. This development can be described as a shift from a journalism of information to a journalism of witnessing and deliberation.

While the communicative act of informing refers to 'the business or practice of disseminating information about contemporary affairs of general public interest and importance' (Schudson 2003, 11) and privileges an ideational focus on objective fact over the interpersonal focus on subjective value, the acts of witnessing and deliberating rely on the reverse: the interpersonal over the ideational. On the one hand, witnessing connects people through the voicing of victimhood (Peters) and its function is to turn local testimonies of human suffering into legitimate news discourse so as to invite our judgement and emotion towards it. On the other hand, deliberating is about voicing opinions, justifications, or appeals, and intervenes with the world through inviting us to join networks of conversation or action; as Bennett *et al.* put it, journalism can facilitate public deliberation, on the condition that 'when news accounts report diverse voices (access) . . . identify and comparably value those voices (recognition) and . . . invite those with opposing views to respond directly to each other (responsiveness)' (Bennett *et al.* 439). Both witnessing and deliberation inevitably retain a link to reporting real-world events, but they subordinate this function to the moral-political appeal that stories of suffering make on us as active and compassionate citizens (Zelizer; Frosh and Pinchevski 2009).

When we speak of the new performativity of journalism, therefore, we speak about the digitally mediated, institutionally conferred acts of witnessing and deliberation and the ways in which these acts attribute agency to those who speak and to those who are addressed through them. Even though more open and pluralistic than the traditional performativity of informing, this convergent performativity remains nonetheless a structure of symbolic power. This is so insofar as it continues to operate within Western political economic and institutional conditions that, at least partly, may define who is entitled to speak, what to say, and how to connect to those he or she addresses. In this sense, despite its promise to voice the plight of the victim, the journalism of witnessing and deliberation has the potential to regulate the attribution of voice and agency to certain victims rather than others, as well as facilitate the constitution of certain communities of recognition over others.

Whether and to what extent convergent journalism might do so depends on how the voice of victimhood circulates across three distinct but interrelated structures of global mediation: (i) the *remediation* of this voice from social media onto one of the major global news platforms of the West (BBC); (ii) the *intermediation* of the social media platforms (such as Twitter or Facebook) through which such voice is already organized into networks of communicative activism (e.g. NGO coordination or social movement protest); and, finally, (iii) the possibility for the *transmediation* of this voice from the symbolic sphere of communication to the sphere of physical action. This emphasis on the complex digital structure of mediation is crucial, because it suggests that the symbolic power of witnessing and deliberation cannot be determined once and for all, but has specific conditions of possibility. Instead of rushing to celebrate the new audibility of the voice of victimhood, as many do, therefore, we need to examine these conditions on a case-by-case basis, asking the question of how the voice of suffering may challenge existing hierarchies of life and place and that might reproduce them.

The digital voicing of victimhood: Haiti and Egypt

I focus on two crucial cases of transnational reporting, the Haiti earthquake (2010), and the Egypt uprising (2011), which both share key features and are sufficiently different to warrant a comparative analysis with rich implications. On the one hand, they are both 'ecstatic' (Chouliaraki, *The Spectatorship of Suffering*), in the sense that the magnitude and drama of human suffering in them interrupted the global flow of ordinary news and involved extensive live broadcasting from the scene of disaster; they involved multiple voices from the scene of suffering, making claims to transnational solidarity and addressing their viewers as a global community of humanity; finally, they consist of a similar complex communicative structure that mixes electronic with digital networking technologies and genres as well as institutional professional with local voice narratives. On the other hand, there is significant variation between them not only in terms of the nature of the event they report on, disaster in Haiti and protest in Egypt, but also, importantly, in terms of the position of each location in existing socio-economic world hierarchies: Haiti is one of the poorest countries in the world while Egypt, at the time characterized by a dynamic and media-savvy youth elite, used to be a relatively prosperous nation that functioned as a link between the Arab world and the West. It is this mix of similarity with variation that makes it possible to compare and contrast the two cases as exemplary of two different articulations of the voice of victimhood, and consequently also of different processes of recognition and community formation. I begin with the disaster news in Haiti before moving to the Egypt protests, focusing upon the categories of *remediation*, how speech acts are structured in the global news flows; *intermediation*, how their structures interact with one another; and *transmediation*, whether they turn into action or not.

The Haiti earthquake

The Haiti earthquake (12 January 2010) was a catastrophic event that caused major damage in Port-au-Prince, Jacmel, and other settlements in the region, causing damage to vital infrastructure necessary to respond to the disaster; this included all hospitals in the capital, air, sea, and land transport facilities, and communication systems. According to the Haitian government and International Organization for Migration report of May 2011, the human loss is estimated at about 316,000, while the number of displaced at up to 1.5 million.

The voicing of victimhood in Haiti occurred primarily in the BBC's live blog platform, which provided constant updates of events for a number of days. As such, it was characterized by three features: (i) its privileging of Western over local voices of victimhood; (ii) its replication of the generic model of crisis communication; and (iii) the interface of online journalism and offline humanitarian activism.

Remediation: The Haiti earthquake introduced live blogging in disaster reporting. This form of real-life, collaborative blogging uses platforms of Western networks, such as the BBC, as online news hubs that aggregate messages from multiple sources into a timeline of event updates (Beckett). Due to its multimedia platform, live blogging enables the online combination of complex written, visual, and aural material, such as eyewitness links to mobile phone footage, 'audio accounts' of survivors, Twitter and email messages, as well as telegraphic journalistic updates and interactive maps of the affected area. The remediation of the Haiti earthquake can be described, in this sense, as the re-dissemination of these different voices of disaster on a global scale, according to the chronological sequence in which they reached the BBC hub.

Given the damage to the Haitian communication infrastructures, the remediation of the disaster, at least initially, was conducted primarily by Western NGOs. Even though they did offer information, these messages were primarily testimonial, providing dramatic descriptions of devastating suffering. A substantial number of such messages came from ordinary people. Even though a few of those came from Haiti, the vast majority came from Westerners who expressed compassion for the victims or communicated their worry about family members who happened to be in the location of the disaster. Rather than witnessing, such voices were primarily deliberative in that they conjured up a shared space for global solidarity towards the earthquake victims to be symbolically performed. At the same time, political and religious elites also expressed compassion with the victims and stated their readiness to assist in aid and recovery operations.

Articulating witnessing with deliberative speech, then, the remediation of the Haiti earthquake construed an emotional public realm, where expert and non-expert voices coexisted without hierarchies in a global space of solidarity for distant sufferers. While this affective space is necessary for catalysing processes of symbolic recognition, its emotionality is not sufficient to the task. This is because this space communicates primarily Western voices of witnessing and deliberation, facilitating recognition with people like 'us' rather than with the actual voices of victimhood in Haiti. In marginalizing the Haitian sufferer in favour of the Western compassionate soul, it deprives the former of any sense of agency while endowing the latter with disproportionate psychological depth and renders the news a site of affective self-expression – a therapeutic communication that connects to its own community of co-viewers while leaving the Haitian outside the Western remit of compassion and care.

Intermediation: By virtue of reaggregating and recirculating messages, the remediation of the Haiti earthquake replicated the structure of crisis communication. This is so because the remediation of NGO and local voice did not simply share emotion, but further participated in the coordination of humanitarian action: 'The earthquake set a number of precedents in terms of . . . the use of new technologies for humanitarian response', the ALNAP report said, 'Many UN and international NGOs and some military actors embraced technologies such as Twitter, Facebook, YouTube and Skype in their work, to coordinate, collaborate and act upon information from the ground generated by people directly affected by the earthquake' (2010: 27).[5]

Intermediation refers here to the practice of major networks capitalizing on these social media networks of the disaster so as to establish themselves as key agents of remediation among them, with a view to facilitating the informational management of the disaster. During the first day after the earthquake, for example, the UN forwarded constant updates of its own missing personnel, Port-au-Prince UNAID staff, in BBC's live blogging platform. While some crisis

5 See www.alnap.org/pool/files/haiti-context-analysis-final.pdf.

communication networks did operate outside major news networks (such as Ushahidi),[6] the intermediation of NGO voices through the BBC points to another key function of the journalism of witnessing and deliberation that goes beyond the therapeutic communication of Western communities: its function as humanitarian activism that seeks to respond to the immediacy of suffering. At the same time, however, this humanitarian function of intermediation situates the disaster into what Calhoun terms an 'emergency imaginary', that is, a collective understanding of the disaster as a 'sudden, unpredictable event emerging against a background of ostensible normalcy, causing suffering or danger, and demanding urgent response' (2). While there is no doubt that saving lives was the most urgent priority in the aftermath of the earthquake, Calhoun's term draws attention to the fact that this priority has a significant cost: it tends to detract attention from the long-term and structural causes of the disaster – 'it calls', as he puts it, 'for humanitarian response not political or economic analysis' (2).

Transmediation: Two processes of transmediation connect the convergent journalism of disaster with the scene of the earthquake: donations as public response to NGOs' appeals for financial support to victims, and relief aid as specialized assistance offered on the ground. Both constitute a transfer from communicative acts to material action, but while donations are typically associated with action at a distance, and so with the transmediation of Western voice into money, humanitarian aid is typically associated with professional practice, and hence the transmediation of NGOs or other international elite actors – governments, religious or for-profit institutions, and, exceptionally, journalists. Both forms of transmediation turned out to be impressive. With $220 million collected in donations in the first week of the disaster in the USA alone,[7] and 2,000 rescuers present from 43 different NGOs on the ground already in the first hours after the earthquake, ample support appeared to be offered.

Yet, criticism emerged regarding both the short- and long-term management of the disaster, with the former focusing on failures in the coordination of immediate aid and the latter on failures to secure recovery both at the level of hygiene (resulting in the 2011 cholera outbreak), but also at the level of absorbing funds: 'In a country sometimes dubbed a "republic of NGOs"', as Claire Provost put it in January 2012, 'only 6% of bilateral aid for reconstruction projects has gone through Haitian institutions, according to UN figures. Less than 1% of relief funding has gone through the government of Haiti'.[8] What such criticism points to is a fundamental weakness in humanitarian relief as a form of global governance, namely that asymmetries in the macroeconomic map of development cannot be compensated for by an emphasis on micro-aid. Despite a

6 For the emergence of novel, citizen-driven crisis communication networks, such as Ushahidi, following the Haiti earthquake: see, www.knightfoundation.org/blogs/knightblog/2011/1/11/new-media-and-humanitarian-relief-lessons-from-haiti/.

7 See http://money.cnn.com/2010/01/18/news/international/haiti_donations/.

8 See www.guardian.co.uk/global-development/datablog/2012/jan/12/haiti-earthquake-aid-money-data.

constant outpouring of aid funds throughout the past 40 years, Haiti remains, indeed, at the bottom of world rankings across a number of wealth indexes. Instead, then, of a politics of continuing dependence, as Collier warned already in 2009, what Haiti needs is a strategic plan for sovereign economic development: 'what is missing', he adds, 'is a practical and focused economic strategy that clearly specifies the actions needed by all the actors that collectively determine whether Haiti will achieve economic security' (4).

In summary, the Haiti earthquake marked a new epoch of convergent journalism in disaster reporting, in that it placed the voices of witnessing and deliberation on a par with the expert voices of journalists while replicating and magnifying existing forms of humanitarian communication involving NGOs and other elites. This structure, however: (i) ignored the voice of victimhood emanating from the scene of disaster, and instead prioritized the voice of social media users in the West; (ii) construed the suffering of Haitians as an emergency, that is, a sudden and unpredictable event devoid of historical or political economic context; and (iii) facilitated a solidarity of salvation, focusing on aid relief, over a solidarity of justice, which would also ask the pertinent question of why such devastation was possible in Haiti, but not, say, in San Fransisco's equally powerful earthquake (2003).

The Egypt protests

The Egyptian protests, January–February 2011, began as a form of non-violent popular resistance, consisting of demonstrations and other acts of civil disobedience, and increasingly mobilized millions of Egyptians around the demand to overthrow the regime of then-President Hosni Mubarak. Despite the longer-term failure of these events to realise the vision, shared by the West, of a stable, moderate, and pluralistic government in the country, and the concomitant installation of a military regime under retired Field Marshall al-Sissi, the attention of this study, falls strictly upon one particular historical moment: Egypt's 'Arab Spring' and its reporting in the 25 January and 11 February temporal frame. During that time, social unrest, accompanied by the deaths of 846 people, led to short-term change – Muslim Brotherhood's government by Mohamed Morsi – but, importantly for this project, gathered the Western world around the cause of the Egyptian people, in what, at the time, appeared to be a call for democracy and a more open and pluralistic society.[9] The convergent journalism of this

9 Later Western assessments of the 'Arab Spring' have been reflexive accounts of disillusionment and critical re-evaluation of those events and their potential, while the future of the country is now approached with a sense of resigned pessimism: 'The heady days of Egypt's "Arab Spring" are now a distant memory (indeed I always doubted that Egypt's revolution would very easily shake off decades of authoritarianism). Now, nothwithstanding the wishful thinking of the Egyptian tourist industry, the future looks bleak for Egypt' (www.huffingtonpost.co.uk/news/egypt-revolution/).

unique and short-lived historical moment of protest and conflict is characterised by: (i) its focus on witnessing and deliberation, this time, however, articulating and legitimizing the voices of victimhood; (ii) its replication of the generic model of political advocacy; and (iii) the interface between online communication and an offline activism of mass demonstrations on the ground.

Remediation: The BBC live blogs consistently situated the local voice in Cairo's Tahrir Square, and broadly in Egyptian streets, at the centre of its communicative structure. However, it was particularly after Mubarak imposed a shutdown of the country's Internet infrastructure for a week (starting 28 January 2011) that global news networks, notably Al Jazeera but also Western ones, became instrumental to the remediation of the voice of victimhood on the ground. While the BBC aggregated and redisseminated a number of diverse voices, from Obama to Hezbollah, and from the Muslim Brotherhood to its own journalist Jeremy Bowen, it regularly also included messages from people who monitored the day-to-day situation and offered accounts of violent (but also peaceful) encounters with the army, testimonies of citizen arrests and persecution, or moving tales of victimhood and heroic resistance.

Available through Twitter and YouTube videos, which were resourcefully accessed by bypassing Egypt's official ICT network, the majority of such messages had a witnessing value, in that they did not simply inform us of activity in the street, but also took a moral stance towards such action: 'The protesters are shouting "Down, down, Hosni Mubarak" and "The people want the regime to fall", reports say'.[10] In so doing, they worked to sensitize not so much the majority of Egyptians, largely cut off from Internet access, but rather 'the international media and the world', as Khamis and Vaughn put it, 'thus ensuring that the regime would not be able to cut them off from the world' (xx). Such acts of witnessing, the authors claim, did not simply connect the West with distant events, but also worked to add authenticity to these events: 'young Egyptians', as Khamis and Vaughn put it, 'were in the thick of it, mobile phones at the ready, often live-tweeting as skirmishes broke out' (2011).

Unlike the Haiti earthquake, then, where local voice was rare, rendering the earthquake sufferer inaudible and invisible, the coverage of the Egypt protests construed the Egyptian youth as an agentive victim in full control of its powerful voice – here used both as a testimony of violence and as a marker of the authenticity of reporting. Similarly to Haiti, such acts of witnessing entail a strong emotional dimension, which invites Western publics to engage with the Egyptian protesters and, potentially, construes a space of transnational recognition between 'them' and 'us' – as, for instance, when a protester tweets: 'Army trying to starve and box in the #tahrir protesters, so orders r everything but shoot, fine, ppl won't back down'.[11] This is, however, a different emotionality.

10 See http://news.bbc.co.uk/1/hi/uk_politics/9380441.stm.

11 See http://news.bbc.co.uk/1/hi/world/middle_east/9390387.stm.

Far from being reduced to an expression of compassion for a voiceless other, it articulates the affective discourse of the Egyptians themselves as an empowered public that speaks out against the regime: 'in regimes where expression is controlled and restricted', as Papacharissi and Oliveira argue, 'it takes a lot of courage to utter affective statements indicating dislike, hatred and anger at a dictator' (xx). What made this discourse particularly forceful in Western contexts, I argue, is the intermediation of the event.

Intermediation: By virtue of remediating local voice from within the Egyptian scene, the reporting of the protests also operated as a parallel network of cyberactivism. This is because the remediation of such voice was not only about sharing emotion, but also about deliberating on a political agenda with a view to mobilizing people to action: 'the goal of such activism', as Howard puts it, 'is to . . . tell stories of injustice, interpret history and advocate for particular political outcomes' (145). Even though Egypt's cyberactivist infrastructure was well in place well before the protests began (Eltahawy 2011), the use of social media as platforms of popular deliberation continued to grow and take shape throughout the course of the events, thereby ensuring that people had 'a sense of ownership' over 'the tools for crafting the revolution's narrative' (Brisson).

Intermediation, in this context, refers to the ways in which convergent journalism capitalized on these already existing networks of online activism with a view to amplifying the voice of the protests on a global scale and, in so doing, 'to empower activists to associate and share ideas with others globally, enabling collaboration between activists in Egypt and Tunisia, as well as between protesters and Arabs in the diaspora; democracy activists in other countries' (Khamis and Wangh). Central to this intermediation of ordinary voice was the Egyptians' appeal to democracy, which injected a strong sense of moral and political significance to the protests: 'The people of Egypt want their freedom, and they want it now', as another tweeting protester put it, 'We have lost all trust in a system that makes promises and does not fulfill them'.

It is precisely this demand for freedom that, unlike the emergency of the Haiti suffering, politicized and historicized the Egypt protests and managed to engage the West in concrete acts of solidarity for justice.

Transmediation: Two types of transmediation link the communicative acts of witnessing and deliberation in protest reporting with the physical scenes of action: the continuing demonstrations in real space, Tahrir Square and elsewhere in Egypt and the Arab world, throughout the three-week period of protests (25 January–11 February), and the parallel demonstrations in many Western capitals in support of the Arab Spring events. While both forms of transmediation consist of the bodily co-presence of publics protesting in the name of solidarity, the difference between Arab and Western transmediations lies in that the former, unlike the latter, involved a strong element of risk: 232 people died in Cairo alone, with the total number of deaths around the country reaching 846 in this 18-day period. Crucial, then, in this shift from online to offline activism was, as Eltahawy put it, 'a mass of youthful protesters' who managed to turn their ordinary voice into an extraordinary act of revolution: 'Every revolution has its square', she says, 'and Tahrir (liberation in Arabic) is earning its name. This is the square Egypt uses to remember the ending of the monarchy in 1952, as well as of British occupation'.[12]

It is, I argue, this persistent and dramatic doubling of the communicative acts of convergent journalism with the embodied performance of self-sacrifice that sparked off the widespread manifestations of solidarity with Egypt around the world. Yet, while the spread of activism in the Middle East at large testifies to the formation of an Arab public unified around a similar demand of regime change, protests in the West point to a distinct process of recognition. This is a recognition that, instead of unifying the West around a voice of its own, à la Haiti, endorses and amplifies the voice of distant, rather than proximal and similar, others. In so doing, it also decentres the boundaries of its own community in the name of a solidarity of justice, thereby further activating meaningful links between 'us' and 'them', under the moral claim to a common humanity: the Occupy Wall Street movement describes itself precisely as an extension of the Arab uprisings, articulating ordinary voice against the injustices of the global financial system (see below).

While the Egypt protests, then, offer good evidence of the power of convergent journalism to reconstitute community around a sense of care and responsibility beyond ourselves, it is important to draw attention to the fact that in Egypt, unlike Haiti, the voice of victimhood was already empowered. Even if not topping global economic indexes, Egypt was, in 2012, regarded as an economically advanced country of the Arab world with a young, well-educated, urban elite whose sociopolitical dispositions greatly converge with Western ideals of democratic governance: 'There is', as Pintak says of Egypt, 'an army of media-savvy activists who have seized on tools like blogs, Twitter, Facebook and other forms of instant messaging as weapons . . . in their battle with entrenched regimes' (Ghannam 56).

To conclude, the Egypt protests, similarly to Haiti, also placed the witnessing and deliberation of the voice of victimhood on a par with the institutional voices of journalists, NGOs, and political elites. Key differences in the communicative structure between the two events, however, led to a different articulation of these journalistic functions, which consequently now managed to: (i) widely reverberate the voice of victimhood, as spoken by the Egyptian protesters, across Western contexts; (ii) construe the Egypt protests as a historical and political event strongly resonating with Western sociopolitical sensibilities; and (iii) prioritize a solidarity of justice that focuses on political transformation over a solidarity of salvation that focuses on saving lives.

12 Quoted in www.guardian.co.uk/commentisfree/2011/jan/29/egypt-mubarak-tunisia-palestine.

Victimhood, voice, and power

In this chapter, I have theorized convergent journalism as a digitally driven form of institutional journalism characterized by a shift in the communicative structure of reporting from informing to deliberating and witnessing. While this shift has also been hailed as a welcome reconfiguration of the power relations of journalism, signalling the interruption of professional narratives by the local voices of suffering, and thus potentially also marking the empowerment of the voices of victimhood in zones of disaster or political oppression, I have argued for a more sceptical, case-driven approach that attends to variations in convergence reporting.

My analysis of two contrasting case studies (Haiti and Egypt) sought to exemplify that the distribution of such voices of victimhood in each empirical context reflects, in fact, a concomitant variation in the power relations of suffering on a global scale. The Haiti earthquake and the Egypt protests are both ecstatic events that make claims to cosmopolitan solidarity, insofar as they invite us to act upon the misfortune of non-Western victims, yet their claims to solidarity radically differ. Whereas the nature of the events, a natural catastrophe and a political uprising, obviously justifies this difference, my argument is that the Western structures of journalistic reporting via which each event is mediated are also crucially responsible for their variation. This is, I argue, because these structures selectively give voice to distant others, silencing the voice of earthquake victims but amplifying the voice of political protesters, and, in so doing, encourage recognition of the active and resistant victimhood of the latter while depoliticizing the historical condition of victimhood of the former.

Specifically, the journalistic iterability of the Haiti earthquake is structured in ways that remediate the ordinary voices of a compassionate West, intermediate networks of crisis communication that focus on the management of the disaster and transmediate an activism of Western donations as well as NGO relief aid. The solidarity of the Haiti earthquake is, as a consequence, a solidarity of salvation that suppresses the voices of victimhood in favour of a Western appeal to compassionate emotion. Rather than downplaying the significance of the humanitarian dimension of the event, my point is, rather, to draw attention to the importance of challenging the assumption that salvation is the only possible response to Haiti's disaster. We need to consider, instead, why the journalism of witnessing and deliberation reproduces the positioning of Haiti within an emergency imaginary, that is, within a dominant explanatory framework for the victimhood of Haitians, which depoliticizes the nation's postcolonial trajectory and relieves global governance institutions of the responsibility for the nation's continuing aid dependency.

In contrast, the journalistic structure of the Egypt protests is structured in ways that remediate the ordinary voice of Egyptians, intermediate networks of cyberactivism, and transmediate into militant forms of civic engagement both in Egypt (and beyond) and the West. The solidarity of this event is, as a consequence, a solidarity of revolution that communicates a human rights appeal for political freedom and social justice. Instead of depoliticization, as in Haiti, this is a story that did more than give voice to Westerners supporting the Egyptian cause. It established the local voices of victimhood as voices of suffering, indignation, and political dissent, and thereby further managed to establish equivalential claims to solidarity between Egypt and the West. In so doing, it rendered 'their' and 'our' protests a common terrain of activism against authoritative structures that limit democracy: 'I am occupying Wall Street', as one American protester put it, 'because it is my future, my generation's future, that is at stake. Inspired by the peaceful occupation of Tahrir Square in Cairo, tonight we are coming together in Times Square to show the world that the power of the people is an unstoppable force of global change. Today, we are fighting back against the dictators of our country – the Wall Street banks – and we are winning'.[13]

What this juxtaposition of these new performativities of convergent news demonstrates is that, *pace* celebrations on the democratisation of voice, digital journalism remains subject to global power relations that control the mediation of voice along the West–Global South axis. While the Egyptian voice, in its rare combination of cyberactivism with self-sacrifice, broke through and catalysed a cosmopolitan community in the name of a common cause, the Haitian one, locked in a passive fate of muteness, did not manage to stake a distinct claim and reverberate in global media. This inability to speak is, of course, associated with the digital divide – 35 per cent of the Haitian population owns a mobile phone while Internet penetration among Egyptians is close to 'saturation point' (i.e. over 80 per cent).[14]

There is, however, another crucial barrier to the articulation of the voice of victimhood – a symbolic barrier that reflects the profound misrecognition of the Global South in a predominantly Western mediascape. Captured in Spivak's pertinent question 'Can the subaltern speak?', symbolic misrecognition refers to the systemic inability of non-Western others to speak out and be heard in the transnational flows of mediation. Even though the West has always possessed the disposition of voice, exercising its agency to define the boundaries of legitimate community around itself, the South does not automatically possess such disposition. Egypt may have managed to speak out, having long prepared the articulation of its ordinary voice in public: 'For at least five years now', as Eltahawy put it, 'they [Egyptian youth, LC] have been nimbly moving from the "real" to the "virtual" world where their blogs and Facebook updates and notes and, more recently, tweets offered a self-expression that may have at times

13 See www.huffingtonpost.com/2011/11/14/occupy-wall-street-consid_n_1093350.html.

14 See www.thedailynewsegypt.com/it-a-telecom/egypts-mobile-market-nears-saturation-at-80-pct-penetration.html.

been narcissistic but for many Arab youths signalled the triumph of "I". I count, they said again and again'.[15] Haiti, however, did not. As a result, it has been unable to participate in a mediation process that would challenge the West to recognize its suffering not only as yet another God-sent disaster, but also as a matter of political injustice and historical responsibility.[16]

Rather than a matter of a technology-driven democratization of voice, then, voice and agency are, crucially, a political matter of injustice, which throws into relief the deep inequalities of power that selectively enable some voices to be heard and recognized as worthy of our solidarity and not others – what I earlier called the symbolic power of mediation. It is, therefore, a matter of crucial importance to draw attention to the ways in which the structures of convergent journalism may now restructure the dominant arrangements of this power and allow for a different distribution of the voices of victimhood in the flows of global mediation: 'overcoming injustice', as Fraser says, 'means dismantling institutionalized obstacles that prevent some people from participating on a par with others, as full partners in social interaction' (Fraser 16). Insofar as convergent journalism remains embedded in structures of power that reproduce the dominant visions and divisions of community, cosmopolitan solidarity will remain, at best, a rare moment of revolutionary resonance between the West and its others, or, at worst, a reverberation of our own pity for these others' suffering – nothing more than a narcissistic form of 'mediated mass self-communication . . . self-generated in content, self-directed in emission, and self-selected in reception by many that communicate with many' (Fraser 248).

Works cited

Beckett, Charlie *The Value of Networked Journalism*. Polis/BBC College of Journalism, 2010. Web. 30 May 2016 <www2.lse.ac.uk/media@lse/POLIS/Files/networkedjournalism.pdf>.

Bennett, Lance W., Victor W. Pickard, David P. Iozzi, Carl L. Schroeder, Taso Lagos, and C. Evans Caswell. 'Managing the Public Sphere: Journalistic Construction of the Great Globalization Debate'. *Journal of Communication* 54.3 (2004): 437–455. Print.

Brisson, Zack. 'Institutional Overview: Independent Media Blog'. *The Reboot: Egypt. From Revolution to Institutions*. 2011. Web. 30 May 2016. <http://thereboot.org/blog/2011/04/18/institutional-overview-independent-media/>.

Butler, Judith. *Excitable Speech: A Politics of the Performative*. London: Routledge, 1997. Print.

——. *Frames of War: When Is Life Grievable?* London: Verso, 2009. Print.

Calhoun, Craig. 'The Idea of Emergency: Humanitarian Action and Global (Dis-)order'. *States of Emergency*. Ed. D. Fassin and M. Pandolfi. Cambridge: Zone Books, 2010. 29–58. Print.

15 Quoted in www.guardian.co.uk/commentisfree/2011/jan/29/egypt-mubarak-tunisia-palestine.

16 But see Al Jazeera 'live blog' on Haiti for a historicizing perspective along these lines: http://blogs.aljazeera.net/americas/2010/01/13/why-haiti-earthquake-was-so-devastating.

Chouliaraki, Lilie. *The Spectatorship of Suffering*. London: Sage, 2006. Print.

——. 'Ordinary Witnessing in Post-Television News: Towards a New Moral Imagination'. *Critical Discourse Studies* 7.4 (2010): 305–319. Print.

Collier, Paul. *Haiti: From Natural Catastrophe to Economic Security. A Report for the Secretary-General of the UN.* 2009. Web. 30 May 2016. <www.focal.ca/pdf/haiticollier.pdf>.

Crowley, J., W. J. Smyth, M. Murphy, and C. Roche. *Atlas of the Great Irish Famine*. New York: New York University Press, 2012. Print.

Fraser, Nancy. *Scales of Justice: Reimagining Political Space in a Globalized World*. New York: Columbia University Press, 2010. Print.

Frosh, Paul and Amit Pinchevski. *Media Witnessing Testimony in the Age of Mass Communication*. Palgrave Basingstoke/New York, 2009. Print.

Ghannam, Jeffrey. *Social Media in the Arab World: A Report to the Center of International Media Assistance*. Washington DC. 2011. Web. 30 May 2016. <www.cima.ned.org/wp-content/uploads/2015/02/CIMA-Arab_Social_Media-Report-10-25-11.pdf>.

Howard, Phil N. *The Digital Origins of Dictatorship and Democracy: Information, Technology and Political Islam*. Oxford: Oxford University Press, 2011. Print.

Khamis, Sahar and Katherine Vaughn. 'Cyberactivism in the Egyptian Revolution: How Civic Engagement and Citizen Journalism Tilted the Balance'. *Arab Media and Society* 13 (2011). Web. 30 May 2016. <www.arabmediasociety.com/?article=769>.

Madianou, M., L. Longboan and J. Ong 'Finding a Voice Through Humanitarian Technologies? Communication Technologies and Participation in Disaster Recovery'. *International Journal of Communication* 9 (2015): 3020–3038. Print.

Meier, Patrick. 'Crisis Mapping in Action: How Open Source Software and Global Volunteer Networks Are Changing the World, One Map at a Time'. *Journal of Map Geography Librairies: Advances in Geospatial Information, Collections and Archives* 8.2 (2012): 89–100. Web. 30 May 2016. <www.tandfonline.com/doi/abs/10.1080/15420353.2012.663739>.

Papacharissi, Zizi and Maria de Fatima Oliveira. *The Rhythms of News Story-Telling: Coverage of the January 25th Egyptian Uprising on Twitter*. Paper presented at the World Association for Public Opinion Research Conference, Amsterdam, 2011. Web. 30 May 2016. <www.insideview.ie/files/rhythms-of-news-storytelling.pdf>.

Peters, J. D. 'Witnessing'. *Media Witnessing* Ed. Paul Frosh and Amit Pinchevski. London: Palgrave, 2001. 23–48. Print.

Rencoret Nicole, Abby Stoddard, Katherine Haver, Glyn Taylor and Paul Harvey. 'Haiti Earthquake Response: Context Analysis'. *ALNAP*, n.d. Web. 18 June, 2016. www.alnap.org/pool/files/haiti-context-analysis-final.pdf.

Russell, A. 'Extra-National Information Flows, Social Media, and the 2011 Egyptian Uprising'. *International Journal of Communication* 5 (2011): 1238–1247. Print.

Sambrook, Richard. 'Citizen Journalism and the BBC'. *Nieman Reports*, 2005. Web. 30 June, 2016. http://niemanreports.org/articles/citizen-journalism-and-the-bbc/.

Schudson, M. *The Sociology of News*. New York: Norton, 2003. Print.

Silverstone, Roger. *Media and Morality: On the Rise of Mediapolis*. Cambridge: Polity Press, 2006. Print.

Spivak, Gayatri. 'Can the Subaltern Speak?' *Marxism and the Interpretation of Culture*. Ed. Cary Nelson and Lawrence Grossberg. Urbana/Chicago: University of Illinois Press, 1988. 271–313. Print.

Taylor, Charles. 'The Politics of Recognition'. *New Contexts of Canadian Criticism*. Ed. A. Heble *et al.* Ontario: Westview Press, 1995. 98–131. Print.

United Nations Office for the Coordination of Humanitarian Affairs. *Humanitarianism in the Network Age.* OCHA Policy and Studies Series. UN Office for the Coordination of Humanitarian Affairs, 2013. Print.

Zelizer, B. 'On Having Been There: Eye-Witnessing as a Journalistic Word'. *Critical Studies in Media Communication* 24.5 (2007): 408–428. Print.

Zelizer, B. *About to Die: How News Images Move the Public.* Oxford: Oxford University Press, 2010. Print.

Index

Page numbers relating to notes contain the letter 'n' followed by the note number(s). References to names beginning with 'De' or 'Von' are listed under the main surname.

www.ingramcontent.com/pod-product-compliance
Ingram Content Group UK Ltd.
Pitfield, Milton Keynes, MK11 3LW, UK
UKHW022014180926
475701UK00003B/359

* 9 7 8 1 1 3 8 4 8 1 9 1 6 *